Text-book of the Diseases of Trees

TEXT-BOOK

OF THE

DISEASES OF TREES

The "Country Life" Library.

TEXT-BOOK

OF THE

DISEASES OF TREES

BY

PROFESSOR R. HARTIG

OF THE UNIVERSITY OF MUNICH

TRANSLATED BY

WILLIAM SOMERVILLE, D.Œc., B.Sc., F.R.S.E., F.L.S.

PROFESSOR OF AGRICULTURE AND FORESTRY
DURHAM COLLEGE OF SCIENCE, NEWCASTLE-ON-TYNE

REVISED AND EDITED, WITH A PREFACE, BY

H. MARSHALL WARD, D.Sc., F.R.S., F.L.S., F.R.H.S.

LATE FELLOW OF CHRIST'S COLLEGE, CAMBRIDGE
PROFESSOR OF BOTANY AT THE ROYAL INDIAN ENGINEERING COLLEGE, COOPER'S HILL

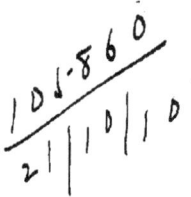

London

PUBLISHED AT THE OFFICES OF

" COUNTRY LIFE," 20, TAVISTOCK STREET, W.C.

AND BY

GEO. NEWNES, Ltd., 7-12, SOUTHAMPTON ST., COVENT GARDEN, W.C.

.

PREFACE TO THE ENGLISH EDITION

[BY H. MARSHALL WARD, D Sc., F.R.S, F.L.S, F R.H S] .

THE foundation of a science of Mycology by Berkeley, de Bary, and Tulasne, pursued by Brefeld, Zopf, and others, has led to a knowledge of the biology of fungi highly creditable to the industrious observers who have explored this domain of the vegetable kingdom, while the gradual building up of the science of plant-physiology from the days of Knight and Hales, De Saussure and Boussingault, to those of Sachs and Pfeffer, has placed us in possession of a vast amount of information as regards normal life processes in plants. Until much more recently, however, it cannot be said that we have had a science of the pathology of plants—*i e* the study of abnormal physiology—of anything like the same importance, in spite of the splendid and progressive attempts of Berkeley, Frank, and Sorauer to found one.

In the particular department he has cultivated, Robert Hartig has succeeded in founding a plant-pathology really worthy of the name, and I would especially emphasize this, that his researches are so thoroughly elucidative of *pathological* phenomena, in that he studies not only the nature of the structural lesions and of the physiological disturbances consequent on these, but also the factors of the environment which throw light on the question No better illustration of this could be selected

than his admirable discussion of the complex phenomenon of
"Leaf-casting" on pp 110–117 of the present work , while his
work on the *Zersetzungserscheinungen des Holzes* is a model of
thoroughness and scientific accuracy and acumen to which all
workers in this branch of botany must look up

In this country we are awakening rapidly to the necessity
of placing ourselves abreast of the new ideas involved in this
compound study of plant-pathology ; but we are perhaps as yet
by no means so alive to the practical importance of the new
discipline as it might have been inferred (from our national
pride in being practical) we should be.

Animal-pathology is studied with zealous and expensive
enthusiasm—I suppose because, being animals, we are at once
alive to its importance ; but plant-pathology, in the real sense
of the term, scarcely obtains recognition as yet, no doubt owing
to our interest in the culture of trees and agricultural produce
having seemed to be less pressing than coming events are likely
to prove it really to be • From this condition—only apparently
apathy—we are doubtless awakening, and, as is usual, when we
English do awake to new necessities, we at once enthusiastically
set to work to recover lost ground

Now, in this department, we have to awaken to some startling
new facts, the practical bearings of which have deeply impressed
our Continental cousins for some years past.

One of these new facts is that we may know a very great
deal about the systematic position and the morphology of
parasitic and destructive fungi without knowing much—or,
indeed, necessarily *anything*—about the diseases and injuries
they induce ; another of these new facts is that pathology—
i e the study of disease—cannot be fruitful unless the student
is experimentally acquainted with plant-physiology, and especially (though by no means only) the physiology of nutrition

To these statements I would add that we have, as a nation,
to force ourselves even more than we have yet done out of
the groove in which plant-physiology is looked upon as a mere
branch of chemistry and physics   It is no undervaluing of

the true status of agricultural chemistry, or of the study of
the physics and chemistry of soils, &c, to insist upon it that
no one can appreciate even the rudiments of plant-physiology
who does not make himself master of the facts of structure
and the essential phenomena of life by experimental investigation ; nor to point out that, as we come to know more about
the physiology and pathology of plants, we learn that the
chemistry of the soil is one of the least important factors we
are concerned with

These truths have to be faced, and in spite of the at first
sight depressing inference that the study of plant-pathology
—and I suppose the same applies to animal-pathology—demands rigorous and active acquaintance with several other
branches of science. As I have stated in substance elsewhere,
we demand that the surgeon or doctor who attends us shall be
qualified properly to do his work, though we are perhaps not
always alive to the extravagance of our demands on his ability
and training ; and just as we cannot expect him to do his work
in diagnosing the disease or injury, and explaining and combating or removing its cause, unless he *is* properly qualified,
by the requisite instruction in the physics, chemistry, structure,
and normal working (*i e.* physiology) of the healthy body and
in the pathology of the case concerned, so can we as little
expect any one to deal with diseased conditions in plants who
is ignorant of their structure and physiology, and the pathological conditions of the case concerned. There is, however,
the comforting assurance that the processes in plants, complex
as they are—and we must not err in underrating this—are
simpler than in animals, and must throw useful lights on all
general problems in Biology

The objection that there are epidemic diseases of plants
which we have as yet failed to prevent or overcome is obviously
no more valid than the cry that we cannot as yet stay the
progress of epidemics of influenza or cholera : the cases are
exactly parallel, and since we do not abandon or depreciate
the study of medicine because medical science is not yet in a

position always to cope as successfully as we could wish with human ailments, so we must not undervalue the importance of the triumphs of the much younger baby science—plant-pathology.

Probably few people in this country are really aware of the enormous strides towards lusty and vigorous youth the new science is now making, and what important contributions to human progress its study is affording.

Educated and properly trained agriculturists and foresters have long been familiar with the fact that great advances are being made in these directions, and perhaps the only fault that a very severe critic could find with them is that they have remained a little too long deterred by the failures which have always to be acknowledged (and met) in a progressive experimental science. That much more general interest in this progress is now evident, however, is best proved by the various publications on the *treatment* of plant-diseases which are springing up around us, for even the very sceptical will admit that, on the one hand, the treatment of diseases depends on knowledge of them and their origin, and, on the other hand, that such eminently practical works would not be published unless they were read.

Foremost among such publications are the reports of the various experimental stations on the continents of Europe and America, and it is a matter of the highest credit and congratulation that the Americans are devoting large sums of money to the experimental study of methods of treatment, based on knowledge of the diseases treated, at several of their enthusiastically planned experimental stations. I need only point to the reports published by the United States Department of Agriculture (Section of Vegetable Pathology), and to the *Zeitschrift für Pflanzen-Krankheiten* emanating under the auspices of the " Internationalen Phytopathologischen Kommission," as showing how necessary it is becoming to have special organs in this branch of science, and to the increasing number of text-books on the subject of plant-diseases and their treatment now being published, as evidence for the justice of the above statement.

Among these latter, Kirchner's *Die Krankheiten und Beschad-igungen unserer Landwirthschaftlichen Pflanzen* stands high in the list as a treatise on the diagnosis and treatment of agricultural and horticultural plant-diseases.   Far more of a classic, however, but dealing more especially with the diseases of forest trees, is Robert Hartig's beautiful text-book now intro-duced to the English public. Another encyclopædic work, Hess's *Fortschutz*, deals more particularly with the "dodges," if I may use the word, practical foresters are devising to combat the principal maladies to which forest trees are subject, and of this work English readers are also promised a translation at an early date.   These more special treatises may be men-tioned as supplementing—and in part supplanting—the more academical and general works of Frank and Sorauer previously referred to.

The great charm of Hartig's book lies as much in the ex-cellent plan and simple method of exposition of the facts and principles concerned, as in the astounding richness of infor-mation it conveys. This is unquestionably owing to Hartig's prominence as the leading investigator and authority in Ger-many in this special branch of knowledge—the fungoid diseases of forest trees.

His pre-eminence as a sturdy and patient inquirer, as an admirable anatomist and physiologist, and as a bold and original thinker, is well known to the few who are acquainted with his special scientific publications, particularly his laborious memoir on the destruction of timber by fungi.   In the present work I think he shows himself also a master of the art of teaching the principles as well as the facts of his subject.

Of course there are points of view to be considered in criticising such a book

The specialist on the Morphology of the Fungi will probably complain of the author's classification of these organisms, and of his somewhat lax use of certain morphological terms ; but it should be remembered that, in the first place, the student's attention is not here directed to the fungus itself, as an object of morphological study, so much as to the action of certain fungi in inducing specific diseases in trees ; and, in the second place, it is assumed that the student is already acquainted with the main facts in the biology of the fungi—including their morphology—before he attempts this particular branch of science

Again, the professed botanist may remark how much is assumed concerning the structure and physiology of the host-plants—the trees—whose diseases are here treated of The reply is, as before, the student cannot extract all, or nearly all, of value from such a work as this, unless he is thoroughly acquainted with the principal facts of the normal anatomy and physiology of the higher plants

A third platform of criticism is that of the " practical forester," who may object that the author gives too little information as to the details of combative or therapeutic treatment of the special diseases To this the obvious reply is that it is not necessarily the duty of the scientific pathologist to devise the particular mode of attack to be employed in special cases—these plans of remedial treatment involve the outlay of money, labour, &c, which vary in different countries and in different cases, and enough has been done by the investigator who indicates the factors involved Special works must be consulted regarding the *details* of treatment, though it seems to me the author, while clearly recognising this, goes even out of his way to give practical hints as to treatment, and has in many cases put the principal factors concerned in the treatment so clearly that every thinking practical man can do the rest himself. No better illustration of the thoroughly practical nature of his writings could be selected than his recommendations for the treatment of Dry-rot

But it is by no means solely on the ground of the information capable of direct application which the book contains that it should be judged I would especially urge the value of this study to the student of botany as calculated both to test his knowledge in other departments of his science and to open out new lines of thought as he considers the interactions between one plant and another, and between both and other factors—living or not—of the environment.

Hartig's ingenious explanation of the spread of the well-known Larch-disease may or may not be accepted in all its details, on the evidence given, and dissent from his explanations of such diseases as "Canker," &c, has been expressed, but I would maintain—apart from my acceptance of the general truth of his arguments—that they teach the student very clearly how to investigate and think out these complicated matters for himself.

We are still decidedly wanting in information concerning many diseases of trees Standing elms and other trees are occasionally found in this country with a species of Hymeno-mycete growing from the trunks six feet or more above the ground · are these parasitic or not, and what is their mode of action ?   How does *Polyporus squamosus* attack timber ?   What are the exact biological relations of *Polyporus fomentarius*, *Fistulina hepatica*, and a number of other forms found in this country, to the trees on which they grow ?

These and numerous other questions await solution, by means of thorough investigations properly conducted in this country, along such lines as Hartig has laid down in Germany, and it should be borne in mind that such studies offer stores of facts likely to be of the utmost interest to investigators in other branches of Botany.   To give one instance only the study of the destruction of the walls of the tracheids, and other elements of which timber is composed, by the hyphæ of fungi, shows that there is considerable variety in the processes of piercing, delignifying, corroding, and dissolving them, and it seems a safe conjecture that valuable information as to the intimate structure of these walls may be derived from the examination of the way the fungus unbuilds them, so to speak.

Among the Ascomycetes and the Uredineæ are numerous questions already framed for investigation, and I know of no department of botanical study more fascinating than the scientific hunting for the heterœcious forms of Æcidiomycetes: the work combines all the excitement of a true hunt with the intense intellectual pleasure implied in the demand for the severest critical observation, and skilful and delicate manipulation of the microscopic cultures.

Again, the whole question of wound-rot, opened up on pp 236–237, is one which demands long and thorough investigation; not only to clear up the many chemical problems involved, but also to explain the exact behaviour of saprophytic fungi and bacteria, and the part they play in the phenomena

My duties as Editor of this work have not seemed to be such as to demand that I should express my own opinions on the subjects raised, and I have almost confined myself to merely noting the occurrence of the principal diseases in this country (since the original is written for German readers), and to adding a few explanatory sentences wherever it has seemed useful in the interests of the lay reader to do so. In some respects Hartig's book is a popular one—by which I mean it appeals to a wide circle of readers not professionally engaged in the study of this branch of science—and it has seemed advisable, therefore, occasionally to interpolate a short note in explanation of some of the more technical terms employed. Short notes are apt to be insufficient in such cases; but it would so obviously have been out of place to overload the author's work with long disquisitions on the matters referred to, that I have been constrained to risk their being occasionally too brief.

Here and there I have ventured, however, to go a step further, and add a reference which may be useful, and this in face of my full recognition of the fact that Hartig's book is an exposition of his own view of his own work rather than that of others.

In all cases I have been careful to place my remarks, more-

over, in footnotes between square brackets, so that the run of
the author's text is uninterrupted.   In one case at least I have
expressed dissent from Hartig's views, but here again the
reader has the option of neglecting the footnote, and at any
rate the matter is one of evidence.

H. MARSHALL WARD.

COOPER'S HILL, *March* 1894.

TABLE OF CONTENTS

SECTION II.   WOUNDS.

SECTION III.   DISEASES DUE TO CONDITIONS OF SOIL.

SECTION IV.   INJURIES DUE TO ATMOSPHERIC IN-
           FLUENCES AND FIRE.

DISEASES OF TREES

INTRODUCTION

DEVELOPMENT OF THE STUDY OF VEGETABLE PATHOLOGY

DURING the present century, and especially during the last few decades, the forests of Germany have been threatened with dangers of a magnitude formerly unknown. These have been occasioned by the gradual relinquishment of natural regeneration, and by the substitution of pure even-aged woods for woods consisting of trees of different species and of various ages, but most of all by the displacement of broad-leaved trees by pure coniferous woods It is especially noticeable that enemies from the animal and vegetable kingdoms find favourable conditions for rapid development in our modern forests, so that the complaints of increasing devastation of woods appear to be by no means unfounded The foresters of the last century had already made themselves familiar with a large number of the enemies and diseases of trees, as is proved by the appearance in 1795[1] of a work which probably contains the first compilation of the observations on plant-diseases scattered throughout the older literature. We may assume from this that a large number of diseases which have only been properly explained during the last few years, e.g. the damping off of seedling beeches, the resinous degeneration of pine-tops, the red-rot of the spruce, &c., were known to foresters more than a hundred years ago, though of course the explanation of the causes was

[1] Schreger, *Erfahrungsmassige Anweisung zur richtigen Kenntniss der Krankheiten der Wald- und Gartenbaume*, &c. Leipzig, 1795. 518 pages.

9

B

bound to be defective in accordance with the position of botanical science at that time

Some fifty years ago a number of able investigators, of whom only Saxesen, Th Hartig, and Ratzeburg need be named here, applied themselves to the study of insects   The life-history of forest insects, their harmfulness or usefulness, soon became the favourite study of many practical foresters, and in a few decades the joint efforts of numerous workers were rewarded by the elevation of Forest Entomology to the position of a much-appreciated subject of scientific instruction, which has become the common property of all educated foresters

The case was otherwise with those plant-diseases which cannot be ascribed to the injuries of animals   Their investigation was delayed until quite recently, for it was only after botanical science, by the aid of its chief instrument, the microscope, had obtained a clear insight into the normal structure and vital phenomena of plants, and especially after the study of fungi had been prosecuted in the last few decades by a series of distinguished investigators, that the examination of the phenomena of disease in the life of plants could be undertaken with a prospect of success.

During the period from 1833 to 1841 three text-books of plant-diseases did indeed appear—namely, those of Fr Unger,[1] Wiegmann,[2] and Meyen[3]—which bear witness that in attempting to explain the phenomena of disease in plants the progress already made in the knowledge of the structure and life of plants was not left out of account, but the erroneous views as to the nature of fungi, and the absolute ignorance of the history of their development which prevailed, impeded progress towards a clear understanding of the processes of disease   Independent investigation was especially interfered with by the mistaken attempt to apply to the study of the diseases of plants the scientific results which J. von Liebig in particular had obtained in the department of agricultural chemistry. After it had

[1] Fr Unger, *Die Exantheme der Pflanzen und einige mit diesen verwandte Krankheiten der Gewachse*   Vienna, 1833

[2] Wiegmann, *Die Krankheiten und krankhaften Missbildungen der Gewachse*   Brunswick, 1839

[3] Meyen, *Pflanzenpathologie   Lehre von dem krankhaften Leben und Bilden der Pflanzen*   Berlin, 1841

been recognized how great is the importance for the welfare of plants of the quantity and condition of the mineral matter in the soil, and how an irrational treatment of the soil, such as *scourging the ground,* in sylviculture, agriculture, and horticulture can and must lead to exhaustion of one or other of the nutritive ingredients, which betrays itself in the stunted growth of the crop, it was supposed to be permissible, though unsupported by any exact investigations, to proceed a step further, and to regard acute diseases of crops, so long as they could not be ascribed to external causes, as the results of the want of one or other of the nutritive substances of the soil The fact that unhealthy symptoms make their appearance quite as often on very fertile soils as on poor ones led to the assumption that a superfluity of nourishment may also be the means of causing diseases in plants

The works of De Bary[1] and Tulasne[2] first opened the way for the investigation of plant-diseases ; and with the appearance of these a new period began, for from that time onwards very great attention has been devoted to the life-history and action of parasitic fungi.   The view hitherto held that all fungoid growths appear only as the result of previously existing processes of disease, or as indications of the incipient death of the part of the plant which is attacked, was shown to be erroneous.

Investigation was now directed chiefly to the diseases of farm and garden crops. Amongst others Jul. Kuhn[3] especially enriched science by a series of most valuable investigations. Further research gained a surer basis with the appearance of de Bary's[4] *Morphology and Physiology of the Fungi*

So far the attention of investigators had been almost entirely directed to agricultural crops, a circumstance which is sufficiently explained by the fact that but few scientific botanists had the opportunity presented to them of carrying their researches into

[1] De Bary, *Untersuchungen uber die Brandpilze und die durch sie veranlassten Krankheiten der Pflanzen mit Rucksicht auf das Getreide und andere Nahrpflanzen.* Berlin, 1853 .

[2] Tulasne, *Selecta fungorum carpologia*   Paris, 1861

[3] Julius Kuhn, *Die Krankheiten der Culturgewachse, ihre Ursachen und Verhutung* Berlin, 1858.

[4] De Bary, *Morphologie und Physiologie der Pilze,* &c   Leipzig, 1866, and *Vergleichende Morphologie und Biologie der Pilze* Leipzig, 1884. .

the forest and of giving their attention to the diseases of trees. The credit of having first stimulated interest in this direction undoubtedly belongs to M. Willkomm.[1] Hallier's attempt to collate the scattered materials in the form of a text-book[2] was subsequently repeated with happier results by P. Sorauer[3] and Frank,[4] whose handbooks are useful compilations, in which the matter diffused through numerous periodicals and works is collected and systematically arranged. My own investigations have been published partly in periodicals and partly as independent works.[5]

THE CAUSES OF DISEASE

In the present state of science it is scarcely possible to draw a sharp line of distinction between those conditions of the plant known, on the one hand, as healthy, and, on the other, as diseased. The development of any plant depends upon a series of external factors of nutrition, and these, such as light, heat, the kind and proportion of the nutritive materials, and of the water and oxygen contained in the soil, of the carbonic acid present in the atmosphere, &c., are available for the plant in very different quantities. When all these external factors influence the development of the plant in the most favourable manner, it is vigorously nourished and flourishes well. But probably the case is never realised when all these factors of life act simultaneously and concurrently in the most favourable manner possible : on the contrary, one or more is sure to be deficient or superabundant, and this causes interference to a greater or less extent with the development of the plant. We cannot as yet say, however, that such plants are

[1] M. Willkomm, *Die Mikroscopischen Feinde des Waldes.* Dresden, 1866, 1868.

[2] E. Hallier, *Phytopathologie. Die Krankheiten der Culturgewächse.* Leipzig, 1868.

[3] P. Sorauer, *Handbuch der Pflanzenkrankheiten.* Berlin, 1874. 2nd Edition, 1886.

[4] B. Frank, *Die Krankheiten der Pflanzen.* Breslau, 1880.

[5] R. Hartig, *Wichtige Krankheiten der Waldbäume.* Berlin, 1874. *Die Zersetzungserscheinungen des Holzes der Nadelholzbäume und der Eiche.* Berlin, 1878. *Untersuchungen aus dem forstbotanischen Institut zu München.* I. Berlin, 1880. III. Berlin, 1883. *Die echte Hausschwamm, Merulius lacrymans.* Berlin, 1885.

unhealthy; it is only when the life-processes have sunk to very small proportions that we speak of a plant as "sickly."

Such sickly plants recover, as a rule, when the deficiency of light, heat, nutriment, or whatever the cause of the sickliness may be, is removed. It is the province of physiology to discover the conditions under which plants thrive best. I do not regard the investigation of the phenomena of mere sickliness as the task of pathology. It is only when the sickly condition leads to the death of some part of the plant that we may speak of actual disease. Suppose, for instance, that the soil of a wood has suffered through removal of litter, a diminution of growth will result, which, however, is not as yet disease; but if a moribund condition of the tops of the trees sets in, we are confronted with the disease known as "top-drying" or "top-drought." This example shows how gradually the condition of sickliness merges into that of disease, and how it is only the partial death of the plant that can be regarded as giving external indication of the latter.

It is quite as difficult to draw the boundary line between healthy and diseased, and between normal and abnormal, in the case of those phenomena which we are accustomed to designate as monstrosities. In the nature of organisms there is a tendency towards variation both morphologically and physiologically, and it is upon this, in fact, that progressive evolution in the organic world depends.

Variation is, therefore, a normal phenomenon, and depends on causes which are probably almost always operative in the earliest stages of the life of the organism before, during, and immediately after the fertilization of the oosphere.

It is impossible to establish a strict line of demarcation between normal variation and malformation; and thus all the phenomena connected with the latter, which we are not in a position to explain, have been separated and grouped together to form the special study of teratology apart from pathology.

In this text-book therefore we shall confine ourselves essentially to describing and explaining those phenomena which bring about the premature death of the plant, or of any part of it, however small.

This limitation leads us to the answer to the question whether plants all die a natural death, or whether they, at least in part, succumb to external influences—that is to say, are subject only to accidental death.

Experience teaches that, at any rate among the more highly developed plants, each individual dies sooner or later, but that in the case of perennial plants, particularly trees and shrubs, the cause of death is always to be found in unfavourable external influences. In the case of the more lowly organisms, which only multiply by division and as yet exhibit no sexual reproduction, one can scarcely speak of a natural death, because each part is as old as the parent organism by the division, &c., of which it was formed. Were a natural limit set to the life of a certain species of plant which can only multiply by dividing, the result would be that when this limit was reached every part, and therefore also the offspring which had originated by division, would perish. It is known, however, that this state of things does not exist. In the case of those plants which are also reproduced by sexual processes many different conditions are met with. In the case of annual plants the vegetative part dies each year, and only the embryos originating from the fertilized oospheres remain alive. When, from these, plants capable of bearing seeds have developed, all that is preserved of them, in their turn, is the formative product arising from the sexual cells. Thus the vegetative part of each plant dies owing to internal causes, though these, in part, depend simply upon exhaustion consequent on the formation of seed. We see then that natural death of the vegetative organs of the plant occurs from internal causes, whereas the sexual cells only die if they have not been fertilized, or if, owing to external causes, the product of fertilization has not given rise to a new plant. Upon the unlimited duration of the life of this part of the plant—that is to say, of those sexual cells which do not fall victims to accidental death—depends indeed continuity in the organic world, in other words, the development and preservation of the vegetable and animal kingdoms.

In the case of perennial plants it is only certain parts that succumb to natural death each year. Amongst herbaceous plants, for instance, it is the parts above ground which thus die off: in the case of deciduous trees and shrubs, it is the outer cortical tissues, the leaves, &c.

The plant-individual proper, however, only dies in consequence of unfavourable external influences. As a matter of fact, every tree is rejuvenated each year by the cambium forming new tissues at its periphery, and by new shoots and buds. It is a matter of experience that the duration of the life of all trees is limited, but it is not proved whether this is to be ascribed to internal causes, or is the result of the innumerable influences which act more or less prejudicially on the plant from without. The reduction and final cessation of the growth in height of a tree, after attaining a certain maximum, must be ascribed to interference with the factors of nutrition, and, in all probability, especially to the fact that the forces which conduct the water and nutritive materials to the highest bud of the tree are limited in their action, and that sooner or later, depending on the specific and individual nature of the plant, these no longer suffice to provide for the continuance of growth in height. If we cut a slip from an old tree, it will pursue the same cycle of development as the parent tree, thereby proving that by vegetative multiplication the life of a plant may be indefinitely prolonged. Hitherto no phenomenon has been discovered from which one may conclude with certainty that internal natural causes of death are peculiar to all, or even to any perennial plants. In this connection the question is at once suggested whether "the feebleness of old age" is a factor which must be regarded at all in considering the diseases of plants. In discussing how diseases arise we shall show that old age, quite as well as youth, may predispose a plant to some disease or other. In itself, however, the feebleness of old age is not a natural condition attributable to internal causes, but is a state induced by external influences. The older a tree is, so much the more numerous are the dangers through which it has had to pass, and so much the greater is the number of its injuries and wounds through which parasites and saprophytes can find an entrance into its interior. Again, the older a tree is, the narrower are its annual rings, and with so much the more difficulty and tardiness does it succeed in occluding a wound. Finally, the older a tree is, the more sluggish are its nutritive processes, because, on the one hand, the soil in which the roots are fixed has become denser, thereby impeding the entrance of air, and, on the other

.hand, one or other of the nutritive materials may be partially exhausted.

With the reduction in the transference of nutrient matters to the crown of the tree, the latter becomes stunted and partly dies, and this is followed by diseases which finally kill it altogether.

There are, however, always demonstrable external influences at work in the matter, so that the question whether the debility of old age is in itself a natural condition manifesting itself, for instance, in the enervation of the organization of a cambium cell, or in the separation of a bud from a tree, must in the meantime be answered in the negative. Thus, when we speak of the natural duration of life of a plant-species, we are to understand the period of time during which a plant is able to live without succumbing to the unfavourable external agencies in the soil and the climate, or to the varied attacks of parasitic and saprophytic organisms

The above considerations lead us to the natural classification of the different kinds of disease which we shall examine in the following pages, according to the external influences which induce them.

1 Diseases induced by Phanerogams.
2 Diseases induced by Cryptogams
3 Wounds
4 Diseases due to unfavourable conditions of the soil.
5 Diseases due to unfavourable atmospheric conditions

In the case of most diseases it is demonstrable that the individuals of a given species of plant, which are subjected to certain prejudicial influences, do not all succumb to these influences to an equal extent, but that certain individuals or varieties prove perfectly or almost perfectly resistant, while others soon become diseased or die. These observations show that it is not the environment alone which determines the origin of a disease, but that, on the contrary, a plant contracts disease only when subjected to definite pre-existing conditions , that a *predisposition* or *tendency to disease* must exist, and that therefore, to a certain extent, the origin of a disease is determined by the co-operation of two factors The first factor is the external cause of the disease, and this is, as a rule, easy of demonstration

The second factor, however, has its inception in a peculiar condition of the organization of the plant, which is either present only at certain times, or is only peculiar to and innate in certain individuals, or, finally, has been acquired under the influence of definite external conditions. All these peculiarities in the organization of the plant may be quite normal in their nature— that is to say, the organism as such appears to be perfectly healthy—in which case the predisposition is said to be "normal." On the other hand, however, the predisposition to disease may be "abnormal," as is the case when the plant is only predisposed to one disease because it is already suffering from another. Abnormal or disease-inducing predisposition may arise, for example, in the neighbourhood of a wound through which alone some particular parasite could gain entrance to the plant. The entire group of infectious wound-diseases may be placed in this category.

Under normal predisposition, therefore, we are to understand every condition, even if only temporary, in the anatomical structure, in the chemical constitution, or in the vital functions of an organism, which, though not in itself prejudicial to the individual, induces a disease when a second, and that an external, factor co-operates in addition, even though the latter is in itself innocuous to the plant.

In addition to these cases of normal and abnormal disposition residing in the organism itself, we may also speak of a predisposition to disease which is due to the locality.

There are a great number of fungi which can only attack a certain species of tree when plants of another species occur in the vicinity on which the particular fungus, at certain seasons of the year, may complete its development. Localities in which many aspens grow impart to the pines a predisposition for the disease known as "Pine-twist" (caused by *Melampsora Tremulæ pinitorquum*). Rhododendrons abounding in a district make the spruces liable to "Leaf-blister" (caused by *Chrysomyxa Rhododendri*), while barberry bushes are associated with the "rust" of wheat. The mere existence of uninterrupted woods, composed of a single species of tree, may give rise to dangers leading to extensive epidemics. Pure larch woods away from mountainous regions almost always succumb to canker, whereas larches mixed with other trees may remain unaffected The climatic conditions peculiar to a given district may render it specially liable to outbreaks of certain diseases Thus in Alpine districts proximity to lakes and narrow valleys specially predisposes to certain fungoid diseases, because the moist air of such places favours the fructification of fungi in a high degree. In the forest one meets with certain localities, so-called "frost-beds," which favour the injurious action of frost. The character of the soil may predispose to definite diseases, in that, for instance, it specially favours the growth of underground parasitic fungi, or the conditions may induce the appearance of "root-rot" In very many cases one can say forthwith of certain localities that they predispose to definite diseases, and the latter must occur when some factor or other of the environment is present, although in other localities the same factor may be harmless to the vegetable world. Of course this predisposition which is linked to the locality only forms a part of the multifarious circumstances favourable to the occurrence and spread of diseases that are to be ascribed to the environment of the plant, and it must not be confounded with the idea of a predisposition to disease in the narrower sense

In the first place, the normal predisposition of plants may consist *in phases of development* which *naturally exist for a time in every plant* To this class belongs *the period of youth* of the plant, and the young condition of its new shoots, leaves, and roots These are at first covered only by a delicate epidermis, which is but slightly if at all cuticularized, and which can offer no resistance to the attacks of parasitic fungi, whereas later on in life, when a cuticle has been formed on the outer cell-walls, and when periderm and bark have been formed on the axial organs, the predisposition for many forms of disease disappears

On the other hand, *later periods of life* may also induce a predisposition to certain diseases Young conifers which possess resin-canals are almost perfectly protected from infection by wood-fungi, at least in so far as these find an entrance only through wounds caused by the removal of branches, because each fresh wound is at once covered by a protecting substance due to the exudation of turpentine   It is not until after the development of duramen, which no longer conducts water, that a predisposition for wood-diseases sets in, because now, when a branch is broken off, the inner wood no longer protects itself against attack by pouring out turpentine, for it is only in the watery alburnum that turpentine and resin are forcibly pressed out of the resin-canals   In the case of trees advancing age is also, as a rule, accompanied by a diminution in the breadth of the successive annual rings, and the result of this is that wounds are not so quickly occluded as when they occur on young vigorously growing trees   It is easy to perceive that, as a consequence, the prejudicial results of injuries are increased as age advances   In this sense alone can we speak of the feebleness of old age, and increasing susceptibility to external dangers in consequence

The condition of vegetation in regard to the season of the year has great influence on the power of the plant to resist dangers' It is well known what low temperatures a plant can stand during the period of winter rest, whereas in spring, after the beginning of vegetative activity, and before it ceases in autumn, it is killed by a few degrees of frost.

The capacity of resisting the attacks of parasitic fungi on the part of the tissues also differs much according to the season of the year.   Between the living cell of the host-plant and the cell of the fungus-parasite there is a struggle, in which (in the case of many parasites infesting the tissues of the cortex or cambium) the latter can only kill the former if this is in the condition of vegetative rest—that is to say, not actively growing, &c.   If processes of metabolism are energetically at work in the cellular tissue of the host-plant itself, it is then enabled to stave off the attacks of the fungus   The action of the latter on the cellular tissue of the host—depending as it does on the secretion of an enzyme *—is only prejudicial when this tissue is defenceless, as it were, owing to the condition of inactivity in which it is found   These cortex-fungi grow only from autumn till spring, and their further development

* [Enzymes are a peculiar class of bodies, often called unorganised or soluble ferments, capable of producing powerful molecular changes in organic substances in presence of water.—ED]

is checked with the beginning of vegetative activity in the host-plant. A similar condition of things is met with in those fungi which at all seasons luxuriate in the wood of trees, and even kill its living cells, but which are incapable of penetrating the living tissues of the cortex till these have succumbed to drought due to the death of the wood, when they may be easily occupied. The tissues of the wood and those of the cortex appear to differ in their power of resisting parasites.

The amount of water in plants, determined by the weather, also influences the development of endo-parasites. During periods of much rain, when the plant-tissues contain more water than during periods of drought, many perennial fungi flourish with special vigour inside the plant. This is particularly evident in the case of *Melampsora Tremulæ pinitorquum* and *Rosellinia quercina*

In contradistinction to those phenomena of predisposition which have been already discussed, and which to a certain extent only appear periodically, there is a second category of peculiarities which are innate, as it were, only in certain individuals or varieties, which are thereby specially predisposed to certain diseases. Variation in the vegetable kingdom may find expression in morphological, chemical, and physiological peculiarities, and in each of these directions forms may tend to occur which are more or less susceptible to one disease or other. As regards the morphological aspect, it need only be called to mind that there are varieties of potato which possess a very delicate skin, others, a thick periderm; and it is easy to explain why the former are far less secure against the attack of the fungus that causes potato disease than those with a thick skin

Amongst the Douglas firs there is a bluish glaucous variety whose leaves, owing to an abundant waxy covering, are much better protected against atmospheric drought than the pure green form. That the latter possesses a predisposition to perish from drought in a continental climate is to be expected from the fact that it is naturally confined to the west-coast region of North America.

That individual differences with respect to the chemical composition, and especially to the amount of water, occur in plants is undoubted, and it may be safely assumed that these differences also involve differences in behaviour towards prejudicial external influences At present, however, we know very little in this connection, and we can in the meantime only conjecture that the explanation of the individual differences in the behaviour of plants towards frost, drought, and even towards the attacks of fungi will partly be found in such chemical differences

Even more striking are the cases where differences in the physiological behaviour of plants serve as disease-inducing conditions. It is well known how certain trees of the same wood awake from their winter rest and become green at different times, although in other respects they are perfectly similar. In a young spruce plantation differences of two or even three weeks may be easily perceived in the opening of the buds of different individuals, and this must be accounted for, in most part, by differences in the heat-requirements of the plants. It is evident that early unfolding of the leaves implies a disposition for injury by late frosts, but it may also become the chief stimulus to the development of fungoid disease If, for instance, the spruce-leaf-rust (*Chrysomyxa*) is, in the spring, at the stage when its spores are being shed, all those spruces whose buds have not begun to elongate into shoots will remain entirely unaffected by the fungus, which is only able to force its way into the delicate leaves of young shoots. A disposition for this disease, therefore, attaches to the individuals which begin to grow early In other years it may happen that those individuals which first begin to grow are so far advanced in development when *Chrysomyxa* sheds its spores that the leaves are already too old to be susceptible to infection In this case it is perhaps just the late varieties that contract the disease.

The observation that amongst the individuals of a plant species there are always some whose requirements as regards heat are less or more than those of others, and that these are therefore disposed to suffer from cold to a greater or less extent, and that, further, demands on the moisture of the air and other factors of growth vary with the individual, has probably led to importance being attached to the place of origin of the seeds which we employ in cultural experiments with exotic species of plants We endeavour to obtain seeds from districts where, in the course of time, varieties have spontaneously arisen whose power of resisting frost, or atmospheric drought, as the case may be, has become enhanced

, A further group of disease-inducing conditions embraces all these peculiarities which have only been *acquired* in the course of the development of the plant, and which may lead to a disease if certain external influences be present. If plants are reared in a moist atmosphere, *e g* in a greenhouse, the epidermal system develops in response to the moist air which surrounds it, so that it is only slightly cuticularized If such plants are placed in a dry atmosphere—for instance, in the air of a heated room—they become sickly, because the transpiration of the leaves is unduly increased

Trees, especially those with smooth periderm, that are reared in a very dense wood, and then suddenly isolated in later life, suffer from scorching of the cortex Such trees possess a predisposition for scorching which is absent in the case of those plants of the same species which have been grown, from youth upwards, in an open or light wood The disposition to disease in this case consists in the fact that the external covering is less strongly developed Plants grown in the shade also prove to be unduly susceptible to the direct action of the sun, in that the chlorophyll in the cells of the upper layers of their leaves becomes destroyed. Oaks grown in a close beech wood, and consequently with small crowns, incur a predisposition for top-drought when they are isolated, whereas, under similar circumstances, trees with full crowns do not suffer from this disease

During the first few years after being transplanted, many trees show a predisposition to be easily " frosted," which is again lost with the development of a strong root-system. On shallow soils evergreens, and especially conifers, are far more susceptible to injury from coal-smoke than those on deep soils, for the reason that their root-system, being characterised by superficial development, is unable to take up water in winter. Desiccation of the leaves in consequence of action of the sulphurous acid takes place in their case much more easily than in that of trees which are able to take up water from greater depths, and this even in winter

All the disease-inducing conditions which have been discussed may be designated as normal, because the peculiarities noted are in themselves quite in accordance with the nature of the plant-organism, and only become prejudicial when some other external circumstance co-operates, and which is termed the cause of the disease.

There still remain to be noticed numerous abnormal disease-inducing conditions which depend on an unsound state of the plant To these belong all those wounds in whose train some disease or other of the interior of the plant may follow

When a tree is pruned it thereby incurs an abnormal predisposition for a series of wound-diseases, infectious or otherwise, which can be got rid of by the application of timely and appropriate—that is to say, antiseptic—dressings Injury to a root, e g. the severance of a rootlet, is in itself damage, but when this leads to decay spreading from it into the stem, we designate such an injury as an abnormal disposition to disease.

Insects of various kinds live in the cortex of sound trees, which they injure, and thus open doors, as it were, to the entrance of parasitic fungi into the interior, so that the trees are ultimately killed

A hailstone strikes the cortex of a tree and injures it This creates an abnormal condition, which may lead to an infectious disease should certain fungi settle on the cortex.

When trees or shrubs are transplanted in any year, and their development is so much retarded by the operation that the new shoots have not completed their development when frost appears —that is to say, when lignification has not been completed— they possess an abnormal disposition to injury from frost Such plants may survive in mild winters, but if intense cold sets in they may die off completely

From what has been said it will be clear how endless are the phenomena which dispose to disease, and also how only one group of these, "the inherent tendencies," possess the character of inheritability. The phases of natural development, which were first discussed, and which are passed through by every plant, may be left out of account in connection with the question of inheritability Neither acquired predisposing causes nor those due to an unhealthy state can, however, be transmitted

from parents to descendants ; at least nothing is known so far
that indicates such an inheritance.   This holds good not only
for the causes but also for the diseases themselves

A transmission, by inheritance, of diseases to descendants is
unknown in the vegetable kingdom   One may without hesita-
tion make use of the seeds of plants suffering from any con-
ceivable disease for the propagation of new plants   In particular one may without scruple collect the seed of such trees as
are dwarfed owing to poverty of the soil   Indeed, as a matter
of fact, this is done, for instance, in the case of the Scotch
pine, the cones of which are gathered by preference from those
trees whose proportions are so diminutive, owing to their growing on barren moors, that the collection of the cones may be
accomplished with ease without climbing the trees   It is only
when a question of individual properties consisting in dwarfed
habit of growth, spiral stems, or other undesirable peculiarities
that are innate in the plant is involved, that the law of inheritance comes into consideration, and then propagators of
plants have to exercise the greatest care.

METHOD OF PROCEDURE IN INVESTIGATING THE DISEASES OF PLANTS

Reference will here shortly be made to the methods of investigation which we have to follow when we wish to determine the
causes of diseases in plants.

In the case of diseases of men or animals the difficulties of
diagnosis are much increased by the fact that in the great
majority of cases the disease of a single organ or part of the
body is followed by secondary phenomena which impede the
discovery of the proper seat of disease   In the bodies of plants,
where the nervous system is absent, a disease as a rule remains
localized, at least at first   The division of labour is not yet so
far differentiated as in the bodies of the more highly organised
animals, where disease of any organ, often even a small one,
involves the whole body sympathetically   A large part of the
body of a plant may be diseased and even killed without the
plant being necessarily perceptibly injured in its general health.
If we have succeeded in observing the disease in its first stage,

the further investigation offers comparatively little difficulty. It is more difficult, as a rule, to determine the true cause of disease and death in the case of plants already dead, although the skilled plant-pathologist will seldom fail to recognize with certainty the true character of a disease.

If we are dealing with injuries caused by animals or plants, we shall discover and recognize them, or at least their traces, with most certainty in the preliminary stages of the disease. In very many cases it is not sufficient, where we are dealing with injuries due to animals, including insects, that we catch the creature at work and seek to observe it and its mode of life in nature, as has hitherto generally been done ; but, and particularly in the case of insect-injuries, we must determine whether the injured plants did not already possess some predisposition to disease before they were attacked by the insects, &c. Especially does this hold good for the great family of the bark beetles, which often only appear in the train of other prejudicial agencies, and especially of injuries caused by parasitic fungi. In the case of parasitic plants, again, it is not to be concluded forthwith from the presence of a fungus in the dead tissues that death has been caused by that fungus. True, where we find the mycelia of fungi vegetating in the apparently *unaltered living tissues* of a plant, there is practically no room for doubt that we have to deal with a parasite ; but even in the latter case the attempt must next be made, by means of suitable infection-experiments, to induce arbitrarily, and in a somewhat artificial manner, the disease that we are seeking to investigate.

If spores or gonidia of the suspected fungus are to be had, we make use of these in carrying out the investigation, after having first proved that they are capable of germinating. Should no material capable of germinating be at our disposal, we must, if possible, undertake artificial cultures in a damp chamber, and await the ripening of spores, or even the production of sporophores.* According to the character of the disease, infection is secured by scattering the spores on the leaves, or by placing them in a wound artificially made in the host-plant. In the

---

*[Spores may be of several kinds, and the term is used as a general one. Gonidia are a-sexual spores. Sporophore is a general term to denote any of the various kinds of spore-bearing structures met with among Fungi.—ED.]

case of diseases of the cortex it is sufficient to make a fine incision with the point of a scalpel, to which a drop of water, with
spores suspended in it, is attached ; in the case of diseases of
the wood the latter must be pierced by the wound, which is
then allowed to absorb the drop of water with its contained
spores

In dealing with diseases of the cortex or wood, infection by
means of mycelium* is the much surer course   Having removed a
small piece of the cortex from that part of a diseased tree where
the mycelium is still young and vigorous— that is to say, from the
boundary between the dead and living tissue, we place it on a
spot in a healthy tree from which a piece of cortex of the same
size and shape has been removed   We may proceed exactly as in
budding roses, but it is generally better if the edges of the piece of
cortex containing the mycelium are brought into intimate contact
with the edges of the cortex surrounding the spot operated upon,
and which, moreover, should be prepared immediately beforehand

Desiccation should then be prevented by applying grafting-wax
or other dressing   If it is desired to infect the wood of the stem
of a tree with mycelium, a small cylindrical block is removed
(by means of Pressler's growth-borer, an instrument specially
adapted for such work) from the boundary between the sound
and diseased wood, because it is usually only in this region that
the mycelium contained in the wood is still capable of such
vigorous growth as to be able to extend beyond the surface of the
infecting block   With the same borer an exactly similar hole is
then made in the sound tree selected for infection, the diseased
cylinder being substituted for that which was withdrawn, and
the hole closed externally with grafting-wax

If, finally, we have to do with parasites which vegetate underground, it suffices, as a rule, to plant a diseased specimen in
immediate proximity to a healthy plant of the same species.   In
doing this greater success will probably be secured by bringing
a root of the diseased individual (known to contain mycelium
still living and capable of growth) into immediate contact with
a root of the plant to be infected

* [The mycelium is the vegetative part of the fungus, and in many cases is
more easily obtained in the requisite quantities than spores are   a rough
equivalent for the word in English is " Spawn " (of mushrooms, &c)—ED]

It would be a mistake to attempt to answer the question whether a fungus is really a parasite or not after the failure of one or a few attempts at infection. Let us only consider how numerous are the factors regulating success even in the sowing or planting of our forest trees, with whose conditions of life we are to some extent familiar. Of the fungus to be investigated, however, we, as a rule, know almost nothing ; we do not know the external conditions of germination, we often scarcely know whether the spores are really ripe, whether they are in too damp or too dry a medium, whether sufficient oxygen is admitted to them, or whether the season of the year is the right one for sowing—for spores, like the seeds of forest-trees, require to rest for different periods after ripening, before they will germinate. What has already been said about the numerous conditions predisposing plants to disease will show sufficiently how, even with the best material for infection, experiments may give only negative results. Since even trained mycologists and pathologists often succeed only after innumerable abortive experiments in making themselves acquainted with the conditions under which a plant becomes infected, it will be clear that it may be regarded as simply an accident when an amateur succeeds at all with an infection-experiment.

When the infection has succeeded, it is not enough merely to follow the course of the disease through its various stages—in doing which, moreover, it is of the utmost importance to compare cases of disease met with in the forest—but it is also necessary to discover the external influences which restrict or further the development of the disease.

This part of the investigation is the most difficult. It demands, very specially, the power of accurate observation ; apparently unimportant accessory circumstances must be noticed and compared ; and, above all things, excursions to the forest must be made as often as possible. Investigations of the diseases of our forest trees will seldom lead to any definite result unless we make careful and extensive observations and comparisons in the forest itself. At the same time, still less prospect of success will attend observations of diseases in the forest if they are not accompanied and supported by exact scientific investigation.

If investigation shows that neither animal nor vegetable organisms are the primary cause of the disease, then the latter must be due to some influence in the inorganic environment If it is suspected that unfavourable properties of the soil are responsible for the disease, the unhealthy tree should be removed, and—if possible, at the spot where it stood—a hole should be dug to the depth reached by the lowest roots During the operation attention is to be directed to the consistency of the layers of soil, and to the quantity of water which they contain, and especially to their greater or less accessibility to atmospheric air In the forest a change in the amount of mineral food, so great as to induce disease in a previously healthy tree or plantation, would occur only under circumstances that would at once attract the attention of the skilled observer For instance, top-drought may be a consequence of the removal of litter or the laying bare of the soil, sickness or death may be occasioned by the presence of injurious substances derived from factories, or owing to flooding with sea-water, &c. Chemical investigation will very seldom be necessary More frequently the cause is attributable to atmospheric influences, such as variations of temperature, moisture, or precipitations, or to lightning, noxious gases, &c If it can be determined when the disease first appeared, the task will often be more quickly mastered by collecting information, and by ascertaining the external conditions, than by investigating the diseased plant, although the latter course will, in many cases, lead to the desired end.

As a rule, diseases produced by animals and plants are characterised by their occurring first of all on single plants or parts of plants, and then gradually extending from these centres ; whereas diseases which are due to the influence of soil or atmosphere generally appear regularly and simultaneously over large areas, because such influences are seldom bounded in the forest by narrow limits or confined to the neighbourhood of single plants

Mistakes are most likely to occur when a disease is preceded by an abnormal predisposition, because this alone, and not the disease rendered possible by it, is apt to be kept in view. It frequently happens that we meet with different diseases on the same tree, each of which is at work independently, and when this is the case we should not at once stop the investigation when a cause of disease has been discovered. Very often we encounter, *e.g.* in the low lands of North Germany, devastated woods of Scotch pines, in which many trees have been killed by *Trametes radiciperda.* More exact investigation, however, often results in the discovery that in the same wood, in consequence of insufficient circulation of air in the soil, root-rotting is much more destructive even than the root-parasite.

Only the most careful research, supported by thorough knowledge of the forms of disease, which are so numerous and varied, can protect us against error.

SECTION I

INJURIES INDUCED BY PLANTS

THIS is not the place to discuss the many conditions brought about by the struggle for existence—for space, food-materials, water, and light—between plants of the same or opposite species. Any plant may prove injurious to another if it makes the same or similar claims on the constituents of the soil. When two plants compete with each other, success does not alone depend upon the rapid rate of growth of any particular species on a given situation, but is determined largely by the rate of growth which characterises *individual* plants ; and it is this which is mainly decisive in pure woods It has long been known that superior individual growth manifests itself in the earliest stages of the life of a tree ; in fact, sometimes—for instance, in the case of the oak—it is recognizable in the size of the fruit.[1] It is therefore of the greatest importance not only to exercise care in the selection of the seed, but also to remove weak plants when transplanting in the nursery. When crowded, all plants must struggle with their nearest neighbours ; but I do not consider that it is the province of vegetable pathology to discuss these conditions : rather do I hold that I should closely confine myself to the consideration of those injuries which consist in the *direct* attack of one plant on the life and health of another.

[1] Th. Hartig established this fact experimentally in the nursery at Brunswick thirty years ago.

PHANEROGAMS

No sharp boundary can be drawn between parasites and plants that are only indirectly injurious owing to their proximity, or to their competition for food-materials, light, and so forth * One gradually passes from the latter to plants which, while not subsisting on the substance of others, still directly attack them, and induce pathological phenomena.

Allusion may be made, for instance, to *Lonicera Periclymenum,*† whose stem, when opportunity offers, winds round young trees with the result that a few years later the descent of the plastic materials in the bast is forced to take place in a definite spiral course With increasing thickness the tree is soon subjected to direct pressure by the twining plant, which prevents the direct vertical descent of the solutions of food-substances coming from the leaves It frequently happens that the part of the stem immediately below that of the honeysuckle is deprived of nourishment, the result being that the cambium in that region gradually dies ; whereas the portion above the passively tightening stem of the honeysuckle on the one hand exhibits very vigorous growth, and, on the other, experiences abnormal alteration in its younger parts owing to the spiral direction imparted to all the organs of the vascular bundles.

While there is no doubt that the immediate cause of the movement of plastic substances in the cortex and bast is the fact of their being produced in one place and utilised in another, necessitating a transference from the place of origin to the place of consumption, still the assumption that the movement of the plastic materials in the bast takes place much more easily and quickly in a vertical than in a lateral direction receives support from the fact just mentioned, and illustrated in Fig 1, as well as from many other phenomena In fact, lateral movement is so difficult as sometimes to induce complete cessation of the

* [In such cases the plants not valued are regarded as " weeds ", but it is obvious that any plant may act as a weed towards others, and a little reflection shows that it may act as a weed towards its own species if crowded, &c —ED] † [Honeysuckle —ED.]

nourishment of the band of cambium situated under the stem
of the honeysuckle.

Triticum repens * may also be mentioned here, the sharp-pointed
rhizome of which has the power of piercing and growing through
the fleshy roots of other plants which it
may encounter in the soil. This has
been specially observed in beds of oak
seedlings, though it may be remarked
that the piercing of the roots has resulted in no apparent damage to the
oaks.

The passage to the true parasites—
that is to say, to those which subsist
entirely on the plastic materials of
other plants—is formed by a group of
plants in which one cannot at first perceive a parasitic existence, seeing that
they are provided with leaves containing
chlorophyll, and take water and inorganic nourishment from the soil with
their roots. While they assimilate plastic
materials for themselves, they also attach
themselves to the roots of other phanerogamic plants from which they abstract
organic substances by means of an absorbing apparatus (*haustorium*) on certain of
their roots. To such plants belong the
Rhinantheæ, a sub-family of the *Scro-
phulariaceæ*. The cow-wheat (*Melampy-
rum arvense*), the common yellow-rattle
(*Rhinanthus Crista-galli*), and the louse-
wort (*Pedicularis*) and eye-bright (*Eu-
phrasia*) furnish well-known examples
of this kind of life. As these plants
are parasitic only on the plants of pastures and meadows, we
cannot here spare time to examine them more closely. The genus
Lathræa, also, which contains the common species *Lathræa
squamaria*, the tooth-wort, has not yet been proved to be wholly

FIG. 1.—An oak-stem which has been entwined by *Lonicera Periclymenum*. The stem of the honeysuckle is visible at *d*, *c*, and *b*. Beneath it the cambium is dead, *e*, and the new wood has been
laid on in the form of a spiral, *f*. Growth is again normal at *g*. From *a* downwards the whole
stem is shown without its bark.

* ["Couch grass" or "twitch."—ED.]

parasitic. Its roots are partly attached to the roots of many different plants, including several trees such as beech, hornbeam, hazel, and alder.

Notwithstanding traces of chlorophyll in the *Orobanchaceæ*, these must undoubtedly be classed as true parasites, which derive their nourishment exclusively from the host-plants to whose roots they are attached. Of the numerous species, some occur so plentifully on cultivated plants as to cause appreciable damage *e.g. Orobanche ramosa* on tobacco and hemp, *O. lucorum* on the barberry and bramble, *O. Hederæ* on ivy, *O. rubens* on lucerne, and *O. minor* on red clover. The parasitism of the yellow bird's-nest (*Monotropa Hypopitys*) is still doubtful, but, as its roots are found in contact with those of conifers and the beech, it is extremely probable that though most of its nourishment is got from the humus a certain amount is also abstracted from these plants. Besides *Monotropa* we have the *Orchidaceæ* that are destitute of chlorophyll, which are all of a saprophytic nature.

Nor can the *Loranthaceæ* be regarded as true parasites, because for the most part they abstract only water and inorganic food-materials from trees and shrubs, organic substances being appropriated to a very limited extent. They possess leaves containing chlorophyll, and behave towards their host in exactly the same way as a scion does to a stock. In fact they yield up a portion of the plastic substances which they themselves have prepared to the host-plant, which employs them for its own growth. Whether, however, this occurs in the case of all, or even most, *Loranthaceæ* is doubtful, but at all events such reciprocal nourishing takes place with *Loranthus europæus*. The manner in which the different species of this family abstract water and nourishment by means of their roots from the plants which they inhabit varies extremely, especially when the exotic species are taken into account.[1]

The best-known species is *Viscum album*, the common mistletoe, which is distributed throughout the whole of Europe, and Asia to

---

[1] See Solms Laubach in Pringsheim's *Jahrbüchern f. wiss. Bot.* VI., pp. 575 *et seq.* R. Hartig, *Zur Kenntniss von Loranthus europaeus und Viscum album*, with a table, *Zeitschrift für Forst- u. Jagd-Wesen*. 1876, pp. 321 *et seq.* Dr. C. v. Tubeuf, *Beiträge zur Kenntniss der Baumkrankheiten*, pp. 9—28. Springer, Berlin, 1888.

Japan It is met with on almost all dicotyledons and conifers, but exibits a preference for certain species, *e g* silver fir, Scotch pine, poplars, and fruit-trees ; whereas on others, *e g.* spruce, oak, beech, Spanish chestnut, alder, and ash, it has been met with either very seldom or not at all [1] With regard to the appearance of this familiar plant, it need only be mentioned that narrow and broad-leaved varieties occur on different species of trees The mistletoe is distributed by thrushes (especially *Turdus viscivorus*), which feed upon the berries and carry them off. The birds disengage the sticky seeds from their beaks by rubbing them against the branches on which they perch, and to which the seeds thereby become attached The seeds, which germinate in spring, first of all develop a kind of sucker, from whose centre a fine root appears which pierces the tissues of the cortex. This main root penetrates to the wood of the branch or stem, which, however, it is too delicate to enter. This then finishes its apical growth in length, but, on the other hand, owing to the presence of meristematic tissue behind the apex (such tissue being situated in the region of the cambium of the host-plant), it is enabled to elongate at the same rate as the branch increases in thickness, by the formation of a ring of wood and of bast ("intermediary growth in length") Owing to the fact that the wood-ring envelops the apex of the root of the mistletoe, the latter appears to bore deeper into the wood each year, but this is really due to its being embraced by the stem as it grows in thickness. The growth in length of this root, as of all the "sinkers" that afterwards originate in the roots that are met with in the cortex, very closely resembles the growth in length of a medullary ray possessing cambium of its own in the cambium mantle that covers the whole stem, and is thus enabled annually to elongate both towards the wood and towards the bast Several lateral roots next appear on that part of the radicle which is situated in the cortex, and these proceed to grow both upwards and downwards in the branch These " Rhizoids " or "Cortex-roots" push their pencil-like apices along the young soft bast, without however coming into contact with or altering the cambium zone The organs of the soft bast are dissolved in front of the point, and it

[1] Nobbe, " *Ueber die Mistel, ihre Verbreitung, Standorte, und forstliche Bedeutung*," *Thorander forstliches Jahrbuch,* 1884

may be taken for granted that the products of solution are absorbed by the cortex-roots and used for their own growth. From investigations made on the Scotch pine and the silver fir, the annual growth in length of the cortex-roots is ·75 mm. in the former case and 1·75 cm. in the latter. The growth in thickness would appear to be somewhat irregular. Once a year, very seldom twice, often only each alternate year, a "sinker" originates on the inner side of the cortex-root near the apex. This wedge-like outgrowth is of the same breadth as the cortex-root, but varies much in thickness, and breaks through the cambium zone until it just reaches the wood of the host-plant, where it elongates in the same peculiar manner as has been already described in the case of the radicle. If the cortex-root with its sinkers is exposed, as is represented in Fig. 2, we may trace back from the apex of the root *c*, and accurately determine how many years have elapsed since the various sinkers have originated, because each year these are em-

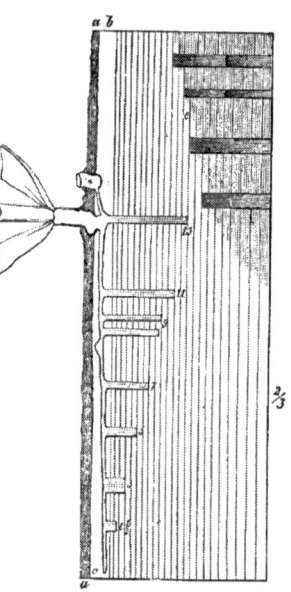

Fig. 2.—Roots of *Viscum album* in *Pinus sylvestris*. The cortex-root, which pushes its apex, *c*, along the bast tissues, *b*, puts forth eight sinkers on the inner surface, and buds and shoots on the outer. The oldest portion has already been pushed out nearly to the dead bark. At *e* the sinkers of a cortex-root which has already been enveloped in the bark are shown.

braced by a wood-ring. Even in the most recent descriptions of the mistletoe we still find, as a rule, Schacht's illustration reproduced, which erroneously represents young sinkers between older ones on the same cortex-root. Water and inorganic nourishment are absorbed by the whole series of sinkers through their lateral surfaces, which are in immediate contact with the water-conducting organs of the wood, and are first of all conveyed to the cortex-root, and through it to the leafy part of the mistletoe. From the peculiar way in which the sinkers increase in length

it is evident that they elongate not only towards the side next
the wood but also towards the side next the cortex. With
the formation of new phloëm-tissues the cortex-roots are constantly being pushed away from the cambium mantle, as may be
seen from Fig. 3. In the case of such trees as the silver fir,
whose stem remains smooth for many
decades before the formation of true
bark begins, the cortex-roots may
thus be pushed away from the cambium mantle without their suffering
any appreciable injury. They may
attain to an age of forty years, a
corresponding age being reached by
the sinkers, whose length increases
in proportion to their age. On the
other hand, trees like the Scotch pine,
which form bark early, show only
short sinkers, of a length of 3-4 cm.,
and an age of twelve to fifteen years.

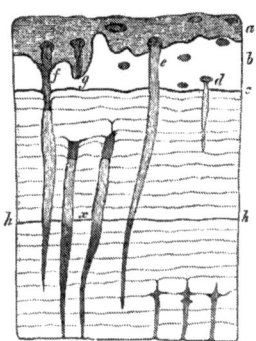

FIG. 3.—Cross section of a stem
of *Abies pectinata* containing
Viscum album. *a*, dead bark
showing dead cortex-roots ; *b*,
region of living bast ; *c*, cambium region ; *d*, cross section
of a cortex-root showing a
sinker six years old ; *e*, a
sinker eighteen years old ; the
cortex-root has lately been
enveloped in the bark, while
the apex of the sinker has
withered in the duramen ; at
f the cortex-root and the portion of the sinker in the bast
have been dead for two years ;
a cortex-root is shown at *g*
which has been dead for six
years. The boundary line
between the duramen and alburnum lies at *hh* ; at *x* two
sinkers are shown, those portions situated in the alburnum
being still alive.

This is to be explained by the fact
that owing to the usually more active
formation of new bast the cortex-
roots are more quickly pushed away
from the cambium mantle. The outer
parts of the cortex are converted
into bark, and as soon as a portion
of cortex containing a cortex-root
is converted into bark, it dries up,
along with that part of the mistletoe
root which it contains, and the connection with the sinker is broken.
This is distinctly brought out in
Fig. 3. The sinker then ceases to
grow, and is covered over sooner
or later by the new wood-rings. Of course the death of a cortex-
root does not take place simultaneously throughout its whole
length. On the contrary, the oldest part—that is to say, the part
situated farthest from the cambium—dies first, whereas those
younger portions which are still enveloped in living cortex

remain alive. These, however, are in the same position as the roots of a tree that has been felled—that is to say, they can no longer conduct nutritive substances to the leafy part of the mistletoe, which must therefore die when its feeding-roots are all confined to the bark. Its place is taken by numerous root-shoots which arise from buds formed on the outer side of those portions of the cortex-roots which are still alive. The mistletoe represented in Fig. 2 is just such a root-shoot. These shoots, which are represented in Fig. 4, form a new root-system

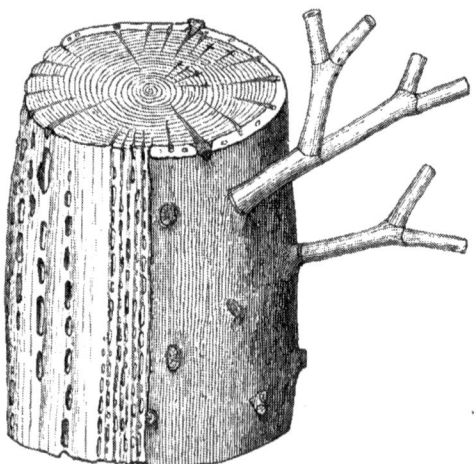

FIG. 4.—Part of the stem of a silver fir showing a group of mistletoe plants. The bark has been removed from one side in order to show the position of the cortex-roots and sinkers.

of their own, and thus it happens that an old stem attacked by mistletoe contains numerous young and old cortex-roots, as well as old and young sinkers. In this way the tree comes to bear as it were a plantation of mistletoes, which is constantly being re-generated by the production of new root-shoots, and which is always taking possession of a larger part of the tree. On old silver firs and Scotch pines it is by no means rare to meet with such mistletoe plantations a yard long and half a yard broad. It ought to be mentioned that the living sinkers begin to die at their apices (Fig. 3) whenever they become enveloped by the advancing duramen Even in the case of the silver fir and spruce it is only the outer wood which conducts water, and in the bole this region seldom embraces more than forty to fifty annual rings, while in the branches it is much narrower.

The damage done by the mistletoe to forest, fruit, park, and avenue trees is by no means inconsiderable. In the Reichswald, in the neighbourhood of Nuremberg, I have seen woods of middle-aged Scotch pines where scarcely a tree had escaped, and where the foliage of the mistletoes competed for effect with the natural foliage of the pines Where practicable, as in orchards, &c , the infested branches should be entirely removed before the mistletoe has had time to spread to any considerable extent Simply breaking off the plants only induces the formation of vigorous root-shoots at the same place

A few words may here be devoted to the genus *Arceuthobium*, of which a species, *Arceuthobium Oxycedri*, occurs in the south of Europe, and also in Austria, where it forms dense bushes on *Juniperus Oxycedrus ,* while in North America quite a number of species attack forest trees, especially the *Abietineæ* These grow in the same way as the European form, or induce the formation of witches' brooms by the rhizoids which live in the cortex causing considerable elongation of the infested branch, from whose cortex numerous shoots 1—2 cm long break through at irregular intervals, as happens in the case of *Arceuthobium Douglasii* [1] In the case of these plants, also, the nutritive substances are absorbed by simple sinkers consisting of a single row of cells, or in other cases by vascular sinkers The injury caused to forest trees by these plants is very considerable ; still one need not anticipate that these parasites will find their way into Europe with the introduction of North American conifers

More interest attaches to *Loranthus europæus*, a parasite specially common in Austria, but also found occasionally in Saxony, the formation of whose roots differs entirely from that of the *Loranthaceæ* already described.

Loranthus europæus is, for the most part, found on the common oak, on which account it is known as oak mistletoe, though it also attacks *Castanea vesca ,* and in Austria, especially

[1] See C v Tubeuf, *l.c*

in the Wiener Wald, it has proved very destructive in stored coppice, where by killing the tops of the oak standards it prejudicially affects their growth in height. An irregular swelling of the size of a man's head (Fig. 5) often occupies the place of the leading shoot. The oblong seeds (Fig. 6, *f*) of the plant, which is deciduous, are affixed to branches by thrushes, as in the case of *Viscum*. There they germinate, and in a few years the base of the parasite becomes completely enveloped in a large excrescence which forms on the tree (Fig. 6, *c*).

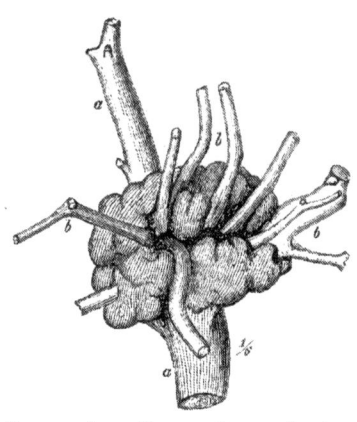

FIG. 5.—A swelling on *Quercus Cerris*, *a*, bearing an old plant of *Loranthus, bb.*

The root-system is to be distinguished from that of the *Loranthaceæ* already described by the fact that the few rhizoids which arise on the radicle always grow downwards—that is to say, in a direction opposed to that of the ascending water—and by these rhizoids

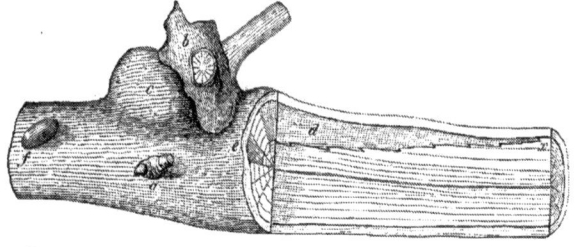

FIG. 6.—*Loranthus europæus* on a branch of *Quercus Cerris*. *a*, a young plant ; *b*, a five-year-old plant ; *c*, an outgrowth of the oak ; *d*, longitudinal section of a root of *Loranthus* ; *x*, apex of the root ; *e*, cross section of a root ; *f*, a seed.

taking up water and food-materials directly from the wood without forming sinkers.

The pointed apex of the root (Fig. 7, *x*) does not grow outside the cambium zone, but in the young wood—that is to say, in the part of the branch that is not completely lignified—and always exactly parallel to the longitudinal course of the xylem elements. The apex of the root, which is flat upon its inner side, advances in a definite region of the young wood, at the same time pressing out, splitting, and dissolving the still

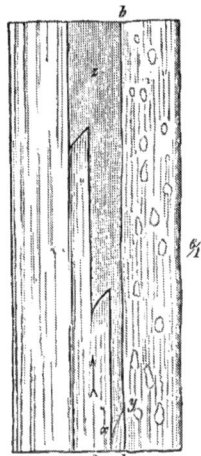

unlignified elements by means of its convex outer surface. This goes on till future progress in the original direction is prevented by the resistance consequent on lignification in the outer layers of the new wood which the roots of the parasite are unable to split off and dissolve. The root, whose apex is thus in a *cul-de-sac*, is forced to form a new growing-point some distance behind the apex—namely, at the place where the convex outer side comes into contact with the cambium zone (Fig. 7, *y*). From this new point growth in length begins afresh, and is continued in a zone situated nearer the periphery of the wood. During the development of an annual ring the root

FIG. 7.—Youngest portion of a root of *L. europæus. a*, cortex and bast; *b*, cambium; *c b*, young wood; *d*, the portion of the wood-ring of the current year in which growth has been completed; *e*, wood-ring of the previous year; *z*, root of *Loranthus*; *x*, the apex of the root; *y*, the point where a new root-apex is forming.

of *Loranthus* (which, of course, can only grow during the period when the cambium produces young wood) is generally thrice compelled to shift the direction of its growth farther out, the result being that the inner side of the root shows a corresponding step-like arrangement, which accords with the advance of the wood, as is shown in Figs. 6 and 7. The distance between two steps measures from 5 to 8 mm., while the annual growth in length of the root amounts to about 1·5 cm. As the roots grow in a direction opposed to that pursued by the ascending water, the latter flows directly from the conducting elements of the wood into the roots of the *Loranthus*, at the points of depression. The root possesses the power of growing vigorously in thickness, whereby it is enabled for a series of years to keep pace with the increase in thickness of the oak-branch, and thus to protect itself against being overgrown. The root usually continues to grow in thickness for eight years, though it occasionally ceases to grow in four, when it is enveloped in the adjoining wood owing to the formation of callus.* Thus, while it still continues to grow at the point, those portions of a greater age than eight years lie embedded in the wood, but they remain capable of performing their functions perfectly and of taking in food-substances, so long as they are not in the region of the duramen (heart-wood), where water is no longer in motion. Even then, however, nutriment may still be furnished to the *Loranthus*. Here and there processes similar to medullary rays run from the roots enveloped in the wood to the cortex, and at this point root-shoots may be formed from adventitious buds, although this occurs but seldom.

The gnarled swelling which forms on an oak-branch attacked by *Loranthus* is a very striking object. While the upper part of the branch ultimately dies, the rugged protuberance increases in thickness, and envelops the whole of the lower part of the *Loranthus* along with its branches. The part of the oak-branch that bears the swelling also increases in thickness, although it possesses no leaves of its own, and there can be no doubt that the products of assimilation of the parasite serve both for its own nourishment and for that of the host-plant.

As it is not expedient to shoot the thrushes even for the purpose of preventing the spread of the seeds of *Loranthus*, we must, in this case also, minimise the evil by cutting off branches which are infested by the parasite.

Although the Dodders, *Cuscuteæ*,[1] which are true parasites destitute of chlorophyll, are for the most part injurious only to herbs, they are still met with on woody plants with sufficient frequency to merit a short description in this treatise. Their seeds germinate in spring on the ground. The young plant perishes unless its long thread-like stem

---

*[Callus is the cushion-like mass of growing tissue which arises at the edges of a wound and eventually covers over (occludes) the damaged surfaces—see Part II. under the discussion of wounds, &c.—ED.]

[1] See Sorauer's *Handbuch*, 2nd Edition, Part II., pp. 32—48. v. Solms-Laubach, *Ueber den Bau und die Entwicklung parasitischer Phanerogamen.* Pringsheim's *Jahrb.* vol. iv.

finds a suitable host-plant, in which case it twines round the-stem of the latter and sends numerous absorbing roots, or "Haustoria," into the cortex Although the root which originally connected the plant with the ground disappears, the dodder nourishes itself by extracting nutritive materials from the host-plant round which it twines by pushing its sucker-roots as far in as the vascular bundles, in which, by breaking up into unicellular threads, they often assume a brush-like appearance If the plants are small they may soon be killed, but in the case of larger plants it is only their development that is interfered with, and, so far, I have not noticed any appreciable damage to woody plants

The *Cuscuteæ* are distributed by means of numerous seeds, which are produced by dense globular inflorescences, situated at some distance apart on the stem , and it has lately been discovered that the plants themselves may survive the winter The only protective measure that is practically applicable in the case of this parasite consists in using seed uncontaminated by dodder At the same time, the eradication of the dodder-plants which are so common along hedges and fences is also to be attended to These are the places where we most frequently meet with dodder, and there too it will oftenest be found on various woody plants. *Cuscuta europæa,** the greater dodder, is the species most frequently met with It is parasitic on almost all trees, as, for instance, *Corylus, Salix, Populus, Prunus spinosa*, but especially on *Humulus, Urtica*, and *Galium.* As the lesser dodder, *Cuscuta Epithymum*, is specially liable to attack clover and lucerne, it is the species most to be feared Besides having numerous other host-plants, *e g. Thymus, Genista,. Calluna*, &c , it has also been met with on *Vitis Cuscuta Epilinum* is commonest on *Linum usitatissimum* The other species are but, seldom met with

* [*C. Europæa* is far less common in this country than is the Lesser Dodder, *C Epithymum*, and *C Epilinum* is not often met with —ED]

CRYPTOGAMS

PSEUDO-PARASITES

Among cryptogams, also, we meet with plants which, although not parasites in the narrower sense of the term, may prove directly injurious to other plants by the manner of the attack which they make upon them. A case in point is furnished by *Thelephora laciniata*,[1] whose thallus* lives on the humus constituents in the upper layers of the soil, but whose sporophores grow up and embrace young plants, as is shown in Fig. 8. Commencing at the ground, they envelop leaves and branches so completely as to smother and kill them. I have found the ferruginous, sessile, more or less confluent sporophore, with its lacerate pileus,† commonest on young spruces, silver firs, and Weymouth pines, on which it ascends

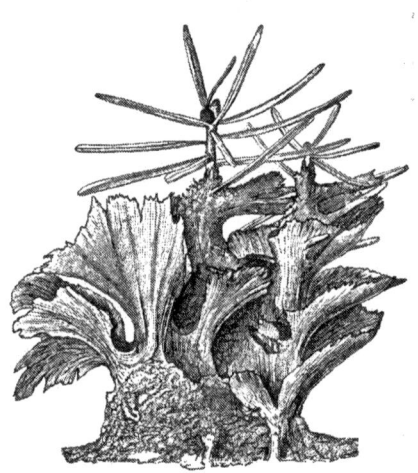

Fig. 8.—Thelephora laciniata.

to a height of eight inches from the ground. For similar reasons, though to a much less extent, trees may be injured by an excessive growth of lichens. A luxuriant growth of lichens on the stems and branches of trees is a sign that the air is permanently humid. It is also connected, however, with the quality of the soil and the rate of growth of the trees, and

[1] R. Hartig, *Untersuchungen a. d. forstbot. Inst.*, I. p. 164.   Berlin, 1880.
*[Thallus is the term applied to the cellular vegetative body of many lower plants.—ED.]
†[The pileus of a mushroom or similar fungus is the expanded upper part, on a portion of whose surface the spores are produced.—ED.]

it is well known that the stems of beeches grown on the best
soils, especially such as are calcareous, bear but few lichens,
whereas on the poorer soils, especially such as are sandy, lichen-
covered stems are very abundant When a beech grows very
rapidly in thickness, the formation of periderm* must also be
rapid, and, since the dead cork-cells on the outer side of the cortex are soon exfoliated and pushed off, luxuriant development
of lichens is impossible Where growth in thickness progresses
very slowly, the dead cork-cells adhere to the cortex for a much
longer period, so that lichens are enabled to grow longer and
develop more vigorously Under such circumstances, too, moisture is longer retained, and this also favours the growth of
lichens The same remarks apply to trees, such as the spruce,
whose outer layers of periderm are cast off as scales, or whose
moribund layers of cortex are thrown off in later life as plates
of bark The slower the growth of a tree, the more slowly do the
outer cortical layers die, and so much the more suitable are the
conditions for the growth of lichens Consequently, although the
presence of lichens·is primarily the sign of a permanently humid
atmosphere, or of a slow rate of growth, it cannot be denied
that they do some small amount of damage to trees During
summer the tree takes in oxygen by means of numerous lenticels,
and this process goes on even in the older parts of the stem.
The presence of oxygen in the interior of the tree is absolutely
necessary for maintaining the processes of metabolic, or chemical
and vital changes. Now, if the passage of oxygen to the lenticels † of the cortex is impeded by a luxuriant growth of lichens
or mosses, we may assume that the tree suffers more or less in
health This may furnish us with a reason for the death of so
many branches of spruces and larches whose crowns are overgrown with lichens.

* [Periderm is the corky covering which replaces the delicate epidermal
layer as the stem grows older Cortex is the green, living cellular tissue
covered by the periderm, &c. For the connection between "periderm" and
"bark," see later in Part II On a two-year-old twig of a tree, about June or
July, we usually find epidermis on this year's growth, and periderm on the
browner, older part—ED]

† [Lenticels are the perforated or pervious corky warts noticed on the
periderm of twigs—e g , they are very evident on twigs of chestnut, elder,
&c —ED]

BACTERIA, OR SCHIZOMYCETES

It was not till a few years ago that bacteria were recognized as plant-infesting parasites, and only in extremely isolated cases has it been placed beyond doubt that these low organisms are the primary cause of disease in plants.*

Whereas the processes of decay, and most of the infectious diseases of man and animals, may be traced to bacteria, the plant-organism is protected against them by the peculiarity of its structure, and especially by the absence of circulatory channels for conducting the nutrient fluids which could serve to distribute any lowly organisms which might happen to be present in the food. It is only by means of the vessels and intercellular spaces that they can distribute themselves in any great numbers in the body of the plant, for in other cases they have to pass through the cellulose or woody cell-walls, which offer great resistance to their attack.

In addition to this, the vegetable juices, most of which show an acid reaction, are unfavourable to their growth. As a matter of fact, bacteria have hitherto been found only in the tissues of plants whose cells are parenchymatous in character and possessed of very delicate walls, as, for instance, bulbs and tubers. Sorauer [1] applies the collective name bacteriosis to diseases due to bacteria. These diseases are characterised by the fact that the succulent parts of the infested plant are converted into a slimy glutinous pulp, which emits a most repulsive stench. Owing to the action of those bacteria which have advanced more rapidly along, and spread out from, the vessels, the delicate walls of the cells are dissolved, being employed, along with their protoplasmic and other contents, in nourishing and fostering the bacteria, whereas the starch is often left intact.

The yellow "bacteriosis" of the bulbs of hyacinths (*Bacterium Hyacinthi*) is a common disease. Here the yellow slimy masses

---

[1] Sorauer, *Handbuch*. 2nd Edition. Pp. 74—112.

* [Russell has recently put together the literature on this subject in a dissertation to the John Hopkins University, Baltimore, 1892.—ED.]

of bacteria, called *B Hyacinthi* by Wakker, occur in the vessels, and completely decompose the surrounding tissues.

Under normal conditions the bacteria do not attack perfectly healthy well-developed bulbs Wounds of some kind are necessary, which may be easily caused in transplanting the bulbs, or the bulbs are previously attacked by filamentous fungi, amongst which a species of *Hyphomyces* almost always accompanies the disease. In a damp situation the bacteria enter the wound and cause it to putrefy

The wet-rot or "bacteriosis" of the potato, which generally appears as an accompaniment of the decomposition of tubers and stalks due to *Phytophthora infestans,* is also a disease produced by bacteria.*

The investigations conducted by Vuillemin a few years ago[1] have shown that *Pinus halepensis* is subject to a disease induced by bacteria which may prove fatal to the tree   The first symptoms are that the stem and branches show small outgrowths which gradually enlarge till they embrace the whole circumference, when the portion of the tree situated higher up dies and withers   When, as is usually the case, these swellings occur on most of the branches, the tree succumbs altogether

The olive, also, suffers from a disease which is induced by a species of bacterium (*Bacillus Oleæ tuberculosis*)[2]

Lately a disease of apple- and pear trees has been described by J Burrill, of Urbana, Illinois, under the name of "blight," the cause of which, according to this investigator, is to be ascribed to the invasion of a bacterium   The disease appears to bear resemblance to the tree-canker produced by *Nectria ditissima* . and as, in the case of this fungus, large numbers of small gonidia resembling bacteria are produced in the cortex, it remains to be seen whether this disease has not been erroneously ascribed to a bacterium

[1] C. R. Séances   November 26th, 1888, and December 31st, 1888

[2] L. Savartane, *Les Maladies de l'Olivier*, *Comptes Rendus*, December 6th and 20th, 1886.

* [It is extremely probable that in these and other similar cases the minute bacteria travel into the tissues down the tubes of the filaments (hyphæ) of the fungus, feeding on the decomposing protoplasmic contents of the latter —ED]

MYXOMYCETES, OR SLIME-FUNGI

Amongst the *Myxomycetes*, several—though the number is a small one—live as parasites, and cause peculiar swellings to form on the roots of their host-plants. To these belongs *Plasmodiophora Brassicæ*,[1] which causes "club-root"* in cabbages, &c. The roots and lower parts of the stems of cabbages which are attacked by this parasite exhibit excrescences which vary in size but are often as large as one's fist. These soon decay, and the enfeebled plants frequently fail to give any return. The disease is combated, on the one hand, by burning the stumps of all infested cabbages, so that the parasite is prevented from spreading in the soil, and, on the other, by ceasing to cultivate cabbages for some years on ground where the disease has appeared.

Alder-roots, even when very young, are generally beset with much-branched tuberous outgrowths, in whose cells Woronin has discovered a fungus which he has named *Schinzia Alni*.

FIG. 9.—Excrescence on a root of the alder, due to *Schinzia Alni.*

Recently Möller[2] has referred the plasmodium-like structures which occur in the cellular tissue of the excrescences of the roots of alders to a Myxomycete belonging to the genus *Plasmodiophora*, which he calls *Plasmodiophora Alni*. Whether this is identical with *Schinzia Alni*, or distinct from though occurring simultaneously with it, cannot be decided without further investigation.

The tubercles on the roots of *Leguminosæ*† and *Elæagneæ*, in whose parenchymatous cells plasmodium-like structures occur, also require to be further investigated.

---

[1] Woronin in Pringsheim's *Jahrb.*, vol. xi. p. 548.

[2] H. Möller, "*Plasmodiophora Alni*," *Ber. Deutsch. bot. Ges.*, 1885, Pt. 3, p. 102.

*[Often termed "Fingers and Toes" and "Anbury."—ED.]

†[These tubercles are caused by symbiotic organisms of quite different nature from Myxomycetes. See *Phil. Trans.* 1887 and *Proc. Roy. Society*, 1889.—ED.]

FUNGI

THE STRUCTURE AND LIFE-HISTORY OF FUNGI GENERALLY

Every fungus consists of a mycelium and a sporophore The former takes in and elaborates the nutrient materials, and discharges all vegetative functions, whereas the sporophores produce the organs of reproduction, which may have a sexual or an a-sexual origin, in the latter case being produced in a vegetative manner by division and abscission, a process analogous to the formation of buds in the higher plants The mycelium has its first inception in a tubular outgrowth which is produced during the germination of a fungal cell, and which by absorbing water, and usually food-materials as well, forms what is called a fungal filament, germ-tube, or "Hypha" The germ-tube is characterised by apical growth, and by the formation of lateral branches, whereby a system of fungal tubes (hyphæ) is formed which is constantly anastomosing, and which has erroneously been compared to a stream with its tributaries and springs. This comparison is not apt, because fungal hyphæ are almost uniform in diameter,* there being usually but little growth in thickness of the oldest part of a system of filamentous mycelia.

In the case of some species no partitions form in the fungal filaments or hyphæ, but as a rule transverse septa, which divide the internal space into chambers, are formed a short distance behind the apex. Such a hypha is said to be "septate" When quite young its contents consist of protoplasm, which is usually colourless, and only at some distance from the apex does a granular appearance manifest itself, which is generally due to the formation of fat globules. The cells of the mycelium are frequently filled with large drops of fat, and this is especially the case when the mycelium assumes a condition of inactivity, in which it remains till growth is again resumed The potato tuber, by storing up reserve materials (in this case chiefly starch), which are not utilized in the formation of new

---

* [Nevertheless, as the author himself points out on the next page, the hyphæ developed later are often progressively finer and finer than those first produced. This is strikingly obvious in the case of some moulds—*e.g*, *Mucor*.—ED

tissues till the following year, behaves in a physiologically similar manner. The fatty oil is not unfrequently coloured, and especially in the case of "rusts," whose oil is of a golden yellow colour, a yellow hue is imparted to the tissues of the leaves and cortex in which the mycelium grows. Usually drops of cell-sap, or so-called vacuoles, also appear at an early stage in the protoplasm, and these, by forcing most of the protoplasm against the walls, impart a frothy appearance to the contents.

It is only when nitrogenous food-materials are present in abundance that the contents of the hyphæ are retained for a long time. This occurs when mycelia vegetate in or amongst the tissues of the cortex, bast, or leaves, which for the most part consist of parenchymatous cells. On the other hand, the contents disappear early when the mycelium vegetates in tissues containing little nourishment, as is markedly the case in the wood of trees. When the mycelium of a fungus spreads in the interior of a tree, it finds abundance of nitrogenous food-materials in the contents of the cells of the medullary rays and the wood-parenchyma. It is thereby enabled to produce vigorous hyphæ, even when traversing the empty lumina of tracheïdes, wood-fibres, or vessels. When the hyphæ have to pass through regions of tissue containing no proteids, their apices are supplied with protoplasm which is sent forward from behind at the expense of the older parts of the hyphæ. The latter are therefore soon emptied, and become filled with air. Although the empty mycelial hyphæ persist for some time, they ultimately disappear under the decomposing influence of the fungus itself. The consequence is that one may frequently fail to find anything of the fungus itself, although numerous punctures in the walls of the cells show clearly that the fungus had formerly been present in that part of the tissues. In proportion as the mycelium develops in the wood, so does a dearth of proteids for the production of new fungus-protoplasm set in, and this is strikingly manifested in the diminished thickness of the new hyphæ.

The walls of the hyphæ, which consist of fungus-cellulose, are at first very delicate, though in the course of time they occasionally attain such a thickness that the lumen almost entirely disappears. In this way it sometimes happens that a fungus-body which consists of these thick-walled hyphæ becomes almost as hard as stone.* On the other hand, there are instances of the entire walls—or only their outer, less frequently their inner parts—being converted into a mass of slime, and under certain conditions the walls, when treated with iodine, become as blue as starch would under similar circumstances. This occurs, for instance, in the mycelium of *Hysterium*, and the apices of the asci of *Rosellinia quercina*.

At first the hyphæ are almost always colourless, but in later life the walls very often assume a light or dark brown colour. In rarer instances other colours are produced, *e.g.* the blue green of *Peziza æruginosa*, which causes the so-called green-rot in the dead wood of the oak, beech, and spruce. Sometimes the coloration is confined to the outer or to the inner layers of the cell-wall. The mycelium, which increases acrogenously and produces lateral branches, generally remains in a filamentous condition—that is to say, the mycelial filaments remain isolated, or, at most, coalesce only at the points where they cross each other.

A mycelium which vegetates on the outside of leaves, fruits, &c., as is the case for instance with the mildews (*Erysiphe*), is said to be epiphytic. When it vegetates in the inside of plants it is called endophytic. In this case it either grows from cell to cell by piercing the walls (intracellular), or it advances between the cells (intercellular). In the latter case it behaves, as a rule, like most epiphytes, sending out short branches, known as sucker-tubercles or haustoria, into the interior of the cells, in order to extract the nutrient contents.

When the opportunity is presented for the filamentous mycelium to develop vigorously outside the nourishing substratum—as happens most frequently in the case of the wood-inhabiting *Hymenomycetes*—it forms a skin-like layer, which often attains large proportions. In other cases it may fill cracks or other cavities in the stems of trees. Such layers, crusts, and masses of fungal growth are best known in the case of *Polyporus sulphureus, P. vaporarius, P. borealis, Hydnum diversidens, Trametes Pini, Merulius lacrymans*, &c.

* [Such indurated masses of fungus-mycelium are usually termed *Sclerotia*, in reference to their hardness: they commonly serve as storehouses in the sense indicated on p. 40.—ED.]

Then, again, the mycelium frequently assumes the form of branching strands, which enable the fungus to traverse strata containing little if any nutriment. In such a case the strands are either formed by the loose union of similar hyphæ, when they are called *Rhizóctoniæ*, or they are peculiarly constructed of various kinds of organs. The strands of the dry-rot fungus— *M. lacrymans*, for instance—possess, first, organs with wide lumina and perforated transverse walls which resemble vessels ; secondly, thin sclerenchymatous filaments ; and, thirdly, delicate hyphæ rich in protoplasm, and provided with clamp-cells. In addition to such strands we have the so-called Rhizomorphs, which, externally, present a close resemblance to the fibrous roots of higher plants, while their internal structure displays peculiarities which depend entirely upon the species of fungus to which they belong. The best known of these are the rhizomorphs of *Agaricus melleus*, which, when they have room to develop, assume a round shape. In the cortical tissues of living trees they spread out in a fan-like manner. Their internal structure shows characteristic features, by which they may at once be distinguished from the rhizomorphs of other fungi, *e.g. Dematophora necatrix*.

Functions similar to those of the tubers and rhizomes of higher plants are to be ascribed to the so-called sclerotia. These are peculiarly constructed masses of mycelium, in which rich stores of nutriment, especially protoplasm and oil, are deposited. After remaining quiescent, it may be for a long time, they germinate on the recurrence of favourable conditions, and produce either a new filamentous mycelium or the sporophore of the special fungus.

The simplest form of such resting-mycelia is represented by the cell-groups of *Cercospora acerina*. Then come the sclerotia of *Rosellinia quercina*, and the well-known sclerotia of *Claviceps purpurea*.*

The sporophores which spring from the mycelium bear the organs of reproduction—that is to say, the spores which give rise to new individuals. The same species of fungus frequently produces different kinds of reproductive organs, which develop

* [Rhizomorphs are also, in a sense, extended Sclerotia—see also pp. 40 and 41.—ED.]

on or in variously shaped sporophores The shape of the sporophore is much more characteristic of the species than the mycelium, and as the sporophore (which often grows to a large size) is almost always outside the nutrient substratum, whereas the mycelium is hidden in it, the uninitiated often regard the sporophore as the whole fungus, and pay little or no attention to the mycelium

When the sporophore consists only of single filaments springing from the mycelium, it is called a simple or filamentous sporophore, whereas the compound fungus-body goes by the name of a compound sporophore. On account of the great variety in shape and structure exhibited by the sporophore, it would be going beyond our limits were we to consider it more closely at this time * Cells which are called spores are separated off in some way or other in or on the sporophore, and these by germinating give rise to new individuals. The cells, from which spores directly originate, are known as sporogenous cells The spores are produced either internally, as in the case of the sporangia of the *Phycomycetes*, and the pouches or asci of the *Ascomycetes*, or by apical abscission, in which case the mother-cell is often called a basidium.

In the case of some groups of fungi, sexual processes have been proved to exist.† The course of development, as in other plants, has been divided into two sections (generations), of which the one called the a-sexual generation begins with the germination of a sexually fertilized cell, and leads to the production of spores (oospores , zygospores) The germination of these spores gives rise to the second generation, which, in form and development, is essentially different from the a-sexual plant It ends with the formation of the male and female sexual apparatus and sexual cells, and on this account is called the sexual generation Spores which do not mark the close of the a-sexual generation, but which, like buds, brood-cells, and other

*[The student may be referred to the works of De Bary, Zopf, and Von Tavel for details —ED]

† [Such a book as this is, of course, not concerned with the morphological details of this difficult and involved matter, and the student is referred to the works of Tulasne, De Bary, Zopf, and Brefeld for particulars of the subject. The outcome of recent researches is to show that sexuality has disappeared in the case of most fungi.—ED]

organs of vegetative propagation, produce the same plant-form as that from which they themselves sprung, are called gonidia Following the example of De Bary, this term may be taken to replace that of conidia, introduced by Fries

The gonidia serve chiefly for the rapid propagation of fungi during the growing season, whereas, in general, the sexual spores serve to carry the species over from one year to another

I may here briefly sketch the mode and conditions of life of the fungi Just as in the case of phanerogams the germination of seeds, and the length of time during which they will retain their vitality, are much influenced by external factors, so in the case of spores and gonidia the power to germinate—varying with the different species—appears either immediately after ripening, or not till after the lapse of a long period of rest.

On the other hand, in the case, for instance, of the gonidia of the rust-fungi, the power to germinate is lost a few days after ripening, whereas the oospores of *Phytophthora omnivora* may remain dormant in the ground for at least four years, without losing their vitality.

The demands as to heat are not so great as in the case of the higher plants, and thus it is that we see the most luxuriant fungus-vegetation in autumn, at a time when the growth of trees has ceased The optimum temperature for fungi, as for other plants, varies very much, but in this connection we still await the results of reliable investigations In the case of those fungi which concern us here a temperature over 212° F. (100° C.) is undoubtedly always fatal

One vital condition, of extreme importance for fungi, is a high degree of humidity of the air or of the substratum in which they develop This is due not only to their requiring large quantities of water, but also, and much more, to the ease with which the mycelia or young sporophores die in a dry medium from the effects of excessive evaporation. On this account it is very seldom possible for the mycelium to develop in the open air. It is for this reason also that in all the rusts and smuts, and even in the case of a great number of *Discomycetes*, the sporophores—which usually require to scatter their spores outside the plant—

are formed under the protection of the epidermis of the host-plant, which is ruptured only after the spores have ripened.

The fact that in summer, in spite of a more favourable temperature, far fewer so-called " Toad-stools " spring from the ground than in October, when the atmosphere is relatively much more humid, shows clearly how dependent on a constant supply of moisture in the air is the development of sporophores that expand entirely outside the substratum.* The extensive distribution which the larch-fungus, *Peziza Willkommii*, has experienced in the plains of Germany is almost entirely due to the abundant production of fructifications and spores which have ripened perfectly in the moist, stagnant air of the dense low-lying woods; whereas in the breezy Alps the fructifications almost always wither before they have had time to mature.

Not only does a moist atmosphere affect the ripening of the fructifications and the germination of the spores outside the plant, but it also appears to have great influence on the development of the fungus even inside the plant. This assumption is at least supported by the fact that *Cæoma pinitorquum*, which is a perennial in the shoots of the pine, assumes the proportions of a plague when the month of June is wet, but causes scarcely any appreciable damage when the weather is dry.

As regards their adaptations for nutrition, fungi may be arranged in two great divisions. Parasite is the term applied to those fungi which draw their nourishment from living organisms; saprophyte, to those which live on dead bodies. It is not possible, however, to draw a sharp line of demarcation between these two categories. To begin with, it may often be disputed whether an organic body is to be called dead or living. By far the greater part of the wood of trees is made up of dead cells, the walls of which alone remain; and only a relatively small part, consisting of the parenchymatous cells of the wood and medullary rays, remains alive and contains protoplasm. Seeing that many fungi live only on the old stumps of trees and on trees that have long been felled or otherwise killed, whereas others destroy growing trees, it would

---

* [The whole subject needs thorough investigation, however, and it would be particularly valuable to have more information as to the importance of sunlight and other factors in this connection.—ED.]

appear to be necessary that we should regard the sound wood of a growing tree as being alive, even although only a portion of its cells may exhibit the phenomena of life.* In many cases it is difficult to decide whether wood—*e g* the duramen in many trees —was actually living when attacked by the fungus-mycelium, or whether its parenchymatous cells were then dead But apart from those doubtful cases, in which it is difficult to decide at once whether a fungus is existing as a parasite or as a sapro-phyte, there are many fungi which occupy a position somewhere between those which are strictly saprophytic and those which are strictly parasitic Numerous fungi are in a position to complete the whole course of their development as saprophytes, though, under certain circumstances, they may also live in a purely parasitic manner *Agaricus melleus* and the genus *Nectria* may serve as examples Such fungi are designated facultative parasites Other fungi, which, as a rule, go through the whole course of their development as parasites, but which are capable of growing as saprophytes, at least during certain stages of their existence, are designated facultative saprophytes To this group belong, for instance, *Phytophthora omnivora* and *Cercospora acerina* We have thus to distinguish four groups 1 Obligate saprophytes. 2. Facultative parasites 3 Facultative sapro-phytes. 4 Pure—that is to say, strictly obligate—parasites, which can only grow parasitically, *e g.* the group *Uredineæ*

The spread of an infectious disease may take place in two distinct ways, either by infection caused by the mycelium, or by infection caused by the spores, including the gonidia.

Infection by the mycelium is met with in nature most frequently in the case of those parasites which grow below ground This is to be explained by the fact that the varying amount of moisture in the air admits of the development of the mycelium above-ground only in exceptional cases, as, for example, in *Herpotrichia* and *Trichosphæria*

In the case of infection by the mycelium, it is, to a certain ex-tent, the same individual fungus that spreads from root to root and

---

* [In many such cases the destructive fungus may be looked upon as a *Saprophyte*, when viewed with regard to the immediate seat of its action— *e g*, wood—but as a *parasite* with regard to the tree as a whole, whose life is destroyed in consequence of the secondary results of the damage.—ED]

from branch to branch. Thus, when a disease spreads in a wood in this way, it does so with relative slowness, but, in dense woods at least, it is, as a rule, characterised by the death of all or most of the trees inside the local area of distribution. The result is that blanks, varying in size, gradually occur in the wood

In the case of *Trametes radiciperda*, the most dangerous enemy of spruce and pine plantations, contact of the diseased root containing the fungus with the sound root of a neighbouring tree is necessary in order that the latter may be penetrated by the mycelium which protrudes from between the bark-scales. In the case of *Agaricus melleus* mycelial strands, in the form of rhizomorphs, spring from the diseased roots, and proceed to spread underneath the surface of the ground. The roots of sound conifers that are encountered are embraced, and an entrance is effected between the bark-scales : these are forced off by means of the conical apices of the rhizomorphs, which then bore into the living tissues.

In the case of *Rosellinia quercina*, which destroys the roots of the oak, the delicate filiform mycelium—which here and there forms rhizoctones—spreads during moist warm weather from the diseased plant into the upper layers of the soil, where it attacks and destroys the roots of neighbouring plants in a manner which will be described more fully later on On account of the mycelium being capable of forming small round sclerotia on oak-roots, and of assuming a resting condition, the parasite is afterwards enabled to resume the growth which has been interrupted by such unfavourable conditions as cold or a temporary lack of moisture in the soil

Dematophora necatrix spreads in a similar manner in vineyards

The distribution of a parasite by spores and gonidia is not, as in the case of infection by the mycelium, confined to plants in the immediate neighbourhood, although these are certainly most exposed to the danger of infection. It may, in fact, happen that trees at a great distance are infected, while those in the immediate neighbourhood remain sound When treating of special cases we shall have occasion to bring into prominence how various are the conditions that influence this question, and, in particular, how animals and men, by spreading the spores, may induce the outbreak of an epidemic   Here a few examples may be cited in illustration of this point.

Phytophthora omnivora produces spores (in this case called oospores) in the interior of the seedling, as the result of sexual fertilization.   When the plants decay, these spores get into the ground, where they may rest for a series of years and produce the disease afresh, should the right kind of seedlings be present But, in addition to these oospores, the parasite produces numerous gonidia on the surface of its leaves.   These are capable of germinating at once, and are blown by the wind, or conveyed by animals or men, to plants in the neighbourhood, the result being the formation of new hotbeds of infection. ·

In the case of *Trametes radiciperda*, which, on the spruce at least, almost always produces its sporophores in holes in the ground, new centres of infection are usually established by spores that have been distributed by mice

The smut of wheat is generally induced by employing seed, to the outside of which spores of the smut-fungus have adhered, but it may also be caused by manuring with fold dung if infected straw has been used as litter

The conditions become most interesting in the case of heterœcious rust-fungi—that is to say, parasitic fungi which complete the various phases of their development not on the same plant but on two different species   Here mention need only be made of the connection between the fungus of the barberry and rust of wheat, or between *Æcidium abietinum* and *Chrysomyxa Rhododendri* and *Chrysomyxa Ledi*, or, finally, between *Æcidium columnare* and *Melampsora Goeppertiana*   In the case of these parasites the occurrence of the disease depends on the presence of both host-plants . still De Bary has demonstrated that in cases of necessity *Chrysomyxa Rhododendri* may exist without spruces, and it appears to me to be beyond doubt that *Melampsora Goeppertiana* is able to develop without the silver fir   We know only one or other of the stages of development of a series of rust-fungi, and it remains to be determined what the other fungus-forms are with which they stand in relationship

The method of attack of parasites, also, reveals the most marked differences   Whereas the epiphytes—whose mycelium vegetates externally on the epidermis of leaves, fruits, and stems —send only delicate absorbing organs into the interior of the

E

epidermis, the endophytes must send either their germ-tubes, arising from spores germinating externally, or else their mycelia into the interior of the plant

According to the mode of attack, we may divide parasites into two main groups   The first comprises those which have the power to attack uninjured plants , the second, those which can effect an entrance only through a wound   It is those belonging to the latter group which are accountable for infectious wound-diseases   The former are partly confined to the very early stages of development of the plant, or of the shoots, leaves, or roots , in rarer instances they also force their germ-tube into the stomata and lenticels of more mature leaves and shoots   It is only when the mycelial growths are very vigorous, like those of *Agaricus melleus* and *Trametes radiciperda*, that they are able, by entering between the bark-scales of the root and forcing them apart, to bore even into cortical tissues covered with corky layers.

The mode of attack of *Rosellinia quercina* affords one of the most interesting examples of this kind   The main root of the young oak is protected against external attack by a corky mantle of considerable firmness   The mycelium of *Rosellinia* is consequently able to get at the interior only by first killing the fine lateral roots, and as these traverse the corky layer the hyphæ form breaches in the protective covering.   At the points where the lateral roots pierce the corky mantle the mycelium develops fleshy tubercles, which then send one or more processes through the breach into the interior of the root   It is only some time afterwards that the destructive filiform mycelium is formed at the apex of these processes

Wounds admitting of the entrance of parasites into the interior of trees arise in many ways   Reference need only be made here to such agencies as animals, man, hail, wind, snow, &c.

The effects produced by parasites on the tissues of the host-plant can be explained only by assuming that in each species of fungus a peculiar enzyme (ferment) is produced in its protoplasm, which by being excreted through the hyphæ is communicated to the adjoining cells *

Very often the mycelium vegetates in living parenchymatous

* [That such enzymes are really formed and excreted by the protoplasm has been proved   For instance, *Botrytis* excretes an enzyme capable of dissolving cellulose—see *Annals of Botany*, 1888, " A Lily-disease "—Ed]

tissues without producing any appreciable effect on them. Especially is this the case when the cells have already attained the condition of permanent tissue before the mycelium has appeared in or between them.

The mycelium of *Calyptospora* has no apparent action on the permanent tissues of *Vaccinium Vitis-Idæa*; whereas, in very young shoots, it causes enlargement of the parenchymatous cells of the cortex, with the result that very remarkable swellings are produced on the stem.

One of the most frequent results of the action of fungi is that a stimulus is given to cell-division. Mention may be made of the swellings on the stems of silver firs whose cortical tissues are infested by *Æcidium elatinum*, of the swellings on the stems of junipers owing to *Gymnosporangium*, &c. Still more frequently the infested parts are stimulated to display altogether abnormal growth. Flowers, fruits, and portions of stem of various species of plants are transformed in a most peculiar manner by fungi belonging to the genus *Exoascus*. It does not necessarily follow, however, that their vitality is thereby prejudicially interfered with (*e.g.* witches' brooms of the hornbeam, &c.)

Changes in the cell-contents are often noticed which are indirectly induced by fungi. This is the case, for instance when the mycelium of *Hysterium macrosporum* kills the elements of the bast at the base of spruce-leaves, thereby destroying their capacity of conducting plastic materials, while the other parts of the leaves still live and assimilate. The result is that on account of the newly formed carbo-hydrates not being able to get away from the leaf, all the cells become packed full of starch.

The tannin which is dissolved in the cell-sap offers excellent food for the mycelium of *Polyporus igniarius*, being absorbed first of all by the hyphæ which penetrate the sound oak-wood, after which it undergoes metabolic changes in the youngest parts of the mycelium. The occurrence of mycelia in oak-timber is therefore followed by the disappearance of tannin, the smell of which has long been regarded by practical men as a proof of the sound condition of the wood. The conversion of a portion of the cell-contents or of the cell-walls into turpentine under the action of the hyphæ of *Peridermium Pini* is also interesting. Although it often happens that the starch-grains disappear very soon from

amongst the cell-contents, as, for instance, in the case of attack
by *Phytophthora omnivora*, it also not unfrequently occurs that
starch resists the destructive influence of wood-parasites longer
than the thick lignified walls of the cells in which it is contained.
In fact the manner of decomposition of the starch-grains varies
exceedingly according to the species of fungus that attacks them.
Similarly as regards the cell-walls. The solvent action of living
hyphæ is manifested in two distinct ways. Where a hypha
touches a cell-wall it dissolves the particles of calcium oxalate
contained therein, exactly as a root-hair, by means of the
acid solution which it exudes, dissolves the particles of calcium carbonate with which it comes into immediate contact.
This action is confined to the surface of the cell-wall which is
actually in contact with the fungus-filament. But every parasitic fungus that lives in the wood of growing trees destroys
the wood in a manner peculiar to itself. When one and
the same species of fungus, *e.g. Polyporus sulphureus*, vegetates
in trees of such different species as oak, willow, and larch, it
changes the wood so peculiarly in a short time that at first
sight it is difficult to distinguish these timbers from each other,
although, in a sound state, they are so strikingly different. This
can be satisfactorily accounted for only by assuming that each
species of fungus exudes an extremely powerful and characteristic ferment, which permeates the walls for long distances, and,
to begin with, frequently dissolves only the incrusting substances,
more especially the lignin.

In the accompanying figure (10) the upper part of the wall is still
lignified, whereas the lower part consists of pure cellulose. After
the removal of the lignin the middle lamella, which is most lignified, is the first to disappear, the result being that the various
organs become completely isolated, as happens when sound wood
is treated with potassium chlorate and nitric acid. The hyphæ
which pierce the walls with their apices disappear later on, when
they themselves are dissolved by the ferment. In Fig. 11 is
shown how the elements of the wood of the oak have been completely isolated and dissolved by the action of a ferment.

In the case of other wood-parasites the decomposition takes
place in the following manner. By the extraction of the incrusting substances a zone bordering the lumen is first converted into

cellulose, after which decomposition spreads generally throughout the walls. Thus the walls constantly become thinner, till finally only the corners remain where three tracheids join (Fig. 12). Several wood-parasites, *e.g. Polyporus Schweinitzii* and *P.sulphureus*, induce a form of decomposition owing to which the walls, with the exception of the middle lamellæ, shrink so much as to give rise to numerous cracks which ascend from right to left. By certain adjustments of the microscope we of course see simultaneously the corresponding cracks in that half of the wall which belongs to the neighbouring fibre, and this makes it appear as though the cracks crossed each other. The walls, which are very rich in carbon, assume a brown colour (Fig. 13). We shall direct attention in the special division dealing with this subject to other forms of decomposition, all of which are characteristic for some species of fungus. Here it need only be mentioned that the question whether all the organic parts of the lignified cell-walls require to be absorbed by the mycelium of the fungus before being decomposed into carbonic acid and water, or whether to some extent they are directly oxidized and converted into these substances, cannot at present be finally decided. As a large quantity of oxygen must be made use of during decomposition, its rapidity depends to a great extent on the facilities that are afforded for the entrance of air to the interior of the tree. A certain amount of air is present in every woody fibre. In dicotyledonous trees the air is conducted to distant parts by means of the vessels and intercellular spaces, and in resinous conifers by the resin-ducts ; but in the case of the silver fir and other conifers destitute of resin-ducts the mode by which

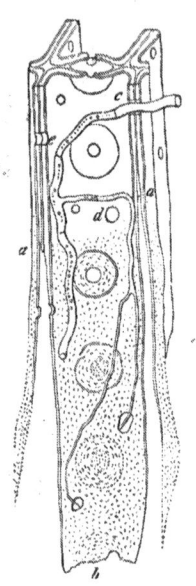

FIG. 10.—Tracheid of *Pinus sylvestris*, decomposed by *Trametes Pini*. The primary cell-wall has been completely dissolved as far as *a a*. In the lower part the secondary and tertiary layers consist only of cellulose, in which lime - granules are distinctly visible, *b ;* filamentous mycelia, *c,* penetrate the walls and make holes as at *d* and *e*.

the entrance of air to the interior of the tree is ensured has yet
to be explained. The carbonic acid which is formed can
escape by the same way as the oxygen entered. To what
extent carbonic acid and oxygen when dissolved in water may
traverse the wood remains to be determined.

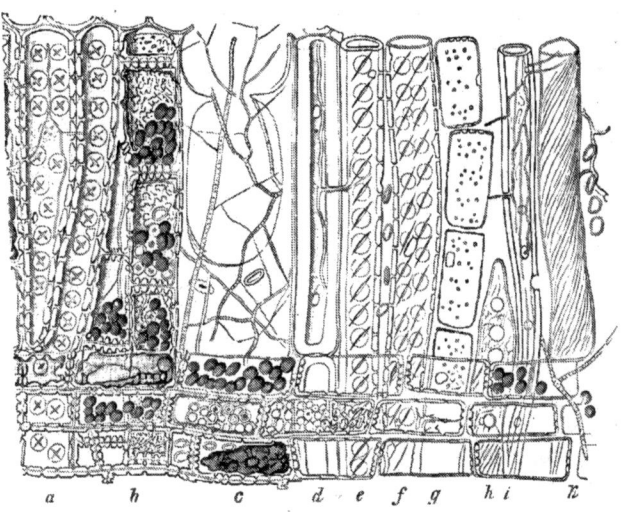

FIG. 11.—Decomposition of oak by *Thelephora Perdix.* *a*, tracheids containing a
few filamentous mycelia, and showing the perforations in the walls which these have
occasioned ; *b*, wood-parenchyma with starch-granules, the latter being in process
of solution, and having to a certain extent disappeared from the neighbourhood
of the cell-walls ; *c*, vessels containing hyphæ ; *d*, sclerenchymatous fibres showing filamentous mycelia and perforations ; *e* and *f*, tracheids which are completely isolated owing to the dissolution of the primary cell-walls ; the thickened
rings of the bordered pits are also found isolated between the tracheids. On
account of the organs being dismembered the openings into the bordered pits no
longer cross each other ; *g*, wood-parenchyma, completely dismembered and
almost entirely dissolved ; *h*, tracheid just before final disappearance ; *i*, sclerenchymatous fibre much decomposed ; *k*, a tracheid whose walls have become
fissured before being dissolved.

In concluding these general considerations, I have still to
discuss the question whether any—and, if so, what—means are
at our disposal for combating the ravages of fungi. I am
convinced that every forester who has received a scientific
education will take a deep interest in obtaining a knowledge of
what tree-diseases are, and how they originate, even though it

may not be possible to apply any practical remedies. It is by
no means the first duty of science to call attention to the
practical value of a new discovery; nor should research be
primarily directed to those fields which promise to yield results

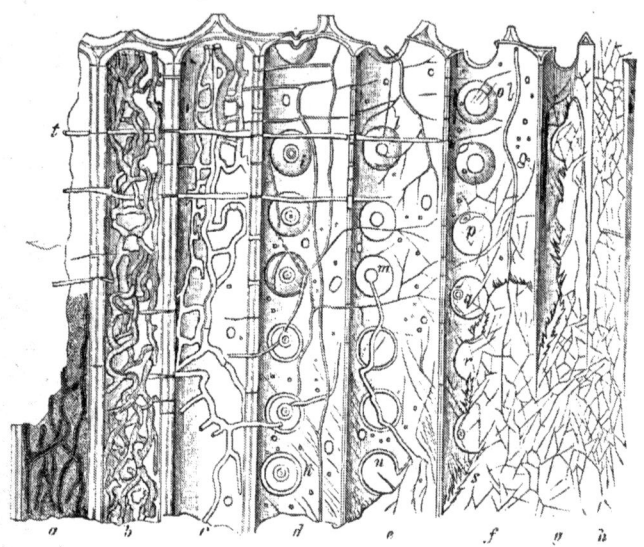

FIG. 12.—Decomposition of spruce-timber by *Polyporus borealis*. *a*, a tracheid containing a strong mycelial growth and a brownish yellow fluid which has originated
in a medullary ray; at *b* and *c* the mycelium is still brownish in colour and
very vigorous. At *d* and *e* the walls have already become much attenuated
and perforated; here the mycelium has been less abundantly supplied with nutriment and the filaments are very delicate; at *f* the pits are almost completely
destroyed; at *g* and *h* only fragments of the walls remain. The various stages in
the destruction of the bordered pits are to be followed from *i* to *r*; at *i* the
bordered pit is still intact; at *k* the walls of the lenticular space have been largely
dissolved, their inner boundary being marked by a circle; at *l* one side of the
bordered pit has been entirely dissolved; at *m* and *n* one sees a series of pits
which have retained a much-attenuated wall on one side only—namely, on that
which is provided with the closing membrane. In making the section a crack
has been formed in this wall. Between *o* and *r* both walls of the pits are found
to be wholly or partially dissolved, only at *p* and *q* has the thickened portion of
the closing membrane been preserved; at *s* the spiral structure of both cell-walls
is distinctly recognizable. These walls when united form the common wall of
the tracheid; at *t* hyphæ are seen traversing the tracheids horizontally.

capable of immediate conversion into hard cash. The duty
of science is nobler and higher than that. But if, in our
search, we succeed in fathoming the mysteries of nature, and,
at the same time, obtain results of practical value to humanity,

then it is our duty to direct attention to these. This I have never neglected to do, and, although I do not under-estimate the many difficulties which foresters will long have to encounter in endeavouring to put into practice the results of scientific investigation, still I hold that, as the guardians of the forest, it is their duty to make themselves acquainted with the results of scientific investigation, and carefully to watch over the health of what is committed to their charge. Not only must they do everything that may prevent disease, but they must also instantly adopt energetic measures to nip an existing disease in the bud, and so prevent its further spread.

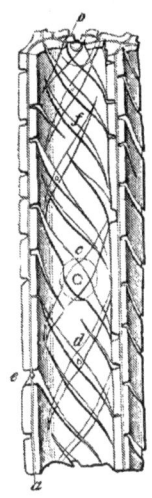

FIG. 13. — Portion of a tracheid of *Pinus* decomposed by *Polyporus Schweinitzii*. Most of the cellulose has been extracted, the walls consisting chiefly of lignin. In drying, cracks have been formed, which however do not extend to the primary wall, *a b*. These cracks are seen to cross each other at the bordered pit *c*, and at the perforations *d* and *e*; a simple fissure is shown at *f*.

As every disease must necessarily be treated differently, this is not the place to enter on the consideration of specific measures. But just as human health is better maintained by the observance of certain general laws, so there are also general rules for the treatment of woods, by following which we may preserve the health of the trees.

The best prophylactic measure against the occurrence and spread of an epidemic is the formation of mixed woods. Infection, both below and above ground, is least likely to occur when every tree is isolated by being surrounded by others of a different species. On ground which is infested by root-parasites, or which contains resting-spores whose vitality is preserved for many years, it may be advisable, under certain circumstances, to abandon the cultivation of some particular species of tree. One should also try to prevent the distribution of spores either by men or animals, and especially so in the sale and purchase of young trees.

In the case of root-parasites, the therapeutic measures to be adopted when a disease has broken out consist partly in promptly pulling up or otherwise eradicating the diseased plants, and partly in isolating the infected area by means of narrow trenches. As a general and most important measure, it is advisable at once to remove from the wood all plants attacked by fungi, so that their spores may not spread infection. Tidiness is the first hygienic law in sylviculture.

Having noted above the more important points that should be kept in view in studying the parasitic fungi, I shall now, in accordance with the plan of this work, pass on to a systematic examination of the parasites that occur in woody plants. As regards fungi that are parasitic on farm or garden crops, I shall shortly refer only to such as are of general practical importance. For plant-parasites not included in this work I must refer to the handbooks of Frank or Sorauer.

Following the most recent classification of the fungi, which distinguishes three groups—namely, *Phycomycetes* (Algal fungi), *Ascomycetes*, and *Basidiomycetes*—I shall begin with the first group. This embraces five orders—namely, *Zygomycetes*, *Entomophthoreæ*, *Saprolegiaceæ*, *Peronosporeæ Chytridiaceæ*, and *Ustilagineæ*.*

Of these orders there are only two that need be considered here.

PERONOSPOREÆ

The *Peronosporeæ* are true vegetable parasites, whose mycelium ramifies in the tissues of higher plants, the hyphæ being for the most part intercellular, though occasionally also intracellular. Special absorbing organs (haustoria) are employed for abstracting the nutriment from the living cells, which consequently die after a shorter or longer period. The sporophores which spring from the mycelium either grow through the stomata or burst through the epidermis. These in various ways form sporangia, which produce gonidia, often motile.

Having moved about for some time in a drop of water as swarm-spores, the gonidia develop a germ-tube, though the sporangia may also germinate directly without having first produced swarm-cells in their interior.

* [For details as to the classification of fungi the reader may be referred to the text-books of De Bary, Zopf, and Von Tavel.—ED.]

In the tissues of the host-plant, though occasionally outside of it, female sexual organs (oogonia) originate on the mycelium, and during fertilization the male sexual organs, called pollinodia or antheridial branches, are brought into contact with these oogonia The antheridia send a minute process (the fertilizing-tube) into the interior of the oogonium, which is fertilized by its protoplasm receiving a small portion of the contents of the antheridium This gives rise to the formation of the egg-spore (oospore), which is provided with a thick cell-wall

While the gonidia, being easily detached and carried by wind or animals, provide for the rapid distribution of the parasite during summer, the oospores reach the ground in the dead and decaying parts of plants There they pass the winter—indeed, in such a position they may remain alive for a number of years—after which they either germinate directly, or first of all produce sporangia with zoogonidia.*

PHYTOPHTHORA OMNIVORA (SYN, PHYTOPHTHORA FAGI, AND PERONOSPORA SEMPERVIVI).[1]

The disease caused by this parasite was noticed in forestal publications over a hundred years ago as " the disease of seedling beeches," and cannot be unknown to any forester employed in beech woods When seedlings are abundant after a rich seed-year the disease is to be met with over the whole of Germany, and the more plentifully the wetter the months of May and June. The fungus also attacks other broad-leafed trees, e g. Acer, Fraxinus, Robinia, as also herbaceous plants such as Fagopyrum, Clarkia, Sempervivum, &c. The parasite is equally widely dis-

---

[1] I described this parasite in 1875 in the Zeitschrift für Forst- und Jagd-wesen, pp 117—123, under the name of P fagi A detailed account of the history of its development, and of the disease to which it gives rise, along with a plate, was contributed by me to the Untersuchungen aus dem forst-botanischen Institut, 1880, pp. 3—57 In 1875—that is to say, simultaneously with me—Schenk described this fungus under the name of P. sempervivi. In order to settle the question of priority De Bary selected the name Phytophthora omnivora (Beitrage zur Morph. und Phys der Pilze, 1881, p 22).

* [For an account of the Phycomycetes peculiar to Britain the reader may be referred to Massee's British Fungi (Reeve & Co., 1891) —ED.]

tributed in the seed-beds of conifers, where it may be met with on the seedlings of every species.

The disease may attack seedling beeches before they have reached the surface of the ground, in which case a dark discoloration spreads from the primary rootlet, and the plants die off. Or, not till the cotyledons have unfolded does the stem above and below them, or at their base, become dark green and change colour (Fig. 14, *a*, *b*) ; or similar spots may be recognized on the cotyledons (Fig. 14, *c*), or on the primary leaves (Fig. 14, *d*). Should the weather remain long wet, decomposition quickly spreads over the whole plant, while during dry weather the plants wither and assume a reddish brown and scorched appearance. Young sycamores, ashes, and robinias show similar pathological symptoms, and, in particular, very black streaks will frequently be found running up or down the stem from the base of the cotyledons. Frequently it is only the apex of the stem and the leaves that become black, in which case the plant recovers ; but if, on the other hand, the lower part

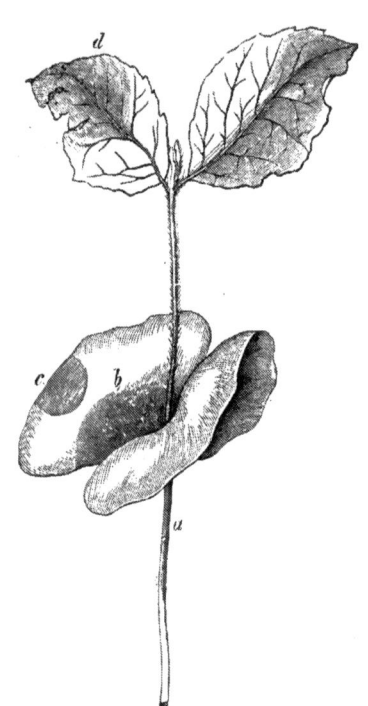

FIG. 14.—Diseased seedling beech. Stem below the cotyledons dark green at *a* ; cotyledons diseased at *b* and *c* ; first foliar leaves showing blotches as at *d*.

of the stem is attacked, recovery is impossible. Where the seeds of conifers are sown in rows, it is not unusual for a large number of the plants to perish before they have appeared above the surface of the ground. The roots and stems usually decay, and the young plants die or wither without any mechanical injuries being observable. It is worthy of note that, owing to the death and disappearance of the whole of the seedlings at certain places, blanks four inches and more in length may be formed in the seed-drills.

The infectious character of the disease may be gathered from the peculiar way in which it is distributed. A diseased plant soon becomes surrounded by diseased neighbours, and thus the epidemic spreads centrifugally in beds that have been sown broadcast, and in two directions where the seed has been drilled. Should a frequented footpath lead through a beech wood that is being regenerated by seed, all the plants growing on the path and along the sides contract the disease and die in a short time. It has also been observed that if the disease has once appeared in seed-beds it usually recurs in succeeding years in a much-accentuated form. The disease is known to be greatly favoured by rainy weather—especially if accompanied by heat—and by any kind of shading, whether produced by standard trees or by artificial covering. The first appearance of the disease in any year can only be due to the oospores of the parasite, which lie dormant in the soil during winter, and infect the germinating seedlings in spring. The mycelium spreads in the tissues of the seedling, and, in the case of the beech, both in the stem and in the cotyledons, the latter being probably attacked as they are being pushed up through the ground. In the tissues of the cotyledons the mycelium is almost entirely intercellular (Fig. 15, *b*), withdrawing the nourishment from the interior of the cells by means of small

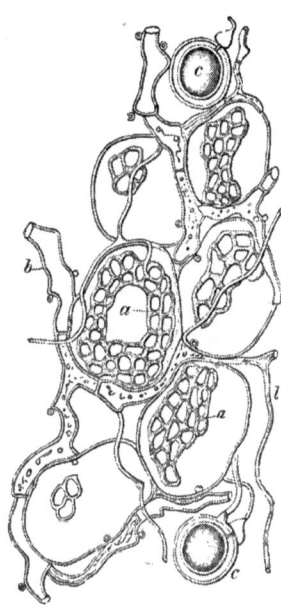

FIG. 15.—Cellular tissue from the cotyledon of a diseased beech. The starch-grains have been abstracted from the protoplasm which has withdrawn from the cell-walls, *a ;* the mycelial filaments, which are of varying thickness, *b b*, grow intercellularly, and are provided with minute haustoria ; each fertilized oogonium contains an oospore, *cc.*

roundish haustoria. The consequence is that the starch-grains soon disappear, and the protoplasm dies and contracts from the cell-walls (Fig. 15, *a*). While the fungus continues to spread in the plant, numerous hyphæ break through the epidermis to become sporangiophores (Fig. 16). The swelling of the extremity (Fig. 16, *f*) gives rise to a lemon-shaped sporangium, which is provided with a papilla at the apex, and a short pedicel at the base (Fig. 16, *g*). After its abscission from the stalk the latter elongates afresh to produce a second sporangium (Fig. 16, *g*, *h*), and meanwhile the first generally drops off (Fig. 16, *i*). Should the sporangia come into contact with water—as, for instance, a drop of rain or dew which has lodged about the cotyledons—they germinate directly, putting forth one or more germ-tubes, which generally proceed to bore into the epidermis of the host-plant. In other cases the protoplasmic contents of the sporangium form a large number of extremely

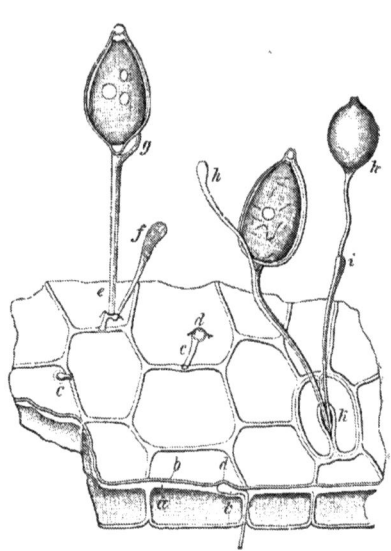

FIG. 16.—Epidermis of a diseased cotyledon of the beech. *a*, the external wall of an epidermal cell; *b*, the cuticle; *c*, a hypha which has intruded itself between the wall and the cuticle; at *d* it pushes up the latter; at *e* it appears on the surface, and at *f* it forms a sporangiophore. After producing the first sporangium it branches at *g*, to form a second *h*, while the first drops off at *i*; a stoma is shown at *k* from which sporangiophores project.

minute and very active gonidia (swarm-spores, or zoospores—Fig. 17, *c*), which are capable of free movement after the apex of the sporangium has been dissolved. For some hours these swim about in a drop of rain with all the activity of infusoria, until they settle on the epidermis of the host-plant, when they germinate with one or even four tubes (Fig. 17, *a*, *b*). Sometimes the zoospores germinate in the interior of the sporangium when their germ-tubes may either break through the lateral walls or push out through the open apex of the sporangium (Fig. 17, c). In either case the germ-tubes creep about for some time on the epidermis of the host-plant, after which they force their way into the interior, and especially at those places

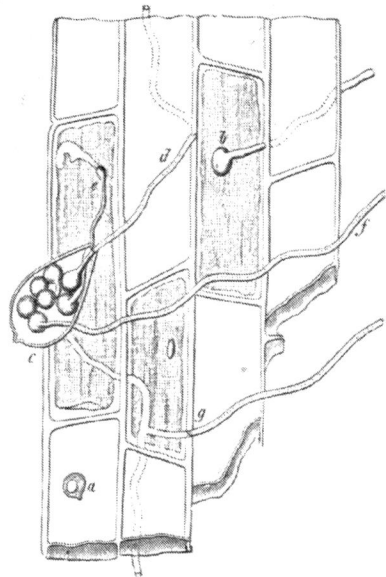

where the lateral walls of the epidermal cells are situated (Fig. 17, b, d). Less frequently the germ-tubes reach the interior by first traversing an epidermal cell (Fig. 17, e). Under favourable circumstances the development of the parasite may have progressed so rapidly in the plant that three or four days after infection new sporangiophores may make their appearance.

The sporangia, and the swarm-cells that form in them, serve to spread the disease during the months of May, June, and the earlier part of July. They either fall directly on to neighbouring plants, or are carried by the wind. Their distribution is greatly assisted by animals—as, for instance, by mice

Fig. 17.—The surface of the stem of a seedling beech. At a b zoospores are seen which germinate and send their germ-tubes into the interior at a point where the common wall of two epidermal cells abuts on the surface ; c, a sporangium whose zoospores have germinated, d f, in its interior ; at e a germ-tube has grown directly into an epidermal cell ; at g a germ-tube has reappeared on the surface.

(in the seed-beds)—and game, but most of all by man. The death of all plants along a path is the result of the sporangia and swarm-cells adhering to the trousers or coats of passers-by, and afterwards dropping off farther along the path.

From what has been said, the favouring influence of rain, shade, &c., is sufficiently evident. In dense seed-beds the hyphæ grow directly from one plant to another, and this offers a simple explanation for the total destruction of all the plants at certain parts of the bed

As the result of the sexual act the oospores originate in the tissues of the host-plant in the following manner In the intercellular spaces of the leaf-parenchyma of the .beech, globular swellings appear at the apex of numerous short hyphal branches, and become oogonia , while smaller so-called antheridia originate in like manner either at the apex of special hyphæ, or on the basal portion of the stalk of the oogonia In each case a transverse septum delimits the organ from its stalk (Fig 15, *c c*). The antheridium having very early laid itself against the outer wall of the oogonium, and the most of the protoplasm of the latter having become aggregated to form an oosphere, the antheridium next develops a short process, the fertilizing-tube, which it pushes into the interior of the female organ as far as the oosphere A part of the contents of the antheridium is then transferred to fertilize the oosphere, which is thereby converted into an oospore.

In the roots of conifer seedlings oospores are formed not only in the cortical parenchyma but also in the interior of the tracheides, when, in consequence of the restricted space, they frequently assume an elongated form.

The oospores reach the ground in the decomposing parts of plants, and there they may remain capable of germinating for at least four years Some soil taken from a diseased beech seed-bed in 1875, having been distributed in water and poured upon a bed of seedling beeches, caused disease and death of the germinating plants not only in 1876 but also in 1878, and even in 1879

The practical measures at our command for combating the disease follow from what has been said. In order to guard against the outbreak of an epidemic, we must avoid sowing seeds on ground where the disease has once proved destructive, though we may cultivate transplants on it The oospores that remain in the ground will prove destructive only to seedlings. Should the disease appear in a seed-bed, all contrivances for producing artificial shading must be removed, as they prevent the rapid evaporation of water from the surface of the cotyledons. All dead and visibly diseased plants should be removed If a number stand close together, the distribution of the sporangia and

gonidia may be most quickly prevented by heaping on earth   If
the diseased plants occur singly they should be carefully pulled
out and buried in a firmly trodden trench, in order to guard
against the dissemination of the sporangia   In traversing the
bed the spread of this disease ought to be obviated as much as
possible by the workman not allowing his boots subsequently to
come into contact with healthy plants.   The seed-bed should
also be inspected daily

PHYTOPHTHORA INFESTANS.   THE POTATO DISEASE.

Although the fungus which produces the potato disease had
been introduced from North America before 1845, it is only
since that year that it has assumed the dimensions of a plague in
Europe, where it always causes great loss in wet years.   In the
mode of its distribution and in its dependence on wet weather it
very closely resembles *P omnivora*   A characteristic feature is
the occurrence on the leaves of black blotches, which, constantly increasing. in circumference, and finally embracing the
stems, may bring about the premature death of the parts of the
plant above ground.   Although the tubers of diseased plants are
generally more or less affected, still this is sometimes the case
only to a small extent, being recognizable merely by a few brown
specks on cutting into the tuber   During wet years the tubers
often rot for the most part in the field, those that are less
attacked decaying in the cellar or pit during winter.   These
changes (wet-rot) are to a large extent due to the action of
bacteria *

The mycelium of *P infestans* passes the winter in the tubers,
and when these are planted out it grows into the sprouting shoots
invading the tissues of both stem and leaf   On examining the
neighbourhood of the black blotches, one recognizes, even with
the naked eye, a zone which is distinguished by its mouldy
appearance   Here are to be found the numerous sporangiophores,
for the most part projecting from the stomata   They agree
in shape with those of *P omnivora*, and bear similar but more
numerous sporangia, which convey the disease to sound plants,
and are even carried by the wind to adjoining fields   There is

* [See footnote on p 38 —ED]

no doubt that they are also brushed off and distributed by animals, as, for instance, by hares. The germination of the sporangia, or their production of swarm-spores as the case may be, agrees generally with that of the allied species The sporangia, however, reach the ground in large numbers, and are carried down to the tubers by the rain-water. Should the ground remain wet, infection follows upon the development of the germ-tube The fact that varieties of potatoes with thin skins are more easily penetrated by the germ-tube of the fungus than those having thick skins may explain how it is that the latter suffer less from disease

The formation of oospores, which I have demonstrated in the case of *P omnivora*, has not yet been discovered in the potato fungus, and possibly it may not exist Seeing that the mycelium passes the winter in the tubers, the existence of the fungus does not in this case depend on the formation of oospores. The occurrence and spread of the disease is most of all influenced by the humidity of the air and soil, because, in a moist environment, sporangia are abundantly produced on the leaves, and the germination of the sporangia and gonidia, both above and below ground, is greatly favoured.

If dampness prevail during storage in winter, numerous sporangiophores are produced on the tubers, especially in the region of the eyes, or where a wound may happen to occur ; and by means of the sporangia that are formed the disease may be conveyed to previously sound tubers even at that season of the year

PERONOSPORA VITICOLA

A decade or two ago this parasite of the vine was introduced from America, and in the interval it has rapidly spread through the vineyards of Europe

Its American designation of mildew, or grape-vine mildew, has been changed in France to *mildiou*. In Germany it is called the false mildew of the vine (*falscher Mehlthau der Reben*).

The disease is characterized by the occurrence of large grey patches on the under side of the leaves, while on the upper side the infested spots become yellow or reddish. The diseased spots dry up, and the leaves are shed prematurely During

F

rainy weather the disease spreads rapidly, but dry weather at once retards further progress. The fungus passes the winter in the form of oospores, which are produced in the diseased leaves. During summer the distribution is effected by sporangia and zoospores, as in the case of *Phytophthora*. Infection takes place chiefly on the young shoots and leaves, the epidermis of which is but slightly cuticularized. The disease proves the more destructive to vines and grapes the earlier in the season it appears, and especially so when favoured by wet weather.

It is not improbable that other species belonging to the genera *Peronospora* and *Pythium* do injury to young trees. It is especially desirable that investigations be instituted to prove whether *Pythium de Baryanum*—which in crowded beds causes the death of many agricultural plants—is also injurious in the seed-beds of dicotyledonous and coniferous trees.* The genus *Cystopus* also belongs to the *Peronosporæ*, the best-known species of which is *Cystopus candidus*, which produces the white-rust of crucifers.

USTILAGINEÆ †

Although this order contains only fungi which are parasitic on herbaceous plants, especially grasses, still the diseases which they produce are of sufficient importance to require a short description here.

In the every-day language of the farmer, Smut is a term applied to the most varied phenomena of disease in plants. In the narrower sense of the word, however, the term is restricted to those diseases which produce a dark brown mass of spores in certain parts of plants, especially flowers and fruits, less frequently on leaves, stems, and even roots. In the particular part of the plant that is occupied by the copious mycelia of the smut-fungus this spore-powder is formed by the abscission or abjunction of abundantly developed fungus-filaments, the tissues of the plant itself being almost completely destroyed.

The mass of spores is either formed on the surface of the

* [An allied form was exceedingly destructive in seed-beds of Cinchona in Ceylon in 1880–1881.—ED.]

† [For the British forms of Ustilagineæ see Massee, *op. cit.*, and Plowright, *British Uredineæ and Ustilagineæ* (Kegan Paul & Co., 1889).—ED.]

plant or it remains enclosed by the epidermis, in which case it appears as a black semi-transparent swelling.

The spores of smut may retain their capacity for germination for several years. On the recurrence of favourable conditions they usually produce a stout germ-tube called the promycelium (*vorkeim*), which, after attaining a length equal to two or three times the diameter of the spore, forms a number of smaller spores, known as sporidia, at its apex or on its sides.

Frequently the promycelium breaks up directly into a number of sporidia. In the case of those species which produce whorls of sporidia at the apex of the promycelium, a process of fusion takes place between adjoining sporidia, and these afterwards drop off in pairs.

When a germinating smut-spore or sporidium comes into contact with a suitable young host-plant, it sends its germ-tube through the epidermis, and thus gets into the tissues of the stem, where the mycelium grows upwards, chiefly intercellular, without producing any apparent damage. It is only in the parts of the plant where spores are formed that the tissues are destroyed.

Those smut-spores which fall to the ground before or during harvest usually germinate at once, and perish in the absence of suitable young host-plants.* This being the case, the disease persists from year to year, for the most part, owing to the employment of seed to which smut-spores adhere externally. When the corn is being threshed the detachment of the spores from smutted plants offers ample opportunity for the contamination of the seed-grain. Frequently, however, the spores are conveyed to the field in manure which has been made with smutted straw.

On account of the germination of the smut-spores being dependent in great measure on moisture in the air and soil, the occurrence of the disease is favoured in a soil whose physical condition—either naturally or owing to the liberal application of farm-yard manure—enables it to retain large quantities of water.

It follows from what has been said that attention should first

* [Brefeld has shown that the "sporidia" may reproduce by budding saprophytically during long periods in the manured soil.—ED.]

be directed to preventing the transference of smut-spores to the field   To secure this, seed which is as clean as possible should be used   If this cannot be had, the adhering spores should be killed by steeping the seed-grain for twelve to sixteen hours in a one-half per cent solution of cupric sulphate   Further, the use of smutted straw for manure should be avoided.

The most important kinds of smut (brand) are :—

THE COAL-BRAND, STICKY-BRAND, STINK-BRAND, OR BUNT of wheat (*Tilletia Caries and T lævis*)—which besides attacking wheat is also found on quickens, wall barley, and meadow grass (*Poa pratensis*)—is characterized by the fact that the spore-powder (which emits a disagreeable smell when fresh) remains enclosed in the grains till the time of harvest   The bunted grains being bruised in threshing liberate the spores, which adhere to the sound grains, and, both being sown, the young plants become infected

The DUST-BRAND (*Ustilago*) is the most destructive genus, and also contains the greatest number of species. *Ustilago Carbo* attacks not only oats, wheat, and barley, but also a large number of meadow grasses   It completely destroys the ovary, and usually the paleæ as well, so that brown spore-powder escapes on to the stalk.

Ustilago destruens, the Millet-brand, destroys the panicles of the millet while they are still enclosed by the highest leaf-sheath.

Ustilago Maydis, the Maize-brand, produces large swellings, completely filled with dark brown spore-powder, on the stem, leaves, and cobs of the maize.   Numerous other species occur on grasses, herbs, and bulbous-rooted plants

The STEM-BRAND (*Urocystis*) is frequently met with, and especially the brand of rye-stems, *Urocystis occulta*   It is very conspicuous, on account of the highest internode of the rye-stem rupturing longitudinally, and allowing the black spore-powder to escape.

Other forms often met with are *Urocystis Violæ*, *U Anemonis*, and *U Cepulæ*

ASCOMYCETES SAC FUNGI

This second group of fungi has obtained its name through the spores being produced in the interior of sacs (asci) In some cases the sporocarp results from a sexual process.* The fungi belonging to this group are very numerous, and are arranged in four orders—the *Erysipheæ*, *Tuberaceæ*, *Pyrenomycetes*, and *Discomycetes*

THE MILDEW FUNGI, ERYSIPHEÆ

All the mildew fungi are true parasites Their mycelium vegetates on the surface of plants—that is to say, on the epidermis of leaves, fruits, and stems, and obtains its nourishment by means of haustoria from the interior of the epidermal cells, which consequently turn brown and die The ascocarps which are developed on the mycelium are usually globular, and completely closed—that is to say, unprovided with an apical or other opening,† and may be recognized with the naked eye as small dark specks. These hibernate and carry the fungus over to the following year, while in the course of the summer gonidia are formed by abscission on numerous simple erect hyphæ These are at once capable of germinating, and spread the disease during the period of growth On account of the interwoven mycelia and gonidiophores, when luxuriantly developed, forming a fine grey meal-like covering on the upper surface of the leaf, the term " Mildew " has been applied to the disease

As a preventive measure, the burning in autumn of leaves infested by the cleistocarps of the fungus has been recommended, while sprinkling sulphur on the diseased parts after the mildew has appeared in summer is said to be efficacious Unfortunately no scientific investigations regarding the action of the powdered sulphur on the mycelium of the fungus have as yet been undertaken.

* [The Sporocarp (in this case termed an Ascocarp) is often a very complex body The question as to its origin and morphological nature cannot be discussed here, and the reader is referred to the special works of De Bary, Brefeld, &c., already quoted —Ed]

† [These closed Ascocarps are termed *Cleistocarps*, in distinction from the perforated *Perithecia* of the Pyrenomycetes and the open *Apothecia* of the Discomycetes.—Ed]

The numerous species of mildews have recently been arranged in several genera according to the number of asci in the cleistocarp, or according to the number of spores in the ascus, or, finally, according to the structure of the so-called appendiculæ, which are peculiar filiform radiating processes of certain cells of the wall of the perithecium. Here we need only allude to a few species

Erysiphe (Phyllactinia) guttata forms the mildew of *Fagus, Carpinus, Corylus, Quercus, Betula, Alnus, Fraxinus, Lonicera, Pyrus communis,* and *Cratægus* The cleistocarps are furnished with appendiculæ which are straight, unbranched, and thickened in a bulbous manner at the base, and internally produce several asci, each containing two spores In beech woods this parasite sometimes causes premature withering of the leaves

Erysiphe bicornis (Uncinula Aceris) very often injures the leaves and young shoots of *Acer* I have encountered this species most frequently on *Acer platanoides* and *A campestre* It covers the whole of the leaf, or forms large greyish white blotches on one or both sides (the black patches on these leaves are due to *Rhytisma acerinum*). The cleistocarps possess several asci holding eight spores, and the appendiculæ are simply forked at the apex The gonidia are elliptical in shape. Even so early as August the leaves of the maple are often completely covered with these white patches

Erysiphe Tulasnei is closely related to the former species, but occurs only on the upper side of the leaves of the Norway maple The gonidia are globular. *Erysiphe (Uncinula) adunca* produces the mildew of the leaves of willows and poplars

Erysiphe (Sphærotheca) pannosa forms the well-known mildew on the shoots and leaves of the rose. In wet years especially it is necessary promptly to pluck and burn the diseased leaves

Oidium Tuckeri, the fungus which causes the disease of the grape, was observed in England for the first time in 1845, but has since spread throughout all the vine-growing countries of Europe The mycelium grows on the leaves, shoots, and fruit When the last is attacked the epidermis dies and loses the power of expansion, so that as the berry grows the epidermis is ruptured, and the grapes in consequence begin to decay. So far only the gonidia have been discovered, and it remains to be determined how the fungus survives the winter.

THE TRUFFLES, TUBERACEÆ

The Truffles are distinguished by having round subterranean closed fructifications (cleistocarps), in which the asci are produced on hymenia which clothe the surfaces of contorted passages. Gonidia and sexual organs are unknown.

Through the investigations of Rees[1] it was first established that the stag truffle, *Elaphomyces granulatus*, develops its mycelium parasitically on the roots of pines. It is further known that the edible species of truffle of the genus *Tuber* are parasitic on the roots of the oak and beech. Frank has recently devoted much study to the occurrence of fungal growths on the roots of phanerogamic plants, especially *Coniferæ* and *Cupuliferæ*, and has proved that mycelial growths are widely distributed on the tender apices of the roots of trees. The outer surface of young roots may be so closely covered by the mycelium, which penetrates into and between the cells, as to form a dense fungal mantle. Owing to luxuriant branching and growth of the tissues the infested roots to some extent display abnormal forms, while a sort of symbiotic condition arises similar to what we find associated with many other plant-parasites. When the cortical tissue of the roots has been infested by the fungus for some time, it dies, and should the fungal filaments penetrate into the internal tissues the roots themselves die off entirely. Frank has designated these phenomena by the name *Mycorhiza*, or fungus-root. It has not yet been determined how many species of fungi take part in these phenomena, and, especially, whether fungi belonging to other groups besides the *Tuberaceæ* form *Mycorhiza*. Frank holds the view that these root-fungi, by assisting in nutrition and by conveying organic plant-food from the soil, play an important part in the life of trees.*

[1] Dr. M. Rees and Dr. K. Fisch, *Untersuchungen über Bau und Leben der Hirschtrüffel, "Elaphomyces,"* 1888.

*[The best account of Frank's views for the student is in his *Lehrbuch der Botanik*, B.I. 1893.—ED.]

Whether this view will receive confirmation in the future remains to be seen, but in the meantime its correctness is open to grave doubts In the first place, it has not yet been proved that trees can take in organic food-substances by their roots , and, in the second, it has been established that trees are very well nourished without the aid of *Mycorhiza*, and that, besides the infested roots, there is always a very large proportion of roots entirely free from fungoid growth.

PYRENOMYCETES

In the case of *Pyrenomycetes* the hymenium bearing the asci usually lines the inner surface of roundish or flask-shaped receptacles, called perithecia, which are distinguished from the cleistocarps of the preceding by having an aperture at the apex through which the spores escape The numerous genera may be divided into two groups, according as the perithecia stand singly (simplices), or grouped in large numbers on a common cushion, or sunk in a stroma (compositi)

The following species, being noteworthy parasites, deserve closer attention

TRICHOSPHÆRIA PARASITICA [1]

This parasite is chiefly met with on the silver fir, though, according to v. Tubeuf, it also occurs on the common spruce and hemlock spruce. It is to be found wherever the silver fir is indigenous Its colourless perennial mycelium grows on the under side of the branches, from which it spreads to the under side of the leaves, knitting them firmly to the branches. On this account the leaves, instead of falling off on dying, remain attached to the branches (Fig. 18)

On account of the mycelium being confined to the lower side of the branch, most of the leaves that are met with on the upper side survive during the first year at least (Fig. 18, *a*) The mycelium encroaches on the new shoots as they are formed, and,

[1] R Hartig, *Ein neuer Parasit der Weisstanne,* " *Trichosphæria parasitica.* ' *Allgem Forst- und Jagd-Zeitg* , January 1884

the young immature leaves at the base of the shoot being killed, subsequently shrivel up. The leaves on the middle and apex of the shoot, being reached somewhat later by the slowly advancing mycelium, retain their shape.

The cushions which are formed by the mycelium on the under side of the leaves are at first white, but afterwards turn brownish (Fig. 19, *b b*). They only partially conceal the bluish lines which are met with on the under side of the leaves of the silver fir. In the course of time very minute perithecia are formed on these cushions (Fig. 20).

The cushion originates in the following way. From the hyphæ that cover the leaf (Fig. 21, *a*) numerous branches, *b*, are sent out towards the epidermis, and these form a fleshy cushion, *c*, consisting of parallel hyphæ closely united to each other. At the point, *d*, where it reaches the epidermis of the leaf, each hypha sends a fine

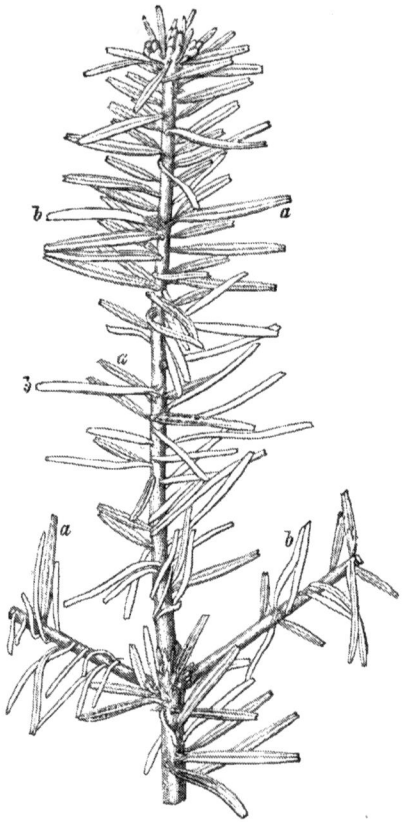

FIG. 18.—Branch of the silver fir attacked by *Trichosphæria parasitica*. *a*, healthy leaves; *b*, dead and brown leaves whose bases are attached to the branch by the fungus-filaments. On account of their not being fully formed when attacked by the fungus the dead leaves towards the base of the shoot have shrivelled up.

rod-like haustorium into the outer wall, *e*, of the epidermal cells, and owing to the secretion of a ferment these cells and the stomata, *f*, are killed and become brown. The cells of

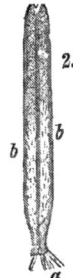

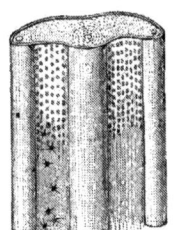

FIG. 19.—Lower side of a leaf of the silver fir attacked by *T. parasitica*. At *a* the colourless mycelium spreads from the branch on to the lower side of the leaf, on which it forms white cushions, *b b*.

FIG. 20.—Part of the leaf of a silver fir, on the left side of which the cushion bears a number of small perithecia.

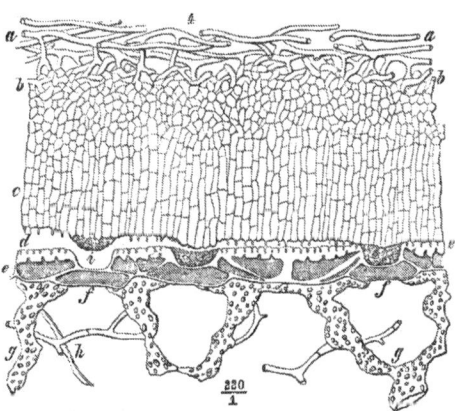

FIG. 21.—Mycelial cushion of *T. parasitica* on the under side of the leaf of a silver fir. The filamentous mycelium *a* sends down numerous branches at *b* to form a cushion *c*, consisting of parallel hyphæ; where the hyphæ reach the surface of the leaf each sends a rod-like haustorium, *d*, into the outer wall of the epidermal cells, *e e*; at *d* the cushion has been somewhat raised from the leaf, so that several of the haustoria have been pulled out of the epidermis; the epidermal cells *f f* have become brown. Although the filamentous mycelium *h* has penetrated the chlorophyllous cells of the leaf-parenchyma *g g*, these do not become brown till somewhat later; the mycelial cushion grows into the depressions at the entrance to the stomata *i*, where however it is unable to form haustoria; at these places it becomes coated with the adhering waxy granules.

the interior, *g*, which contain chlorophyll, do not succumb for some time to the action of the mycelium, *h*, which here and there effects an entrance. The depression at the entrance to the stomata, being lined with waxy granules, prevents the entrance of any haustorium, *i*. The dark brown perithecia (Fig. 22) which ultimately arise on the cushion are scarcely recognizable with the naked eye. They are

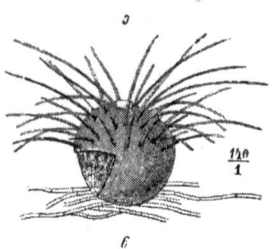

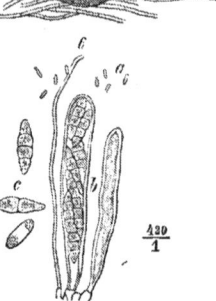

FIG. 22.—Perithecium of *T. parasitica*. The dark brown sphere shows a round aperture at its apex, and bristle-like hairs which project from its upper half. A portion of the wall has been removed from the lower left-hand side in order to show the pale contents, which consists of asci and paraphyses. These are shown more highly magnified in the lower part of the figure ; *a* representing rod-like bodies which are often present ; *b*, asci with spores, and *c*, isolated spores.

FIG. 23.—*Herpotrichia nigra* on the spruce ; half natural size.

characterized by having bristle-like hairs distributed over the upper half. In the interior of the perithecia are often to be found small rod-like organs, *a*, besides the asci, *b*, which hold eight grey spores, usually consisting of four chambers. Should these spores succeed in obtaining a suitable footing on the branch of a silver fir, they speedily germinate and produce the disease. The mycelium spreads parasitically from the point of infection in all directions, so that large branches may be eventually entirely defoliated. In dense young woods it even spreads from branch to branch, while fresh centres of disease are produced by the distribution of the spores

Seeing that young woods which have been naturally regenerated may suffer severely—and especially so where they have been formed under shelter trees—it is desirable that diseased branches should be pruned off This treatment has produced good results where practised on a large scale

HERPOTRICHIA NIGRA [1]

This parasite is met with in the higher mountain ranges, where it chiefly attacks the spruce, mountain pine, and juniper. In the woods of mountain pine, large blanks are met with, which, on a cursory glance, give one the impression of having been completely charred In nurseries at high elevations, where the young spruces are buried under snow during winter and spring, it often happens, directly after the snow has melted, that the plants are overgrown and killed by the dark brown mycelium. This is especially noticeable when the young trees have been laid prostrate on the ground.

In the spruce woods of the Bavarian Forest one often finds that the fungus has killed the young seedlings over large areas either entirely or to the height of twelve or fifteen inches The dark brown mycelium envelops the whole branch or plant, knitting the leaves completely together (Fig. 23).

.Instead of forming a definite cushion, the mycelium embraces the leaves irregularly (Fig 24, b), and on these the perithecia are also produced (a) Dark brown tuber-like bodies are formed over the stomata (Fig 25), while the mycelium also spreads over the surface of the leaf and sends haustoria into the outer walls of the epidermal cells, which consequently die and become brown The deeper-lying parenchymatous cells are also killed by the fungus, even before any mycelial threads have gained an entrance through stomata on other parts of the leaf, and penetrated into the interior

The surface of the dark brown comparatively large perithecia,

[1] R Hartig, *Herpotrichia nigra n sp All Forst- und Jagd-Zeitg*, January 1888

Fig. 24, is beset with numerous branching hyphæ, which are specially abundant on the lower part, near the point of contact with the mycelium. These black spheroid bodies are frequently nearly hidden by the mycelium. In the asci the spores are arranged in two rows. At first, and apparently also when mature, they consist of two chambers, but at last four chambers are formed. These spores germinate with great readiness.

It is an interesting biological point that the fungus grows, especially when the temperature is low, under the snow or during the time it is melting, because, under such circumstances, the air is completely saturated with moisture. The frequency of the disease at high eleva-

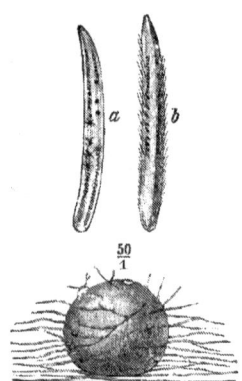

FIG. 24.—*a* and *b*, two spruce leaves attacked by *H. nigra*, twice natural size. The brown mycelium forms black tuber-like bodies in the stomata, which however are much smaller than the black perithecia, one of which, magnified fifty times, is shown in the lower part of the figure.

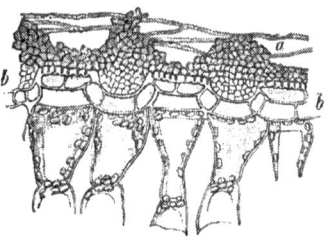

FIG. 25.—The growth of the mycelium of *H. nigra*. The filamentous mycelium *a* develops a granular mycelium on the surface of the leaf, and this covers the stomata with tuber-like bodies, rod-like haustoria being sent into the outer walls of the epidermal cells.

tions has led to the general adoption of the practice of forming spruce nurseries at low altitudes. It has also been found a good plan to look over the nurseries immediately after the melting of the snow, and to raise up all prostrated plants in order that they may be exposed to the wind. It would also be a step in the right direction, in planting out trees, to set them on hillocks and similar elevations, and to avoid placing them in hollows and other depressions.

ROSELLINIA QUERCINA [1]

The oak-root fungus, *Rosellinia quercina*, is one of the most interesting of parasites, and especially so because its mycelium displays the same diversity of form as that of *Agaricus melleus* The mycelium is one of those parasitic mycelial forms which were formerly referred to a special genus, *Rhizoctonia*.

The disease produced by *Rosellinia quercina* appears only to attack the roots of oaks from one to three years old, but it is very prevalent, especially in north-west Germany. In oak seed-beds it gives indications of its presence by the young plants becoming pale and withered, especially during rainy seasons The leaves near the apex of the shoot are the first to wither, but later on the lower ones go too If a plant showing the first symptoms of the disease be lifted out of the ground, we perceive a few black spheroid bodies of the size of pin-heads situated on the tap-root, especially at the points where the delicate lateral rootlets are met with (Fig. 26) It is also observed that, at certain points, the roots are closely embraced in a web-like fashion by delicate ramifying strands which resemble so many threads These are the *Rhizoctoniæ*, which penetrate also into the adjacent soil, and, as we shall see, spread the disease underground from root to root In the neighbourhood of these black tubers, and wherever the *Rhizoctoniæ* have been closely in contact with the surface of the roots, the cortex turns brown The apex of the tap-root is often quite rotten, but even plants whose roots remain alive to the tip display the pathological symptoms already described

Upon older plants that are already dead the *Rhizoctoniæ* are no longer white, but brown, and there the black spheroid bodies are often to be recognized in large numbers Sometimes the latter are also to be found on the lower part of the stem—that is to say, on the epicotyledonary axis: they may be most easily discovered after the plant has been very carefully washed, because then the lustre of the black tubercles readily betrays their presence During damp warm weather all the plants on patches a yard or so in diameter may become withered and die

[1] R Hartig, *Untersuchungen aus dem Forstbot Institut*, I. pp 1—32

Where the seed has been drilled, the disease spreads from the point of attack in two directions; where sown broadcast, it spreads centrifugally in all directions. Should dry weather intervene, or on the approach of autumn, the disease ceases to spread, but on examining the roots of plants apparently sound situated in close proximity to those already dead one will be able to recognize numerous examples of the pathological symptoms which have been already indicated. If such diseased plants are transplanted in the following year, it will be a question of weather whether they die, and possibly transmit the disease to neighbouring trees, or form a new tap-root, if the apex was destroyed by the disease, and, after remaining stunted for some years, slowly recover.

If a dead plant be placed in a damp warm chamber, or be planted in July in the middle of a bed of healthy young

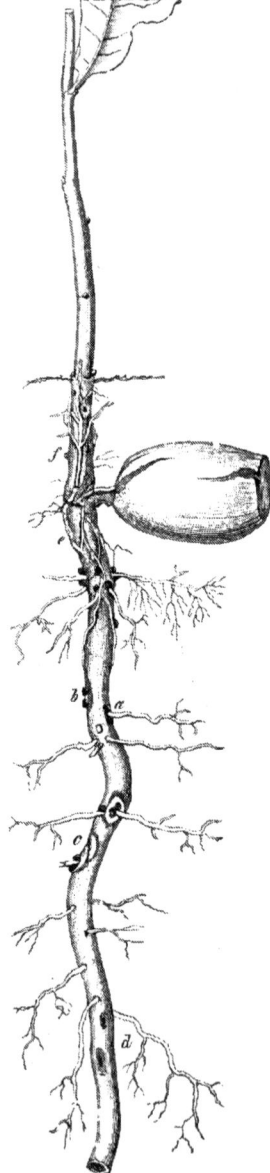

FIG. 26.—Seedling oak attacked by *Rosellinia querrina*. A few of the lateral roots are still healthy, but most of them have been killed by the filamentous mycelium. At the places where the tissues of the tap-root are traversed by the lateral roots, infection-tubercles, *a*, *b*, have been formed. In their neighbourhood the cortical tissues have become brown, and the periderm is frequently withered, *c*. It is but seldom that the infection-tubercles appear at other parts of the root, as at *d* and *f*. Both above and below the acorn the cortical tissues have turned brown, and strands of *Rhizoctonia*, *e*, ramify over the surface.

seedlings a few months old, a mycelium is very soon developed from the black tubers—which we may call resting-mycelia (Sclerotia)—which breaks through the bark at different places and forms a dense whitish-grey mildew-like tissue, and also spreads rapidly over the surface of the ground (Fig. 27). This mycelium consists of septate hyphæ, which are at first colourless but afterwards turn brown. These, after a time,

arrange themselves side by side, grow together laterally at places, and form the fine strands called *Rhizoctoniæ*, which consist of numerous individual hyphæ very loosely united to each other. Should such a mycelium—whether in the form of isolated hyphæ or of *Rhizoctoniæ*—come into contact with the sound roots of a neighbouring plant, it embraces them in its meshes, and bores directly into such of the cortical cells as are still alive. These are found in the delicate lateral rootlets and near the apex of the tap-root. The mycelium penetrates as far as the medulla, should such be present, and in a short time kills the root. In the living cortical parenchyma of the tap-root—which is only to be found on

FIG. 27.—Oak root enveloped by the mycelium of *R. quercina*, *a*, on which perithecia have developed at *b*.

the lowest and youngest parts—the cells become plugged up with a luxuriant growth of pseudo-parenchymatous tissue, which, owing to the occurrence of numerous oil-globules, may be recognized as a resting-mycelium. These bodies, which germinate under favourable conditions, may be designated chambered sclerotia. On account of the formation of a periderm layer in its cortex, the older parts of the tap-root are protected against the direct attack of the parasite. The outer cortical cells being partly shrivelled up and partly cast off, there remains but one path of entrance into the interior of the root. After the fine lateral roots that pierce the corky covering have been killed by the parasite, openings or breaches are left at certain points, through which the parasite effects an entrance, and this it accomplishes in a peculiar manner (Fig. 28). At such places—frequently both above and below the base of the dead root—fine white mycelial outgrowths are first formed. These develop into fleshy tubers, ultimately possessing a dark brown covering, which send several fleshy processes into the tissues of the oak root (Fig. 28, c, d).

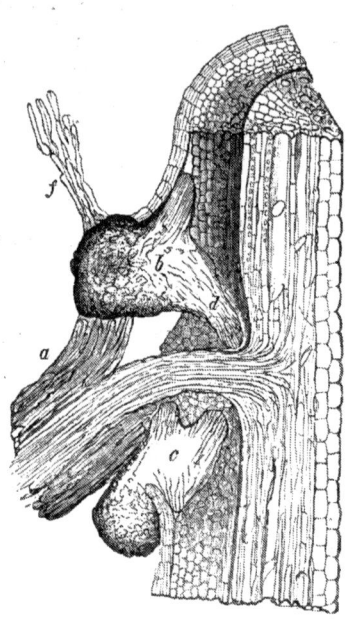

The adjoining cortical tissues are killed and become brown (Fig. 28, e). Should dry or cold weather intervene, the host-plant gains time to form a new layer of cork in the neighbourhood of the infecting tubers along the line that marks the limit of living tissue. In this way the plant may be, for the time, saved. Should the conditions of growth remain favourable for the fungus, however, the fleshy protuberance pushes out a fine filamentous mycelium, which

FIG. 28.—Point of infection by *R. quercina*, magnified twenty times. The delicate lateral rootlet *a*, which has been killed by the filamentous mycelium, displays fleshy infection-tubercles, *b c*, at the place where it has ruptured the periderm of the tap-root. These tubercles send processes, *d*, into the internal tissues. The adjoining cellular tissue is brown, *e*, but free from mycelium. A *Rhizoctonia*-strand, *f*, has been produced by the upper tubercle, which has consequently parted with a portion of its nutritive substance.

spreads through all the tissues of the root and kills it.

In the sclerotia the parasite possesses a means of existing from one year to another, and of resisting the periods of drought during summer which kill all filamentous mycelia as well as

G

the sporophores that may be in process of development upon them

In summer the mycelium that vegetates on the surface of the ground produces gonidia on the whorled branches of gonidio-phores, and these, by being carried on the skins of mice, &c, may originate new centres of infection. But besides these, black spheroid perithecia, about the size of a pin-head, are produced either on the surface of the diseased oaks themselves or on the surface of the ground in their neighbourhood (Fig. 27, *b*)

It is probable that the spores which are formed in the pere-thecia do not as a rule germinate and reproduce the disease till the following year

Generally speaking, it is only in wet years that the parasite does much damage. It may be combated by digging trenches round the diseased spots in the seed-bed so as to isolate them One should avoid transferring diseased plants from the seed-bed to the plant-bed

Rhizoctonia violacea, which kills saffron and lucerne, has not yet been scientifically examined in its different stages of develop-ment, and it remains to be determined whether this parasitic mycelium belongs to a form related to one of the foregoing fungi or not Fuckel's statement that this mycelial form belongs to the fungus *Byssothecium circinnans* appears so utterly improbable that it is not worth while to take further notice of it On the other hand, I feel called upon to describe here the following important parasite of the vine.

DEMATOPHORA NECATRIX* THE VINE-ROOT FUNGUS[1]

Amongst the numerous enemies of the vine, the root-fungus, *D necatrix*, occupies a prominent position The disease which it induces is known as Wurzelpilz, Weinstockfäule, Pourridié de la Vigne, Pourriture, Blanc des Racines, Blanquet, Champignon blanc, Aubernage, Mal nero, and Morbo bianco, and is dis-

[1] R Hartig, *Dematophora necatrix n. sp*, *Untersuchungen aus dem Forstbot Institut zu München*, III., 1883.

*[Viala has published a very thorough investigation of this disease and the devastations it causes in the south of France, &c "*Monographie du Pourridié des Vignes et des Arbres fruitiers*," 1891 —ED]

tributed throughout France, Italy, Switzerland, Austria, and south-west Germany.

Amongst the root-diseases of the vine, that which is caused by *Phylloxera vastatrix* is generally known. Very similar pathological symptoms occur on the stems of plants that are attacked by the vine-root fungus, and confusion often enough results.

Whether *Agaricus melleus* also is injurious to the vine—as has been maintained—I am not in a position to say, because, so far, no specimens have been forwarded to me in which the fungus could actually be identified. On the other hand, it appears as though, in very wet years and on heavy ground, "root-rot" may arise as a result of asphyxia—that is to say, owing to deficiency of air in the soil. On such suffocated vines a fungus, *Roesleria hypogæa*, often occurs, which, it appears to me, is most probably saprophytic in character.

The parasite that we are here discussing spreads in the vineyards from plant to plant by means of its underground mycelium, so that we often hear of great damage being done. Other plants that are cultivated in the vineyards, such as fruit-trees, potatoes, beans, beet, and the like, also fall a victim to the fungus. During my investigations I found that the mycelium could at once kill young maples, oaks, beeches, pines, spruces, &c.

On plants where the mycelium is vigorously developed, as in the case of the vine, Fig. 29, and the young maple, Fig. 30, it forms a luxuriant snow-white mass of a woolly or strand-like texture, which adheres to the outside of the plants, though it may also spread in the ground to long distances. Where this mycelium encounters the fine fibrous roots of other plants, it kills them, and, at their base, bores into the interior of the larger roots, Fig. 31 *a*, spreading afterwards in their interior in the form of peculiar rhizomorphs, Fig. 32, and killing all the adjoining tissues. In the soft cortical tissues of the vine-root they retain their strand-like appearance, and by ramifying laterally and outwards they envelop the root in a network of strands, Fig. 33.

In structure these rhizomorphs are entirely different from those of *Agaricus melleus*. In Fig. 34 I have represented somewhat diagrammatically the apex of one of these rhizomorphs, and refer for details to the description appended to the illustration.

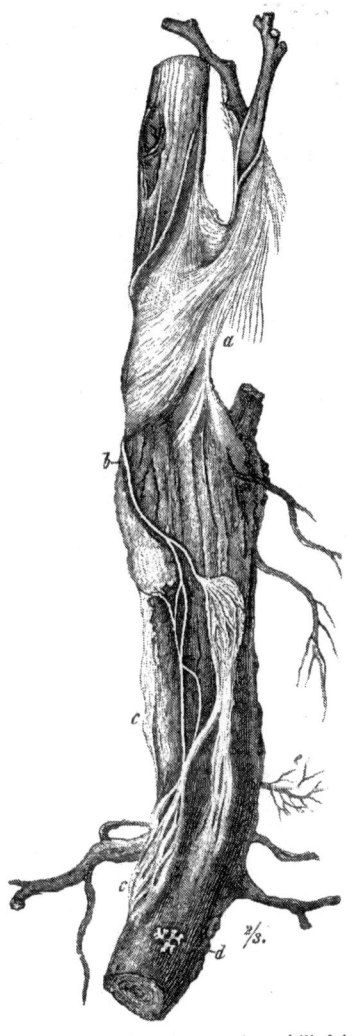

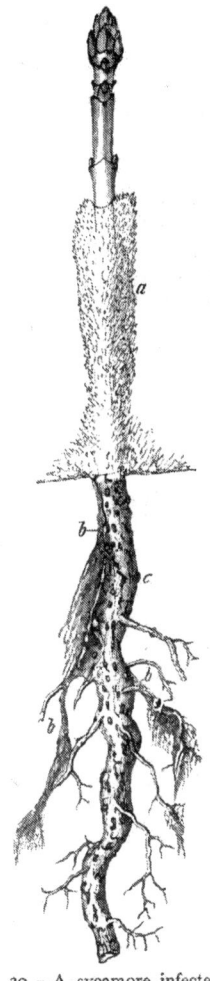

FIG. 29.—A vine that has been killed by
D. *necatrix*, and afterwards kept for a
long time in a moist chamber. The filamentous mycelium, *a*, assumes the character of white *Rhizoctonia* strands, *b*,
which anastomose, *c c*. At *d* and *e* rhizomorphs grow out from the interior.

FIG. 30.—A sycamore infected by
D. *necatrix*. The portion above
ground is represented some fourteen days anterior to the rest.
The plant is enveloped in the
white woolly mycelium, *a*; on
the subterranean portion *Rhizoctoniæ* consisting of dark mycelium, *b b*, are to be seen. Numerous sclerotia, *c*, project from
the cortex.

The branches of the rhizomorph directed outwards break through the cortex from within and form a new filamentous mycelium, which penetrates into the soil ; or, in other cases, they swell up under the cortex to form tuberous sclerotia, Fig. 33 *b*,

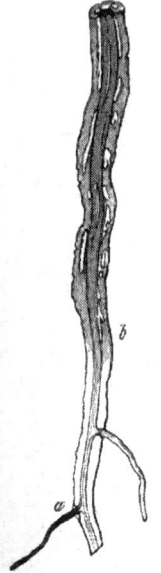

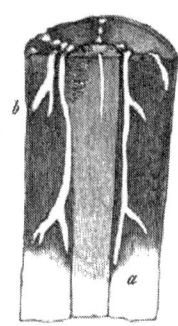

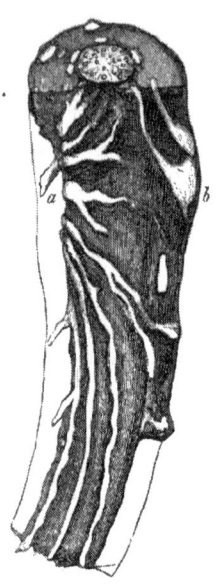

FIG. 31.—Longitudinal section of the root of a vine whose upper part has been killed by the rhizomorphs of *D. necatrix* as far as *b*, and whose lower portion shows an infection-spot at *a*.

FIG. 32.—Magnified five times. Boundary, *a*, of the healthy and diseased parts of the root. The rhizomorphs send out lateral branches, which may occasionally reach the epidermis, as at *b*.

FIG. 33.—A large vine-root infected by *D. necatrix*. A portion of the cortex has been carefully removed so as to show the rhizomorphs which begin to appear at *a* ; at *b* the mycelial tubers, which resemble sclerotia, are formed, and on these the gonidiophores ultimately develop.

which sometimes break through the cortex and appear in rows upon the surface, Fig. 35.

On these tubers the gonidiophores are developed in the form of bristles, at whose apex the gonidia are abscinded, Fig. 36.

It also happens very frequently, however, that these sporophores are developed on the filamentous mycelium which clothes the diseased plant, or foreign substances, in the form of *Rhizoctoniæ* or otherwise

The perithecia of this species have been discovered by Viala.

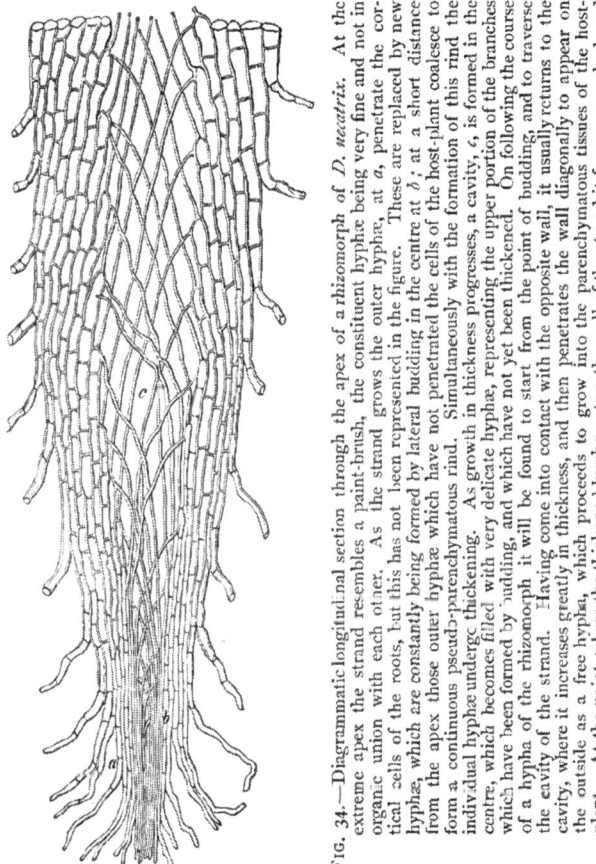

Fig. 34.—Diagrammatic longitudinal section through the apex of a rhizomorph of *D. necatrix*. At the extreme apex the strand resembles a paint-brush, the constituent hyphæ being very fine and not in organic union with each other. As the strand grows the outer hyphæ, at *a*, penetrate the cortical cells of the roots, but this has not been represented in the figure. These are replaced by new hyphæ, which are constantly being formed by lateral budding in the centre at *b*; at a short distance from the apex those outer hyphæ which have not penetrated the cells of the host-plant coalesce to form a continuous pseudo-parenchymatous rind. Simultaneously with the formation of this rind the individual hyphæ undergo thickening. As growth in thickness progresses, a cavity, *c*, is formed in the centre, which becomes filled with very delicate hyphæ, representing the upper portion of the branches which have been formed by budding, and which have not yet been thickened. On following the course of a hypha of the rhizomorph it will be found to start from the point of budding, and to traverse the cavity of the strand. Having come into contact with the opposite wall, it usually returns to the cavity, where it increases greatly in thickness, and then penetrates the wall diagonally to appear on the outside as a free hypha, which proceeds to grow into the parenchymatous tissues of the host-plant. At the point where the thickened hypha enters the wall of the strand it forms a new bud, and the hypha which this gives rise to behaves in a manner similar to that already described.

They form only on vines and fruit-trees that have been dead and decayed for a long period. It is only in soil that has dried slowly that they are to be found. Associated with bristling appendages bearing gonidia the perithecia appear partly on sclerotia and partly on the mycelium. Between the surface of the ground and the depth of some two inches they form clusters of small spheroid bodies round the vine or tree. The sporocarps, which are very hard, deep brown in colour, approximately spheroid in shape, and 2 mm. long, are provided with short stalks. They are completely closed, and enable us to refer *Dematophora* to the *Tuberacei*. The elongated filiform asci, however, which swell out on one side like a lop-sided turnip to enclose the eight spores, distinguish this parasite from all known *Tuberacei*. *Dematophora necatrix* is thus the sole representative of a new genus of *Tuberacei*.

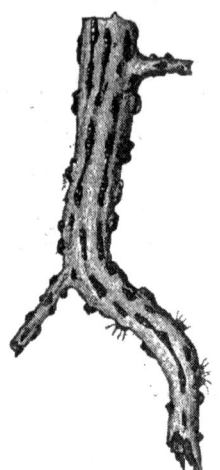

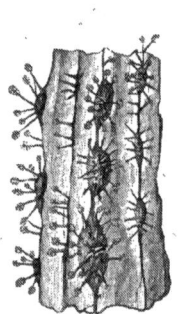

FIG. 35.—Root of a vine showing numerous sclerotia-like tubers, on which a few bristle-shaped gonidiophores have developed.

FIG. 36.—A portion of Fig. 35 after the gonidiophores have been formed; magnified five times.

The method which I at first recommended of starving the parasite by means of isolating trenches, &c., having proved too tedious a process, it remains to be seen whether the impregnation of the poles with creosote can do anything to combat the disease in the vineyards.

CUCURBITARIA LABURNI[1]

This parasite frequently gains an entrance through wounds on *Cytisus Laburnum*, destroying the cortex and branches for considerable distances, and even killing the whole plant. Besides the dark brown spheroid perithecia, which are arranged in groups,

[1] *Cucurbitaria Laburni, auf Cytisus Laburnum.* Freiherr v. Tubeuf. Cassel, Fischer, 1886.

we meet with the most varied forms of gonidia, which are produced either free on the stroma, or in the interior of cavities in
the stroma, or in pycnida. Owing to the ease with which all
these organs of reproduction germinate, the parasite is frequently
very abundant

In a similar manner, *C Sorbi* appears to attack the bark of
Sorbus Aucuparia

Here allusion may be made in a few words to the " Disease-
blotches" on the leaves of numerous trees, shrubs, and herbs
These often occur in great abundance in autumn, the leaves being
covered by numerous sharply defined blotches, which are usually
circular in outline and brown in colour, and frequently surrounded
by a red margin   They are generally due to fungi belonging to
the family *Sphærelloidea*, and especially to the genera *Sphærella*
and *Stigmatea.*

The gonidia are formed on the living leaves, but the perithecia
only on the dead parts of plants, and usually not until the spring
after the leaves have fallen

Sphærella Fragariæ produces the diseased blotches on the
strawberry

S punctiformis and *S maculiformis* produce brown blotches
on the leaves of the oak, lime, and hazel

S Fagi produces blotches on the leaves of the beech, &c

Stigmatea Mespili induces brownness in the leaves of the pear.

Stigmatea Alni is the cause of blotches on the leaves of the
alder

Gnomonia belongs to an allied family, *Gnomonia erythrostoma,*
producing a brown colour in the leaves of the cherry   The infected leaves die prematurely, but do not fall off   On these are
developed the perithecia with their unicellular tubular spores. It
is advisable to remove during winter all leaves that may be
hanging on the trees

A parasite, *Valsa Prunastri*, frequently proves injurious to the
apricot, cherry, and sloe   The fungus infests the cortex, and
causes the death of the branches   The form producing spermatia
is the first to appear, and ejects its tendril-like masses of spermatia ; while later—namely, in the following spring—the perithecia develop in the dead cortex

NECTRIA

The genus *Nectria* contains a number of parasitic fungi which produce their perithecia—which are usually red, and grouped in considerable numbers—on the surface of a pseudo-parenchymatous wart-like stroma. Before the perithecia make their appearance, this same stroma serves for the production of numerous gonidia. The gonidia-bearing stroma was formerly referred to a special genus called *Tubercularia*.

The following three species belonging to this genus are facultative parasites, which, like so many other parasites, can also live as saprophytes.

NECTRIA CUCURBITULA [1]

Like all the Nectrias, *N. Cucurbitula* is one of those parasites which, as a rule, can gain access to the interior of a host-plant only through a pre-existing wound. Here the host-plant is usually the spruce, in rarer instances the silver fir, Scotch pine, &c. The means of entrance which the parasite utilizes in the forest are chiefly the injured spots due to *Grapholitha pactolana*, Fig. 37, though, less frequently, it also enters through the abrasions caused by hail, or the crack at the base of a branch whose bark in the upper angle has been slightly torn by the depression due to an accumulation of snow.

The germinating ascospores or gonidia push their germ-tubes into the tissues of the cortex, and the ramifying mycelium ultimately develops most luxuriantly in the sieve-tubes of the soft bast, Fig. 38 *b*, or in the intercellular spaces between them, Fig. 38 *c*. The mycelium is met with in bast tissues that are apparently perfectly sound and fresh. The brown colour does not appear in the tissues for some time afterwards. The fungus would appear to make progress, for the most part, only when growth is at a stand-still in the cortical tissues. It generally ceases to advance when the plant and its cambium awake to renewed activity. From this we must assume that the power of resistance of the living tissues of the host-plant is

[1] R. Hartig, *Untersuchungen*, I. p. 88.

greater during the season of growth than at other times. As may be seen from Fig. 37, the parasite may advance longitudinally more than $2\frac{1}{2}$ inches during a growing season. Laterally the seat of the disease seldom advances more than $1—1\frac{1}{2}$ inch. The tissues that have been killed by the fungus become separated from the

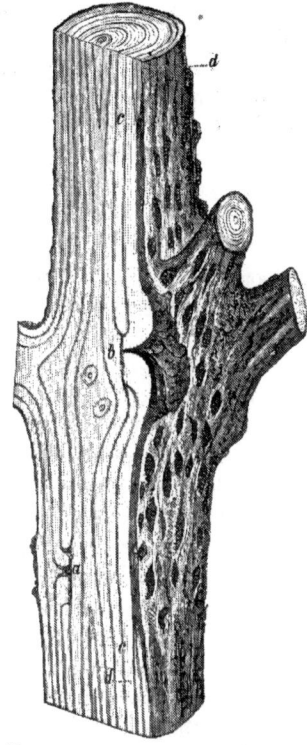

FIG. 37.—A spruce attacked by *N. Cucurbitula*. At *a* a wound due to a hailstone has healed over without becoming infected ; *b*, the gallery of a larva of *Grapholitha pactolana*, over which a callus has been formed, but where infection has occurred two years later ; the mycelium has spread from *c* to *c* in the cambium, and from *d* to *d* in the cortex ; numerous groups of perithecia have appeared on the dead cortex.

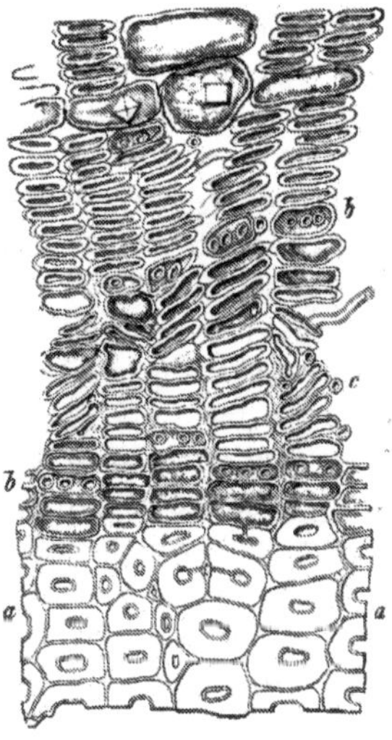

FIG. 38.—Cross section of the cortex and wood of a spruce infected a short time previously ; *a*, the wood. *b b*, the sieve-tubes containing one or more mycelial filaments ; *c*, mycelium in the intercellular spaces ; magnified 420 times.

living parts by the formation of a layer of cork which prevents the further progress of the parasite in the following year. If the cortex that has been killed be exposed to wind and sun, it dries up even so early as the beginning of summer. When the part of the tree that is attacked is thin, the wood also dries up, and the top of the tree dies and becomes yellow and withered. Very frequently one meets with such withered tops in young spruce woods without being able to find a trace of the perithecia, which only attain maturity when the cortex in which the mycelium is hidden is constantly kept moist. When this occurs—as often happens on the lower parts of the stem, where the cortex is kept moist by the shade and protection of the branches—a large number of white and yellow cushion-like stromata develop on the dead tissues. These, which are about the size of pin-heads, break through the outer cortical and periderm layers, or remain hidden amongst the loose bark scales. These cushion-like stromata first of all produce large numbers of gonidia, but later on numerous red melon-shaped perithecia are formed, whose ascospores are usually disseminated in winter or spring, when they find their way to the injuries caused by *G. pactolana*, or to other wounds.

With the disappearance of the moth—as, for instance, in consequence of the severe winter 1879—80, in which the caterpillars were, for the most part, frozen—the injury due to this *Nectria* is of course also diminished, because it has fewer opportunities for infection. Spruces which are attacked only by the moth and not by the fungus hardly ever perish, but after being crippled for a few years recover completely. Spruces which are attacked by *Nectria* only on one side may also recover, because in the course of time a callus forms over the injured part. The damage, however, which is done to young spruce woods by the trees dying at the top is so great that it seems advisable to limit the spread of the parasite by cutting off and burning all such tree-tops as are attacked by the fungus.

NECTRIA DITISSIMA [1] *

It is the dicotyledonous trees that are chiefly attacked by this fungus, many of the varied forms of disease which are usually

[1] R. Hartig, *Untersuchungen*, I. p. 209, Plate VI.

* [This fungus is very common in this country, and I have frequently observed and examined its undoubted connection with the canker of apple and other trees.—ED.]

embraced under the term "Canker" being due to *N dissima*
This canker-fungus appears most frequently upon the beech, oak,
hazel, ash, hornbeam, alder, maple, lime, apple, dogwood, and bird-
cherry Although as a rule this parasite only gains an entrance
to the cortical tissues of trees through wounds, I have also been
able to infect young leaves by means of gonidia and ascospores
Abrasions caused by hailstones are probably the commonest kind
of wounds, Fig 39 Should no infection supervene on such a
wound, a callus forms, and occludes the injured part in a short time,
Fig. 39 *a* If, however, it is infected by the gonidia or ascopores
of *Nectria*, death and brownness spread in all directions, but most
rapidly in the direction of the long axis of the stem Although
in rare instances the mycelium may advance 3 cm. in a year, it
is comparatively seldom that the annual rate of progress in any
direction exceeds one third of that amount The apparent
deepening of the diseased spot in the course of time is to be explained from the fact that not only does the contiguous healthy
tissue continue to increase in thickness, but it even displays an
augmented rate of growth. This is satisfactorily enough explained when we remember that during their movements in the
bast the plastic materials assimilated by the leaves are necessarily confined to the sound side of the stem. As the canker-
spot dries up, their passage is chiefly confined to its margin, which
is consequently very richly nourished, and projects as a well-
marked prominence Thus in the course of years very striking
malformations are formed

It also frequently happens that the base of a lateral branch,
whose cortex has been injured in the upper angle, proves the infection-spot from which death of the tissues annually proceeds,
Fig 40 In the case of the hazel especially it often happens that
in pulling down the branches to get at the nuts a split is formed
at the point of bifurcation This then develops into a canker-
spot, which constantly increases in size, as is represented in
Fig 41

I believe that I am justified in assuming that under certain
circumstances, with which I am not yet familiar, the mycelium
spreads from the cortex to the wood, in which it progresses upwards, and at certain places attacks the tissues of the cortex and
cambium from within In this way canker-spots may be pro-

duced without the part of the tree on which they occur having
been previously injured, Fig. 42. The familiar state of things
where certain trees are covered with canker-spots, while adjoining
trees of the same spe-
cies are tolerably clear
of them, can hardly be
explained in any other
way than by assuming
that the fungus travels

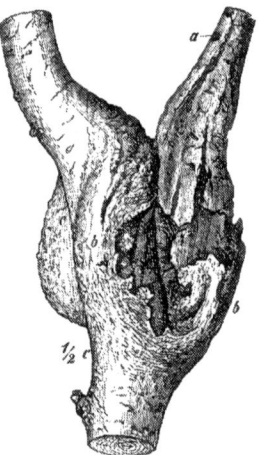

FIG. 39.—Branch of a beech showing two hailstone wounds, of which the upper one, *b*, has been infected by *Nectria*, while the lower one, *a*, has escaped infection and has been occluded by a callus.

FIG. 40. — Hornbeam infected by *N. ditissima*, which has entered at the angle formed by the branch and the stem ; natural size.

FIG. 41. — Hazel showing the canker due to *N. ditissima*, the spores of which have germinated in the bifurcation of two branches which have been somewhat pulled asunder ; *a, b, b*, the boundary of the canker-spot, where red perithecia are abundant ; *c c*, the healthy side of the branch ; half natural size.

in the wood. This subject, however, requires further investigation.

As the mycelium spreads in the cortical tissues of trees, it
produces innumerable extremely minute gonidia resembling
bacteria, which apparently assist in no small degree in the

almost complete decomposition of the tissues of the cortex, with
the exception of the outer periderm layers. Only on those
parts of the cortex which have been killed during the past year

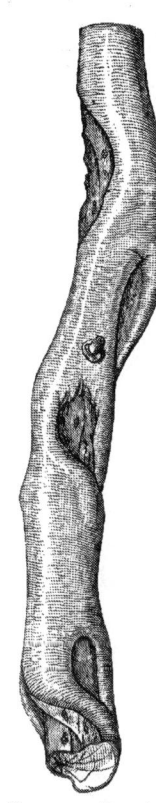

—that is to say, on the periphery of the
canker-spot—do white gonidia-bearing stromata appear. These had already been observed by Willkomm in his investigations
into the canker of the beech, by whom they
were designated *Fusidium candidum*. On these
the minute deep-red perithecia originate, but
they can only be discovered after careful
search. They are found partly in groups and
partly singly on the dead cortex, and especially
in the fine fissures, Fig. 40. One sometimes
searches for them for a long time in vain upon
the older canker-spots, for the reason that
these have ceased to increase in size at all parts
of their circumference. In Fig. 43 the canker-
spot is increasing in size only in the upper
left-hand corner, and it is only there that the
red perithecia are to be found in abundance.

In the case of the canker of the beech, I
have frequently observed that sooner or later
the mycelium ceases to advance at certain
places, in consequence of which the shape of
the canker-spots becomes exceedingly irregular. Here and there the canker spreads for a
series of years, but finally the diseased spots
may be entirely covered over by a kind of
callus. See Figs. 43 and 44.

Fig. 42.—Branch of
a beech showing
numerous canker-
spots, which do
not appear to have
been preceded by
any cortex wounds.

It may also be remarked that the parasite
is distributed throughout the whole of Germany, and that canker of the beech especially
is met with from the Island of Rügen to the
south of Bavaria, being very prevalent, for
instance, in the neighbourhood of Munich.
Young trees from five to ten years old, as well as trees 140 years
of age, may be attacked by the disease, which, however, in the
latter case, is confined to the twigs and branches of the crown.

Climatic conditions, especially frost, are essentially without influence on the disease, and the same is true as regards the soil. Although the damage inflicted by this parasite is by no means small, still I doubt if, in practice, anything can successfully be done to combat it. The injured trees remain alive as a rule, and at least yield firewood. Their removal in the thinnings is certainly advisable, so long as the ground is not thereby injuriously exposed. In oak woods also, whenever thinning and

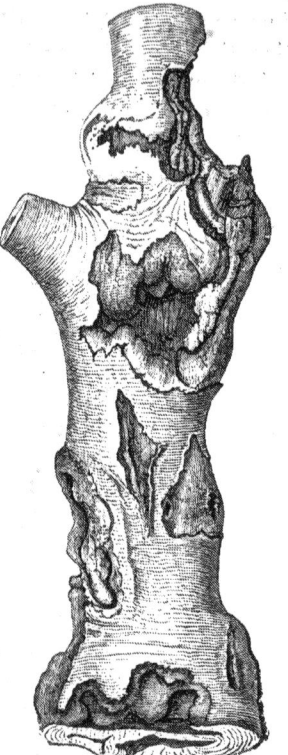

FIG. 43.—A stem of the beech, half natural size, showing numerous canker-spots; these, however, are increasing in size only at certain places, and it is only where increase is taking place that the red perithecia are to be found.

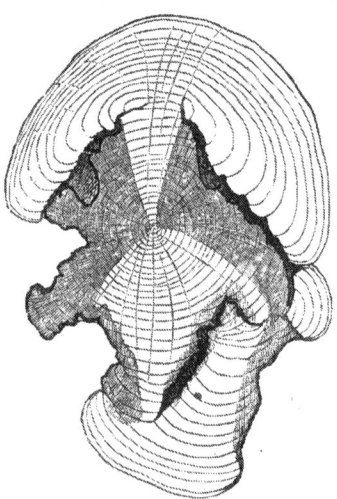

FIG. 44.—Cross section taken from the lower end of the beech stem represented in Fig. 43; natural size.

opening out are undertaken with a view to underplanting, the cankered trees should be the first to be removed. I cannot advise, however, that one should go so far as to fell all cankered trees, if this should mean the formation of large blanks in the wood.

Very frequently *N ditissima* is found associated with *Aphidæ*.[1]
Lachnus exsiccator produces large galls in the cambium of the
beech, and when these afterwards burst open they present the
opportunity of infection to the fungus The mycelium spreads
in the cellular tissues with extraordinary rapidity The beech
Aphis, too, *Chermes fagi*, which clothes the stem with a white
woolly covering, is often associated with the fungus, which, under
these circumstances, quickly kills the cortex, without producing
canker-spots

NECTRIA CINNABARINA [2] *

This *Nectria* is certainly one of the most widely distributed
of fungi, and finds its way on to almost all dicotyledonous trees
and shrubs when they have been killed by frost. Besides living
saprophytically, it also occurs as a parasite, and that most frequently on the maple, lime, and horse-chestnut Infection usually
occurs at branch-wounds, though also very frequently at root-
wounds, which cannot be avoided when transplanting either large
or small trees The mycelium of this fungus, which grows rapidly
upwards in the vessels, penetrates into all the elements of the
wood, decomposing the starch, and leaving a green substance behind, Fig 45 The consequence is that the wood turns black,
while the cambium and cortical tissues remain sound. The wood
becomes unable to conduct sap, the leaves wither prematurely in
summer or drop off, and the cortex of the youngest shoots
dries up after the wood is completely dead In autumn or the
following spring the cinnabar-coloured stromata that bear the
gonidia appear grouped together in large numbers on the dead
cortex On account of their size and colour they are conspicuous even from a distance. The large rough perithecia which are
formed later are much darker red in colour

It is interesting to note that this fungus cannot injure the

---

[1] *Untersuchungen aus dem Forstb Inst zu Munchen*, I pp 151—163

[2] H Mayer, *Ueber den Parasitismus von Nectria cinnabarina. Un-
tersuch a d Forstb Institut zu Munchen*, III

* [This fungus is extremely common on black currant and other trees in
England It is the species which, in its gonidial form, is so often observed
on pea and bean sticks, dotting them over with scarlet points —ED]

living cambium and cortex. It is, in fact, only able to invade them when they have been killed either by frost or by the want of water consequent on the wood drying up centrifugally under the influence of the mycelium of the parasite.

The simplest way to limit the increase of the parasite is to cut off and burn twigs and branches that are bearing gonidia and perithecia. The immediate application of tar or grafting-wax to wounds of all kinds is the best safeguard against infection.

POLYSTIGMA

The various species of *Polystigma* induce the formation of red fleshy blotches on the leaves of trees belonging to the genus *Prunus*. *Polystigma rubrum*[1] occurs on the leaves of the plum and sloe. On the under side of the leaves, which in summer display the large deepred fleshy blotches, numerous small punctures will be found. These are the orifices of the spermagonia, which are buried in the leaf-parenchyma, and from which hooked colourless

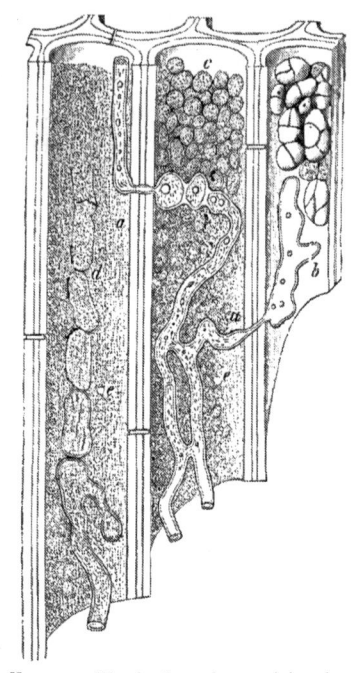

FIG. 45.—Wood of maple containing the mycelium of *N. cinnabarina*; magnified by 1200. The vigorous mycelium, *a a*, traverses the elements and dissolves the starch-grains, *b c*, first attacking the granulose. As the cellulose and the mycelial filaments, *d*, are decomposed, a green solution appears in the interior of the elements. The walls are much perforated, as at *e e*. (After H. Mayr.)

spermatia afterwards appear. The perithecia only occur upon the leaves between their fall and the following spring. By sowing the ascospores on young plum-leaves new spermogonia are obtained in six weeks. The best preventive measure is to

[1] Tulasne, *Selecta Fungorum Carpologia*, II. p. 76.

H

get rid of the infected leaves by raking them together and burning or burying them

Polystigma fulvum attacks *Prunus Padus* and *Amygdalus* This parasite is specially destructive to almond-trees, the yellow patches frequently embracing more than half of the whole leaf-surface. As the perithecia are formed on the fallen leaves in the following spring, it is advisable to burn them

Polystigma ochraceum is parasitic on the leaves of the wild cherry

CLAVICEPS PURPUREA [1] ERGOT

Mention may also be made here in a few words of that disease of cereals which, from the appearance of peculiar sclerotia or mycelial tubers, is designated ergot.

The well-known black bodies that accompany ergot, and which occur on many species of *Gramineæ*, fall to the ground when the crop is reaped. There they pass the winter, and after germinating in the moist soil in the following spring each sclerotium generally produces a number of long-stalked spherical sporophores. Sunk over the whole surface of these reddish spherical bodies are to be seen numerous flask-shaped perithecia, whose orifices project somewhat above the general surface Each ascus holds eight filamentous spores, which reach the open air by being pushed out through the orifice Should a filamentous spore chance to reach and germinate on the flower of a cereal, the germ-tube forces its way into the ovary, where the mycelium develops in the tissues and almost completely consumes them. The ovary, which is entirely enveloped in mycelia, displays on its surface brain-like corrugations, which are the gonidial stromata The gonidia, which are very small, oval, unicellular, and colourless, are imbedded in a sweet mucilaginous fluid which is secreted by the gonidial stromata, and appears in drops between the parts of the flower, being known as honey-dew. This gonidial form of the parasite was formerly designated *Sphacelia segetum* Only after the formation of gonidia is finished does the ergot proper appear, and this it does

[1] Tulasne, *Ann des sci nat*, 3rd ser, vol. xx. p 56

at the base of the ovary, though completely independent of it. Morphologically it is essentially distinct from *Sphacelia segetum* in having a peculiar pseudo-parenchymatous structure. The original tissues of *Sphacelia segetum*, with possibly some remnants of the ovary, die completely, and adhere for a short time to the apex of the ergot.

From what has been said, it will be seen that the disease is spread partly by the sclerotia that hibernate from year to year, and partly by the innumerable gonidia which, suspended in the solution of honey-dew, are carried by various species of insects to the healthy graminaceous flowers where they germinate and which they infect.

On account of the sclerotia that reach the fields in the seed being still capable of germinating in spring, the farmer endeavours to prevent the disease by using clean seed-corn. The ergot should also be gathered before harvest, and this is accomplished at little cost, because it fetches a good price.*

AGLAOSPORA TALEOLA [1]

Amongst the many forms of canker met with on the oak, some of which still await investigation, the one that is caused by *Aglaospora Taleola* is characterised by a number of striking peculiarities. It would appear to be confined to woods under the age of forty years, and it is only so long as oaks are without true bark that they are liable to attack. The disease manifests itself in the following way. Both on the dominant and the smaller trees large patches of the smooth cortex die and become brown, but as this usually occurs only on one side of the stem the whole of the tree does not succumb. As the cortex often dies over long distances and on various sides of the tree, patches of sound cortex are to be met with surrounded on all sides by dead tissue (Fig. 46, 1, *a*). A year afterwards numerous round or oval cushion-like stromata appear in the dead cortex. Later on these break through the periderm in one, two, or three places, so as to open up external communication with the gonidiophores

[1] *Forstlich-naturwissensch. Zeitschrift*, January, 1893.
*[Owing to its use in medicine.—ED.]

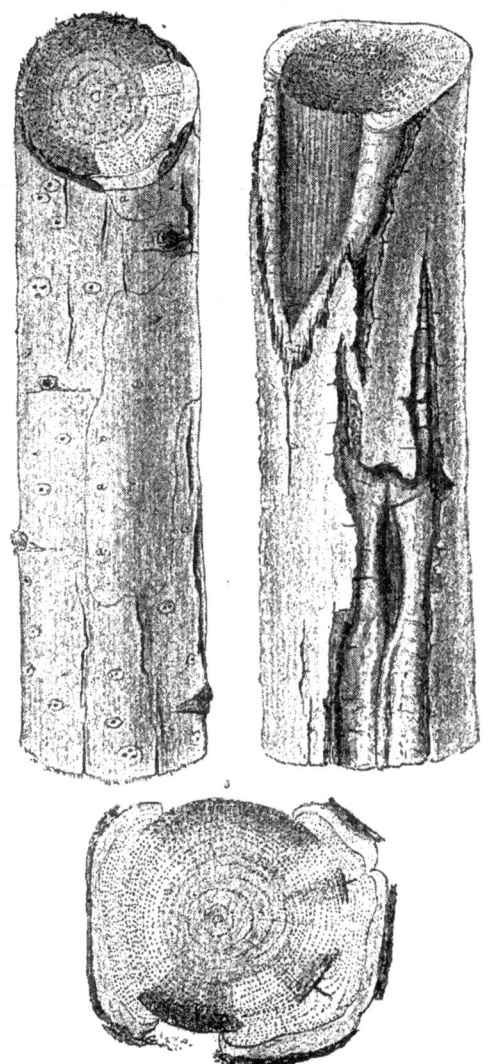

FIG. 46.—Portions of oaks, thirty-five years old, attacked by *A. Taleola;* two thirds natural size. No. 1 has been attacked for one to two years, and still shows some sound patches, as at *a a.* Numerous stromata are visible on the dead cortex. No. 2 has been suffering from the disease for four years. In the upper portion a canker-spot will be seen which is still unhealed, while below another is shown which is nearly closed. No. 3 represents a cross section showing three canker-spots, five, eight, and ten years old respectively.

and the openings of the perithecia (Fig. 47, *a*). When the periderm is removed, the stroma appears in the brown cortex as a dark brown mass of tissue (Fig. 47, *b*). If a section be made of the latter (Fig. 47, *c*), a black line will be perceived which separates the tissues of the cortex from those of the fungus. For each of the openings that appear at the surface one will generally recognize three perithecial chambers in the stroma.

If a section is made at right angles to the stroma so as to expose the longitudinal view of the aperture of a perithecium (Fig. 48), it is seen that the bounding line consists of dark brown mycelium (*a*), which, be-

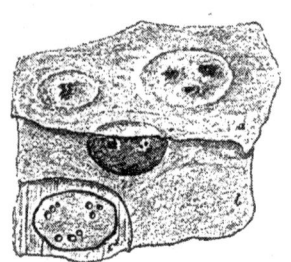

FIG. 47.—Cortex with stromata, which at *a* are covered by the periderm ; at *b* the periderm has been removed ; *c* shows the cross section of a stroma ; magnified five times.

ginning beneath the surface of the dead periderm, separates the whole stroma from the cortex, and even traverses the outermost sclerenchymatous bundle (*b*). The tissues thus enclosed consist of decomposed cortex and a large quantity of mycelium. The flask-shaped perithecia unite at *d* to form a common neck, the aperture of which breaks through the periderm. In the outer layers of the cortex (*c*) close beneath the periderm are the gonidiophores, which disperse numerous gonidia by abstriction.

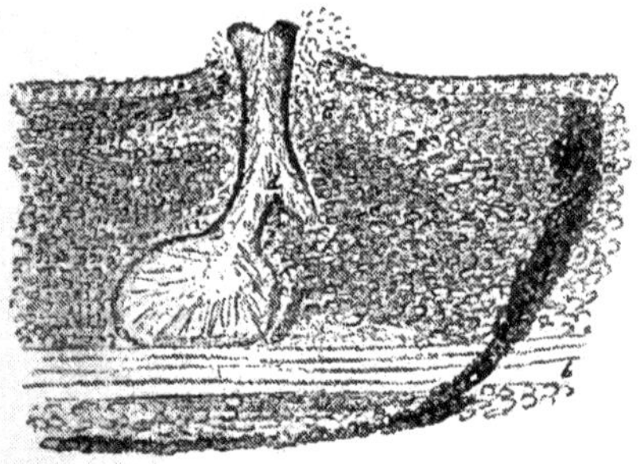

FIG. 48.—Cross section of a stroma. *a* represents the bounding zone consisting of mycelium; *b*, the sclerenchymatous strands of the cortex ; *c*, the gonidiophores ; *d*, the point where several perithecia unite.

The gonidia are sickle-shaped (Fig. 49, *a*), while the ascospores that are produced in the perithecia are bicellular and provided with peculiar filamentous appendages (Fig. 49, *b*). Three such appendages spring from the middle of the spore, and one from each end. It is the gonidia and spores that infect the cortex. It would appear that before infection can occur the periderm must be slightly injured, and this happens with great frequency in thick oak woods owing to the rubbing of the branches of adjoining trees against each other. Soon after the cortex has been killed the alburnum becomes brown, and it frequently happens that absolute decomposition sets in, in the course of the year. The sound portions of the tree begin to form a callus along the edge of the dead part, so that sooner or later the latter is again covered over. The dead fibrous cortex maintains its position for some years, but in the end it is entirely cast off, so that the dead wood becomes visible (Fig. 46, 2). Of course the same tree may in the course of years be repeatedly infected at various points, as the accompanying cross section (Fig. 46, 3) shows.

FIG. 49.—*a*, gonidia, and *b*, asci of *A. Taleola.*

This disease is accountable for the death of a great number of oaks, and renders frequent felling and strong thinning necessary. The dominant fast-growing trees recover from their injuries more rapidly than those of slower growth, the consequence being that one is left with a thin wood, consisting for the most part of the largest trees.

When the disease appears in a young oak wood, it is advisable at once to fell the infected trees, except where they belong to the dominant classes. The latter are thus stimulated to increased growth and enabled to recover from their wounds, and this result will follow with the greater certainty if the wood is underplanted with beeches or some other soil-improving species. The chances of infection are also thereby reduced, partly owing to the removal of the diseased trees, and partly because there are afterwards fewer opportunities for the occurrence of wounds induced by friction.

Plowrightia morbosa[1] (Cucurbitaria morbosa). The

---

[1] W. H. Farlow, "The Black-knot." *Bull. of the Bussey Institution. Bot. Articles*, 1876, p. 440.

Black-knot of Stone-fruit Trees. Although this disease has hitherto been met with abundantly only in North America, still it may find a place here, because experience has taught that the diseases of cultivated plants may be very easily transported to us from other parts of the world. It makes its presence known by the occurrence on the twigs, of plums and cherries, of hemispherical swellings, which project to about $\frac{2}{3}$ of an inch and are usually congregated in groups.

The surface of the swellings is covered by the gonidia of the parasite. The ascophores, which ripen in January, are in the form of round prominent black capsules. The twigs that are beset with knots should be removed as completely as possible and burned.

Physalospora Bidwellii is a parasite of the vine which has been constantly spreading in France since 1885. The disease, which is known as "Black-rot," is usually confined to the berries, the young tendrils and stalks of the bunches being attacked only in exceptional cases. It makes its appearance a short time before the grapes ripen, when it may be recognized by the appearance of a small round sooty blotch, which on enlarging assumes a reddish colour, getting more intense towards the centre. In a day or two the berry is entirely destroyed, and three or four days later it assumes a dark colour and becomes perfectly withered. The skin and succulent tissues become wrinkled and shrunk and adhere to the seeds, without, however, showing any wounds. Thus it is not a case of decomposition but of withering. Gradually but slowly the disease spreads from bunch to bunch and grape to grape. Its occurrence would appear to depend on a high temperature and a humid atmosphere.

The perithecia, pycnidia, and spermogonia of this parasite are known. The fungus survives from one year to another by means of stylospores which are contained in the pycnidia, and also by means of sclerotia.

Coniothyrium diplodiella, a fungus which attacks the vine, is only known in the form of pycnidia. The disease which it induces has occurred as an epidemic in Italy, France, and Switzerland. The fungus for the most part attacks the branches of the raceme and the stalks of the berries, and these parts frequently become perfectly rotten before the berries themselves are attacked. The diseased berries soon assume a pale colour, and the yellowish white appearance is so characteristic as to have suggested for the disease its popular American name of "White-rot," to distinguish it from the dark discoloration induced by Black-rot. So far no effective method of treatment has been discovered.

Glœosporium ampelophagum (*Sphaceloma ampelinum*) produces the "Anthracosis" of the vine. On all parts of the plant are observed brown blotches which rapidly become black. These soon turn to depressions surrounded by a ridge. Later on, when the blotches and surrounding tissues dry up, projecting portions of the mycelium bearing gonidiophores make their appearance on the surface as small white spots. Pycnidia are to be found in the ridge. Anthracosis finds the conditions best suited to its development in warm situations after prolonged damp weather.

Didymosphæria populina attacks the Lombardy poplar, and produces a disease which is met with in many parts of France and Germany.[1]

In spring a brown blotch on one side of the young twigs situated on the lower branches indicates the point to which the mycelium of the fungus has extended. A little later all that portion which is situated above the original blotch becomes black and bends inwards. The buds situated below the diseased spot produce fresh shoots, which become infected in the following spring. Branches whose shoots are largely infested wither up entirely. The lower part of the tree, which suffers most from the disease, becomes very bushy owing to the abundant production of suckers, consequent on the stimulus imparted to the buds by the destruction of the shoots. These sucker-shoots ultimately succumb to the same fate as their predecessors. As a consequence of this state of things, all the nourishment is used up in that part of the tree, with the result that the top of the infected tree withers before the parasite has ascended so far. In the month of May the pycnidia begin to break through the epidermis to admit of the escape of elliptical hyaline stylospores,

[1] Vuillemin, *Compt. Rend.* 25th March, 1889, and Prillieux, *ibid.* 27th May, 1889.

from which one or two much-septated germ-tubes are developed laterally or terminally. The perithecia, which afterwards predominate, appear at the same time. As such they remain through the winter and the following spring. They are spherical in shape, and measure 0·2 mm. in diameter, and contain paraphyses and asci, the latter having eight bicellular spores.

The disease may be combated by lopping off the lower branches of infected trees.

The gonidium form of this fungus is *Fusicladium Tremulæ*, which develops on leaves that have been infected in the previous spring by the ascospores.

DISCOMYCETES *

The essential difference between the *Discomycetes* and *Pyrenomycetes* is that the asci are not formed on the internal wall of a closed spherical or flask-shaped organ (perithecium), but on the surface of an open saucer-shaped fructification (apothecium). Before the ripening of the spores the asci are, at most, protected by a covering which does not belong to the fructification itself, but is partly formed out of the epidermal layers of the host-plant.

The *Discomycetes* are arranged into several sub-families, amongst which the *Phacideæ* are to be distinguished by the hymenial layer, originating not on the surface of the fungus-body but in its interior, where it remains covered, temporarily or permanently, by the fungal tissues.

Special mention may be made of the genera *Rhytisma* and *Hysterium*, which belong to this group.

RHYTISMA ACERINUM [1] †

This fungus causes one of the best known of the blotch-diseases of the Maples. *Acer platanoides* suffers especially from this parasite, *A. pseudoplatanus* and *A. campestre* in a less degree. On the leaves in July we first of all observe round yellow

[1] Cornu, *Compt. rend.*, lxxxvii. (1878), p. 178.

* [The reader may be referred to Phillips's *British Discomycetes* (Kegan Paul & Co., 1887) for an account of our native forms.—ED.]

† [Very common in this country.—ED.]

marks from one to two centimetres in diameter. In August these begin to turn black (Fig. 50), and the leaves usually fall somewhat prematurely, so that, by the end of September, the trees are, for the most part, leafless.

Not till some time during winter or the following spring do the numerous, somewhat prominent, vermiform apothecia appear on the black blotches of the rotting leaves. During damp warm weather these open by a longitudinal fissure. The disease is very easily produced artificially by laying such black portions of the leaves of the previous year on young maple-leaves during wet weather, or in a moist chamber, in the month of May. The filamentous spores which escape germinate, and produce fresh blotches. As this fungus agrees very closely with the next genus, *Hysterium*, both as regards origin of the perithecia and the development of the black stroma, I will not pursue this part of the subject further here.

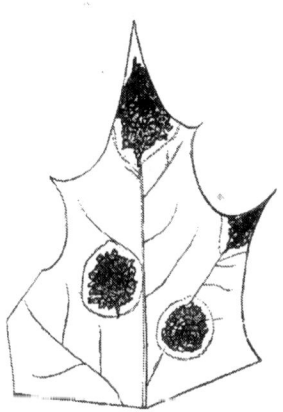

FIG. 50.—Part of a leaf of the Norway maple, showing *R. acerinum.* The black blotches are surrounded by a pale brown zone of dead tissue.

The injury, which consists in the reduced power of assimilation of the leaves, is not so great as to warrant the expense of instituting preventive measures. These would consist in raking together and removing the leaves in autumn. In gardens and parks, where this is done from other motives—for instance, in the English Garden in Munich—one never meets with an example of *Rhytisma*, whereas along the country roads and forest paths in the immediate neighbourhood of the city, where the leaves are left to lie in ditches and hollows, the disease occurs with great intensity.

RHYTISMA PUNCTATUM

This species of *Rhytisma*, which closely resembles the preceding one, is also to be met with on the leaves of Maples. They are to be distinguished, however, by the appearance of the region of the leaf that is occupied by the mycelium: this in the former case is a black blotch, and in the latter consists of black spots on a green ground. In autumn, when the leaves are quite yellow, the green colour of the chlorophyll persists in the blotches for some considerable time.

RHYTISMA SALICINUM

Black blotches similar to those produced by *R. acerinum* often occur on *Salix purpurea, nigricans, Caprea, aurita,* &c. These are caused by *Rhytisma salicinum,* but are of relatively minor importance.

HYSTERIUM (HYPODERMA)

The genus *Hysterium* possesses black elliptical to linear fructifications, which project from the leaves as black, lustrous, wart-like bodies.

The spores are linear, their walls being externally mucilaginous and swollen. In the case of the three following species the germ-tube probably always enters by a stoma. The mycelium spreads between the cells in the parenchyma of the leaves of conifers, which consequently become brown and die. Should the disease attack a leaf near the base at a time when the upper parts are still healthy and capable of assimilating under the influence of light, and should the transportation of the products of assimilation from the leaf be prevented by the death of the elements of the bast, the plastic substances collect in the form of starch-granules in such large quantities as to completely fill up the leaf.

The tissues of the leaves, which are at first pale green, afterwards become brown, and frequently the fructifications do not develop in them for more than a year. The ascogenous fructifications are often preceded by spermogonia, which in the case of the silver fir (Fig. 53) are arranged on the upper side of the leaf in two sinuous longitudinal ridges, whereas the apothecia which produce the ascospores are united on the under side of the leaf to form a single similar ridge. Both originate by the mycelium penetrating into and rupturing the epidermal cells. It then develops luxuriantly and forms a lenticular fungus-body, which afterwards becomes deep brown in colour.

The stroma, which first produces paraphyses and later asci, originates underneath this mycelial body, which is firmly attached to the epidermal cells.

The moister the weather, the more rapidly do the spores ripen. They are disseminated only when a long spell of wet weather has saturated the dead leaves with water and enabled the paraphyses and spore-walls to swell by contact with the water. This swelling leads to the rupturing of the leaf and the formation of a longitudinal fissure, which immediately

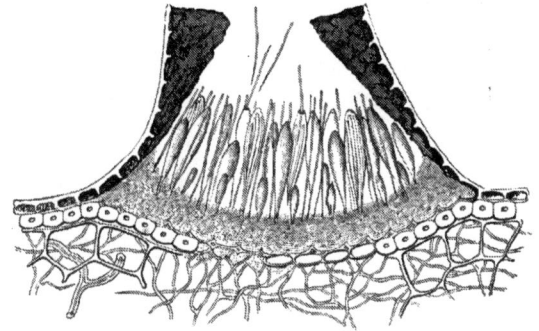

Fig. 51.—*Hysterium macrosporum*, showing a transverse section through a ripe ruptured stroma.

recloses on the occurrence of dry weather or when the spores have escaped (Fig. 51).

HYSTERIUM NERVISEQUIUM[1]

The distribution of this disease is coterminous with that of the silver fir, though I have found it really injurious only in the Erzgebirge, where large woods of silver firs, even of advanced age, had lost the majority of their leaves. Brownness of the leaves is always observed for the first time from May to July, and occurs on the two-year-old leaves which are entering their third year. A few months after the leaves have turned brown the spermogonia develop on their upper side, where two sinuously corrugated black longitudinal ridges make their appearance (right part of Fig. 53).

[1] R. Hartig, *Wichtige Krankheiten*, pp. 114 *et seq.*

Later on the apothecia appear on the under side as a longitudinal ridge on the mid-rib, and ripen in the following April, when the shoot is three years old. A large proportion of the leaves, however, fall earlier, the perithecia being produced on

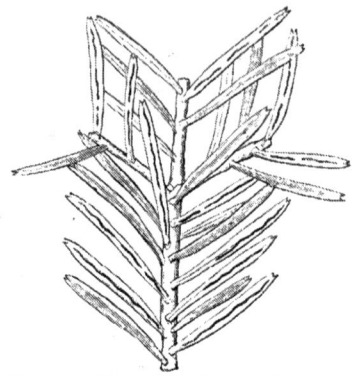

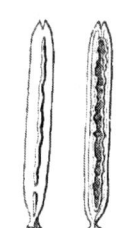

FIG. 53.—*Hysterium nervisequium* on the leaf of the silver fir; the leaf on the left shows the apothecium on the under side, that on the right the spermogonium on the upper side.

FIG. 52.—The under side of a branch of silver fir, showing the perithecia united into a longitudinal ridge.

the comparatively few leaves that remain *in situ*. It may also be remarked that still older leaves may contract the disease.

HYSTERIUM MACROSPORUM [1]

This disease of the spruce produces the "spruce-leaf redness," which in many years occurs with great severity in woods from ten to forty years old.

Its presence may be detected by the leaves of the previous year's shoots turning brown in May, or possibly not till autumn, and by the invariable occurrence of abundant mycelia in the leaves even before they become brown. Leaves which change colour in spring reveal the commencement of the formation of perithecia in July of the same year, and these ripen next spring in April and May. At that time they are present on the two-year-old shoots. I observed this rapid process of development in the humid climate of the Erzgebirge. At Eberswalde, on the other hand, the leaves on the two-year-old shoots do not become

[1] R. Hartig, *Wichtige Krankheiten*, p. 101.

brown till October, and the formation of perithecia begins on
the three-year-old leaves in June of the following year, the spores
ripening in the succeeding March and April. The apothecia
appear as long, straight, lustrous-black ridges, for the most part
only on the two under sides of the leaf (Fig. 55). The spores
are about twice as long as those of *H. nervisequium*. It is
desirable that further investigation should be directed to this
and to the immediately preceding disease, because I have not
yet been able to clear up thoroughly many details in the development of these parasites. Especially has no explanation so far

FIG. 54.—A spruce-branch, showing
brown leaves on the upper two-year-
old portion, and apothecia on the part
that is three years old.

FIG. 55.—Apothecia
on a spruce-leaf.

been offered regarding the phenomenon of the leaves of the
youngest shoots of many spruces first becoming brown and
then dropping off in autumn, so that these shoots become
almost completely defoliated. Instead of long apothecia-
ridges developing on such leaves, small isolated apothecia-
tubercles similar to those of *Hysterium Pinastri* make their
appearance.

HYSTERIUM PINASTRI*

This is a species of fungus which is everywhere present in
pine woods, and has been identified by Göppert [1] as the cause of

[1] Göppert, *Verhandl. d. schlesischen Forstvereins*, 1852, p. 67.
*[Common in England. · ED.]

the pine-leaf cast. Under the name "Pine-blight" (leaf-cast or shedding) the most various diseases have been included. These attack young and old pines, and are characterised by the leaves becoming brown, and usually also by their being prematurely shed. The causes of these diseased conditions are very various. In the first place, frost may actually cause the death of the young leaves of pines. On July 23rd, 1878, large pines, especially such as were growing along the margin of the wood, were so severely affected by frost in the Turoscheln district that those parts of the new leaves which had emerged from the sheath died.

As however the leaves of the Scotch pine do not protrude from the sheath before the beginning of June, late frost can do injury only in very few cases and in very exceptional localities. In many seasons one observes—frequently only on one side, especially the east side, of trees—that all the leaves of the youngest shoots on trees that are much exposed to the wind become uniformly brown, except the lowest part, which is enveloped by the sheath. Whether, in such cases, the injury is always due to actual frost, or even to severe cooling, I am not in a position to determine.

In many cases the browning, death, and shedding of the leaves are the result of drought.[1] In cases where the pine seed-beds have been covered with snow in winter, but which has disappeared after a few warm sunny days without the ground thawing, it will be found that the leaves soon become brown, and that the pines contract "the blight." If one examines the discoloured leaves after the appearance of the first symptoms of the disease, he frequently fails to find any trace of mycelia. It is also characteristic that the brownness is equally distributed over the whole leaf, or spreads back from the apex uniformly to a greater or less distance. In such a case we have to do with a drying up of the leaves, which do not receive a sufficient quantity of water from the frozen ground to compensate for the loss by evaporation that takes place in the clear dry weather of winter. Although erroneously ascribed to the action of frost, the cause is the same, too, in cases where the foliage of *Pinus Strobus*, the spruce, and other conifers, as also dicotyledonous evergreens, becomes

---

[1] Ebermayer, *Die physikalischen Einwirkungen des Waldes auf Luft und Boden*, 1873.

withered on the side of the tree which is exposed to wind or sun
One should certainly not ascribe the withering of spruce-leaves
during winter on the sunny side of the tree to the action of frost,
and there is quite as little reason for relegating to the same
cause the browning of young pines in frozen ground owing to
direct insolation and strong air-currents

In the height of summer, about the month of July, exactly the
same phenomenon may be observed during dry weather when
pines in a drilled seed-bed on sandy soil are left standing for a
second year   Only those pines remain perfectly healthy which are
situated at the sides of the paths—that is to say, at the edges of
the beds   In spring the one-year-old pines remain quite healthy,
as long as the soil retains a sufficient supply of moisture and
growth has not begun. Afterwards growth proceeds both above
and below ground, though most vigorously in the marginal
plants, whose roots can obtain water and nutriment from the
paths as well as from the bed   Should transpiration of water by
the plants in July be greatly increased partly in consequence of
the air being dry and warm, and partly owing to the formation
of new shoots and leaves, and, on the other hand, should the
soil have lost its winter moisture, then the pines wither in exactly
the same way as happens in winter when the ground is frozen
and the sky is clear.   Only those plants remain green which
stand nearest to the paths, or at least to the edge of the bed.

In the nursery at Eberswalde, after a severe early frost in
October, that portion of the ground of the pine seed-beds which
the sun could not reach was still frost-bound at midday.   On
the other hand, the ground which the rays of the sun could affect
was completely thawed and warmed in the course of the fore-
noon.   The seed-beds all over were beautifully green, and very
healthy.

A few days later all the pines in the seed-beds which had been
shaded were brown, whereas those which had been exposed to
the sun remained perfectly healthy.   I am able to explain this
phenomenon only by the fact that the frozen ground prevented
the absorption of water by the roots, whereas the clear sky and
relatively warm air furthered transpiration by the leaves.   In
this case shading had acted prejudicially.

In by far the greater number of cases the pine leaf-cast is

parasitic and epidemic in character, and is to be attributed to *Hysterium Pinastri.* Where " the cast " has become a calamity which year after year overtakes the seed-beds and young woods, it may at once be assumed that the disease is present in this most destructive form.

It may frequently be recognized on young pine-seedlings even in the first autumn by the primary leaves acquiring brown blotches, while the other parts often assume a purple-red colour.

Even at this early stage one always finds the characteristic mycelium of the parasite in the brown blotches. Frequently it also happens in the first autumn that a large number of very small black spermogonia appear on the diseased leaves (Fig. 56, *d, e*), the spermatia of which do not seem to be capable of germinating. After wet summers I have found perfectly ripe apothecia on the leaves of young pine-seedlings even in autumn. As a rule the black apothecia (Fig. 57, *x*), which are much larger than the spermogonia, do not develop till the following year. Everything depends very much on the weather. On account of the dry leaves being unable to offer any nourishment to the fungus, its development, and that of its sporophore, can proceed only during wet weather. Dry summers and cold winters do much to hinder the development and distribution of the fungus, whereas wet summers and mild muggy winters are specially favourable for its growth. During mild winters the blight frequently spreads rapidly in nurseries and in regenerated forest areas. I have never observed the apothecia make their appearance during the first year on the leaves of pines two years old and upwards. They usually appear only in the third year, and generally after the leaves have fallen, though they not unfrequently also ripen on leaves that have remained *in situ.* As regards the manner of distribution of the blight-fungus, it may be mentioned that the ripe apothecia rupture only after long-continued rain. Then the tissues of the leaf have been thoroughly softened, and a plentiful supply of water has been able to reach the apothecia from within. This causes the asci and spores to swell, a state of things which is followed by the forcible rupturing of the apothecium-cover. Long-continued rains, however, do not usually occur except with west winds. They are less frequent with north or

I

south winds. This is to be remembered in instituting preventive measures against the blight. As a rule the diseased leaves of one-year-old seedling-pines die off completely in spring, without however falling off. On the other hand, one finds that all the diseased leaves of the bifo-liar spurs of two-year-old pines suddenly become brown after the advent of warmer weather in March or April. This is followed

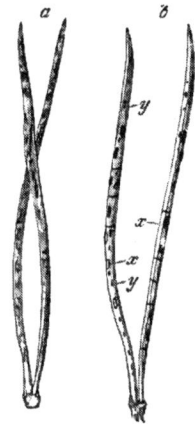

FIG. 56.—A one-year-old pine in spring which has been attacked by *H. Pinastri*. *a*, healthy green leaves; *b*, leaves with a brown apex and green base; *c*, green leaves showing numerous brown blotches; *d*, leaves whose upper portion has become brown during the previous winter, and which now bear the spermogonia of *H. Pinastri*; the basal portion of these leaves has become brown more recently; *e*, leaves that are completely dead and covered by spermogonia.

FIG. 57.—*a*, a one-year-old pine-leaf in April showing brown spots where infected, but still remaining green towards the base; *b*, a dead two-year-old pine-leaf in April with ripe perithecia, *x*, and empty spermogonia, *y*.

by a cast—that is, by defoliation of the dwarf shoots. This shedding, which frequently follows in a few days, is not to be regarded as the effect of immediately preceding unfavourable climatic conditions. It is, in fact, one result of the formation of cork at the base of the dwarf shoots, which are subsequently pushed off when growth is resumed. Seedlings affected by the blight usually perish, and can only recover when about half of the leaves remain green and escape fresh infection. It is decidedly inadvisable to make use of diseased yearling seedlings for planting. Neither is it advisable to use diseased pines two years old and upwards, because they are usually so weakened by transplanting that they soon perish. Diseased plants on a regenerated area may, under favourable circumstances, recover from the disease. This, however, never happens when the mycelium of the fungus has spread from the leaves into the tissues of the stem itself. In particular, if the medulla of the plant has become brown owing to the presence of the mycelium, death supervenes, even although the buds look quite healthy in spring.

Should diseased leaves exist in the crowns of old pines, infection may be easily induced by falling leaves. The young plants are infected either by the dehiscence of the apothecia of the diseased leaves that fall on them, or by the spores that are conveyed to them from the diseased leaves in the descending rain-drops. On this account it is not generally advisable to form pine seed-beds under the drop of old pine-trees.

Infection, in most cases, accompanies wind and rain which in blowing over an infected area catches up numerous spores, and bears them to sound plants. The experience that the disease is most prevalent on very young plants, and in the case of older ones only to a height of about two feet from the ground, is to be explained by the fact that only the air-currents that are close to the ground have the chance of catching up the spores of the fungus and of depositing them upon plants.

In order to raise healthy plants, it is advisable to form pine seed-beds in dicotyledonous woods, or, at least, at as great a distance as possible from young woods affected by the disease of leaf-shedding. Nurseries for seedlings and transplanted trees that have ever shown the disease should only be used for fresh sowings after all diseased plants in the nursery itself, and in its neighbourhood, have been destroyed.

If one is compelled to form seed-beds in unhealthy districts, one should select such situations as do not adjoin, at least on the west side, young diseased woods. If the choice exists, it is advisable to form the nursery in such a position at the edge of the wood that the west winds that impinge upon it shall first have blown over a wide extent of open country. The seed-beds, which are not to be made too large, should be enclosed on the side towards the wood by a perfectly close board fence 6½ feet high. If spruce nurseries are available, containing dense and high beds of plants running from north to south, the pine seed-beds may be laid down between the beds of spruce, so that the latter form a protection against the spores that are borne by the west wind. Burying pines in deep trenches during winter often results in complete smothering of the plants owing to the exclusion of atmospheric oxygen. On the other hand, a light covering of leaves in winter affords good protection against contact with the spores.

In protecting the areas under regeneration against fungal leaf-shed, regeneration by groups, under certain circumstances, gives the best results. Blanks in close pine woods may be very successfully restocked even where the disease destroys everything on larger clear-felled areas. This is undoubtedly due in the first place to the protection afforded against the spore-laden wind. In arranging the direction of felling one must take all possible care to prevent the west wind from blowing over large infected areas before it reaches the part of the wood that is being regenerated. Very extensive seed-fellings, when they adjoin each other, further the epidemic distribution of the disease in any case. Where seed is sown or trees are planted in stripes, it is a good plan to plough the stripes from north to south, and to throw the furrow slice on to the west side. If the furrows run from west to east, the west wind, blowing along them, is sure to carry the spores from diseased plants to sound ones. Where the spruce and Douglas fir thrive, these trees may be planted in stripes running north and south, partly at the edge of the wood, and partly at fixed distances throughout it, to act as screens and prevent the disease spreading. This must be done at least ten years before the final felling of the pine wood.

Areas that are completely overrun by this disease should be planted with Weymouth pines, or some other disease-resisting species, according to the character of the soil.

The Weymouth pine suffers here and there from a leaf-disease which is due to an allied parasite, *Hysterium brachy-sporum* I am not yet able to determine whether *Hysterium laricinum*, which has been observed in great abundance on larches in certain districts of the Alps, is also a true parasite.

The sub-family of the *Pezizeæ* is to be distinguished by cup-shaped or saucer-shaped sporophores, which produce the hymenial layer free on the upper surface

PEZIZA (HELOTIUM) WILLKOMMII [1] *

The fungus which induces the larch-blister is the cause of one of the most destructive and widely distributed diseases of the larch   It was first described by Willkomm,[2] who, however, made a mistake in its identification, and called it *Corticum amorphum*

Corticum, in fact, bears only a superficial resemblance to *Peziza*, and belongs to the *Basidiomycetes*   On the strength of a macroscopic similarity, also, it was next said to be *Peziza calycina*, till I recognized that in this fungus we had to do with a new and still unknown species.   The ascophore is at once distinguishable from that of *P calycina* by its very short cup-stalk.   So much by way of explaining the regrettable confusion of names

The larch is a forest tree which thrives splendidly throughout the whole of Germany, suffering but little from frost, at least not more so than other indigenous trees   Originally, however, its distribution was confined to high Alpine regions, because only there could it offer successful resistance to its enemies   Amongst these enemies are to be classed a number of insects, notably the Larch moth, *Coleophora laricella*   This insect is also found in Alpine regions to a considerable height (over 4,000 feet), and so widely is it distributed, and so

---

[1] R. Hartig, *Untersuchungen aus dem Forstb. Inst* , I pp 63—88

[2] Willkomm, *Mikroskopische Feinde des Waldes*, II. pp 167 *et seq.*

* [Though often overlooked, this fungus is quite common on the diseased Larches in England and Scotland, with all the characters and relations to the "blisters" described by the author   Phillips, *op cit* p 241, gives it as *Lachnella calycina*, and makes no note of its relation to the disease.—ED]

numerously represented, that it is at first surprising why it does
hardly any damage there   This is easily explained from the
fact that at high elevations the transition from winter to
spring is very rapid, and the development of the leaf-fascicles
occupies but a short time   On the plains the larch begins to
display green buds even towards the end of March, but their
further development is often retarded for a long time, until,
in the beginning of May, the growth of the leaves progresses more rapidly.   This is the dangerous period for the
larch, because when the caterpillars awake from hiberna-
tion they begin to devour the green buds, and when growth
proceeds slowly these are largely consumed, and the trees
are, for the most part, defoliated.   On the other hand, when
the leaf-fascicles develop rapidly, a small proportion of the
foliage suffices to feed the caterpillars.   In Alpine regions
the short spring saves the larches from complete or excessive
defoliation, which, especially when often repeated, results in the
crippling and death of the trees   The Larch Aphis also,
Chermes Laricis, damages the foliage of the larch to no small
extent, though not nearly so much as the moth   The disease
which is induced by *P Willkommii* differs entirely from the
crippling which larches experience as a result of the attack of
the moth, aphis, &c.   This parasite is indigenous to high Alpine
regions, where it produces the same disease that has resulted in ..
the destruction of innumerable woods in Germany, Denmark,
and Scotland.   In its native habitat, however, it is only under
special conditions of environment that it destroys whole woods
In order correctly to appreciate this point we must first review
the course of development of the parasite

The spores—which originate in cup-shaped fructifications to
be afterwards described—soon germinate in the presence of
sufficient moisture, with effect not on an uninjured tree, however,
but only on a wound   Such wounds are very often due to hailstones, or to the dwarf-shoots being devoured in spring—as was
mentioned above—or they are formed in the upper angle of
the base of a branch (Fig 58, *b*) owing to its depression under
accumulations of snow or hoar-frost   From such wounds the
vigorous, copiously ramifying, septate mycelium spreads in the
soft bast, partly between and partly in the cells advancing in

the sieve-tubes, and killing and browning the tissues. The mycelium also grows into the wood, and even penetrates as far as the medulla.

That portion of the cortical tissues which has been killed during the first year dries up and appears as a depression, especially after growth in thickness has been resumed by the healthy part of the tree (Fig. 58).

In summer the growth of the mycelium ceases, and an unusually

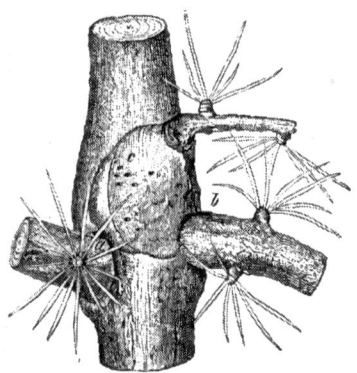

FIG. 58.—A canker-spot that has been recently formed in the upper portion of the stem of an eight-year-old larch from the Tyrol. Infection has occurred above the branch, *b*, where a crack has been formed in the tissues, owing to the branch having been depressed under a load of snow. Numerous immature ascophores, *c*, have already formed on the dead cortex.

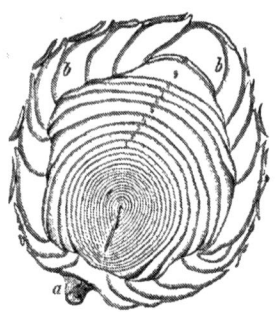

FIG. 59.—Cross section of a well-grown larch which has been attacked by *P. Willkommii*. Infection had occurred ten years previously at the dwarf shoot, *a*. Each year the mycelium advances in opposite directions, in spite of the fact that a layer of cork, *b b*, is formed at the beginning of each growing season along the boundary of the living tissue. In the immediately preceding year a very small quantity of wood had been formed.

broad layer of cork is formed for the protection of the tree along the boundary between the sound and diseased tissues. These layers of cork (Fig. 59, *b b*) which form between the dead and living tissues induce external rupturing of the cortex at points along the boundary of the canker-spot (Fig. 60), the result being that turpentine flows from the interior of the tree. Year by year the canker-spot enlarges along its whole periphery, rather more rapidly, however, longitudinally than horizontally, and it is probably the vital activity of the

cortical tissues which in summer causes a temporary inter-
ruption to the progress of the parasite. In autumn the
mycelium again succeeds in entering the living bast, either
through the cambium region or by way of the wood, so that,
as a matter of fact, the layer of
cork is only of slight service. In
proportion as the passage of the
plastic substances is confined to
one side of the tree, growth of
the wood and bast is stimulated
at that part (Fig. 59). Thus the
conflict between parasite and
host-plant may remain long un-
decided, and in the Tyrol I found
larches still alive with blisters of
a hundred years' standing.

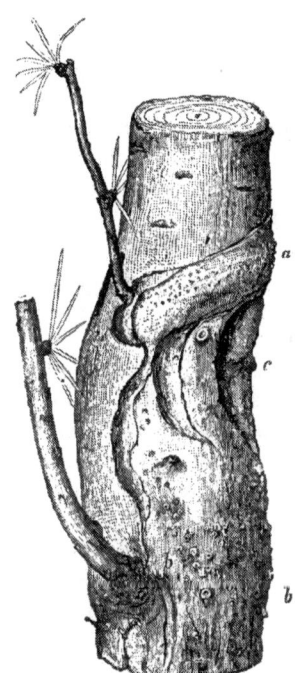

Should the parasite advance relatively quickly, and, at the same
time, should the growth of the tree
at the affected part be slow, then
the canker-spot soon embraces
the whole stem or branch (Fig. 59),
and the tree dies above this spot.

By artificial mycelial infection
one may, almost without fail,
produce a blister on any part of
a sound larch.

Soon after the death of the
cortical tissues, the cushion-like
stromata of the parasite originate
in the form of small yellowish
white pustules of the size of a
pin-head (Fig. 58 c, Fig. 60 a). In
the interior of these stromata,

FIG. 60.—A canker-spot of two
years' standing, close to the collar,
and hidden by the grass. On the
upper portion, which is exposed
to air-currents, the stromata are
abortive; but in the lower portion, which has been kept moist,
they have developed to form
vigorous ascocarps.

and partly on their surface as
well, vermiform passages or roundish cavities are formed, the walls
of which are covered with innumerable club-shaped sterigmata, at
whose apex extremely minute cells originate. Whether these
organs, which appear to be incapable of germination, are

abortive gonidia, or are to be classed with spermatia, remains, in the meantime, undetermined. In this place it is specially important to emphasise the fact that they are incapable of assisting in the distribution of the parasite.

The small stromata are very readily affected by a dry atmosphere and by air-currents, in which they quickly wither and die. They develop only when constantly surrounded by moist air. Under such circumstances they produce the well-known cup-shaped ascocarps (Fig. 60, *b b*). These possess a hymenium of a fine red colour. The hymenium consists of innumerable asci surrounded by filamentous paraphyses. Eight colourless spores are formed in the interior of each ascus. The fact that the mycelium penetrates even into the wood, and kills it, explains why one or a few small blisters may greatly interfere with the growth of the whole stem. Numerous cup-shaped ascocarps ultimately make their appearance on the dead cortex, and these are met with even when blisters are absent.

In muggy situations the larches soon become diseased, and die in a few years without any large blisters making their appearance. The cup-shaped ascocarps of the parasite appear upon the cortex. It looks as though the large quantity of water present in larches whose transpiration is interfered with greatly favours the development and spread of the fungus in the wood, and that the disease consequently spreads throughout the whole plant.

The foregoing descriptive sketch of the results of my investigations may suffice to explain the recognized facts connected with the occurrence and distribution of the disease.

The larch-blister has been indigenous to high Alpine regions from time immemorial. It occurs, however, with marked intensity only in damp muggy valleys in immediate proximity to lakes (*e.g.* the Achensee in the Tyrol, &c.), though on plateaus it may also destroy a small tree here and there. Owing to the prevalence of air-currents, freely exposed ascocarps never ripen on plateaus and valley-slopes. The ascocarps ripen only on those blisters which are situated at the foot of the stem close to the ground, or on blistered branches that are in contact with the earth. This is owing to the surrounding high grass sheltering the young ascocarps against air-currents, and so keeping them moist.

In the early decades of this century, when the larch was planted in various parts of Germany, the enemy was left behind in its native habitat, and the trees flourished to perfection   Probably every old forester knows some groups of larches of the most stately growth which date back to that period.   In consequence of these satisfactory results, the larch was generally planted throughout the whole of Germany.   Most excellent results were obtained, even where the inferior quality of the soil held out but a poor prospect of success

But after woods of all sizes had been established from the foot of the Alps to the coasts of the North Sea and Baltic, the fungus spread downwards from the Alps, to find everywhere the most favourable conditions for its development.   These consisted of dense young pure woods, groups that had been formed in replanting up old beech woods, moist stagnant air, wounds caused by the moth, &c.   Commerce also assisted to intensify the evil, diseased larches being sent out from the nurseries and transported from district to district

Under these conditions the fructifications of the fungus attained to luxuriant development and ripened their spores on the blisters, while the spores found ample opportunity of germinating, and of infecting the trees in the close pure woods   To-day but few of the many promising young woods remain   The larches have maintained their ground best in those woods where a few were introduced as advance-growth.   The air circulating in the freely developed crowns has not only kept the disease in check, but has also prevented the spores from ripening on diseased specimens

Supposing that we have to do with a diseased larch wood, it is first necessary to determine whether the damage is entirely due to the moth or whether it is a case of fungoid blister

Often enough both will appear in company   If it is simply a case of stunting in consequence of the attack of the moth, pruning away the branches till only the vigorous upper part of the crown remains may - be permanently beneficial.   The upper branches will grow vigorously, and may form a good, permanently healthy crown, especially as the moth is most destructive on the lower branches

If it is a case of fungoid injury, pruning may assist somewhat only if the bole as a whole, and especially the part in the crown, is sound. If a tree is in vigorous growth, the smaller blisters low down on the stem, although they increase in size, will induce death only at an advanced age.

Blisters on the branches are, in themselves, of less importance. They merely contribute to the danger of the further spread of the disease by means of spores.

As regards the future cultivation on plains and at moderate elevations of this so essentially valuable tree, the following points may be noted in the light of what has been said. It should only be grown singly—that is to say, it should form but a small part of a mixture, and it ought, if possible, to be planted somewhat in advance of the other trees. It should never be planted in pure woods, and should always occupy an open situation. Where diseased woods are present in the immediate neighbourhood, it is better to abandon the idea of cultivating this tree. The greatest caution is to be exercised in procuring young trees from outside sources, and plants showing any signs of disease in the seed or plant beds must at once be removed and burned.

RHIZINA UNDULATA * FR.   THE ROOT-FUNGUS [1]

On the light sandy soils of Germany, France, &c., especially in pine and other coniferous woods, one not unfrequently meets with numerous ascophores of *R. undulata* growing on the ground. These bear a considerable resemblance to a morel (Fig. 61). In diameter they vary from two thirds of an inch to two inches. The broad ascophore (Fig. 61, *a*) is undulating and chestnut brown on the upper surface, diverse in shape, of a velvety lustre, and glutinous in wet weather. The under side (Fig. 61, *b*), which is destitute of a stalk, is pale yellow and woolly, and is frequently united to the subterranean mycelium by means of numerous loose mycelial strands (Fig. 62). If a section be made of the ascophore, it will be found that towards the upper surface the hymenium (Fig. 63) is composed of asci, each containing eight spores, amongst which filamentous septate paraphyses, clavate towards the apex, will be made out (Fig. 63, *a*). Besides these there are present numerous non-septate secreting-tubes (*b*), which project a little above the surface of the hymenium. These are filled with a

[1] R. Hartig, *Naturwissenschaft: Zeitschrift*, August 1892.
* [This occurs on heaths, &c., in England.—ED.]

brown secretion which pours over the surface as a slimy glutinous substance, swarming with bacteria.   The bacteria also find their way between the paraphyses, so that it is scarcely possible to get a culture of spores that is free from them.   It is these, too, which induce the rapid decay and solution of the entire ascophore.

The spores (Fig. 64, *a*) are spindle-shaped and pointed at both ends, and the wall of the spore is thickened at both of the ex-

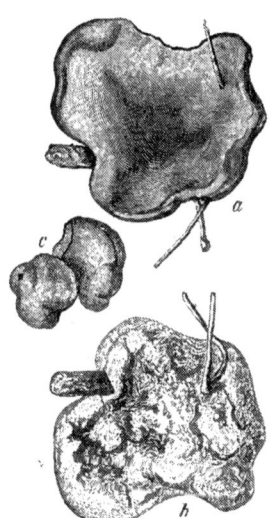

tremities.   Before germinating, each spore generally contains two large drops of oil.

Ascophores of *Rhizina* were sent to me ten years ago from Silesia, with the remark that in a young pine wood where many of the plants had died the fructifications of this fungus appeared on the surface of the ground in the neighbourhood of the dead trees.

FIG. 61.—*a*, the upper side, and, *b*, the under side of a sporophore of *R. undulata;* *c* is a small fungus-body.

FIG. 62.—Section of a sporophore.

My request that a few dead trees should be forwarded for investigation was not complied with, so that it was only two years ago, on receipt of material from Herr von Blücher, forester in Schwerin, that I found myself in a position to make a more intimate acquaintance with the parasite and its life-history.

In the beginning of August 1890, Herr von Blücher and Herr von der Lühe sent me numerous ascophores of the parasite, as well as diseased and dead conifers, along with information regarding the occurrence of the disease at Schildfeld, near Bennin, in Mecklenburg-Schwerin.   The diseased and dead plants were specimens four to ten years old of *Abies pectinata, Tsuga Mertensiana, Pseudotsuga Douglasii, Picea Sitkœnsis, Pinus Strobus,* and *Larix europœa.*

The part of the wood that was attacked extended to about 2½ acres. In the winter of 1889-90 the wood which then existed —namely, a thin stocking of pines, larches, and spruces about fifty years old—was stubbed, and in the spring of 1890 the area was replanted chiefly with three- to four-year-old plants, which were inserted partly in pits and partly in notches.

In the month of June disease had appeared among the plants. The leaves

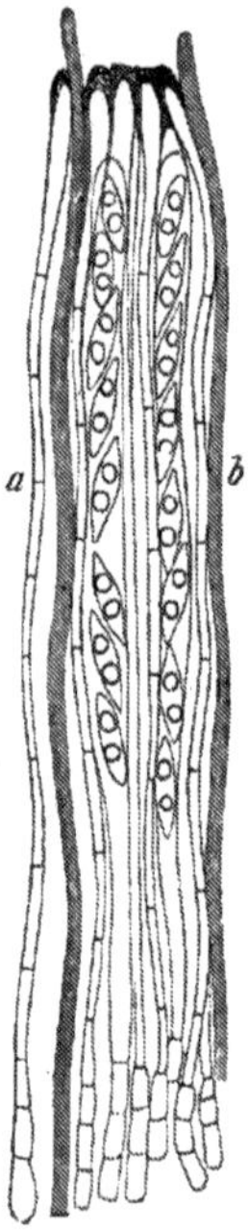

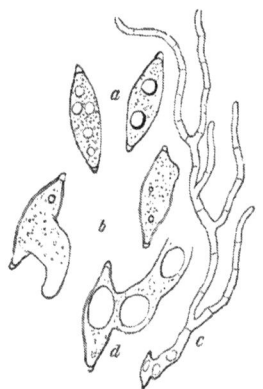

FIG. 63.—Hymenium, consisting of *a*, paraphyses ; *b*, secreting-tubes ; *c*, asci, which contain eight spores each.

FIG. 64.—*a*, spores of *Rhizina ; b*, ditto, twenty-four hours after sowing ; *c*, ditto, twenty-four hours later ; *d*, the spore *c* more highly magnified.

rapidly died and fell off, and the fungus appeared to be gradually spreading over the area. The ascophores were found almost exclusively at a distance of about ten inches from the plants, but on the surface of what had been the pit. But between the plants also, on the bare ground covered with raw humus, numerous ascophores were met with. The soil was sandy in character, covered with raw humus and bilberry-bushes.

The above report refers only to conifers attacked by the parasite. Professor Crié of Rennes was good enough to send me more than once the roots of diseased plants of *Castanea vesca.* On one of these I found *Rhizina undulata* luxuriantly developed.

On removing a diseased or dead plant from the ground, one will find that a large quantity of sandy soil is firmly held amongst the roots by means of numerous fungus-filaments, but that no outpouring of resin whatever is visible (Fig. 65).

On the roots being isolated and carefully examined, it will be found that peculiar mycelial

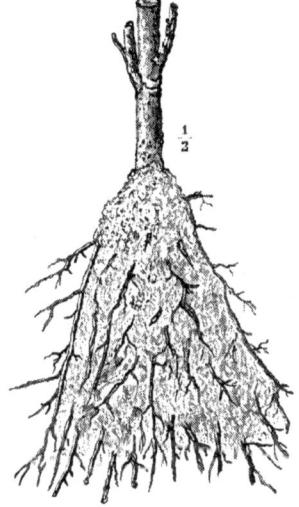

FIG. 65.—The roots of a silver fir which has been killed by *Rhizina.*

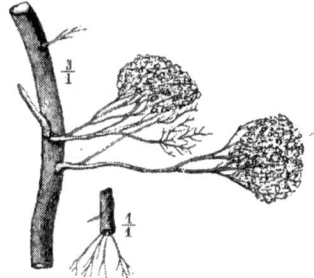

FIG. 66.—Mycelial growths resembling *Rhizoctonia,* which are met with on the roots of plants infested by *Rhizina,* magnified by 3. Mycelial strands protruding from the cut surface in moist air. Natural size.

bodies resembling *Rhizoctonia* project from the cortex. At a distance of two to three fifths of an inch these begin to ramify, and ultimately divide into filamentous mycelia (Fig. 66). If one cuts off a root and makes a culture in a moist chamber, it will be found that such mycelial bodies will form in large numbers on the cortex, or on the cut surface of the wood. These ramify in the usual way and end in a fine point (Figs. 66 and 67), and are always brilliantly white in colour.

A microscopic investigation will reveal the cause of this colour, which is due to drops of ethereal oil adhering in great numbers to the external filaments, or to the apices of the fine hair-like filaments which stand more or less at right angles to the mycelial strands (Figs. 68 and 69).

These short simple or compound hairs produce a large drop of ethereal oil at the apex, which finally ruptures the elastic cell-wall at the end of the hair, and flows out. The hair thus comes to have a funnel-like aperture at its apex (Fig. 69, e).

I am not aware of attention having previously been called to the formation of ethereal oil in the form of drops by fungi. The oil is immediately dissolved by alcohol. As the mycelial filaments in the periphery of the strands contain numerous small oil-drops, it would appear that this ethereal oil is also exuded from the lateral walls of the hyphæ, although it is quite possible that this has gradually found its way thither from the apex of the hairs. When the filamentous mycelia that envelop the soil-particles are examined, it will be found that most of the thin threads possess numerous clamp cells, and are somewhat brown in colour.

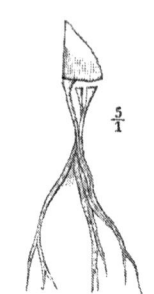

FIG. 67.—Mycelial strands of *Rhizina* which have been cultivated in moist air. They are partly separated from the wood.

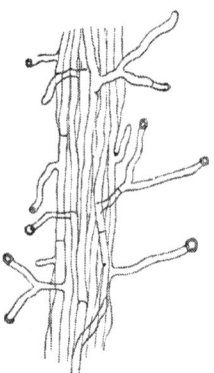

FIG. 68.—A mycelial strand bearing hairs.

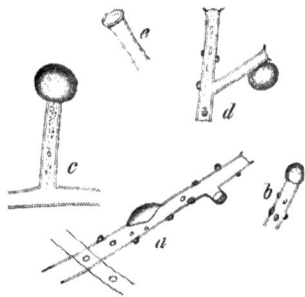

FIG. 69.—*a*, a mycelial filament with an oil-drop attached ; *b*, ditto, with an oil-drop at the apex ; *c*, a hair with a large oil-drop ; *d*, a bifurcated hair from whose apices the oil-drops have become detached ; *e*, apex of a hair viewed from above.

Although I have much diffidence in maintaining that this feature, which otherwise is peculiar to the *Hymenomycetes*, is characteristic of this parasite, still I cannot doubt that these filaments with clamp cells belong to it. However, I will not maintain this as an absolute fact, especially as clamps do not occur either in the interior of plants or in the mycelia produced by germinating spores of *Rhizina*

My first cultures were undertaken on August 19th, 1890, with fresh spores, which I sowed partly on a gelatine extract of fruit and partly on humus sandy soil. These produced no result

On repeating the culture with numerous spores on September 18th, only a single one germinated. On the other hand, germination was general in twenty-four hours in a seeding on gelatine extract of fruit which was undertaken on November 18th. These germinating spores are shown in Fig. 64, *b*. The extraordinarily thick germ-tube proceeded from the lateral wall of the spore, and from the first its diameter was as great as that of the spore itself. After only forty-eight hours the germinating spore had reached the stage which is represented, slightly magnified, in Fig. 64, *c*.

The stout much-branching mycelium is septate, and resembles in every respect that which is found penetrating the healthy cortex of slightly or much-diseased plants   Under such circumstances it grows between the cells of the parenchymatous tissues, while in the soft bast its progress is partly intercellular and partly intracellular, the sieve-tubes being frequently packed full of a dense filamentous mycelium   In the process of time the mycelium kills the tissues of the cortex and soft bast, whose elements become brown and completely dismembered, or, in other words, isolated   The development is so luxuriant that it forms, in certain places, a pseudo-parenchymatous fungus-tissue, consisting of vesicular swollen cells. This however is speedily destroyed as soon as the tissues between the wood and periderm become almost completely decayed   In this process of decay very minute organisms resembling *Micrococcus* play an important part   When employing a high power, the whole field of view sometimes swarms with these minute cells, whose diameter does not exceed 1 to 1 5 micromillimeters These originate (Fig 70) on very small stalks resembling sterigmata, which project some from the lateral walls and some from the apices of the filamentous mycelia. Subsequently they appear to increase by budding.

It is very desirable that foresters, especially in sandy districts, should direct their attention to the occurrence and biology of this parasite.

The term "Soil Canker" has been used for twenty years to designate all those diseases in young and old woods where no indications above ground can be referred to as a cause. Such diseases have their seat below the surface, and gradually spreading from the first point of attack they occasion blanks and gaps in woods and nurseries. During the last twenty years I have described a whole series of parasitic fungi which induce such diseases. These include *Agaricus melleus, Trametes radiciperda, Polyporus vaporarius, Rosellinia quercina, Dematophora necatrix*, and *Phytophthora omnivora* (in the narrow sense). To these must now be added *Rhizina undulata*.

The various species of *Vaccineæ* are attacked by parasites of the genus **Sclerotinia**.[1] The gonidiophores appear in spring on young leaves and stems, which consequently become brown, in

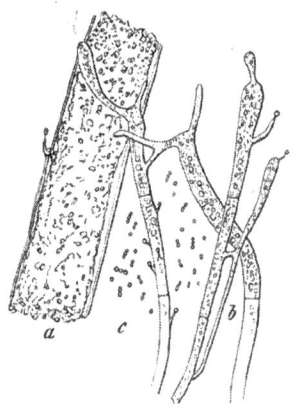

FIG. 70.—Mycelium of *Rhizina* from the cortex of the silver fir. *a*, a filament of average thickness; *b*, very thin filaments; *c*, gonidia resembling *Micrococcus*. Magnified 1500 times.

the form of a mould-like covering which emits an almond-like perfume. The insects that are thereby attracted convey the gonidia to the stigmata of the flowers of the *Vaccineæ*. A sclerotium is formed in the berries, which become brown, dry, and "mummified" and drop off, and from them there develop in the following spring one or two long-stalked chestnut brown cup-like ascocarps. The ejected ascospores infect the young shoots, and again produce the gonidium-bearing form.

[1] Woronin, *Ueber die Sclerotienkrankheit der Vaccinienbeeren*, 1888.

K

Sclerotinia Vaccinii is parasitic on *Vaccinium Vitis Idæa ;*
S. Oxycocci, on *V. Oxycoccos ; S. baccarum,* on *V. Myrtillus ;*
S. megalospora, on *V. uliginosum.*

Of still greater importance, from an agricultural point of
view, is *Peziza ciborioides* (*Sclero-*

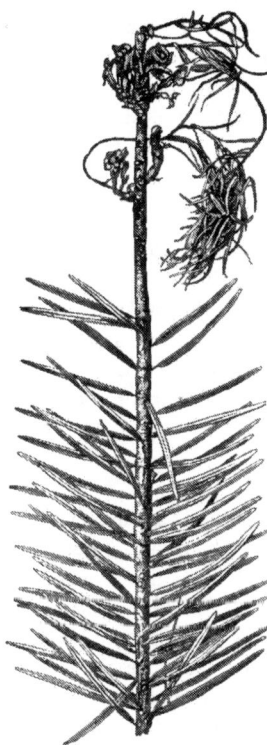

tinia Trifoliorum), the clover-can-
ker, or the sclerotium disease of the
clover.   This parasite is interesting
from the fact that on clover-plants
infested by the mycelium sclerotia
from 0·1—1 cm. in size are formed,
and these produce ascocarps in the
following year in July or August.

A similar course of development
is found in *Peziza Sclerotiorum*
(*Sclerotinia Libertiana*), which produces the sclerotium disease of the
beetroot and carrot.

The best known is *Peziza
Fuckeliana,* through its gonidium-
bearing form *Botrytis cinerea,** the
vine-mould, which finds its way on
to various plants in forcing-houses
and conservatories, producing a
loose grey mycelial covering and
killing the twigs.

For some years a species, *Botrytis
Douglasii,*[1] has proved injurious to
the Douglas fir, which is now generally cultivated in Germany.   In
seed- and plant-beds especially,
where infection by lateral contact
is such an easy matter, one often
notices that the young incompletely
developed shoots die and become brown.   The shoots of the

FIG. 71.—Branch of the Douglas
fir, the youngest shoot of which
has been killed by *B. Douglasii.*
The apex of the shoot of the
previous year has also been
killed.

[1] *Botrytis Douglasii* n. sp., C. Freiherr v. Tubeuf, *Beiträge zur Kenntniss
der Baumkrankheiten.* Berlin, Springer, 1888.

*[Several forms of *Botrytis* are common and destructive parasites in our
green-houses and gardens.— ED.]

previous year may also die back for a certain distance (Fig 71).

One afterwards observes, both on the leaves and on the twigs, small black sclerotia not larger than a pin-head   In a moist chamber these germinate and produce the gonidiophores of *Botrytis*. The gonidia germinate easily, and infect the tender shoot of the Douglas fir. Tubeuf's researches show that silver firs, spruces, and larches were also infected by this fungus, and it remains to be determined whether diseases in the forest may not also be induced by it.

GYMNOASCEÆ [1]

In the case of the parasites that belong to this sub-family of the *Discomycetes*, there is no proper fructification   The hymenium is a flat layer which occupies the surface of the plant, and consists of free tubes which develop among the epidermal cells, or between the epidermis and cuticle

All the species induce characteristic hypertrophy of the part of the plant that is attacked.

EXOASCUS PRUNI [2] *

This is a widely distributed parasite, which is familiar enough by causing the formation of the so-called " Mock," " Pocket," " Starved," &c, plums.   Its mycelium persists from year to year in the soft bast of the branches of *Prunus domestica, P spinosa*, and *P. Padus*, in which it grows intercellularly, gaining access to and contorting the young leafy shoots. The same is true in the case of the flowers, where malformation of the ovary is recognisable even in the beginning of May. Proceeding from the soft bast the mycelium spreads through the fleshy parenchyma of the fruit, where, on the one hand, it prevents the formation of the stone and seed, and, on the other, induces elongation and the well-known deformation of the

[1] Sadebeck, *Untersuchungen uber die Pilzgattung " Exoascus "* Hamburg, 1884 *

[2] De Bary, *Beitrage zur Morphologie der Pilze*, I p 33

*[Common in this country. Sadebeck has just published an exhaustive monograph on the whole group of parasitic *Exoasceæ* (Hamburg, 1893), revising the classification, and clearing up many doubtful points —ED.]

fruit   Numerous mycelial branches penetrate between the
epidermis and cuticle, where, by the formation of transverse
branches, they form short chambers   In this way an almost
uninterrupted layer of fungal mycelium is formed under the
cuticle. Each fungus-cell next grows outwards to produce a
short cylindrical ascus, and the cuticle after being detached
from the epidermis is ruptured, and the ascogenous layer
becomes completely exposed

Each ascus becomes separated from the basal part, or "stalk,"
by a transverse septum ; and, by free cell-formation, six to eight
roundish spores are formed in its interior, to be afterwards
ejected through the ruptured apex   The spores either germinate forthwith, or multiply by budding, and form a kind of yeast

The pocket-plums decay owing to the concurrence of numerous
saprophytic fungus-forms

Exoascus deformans is closely related to the foregoing species,
but lives partly in the leaves and shoots of *Persica vulgaris* and
Amygdalus communis, and partly in the leaves and shoots of
Prunus avium, *P. Cerasus*, *P Chamæcerasus*, *and P. domestica.*
On these trees, according to the investigations of Rathay,[1] it
causes the so-called witches' brooms   Whether the *Exoascus*
that occurs on cherries is really a new species (*Exoascus Wiesneri*), as Rathay assumes, or whether the distinctions that have
been noted are not perhaps due to differences in the host-plants,
must remain doubtful until infection experiments have been
carried out   Peculiar crumpling is induced in the leaves, similar
to that which is sometimes caused by Aphides   The branches
that have been taken possession of by the fungus anastomose
freely, and usually exhibit decided negative geotropism, while
the basal portion is often hypertrophied.   These constitute
the thunder-brooms and witches' brooms   Towards the base,
the branches of these witches' brooms are often double the
thickness of the branches from which they spring   Towards
the apex, on the other hand, they become normal   A possible
explanation of these phenomena is that, as the mycelium grows
more slowly than the young shoot, it finds immature tissue only

---

[1] Rathay, *Ueber die Hexenbesen der Kirschbaume und uber Exoascus
Wiesneri, Rath , im Sitzber d Wien Akad d Wissensch* , vol lxxxiii , March
1881

at its base, which, under the influence of the parasite, enlarges or increases abnormally. On the other hand, the mycelium arrives too late at the apex of the shoot to be able to exert a similar influence there.

Exoascus Insititiæ produces witches' brooms on *Prunus insititia*.

Exoascus bullatus induces bladder-like swellings, which afterwards become mealy underneath, on the leaves of pear-trees. In the case of the hawthorn it produces formations like witches' brooms, which bear leaves of a reddish colour.

Exoascus alnitorquus (*Ascomyces Tosquinetii*) often appears in great abundance both on the leaves of *Alnus glutinosa* and on the scales of the female catkins of that tree and of *Alnus incana*. Not only does it cause the leaves to become crumpled and corrugated, but also to increase in size in every way. On the cones of the alders it produces pocket-like outgrowths, which, when fresh, are of a brilliant red colour, and remind one somewhat of the pockets of plums (Fig. 72).

FIG. 72.—Malformation of the fruit of *Alnus incana* induced by *Exoascus.*

Exoascus flavus (*Sadebeckii*) causes the formation of yellow blotches, in this case also on the leaves of *A. glutinosa* and *A. incana*.

Exoascus epiphyllus, which infests the leaves of *Alnus incana* and *A. glutinosa*, is only with difficulty to be distinguished from the former species by its broader stalk-cells. It induces sinuous crumplings of the leaves, the outgrowths usually appearing on the upper side.

Exoascus borealis produces witches' brooms on *Alnus incana*. These are very numerous near Munich and at other places in Bavaria. It is probably identical with *E. epiphyllus*.

Exoascus turgidus (*Taphrina betulina*) very often produces witches' brooms on the birch.

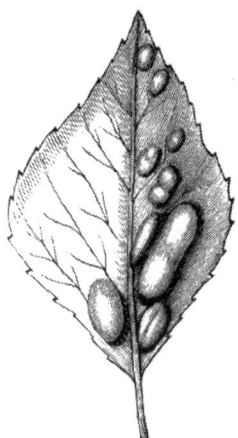

FIG. 73.—A leaf of *P. nigra* affected by *Exoascus Populi*.

FIG. 74.—Malformation of the fruit of *P. tremula*, due to *E. Populi*.

FIG. 75.—A witches' broom of the hornbeam induced by *Exoascus Carpini*. Half natural size.

Exoascus Betulæ (*Ascomyces Betulæ*) produces bladder-like outgrowths on the upper side of the leaves of the birch.

Exoascus carnea produces globular bladder-like swellings on the leaves of the birch.

*Exoascus aureus** (*Taphrina aurea, T. Populi*) produces golden yellow outgrowths on the leaves of *Populus nigra* (Fig. 73) and pocket-like outgrowths on the ovary of *P. tremula* and *P. alba* (Fig. 74).

Exoascus Carpini produces witches' brooms on the hornbeam (Fig. 75).

Exoascus cærulescens (*Ascomyces cærulescens*) produces bladder-like swellings on oak-leaves.

Exoascus Ulmi produces outgrowths on the upper side of elm-leaves.

IMPERFECTLY KNOWN ASCOMYCETES †

The number of those fungus-forms with all of whose stages of development we are not yet acquainted is an extremely large one. In particular a large number of fungi are known to us with whose gonidia—whether on sporiferous hyphæ or in closed organs (pycnidia, spermogonia)—we are familiar, but of whose ascophores we are ignorant, so that we are unable systematically to classify them.

A few of the more important species that occur parasitically on trees, especially on forest trees, may be referred to here.

CERCOSPORA ACERINA.[1]   THE MAPLE-SEEDLING FUNGUS

In rainy years a disease is sometimes conspicuously prevalent, both on maple seedlings in the nursery and on those which have sprung up naturally. It is to be recognized by the cotyledons and first leaves, and also by the shoot axis, becoming black and decomposed, or, if less severe, merely by black blotches

---

[1] R. Hartig, *Untersuchungen*, I. p. 58.

*[I have found this species deforming the ovaries of poplars in Surrey.—ED.]

† [No group of fungi offers more opportunities to the investigator anxious to add to our knowledge of pathogenic forms than the numerous "imperfect" ascomycetes so common on our trees, &c.—ED.]

appearing on the leaves   Even with the naked eye one may often recognize a grey covering on the diseased leaves

On more thorough investigation we perceive a luxuriant mycelial growth in the tissues of the diseased parts, from which innumerable short gonidiophores grow outwards   These produce tufts of long curved multicellular gonidia, which germinate in moist air even in a few hours, and push their germ-tube directly into the epidermis of the maple-leaves, which consequently become brown

The mycelium, which is intercellular, swells up to form large brown mycelial resting-cells and cell-plexuses, which contain oil-drops   These persist during the winter, and carry the disease over to the following year   The fungus is also able to live saprophytically on humus in the soil.

PESTALOZZIA HARTIGII [1]

The disease induced by this fungus, which has often been met with all over Germany, appears most frequently in seed- and plant-beds which are stocked with spruces and silver firs   I described it in the *Allgemeine Forst- und Jagd-Zeitung*, 1883, where I advanced the view that it was due to the formation of ice and the consequent crushing of the cambium   As I expressly stated, the truth of the hypothesis which I there advanced had still to be determined   Von Tubeuf has now proved that here, as in so many cases, we have to do with a parasitic disease   In summer one notices in nurseries of the spruce and silver fir that a number of plants first become pale and then die   If the plants are pulled up, it is seen that the cortex on the parts immediately over the ground is withered, but that, farther up, the stem is swollen as a natural consequence of continued growth (Fig 76)

When the wood dries up or dies at the point where death of the cortex first took place, the plant must perish   On the rind, at the place where contraction is visible, one finds the mycelium of the fungus, and numerous gonidial cushions which develop partly in

[1] C v. Tubeuf, *Beitrage zur Kenntniss der Baumkrankheiten*, pp 40—51, Plate V   Berlin, Springer. 1888

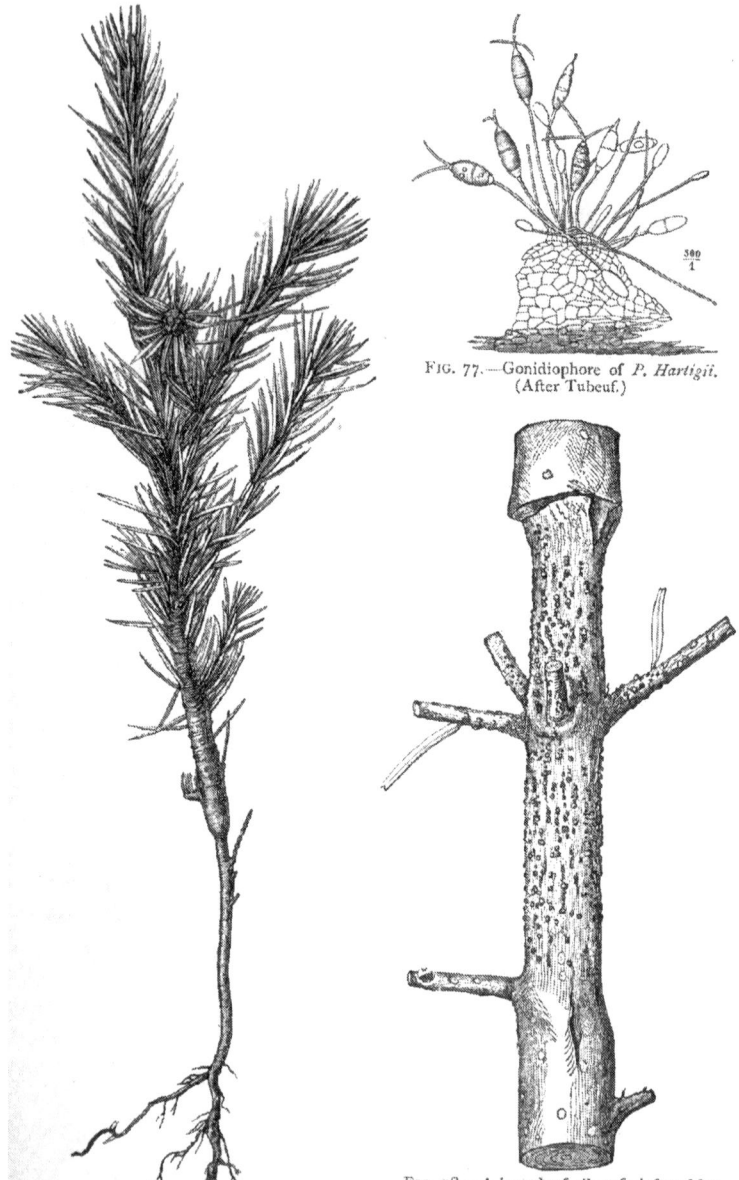

FIG. 77.—Gonidiophore of *P. Hartigii.*
(After Tubeuf.)

IG. 76.—A young spruce which has been infected
close to the ground by *P. Hartigii.*

FIG. 78.—A branch of silver fir infected by
P. abietina. Numerous black tubercles
are visible on the dead cortex.

spheroidal pycnidia, and partly on flat stromata which are disposed in the tissue of the cortex

The characteristic gonidia (Fig 77), which are situated on short or long stalks, are at first hyaline, thin, oval, and uni-cellular, but afterwards become four-celled owing to repeated transverse division. The two middle cells are large and dark, the small stalk-cell and the terminal cell remain colourless The latter pushes out a branched filament which, however, must not be confounded with a germ-tube. It is only one or other of the three lower cells that germinates, most frequently the lower of the two brown middle cells

On account of the general distribution of this disease, and the consequent loss incurred, it would appear advisable carefully to root out and burn all diseased and dead plants that may be found in nurseries.

Similar pathological symptoms have also been observed on young beeches, ashes, and maples I should be glad to receive such plants, in order to prove whether parasites are the cause of disease, and, if so, to determine the species.

PHOMA ABIETINA N SP. THE FUNGUS OF THE CORTEX OF THE SILVER FIR

A disease which has not hitherto been described, but which is extremely common on young and old trees in the Bavarian Forest, is due to a parasite which may temporarily be called *Phoma abietina* The disease may be recognized by both small and large branches of the silver fir becoming pale and withered , in fact, I have occasionally observed diseased spots two inches in diameter on the cortex of silver firs as thick as one's arm. As a rule the disease appears only on branches or on the main axis of the younger classes of silver firs, and attracts atten-tion by the cortex dying right round the branch, as is shown in Fig. 78

Numerous small black pycnidia break through the epidermis and appear on the dead cortex, either as small roundish bodies or as many-chambered, irregularly shaped, black sclerotium-like . tubercles (Fig 79, *a*) Numerous unicellular, colourless, abruptly·

spindle-shaped gonidia (Fig. 79, *b*), which at once germinate in water, develop on the hymenial layer that lines the walls of the cavities of these organs.

Although I have watched the disease every year since 1885, and have sought for the ascophores, I have hitherto been unable to find them. I may, however, remark that in almost all my cultures on silver fir branches a luxuriant growth of the ascocarps of *Peziza calycina* has appeared upon the cortex on both sides of the diseased part. This fact, however, is not sufficient proof of a connection between these two fungus-forms. Attempts to produce the one form from the other by cultural experiments have so far proved abortive.

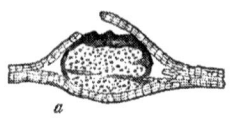

FIG. 79.—*a*, a pycnidium of *P. abietina* which has ruptured the periderm; magnified twenty times. *b*, gonidia magnified 420 times.

The pycnidia ejaculate the gonidia probably for the most part during wet weather in summer and autumn.

It does not appear necessary that mechanical injury of the cortex should precede the entrance of the parasite—at all events, I have never been able to observe such. On old trees a large proportion of the twigs and branches are often brown, a state of things that struck me at once on my first visit to the Bavarian Forest. In the Black Forest also, and at several places in the Bavarian Alps, the disease is to be met with. In the case of the thicker branches nutrition through the wood may still be continued for several years after the cortex has died. For this reason growth in thickness above the dead part is distinctly visible, and causes the cortex to rupture at the boundary of the living and dead parts. When the wood covered by the dead cortex dies and dries up, the passage of water ceases, and the branch dies above the seat of the disease.

Should the fungus attack one side of the branch only, the dead cortex is exfoliated, and the formation of callus commences along the healthy margin.

GLŒOSPORIUM NERVISEQUIUM [1] THE PLANE-TREE FUNGUS

Plane-trees (*Platanus*) suffer very frequently from a disease which is characterised by the leaves acquiring brown blotches and dying. From the middle of May onwards one observes that death sets, in at certain places, and continues along the nerves of the leaf. Small black spots may then be observed appearing on the dead parts, which are the gonidial cushions of *Glœosporium nervisequium.*

Unfortunately we still know very little regarding the development of this fungus, for even trials at infection have not yet succeeded

THE FUNGUS OF THE BLACK (AUSTRIAN) PINE [2]

For a number of years a disease of the black (Austrian) pine has been observed in the south of Norway and throughout the whole of Germany. This disease has constantly been on the increase, but has not yet been thoroughly investigated It is now a considerable number of years since Dr. C. v Fischbach sent me diseased branches, and an opportunity for observing the disease was afforded in the forest division of Freising, near Munich, but the investigation yielded no satisfactory results. This disease may find mention here, especially since Dr Brunchorst's description is now available.

The most vigorously growing Austrian pines show a paleness in the leaves of the previous year's shoots, whose buds, instead of shooting out, die off The disease spreads from the tissues of the shoots, having its inception in the cortical tissues. Here infection is very often brought about, as it appears to me, through the agency of a small plant-mite, which bores through the epidermis into the cortical tissues of the shoot to a depth of 1—2 mm. Infection may, however, also take place easily enough at the base of the leaves, where the epidermis is thin

---

[1] Dr Fr. v Tavel, *Bot Zeit*, 1886, No. 49

[2] Dr. C. v. Fischbach, *Eine neue Krankheit der Schwarzkiefer Centralblatt für das gesammt Forstwesen*, 1887, p. 435 Dr Brunchorst, *Ueber eine neue verheerende Krankheit der Schwarzföhre.* Bergen, 1888

Black pycnidia, with gonidia similar to those of *Fusidium*, develop at the base of the dying leaves, and on the wounds that result from the separation of the leaf-fascicles.

Dr. Brunchorst has not yet been able to observe perithecia, nor has he hitherto succeeded with infection-experiments. Not only has the death of single pines been noticed, but in many cases, especially in Norway, the destruction of large woods has been recorded.

It is strongly to be insisted upon that whenever this disease appears in young woods of the Austrian pine, all diseased shoots should be cut off and burned.

SEPTOGLŒUM HARTIGIANUM SACC [1]

In the neighbourhood of Munich the branches of the English maple (*Acer campestre*) suffer from a disease which kills them off before the young shoots develop in spring. In the middle and lower parts of the crown especially, it frequently happens that more than half of the previous year's shoots perish. On these it will be found that the periderm has been ruptured by oblong cushion-like fungus-bodies.

The disease almost always confines itself to the youngest shoots, the two-year-old shoots being infected only in very exceptional cases. Infection takes place in May and the beginning of June, when the young shoots are still tender and unprovided with periderm. When the spores of the parasite (Fig. 80, *6*) come into contact with a young shoot, they germinate within a few hours. The spore represented in the figure had lain in water for five hours only, at the end of which time it showed large germ-tubes at both ends. The mycelium bores into the cortex, and takes possession of the shoot for a distance of 2—4 inches, but does not kill it in the same year. Even when the leaves are shed in autumn there are no external symptoms of disease. In spring, the buds of the diseased shoots swell up, as a rule, but soon wither. At that time the mycelium is to be found growing vigorously, not only in the diseased cortex, but also in the medullary rays and the vessels of the wood. It grows both intercellular and intracellular, and pushes numerous

[1] R. Hartig, *Forstl. Naturwiss., Zeitschrift*, August 1892.

short stout lateral branches, which resemble haustoria, into the interior of the parenchymatous cells.

Colourless stromata of a fleshy, pseudo-parenchymatous structure (Fig. 80, *3*) form in the cortex beneath the periderm. In cross section these measure 0·3—0·6 mm., while longitudinally their length varies between 1 and 4 mm. In the month of May the periderm ruptures longitudinally, and reveals the sporogenous

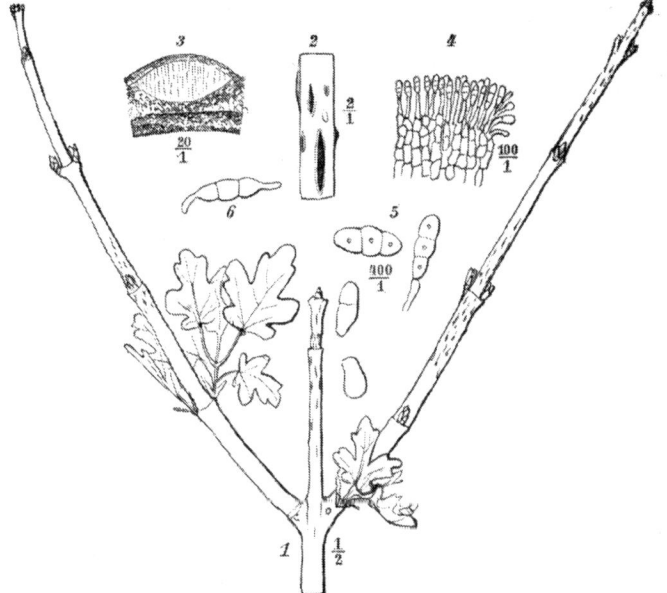

Fig. 80.—Septoglœum Hartigianum.

.ayer as a greyish green cushion, surrounded by the edges of the elevated periderm (Fig. 80, *2*). The surface of the colourless fleshy stroma (Fig. 80, *4*) is formed of cylindrical sterigmata, which frequently enlarge somewhat towards the base. These sterigmata measure 30—35 micromillimeters in length and 6—7·5 micromillimeters in breadth. The gonidia, which are formed at the apex of the sterigmata, measure, when ripe, from 24—36 micromillimeters in length and 10—12 micromillimeters in breadth. In shape they are irregularly oblong-oval, and truncated at both ends (Fig 80, *5*).

In the great majority of cases the gonidia appear to be doubly septate, although occasionally one meets with singly septate examples, and even unicellular gonidia are not unknown. They are of a pale brown colour, and germinate in a few hours, pushing out a thick 'germ-tube from both ends (Fig. 80, 6)

The parasite is distributed in May and the beginning of June by means of the gonidia, which are washed by the rain from the higher diseased shoots on to the young shoots of the lower part of the crown. In other cases the wind may carry them on to distant maples

This destructive parasite of our gardens and parks can only be combated by removing the diseased shoots from the crown in the beginning of May

SEPTORIA PARASITICA, THE SPRUCE-SHOOT DISEASE [1]

Both in young spruce woods and in the seed- and plant-beds of the nursery a disease, which on a cursory examination may easily be mistaken for damage by frost, very frequently attacks the young shoots.

In the month of May, when the young shoots are still succulent and delicate, the disease generally manifests itself (see Fig 81, *a*) by the leaves at the base, or it may be the middle, of the shoot becoming brown and soon dropping off. At first the apex of the shoot remains quite green, but on lateral branches it droops downwards   The disease advances rapidly towards the apex of the shoot, and the base of the young leaves appears dark green (Fig 81, *b*). When held up to the light, it will be seen that the internal tissues of the leaf are dead and shrivelled, and possess a reticulated appearance   Finally the leaves all drop off, or a few dead ones may adhere to the apex of the shoot, as indicated in Fig 82, *a*. The axis of the shoot shrinks more or less according as death had overtaken it in an early or late stage of development   Very frequently the shoot becomes diseased and begins to shrink at the point where its base is enveloped by the scales of the previous year's terminal bud, and this often occurs in the case of shoots that are tolerably well developed. The base of the shoot shrinks, and its internal tissues are so dis-

[1] R. Hartig, *Zeitschrift fur Forst- und Jagdwesen,* November 1890, p 668.

organized by the fungus which causes the disease—as we shall see presently—that the shoot bends sharply over at that point under its own weight, as though it had been fractured at the base. Very frequently death spreads back from the base of the youngest shoot to the apex of the shoot of the previous year (Fig. 81, *c*), in which case the young lateral shoots that are situated there also succumb (Fig. 82, *a*).

As already indicated, this may, in May or early in June, be mistaken for damage due to frost, although the latter is generally confined to certain localities, appears suddenly on a great number of shoots, and is characterised by all the affected leaves dying simultaneously. The disease at present under discussion has no relation whatever to frost. Shoots that have succumbed to this disease also bear a certain resemblance in many cases to those damaged by *Chermes abietis ;* the galls which the latter induces at the base of the shoots being often so small as not to be visible on the upper side, and in both cases there is a deflexion of the shoot downwards.

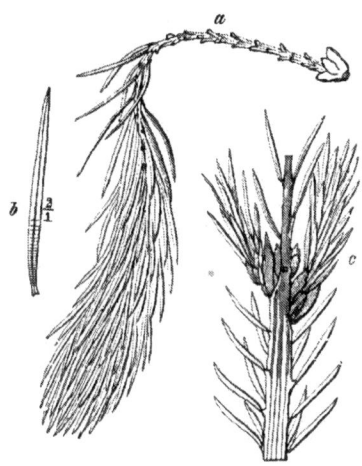

FIG. 81.—*a*, a young diseased spruce branch, the apex of which is still green and fresh. *b*, a leaf attacked by disease towards the base, twice natural size. *c*, apex of a two-year-old shoot, into which the disease has spread backwards from the younger shoot. The brown discoloration of the cortex and pith is indicated by shading.

In the course of the summer the dead shoots display spore-receptacles (pycnidia) in greater or less abundance in the form of very minute black tubercles. These are so small as just to be visible to the naked eye, and are very often to be found only amongst the bud-scales at the base of the dead shoot. In other cases they are also to be met with higher up ; in fact, they are often specially abundant on the shrunken shoot-apex (Fig. 82, *a*). They either rupture the epidermis of the shoot or occur on the leaf-scar on the long pulvinus, where they present a bud-like appearance (Fig. 82, *b*). It also frequently happens that black pycnidia develop on the few dead leaves that have adhered to the shoot (Fig. 82, *a*). These pycnidia, which are uni- or multicellular, produce numerous small gonidia (stylospores) at the apex of subulate sterigmata which spring from the inner wall. These stylospores, which are bicellular, colourless, spindle-shaped, and some 13—15 micromillimeters in size (Fig. 82, *c*), appear as white tendrils on the pycnidia in the month of May, at which time they produce the disease, if borne by the wind or rain to the still tender and non-cuticularized shoots of the spruce.

On May 6th, when growth was active, I infected young spruces by taking a drop of water, in which stylospores were suspended, and placing it by means of forceps amongst the leaves in the middle of a shoot and partly amongst the bud-scales at its base. Infection succeeded in every case, and eight days later death appeared amongst leaves at the infected points, and soon spread in all directions. On the 13th of May,

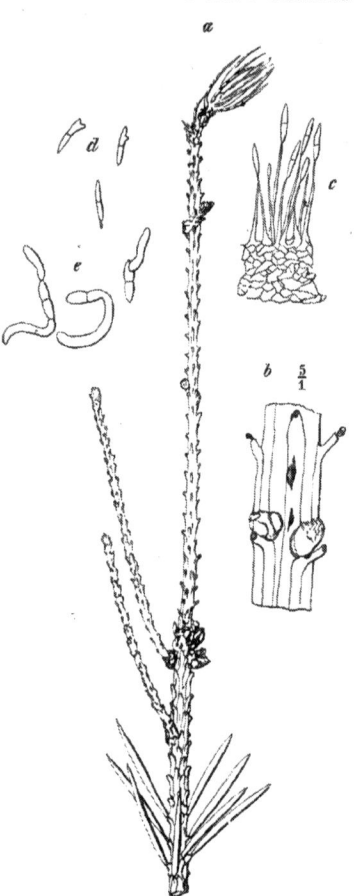

FIG. 82.—*a*, a spruce-leader of which the youngest shoot, the apex of the older shoot, and the two lateral branches have been killed. *b*, pycnidia projecting from the cortex and leaf-scars, magnified five times. *c*, formation of spores in the interior of a pycnidium, magnified by 400. *d*, spores germinating in water. *e*, spores germinating in nutritive gelatine.

L

a drop of water containing spores was placed amongst the scales at the base of a shoot some three inches long, on a twenty-year-old spruce. About twelve days later the shoot was so much diseased as to droop in the manner shown in Fig. 81, *a*.

Spores sown in water on May 6th showed the first symptoms of germination in eighteen hours (Fig. 82, *d*). When sown in nutritive gelatine the spores and germ-tubes were rather more vigorous (Fig. 82, *e*), an extremely luxuriant mycelium with spherical and clavate segments being developed both on a microscope-slide and in a test-tube   Twelve days after sowing, pycnidia with ripe stylospores developed on this mycelium

The culture, which was continued till August 12th, produced a dense mycelial growth, with pycnidia but no perithecia, so that at that time I abandoned the hope of obtaining the latter. An investigation of the diseased shoots showed that the stout vigorous mycelium developed between the cells in the green leaves, and immediately induced death in adjacent cells.   In the shoot axis it penetrated all the tissues, growing as both intra- and intercellular filaments in the pith and cortex, while in the wood it was specially abundant in the annular and spiral vessels.   The development of the parasite is confined to the short period between the beginning of May and the early part of June   Whether the pycnidia will form early or late in summer appears to depend on the humidity of the air, or, in other words, on the occurrence of dry or wet weather.   As already stated, they may ripen in fourteen days, provided the conditions are favourable, as in the case of artificial cultures

Until we obtain the perithecia we must rest satisfied with a provisional name for this new parasite   The character of the pycnidia and spores leads us to place this fungus in the genus *Septoria*, but as there is already a *Septoria Pini* I have named this fungus *Septoria parasitica*   Finally, it may be mentioned that in the spring of 1890 I found this parasite on *Picea Menziesii*, and this makes it probable that it also occurs on other species of spruce.

A NEW PARASITE OF SEEDLINGS[1]

Seed-beds of the pine and spruce are frequently subject to disease in the months of May and June, so that, even where seed has germinated satisfactorily, the plants are more or less decimated, and the otherwise well-stocked drills show blanks as large as one's hand. During wet weather the young plants die and rapidly decay At first only single plants are attacked, but soon the disease spreads more or less rapidly along the whole drill If the weather is dry the diseased plants wither, their yellow colour attracting attention even from a distance During summer, say from the middle of June, the disease ceases, and the dead plants disappear, to leave only the blanks, which are usually ascribed to the ravages of cockchafer grubs, crickets, surface caterpillars, &c I have shown that in most cases these pathological phenomena are due to *Phytopthora omnivora*, which spreads not only by gonidia but also by its mycelium, which traverses underground from root to root, and thus explains the rapid spread of the disease

In 1889 I received a number of diseased pine seedlings from Herr Mantel, forester in Grossostheim, with the information that for some years a disease agreeing with the symptoms just described had appeared immediately after the germination of the seed in his pine seed-beds on sandy land. Some plants which he sent to the forest school of Aschaffenburg were examined, when it was found that, instead of *P omnivora* being the cause of the damage, it was some other unknown disease

An investigation of this new disease showed that it was induced by a different parasite. The mycelium of the parasitic fungus which caused the damage attacked not only the seedlings of the pine but also those of the spruce, alder, birch, &c. In the seed-bed the plants were attacked either at the roots (Fig 83, *a*) or at the hypocotyl (*b*), close beneath the surface of the ground In very dense seed-beds and during wet weather the mycelium also spreads above ground, and infects the cotyledons and the highest part of the stem (Fig 83, *c*) At the point where it comes into contact with the epidermis of

[1] *Forstlich Naturwissensch. Zeitsch.*, November 1892.

the seedling the filamentous septate mycelium, which becomes somewhat brown with age, produces tortuous lateral hyphæ, which ramify abundantly, apply themselves closely to the epidermis (Fig. 84, *a*), and exercise a solvent action on the delicate non-cuticularized epidermis. If one lifts up the hyphæ it will be seen that the epidermis has been dissolved at the points of contact. Without doubt mycelial filaments also bore directly from these points right into the plant.

The stomata form a means both of ingress and egress for the hyphæ. Such a stoma is depicted in Fig. 85, which shows that the sides of the depression leading to the stoma, and the external walls of the epidermal cells, are dissolved at the points where the hyphæ are or have been in close

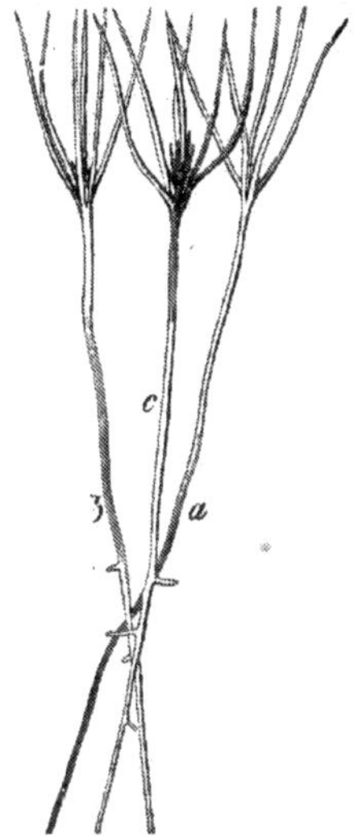

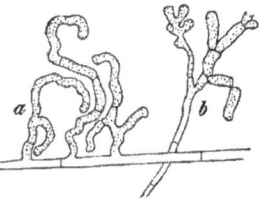

FIG. 83.—Diseased pine seedlings. *a*, a specimen with dead roots ; *b*, ditto with a dead stem ; *c*, ditto with dead leaves and buds.

FIG. 84.—A filamentous mycelium whose lateral hyphæ, *a*, come into close contact with the epidermis ; *b*, a mycelium which has developed in a nutrient solution.

contact. These places appear granulated because the ash constituents of the cell-wall are either left wholly intact or are but partially dissolved. I have proved that under the action of the ferments exuded by wood-destroying parasites the cell-walls also display granulation during the last stages of decomposition, and for the same reasons as those just given. When a diseased plant is investigated on the first symptoms of attack, a vigorous growth of mycelium will be found in all the tissues. Although the green cells do not part with their chlorophyll till some time after death, they easily lose connection with each other, and the stem or root becomes limp At this stage of the disease the interior of the plant is nearly full of a luxuriant mycelial growth. In a short time large numbers of bacteria appear in the tissues and induce complete decomposition, the mycelium of the parasite sharing the common fate. In plants that still appear sound towards the top, the stem or roots frequently retain only the epidermis and the xylem of the vascular bundles I have infected vigorous pine and spruce seedlings, which were taken from dense seed-drills and planted in flower-pots, by laying one or more diseased plants amongst them When a bellglass was placed over the flower-pot all the plants were diseased or dead in four days

The mycelium enveloped the whole plant, and the disease began, for the most part in the upper portion (Fig. 83, *c*) On the other hand, if the flower-pot was left in a room uncovered, infection was induced only by the mycelium growing in or on the surface of the soil and attacking the roots or the lower portion of the stem (Fig. 83, *a*, *b*). All the plants succumbed in eight days, with the single exception of one seedling which remained healthy No results followed trials at infection which I conducted in the end of June on vigorous seedlings As has already been proved in the case of other parasites, it is only when the epidermis is unprovided with a cuticle that it can be dissolved by the mycelium It is known that *P omnivora* also is only destructive in May and June

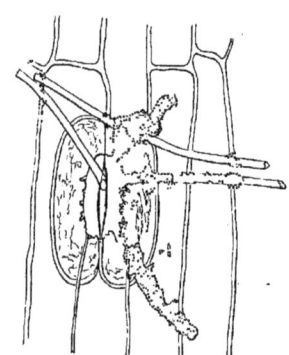

FIG 85 —Epidermis of a pine seedling showing a stoma Solution has taken place wherever the filaments have been in contact

Innumerable gonidia develop in dense bunches on the luxuriantly branching mycelium, and especially in the stomata of the diseased plants. I have represented such a mycelial branch with gonidia in Fig. 86. When ripe they are more or less falcate, pointed at both ends, and generally consist of six cells. In germinating they usually produce two germ-tubes at or near the apices, as is shown in the lower part of Fig 86

The shape of the gonidia makes it probable that the parasite is a species of *Nectria*. A few days after being sown in a gelatine extract of fruit they produce a luxuriantly branching mycelium, whose hyphæ are much septated and anastomose irregularly (Fig. 84, *b*)   This mycelium produces either similar gonidia, or such as are somewhat smaller, less bent and possessed of fewer cells

On being transferred to black bread the mycelium grew so vigorously that the large glass jar in which the culture was conducted was completely filled with a white growth   In the flower-pots also, in which the infected conifer seedlings were growing, the mycelium developed so luxuriantly in the soil as to find its way out at the hole in the bottom and to form a dense mass between the pot and the table   This proves conclusively that the fungus, like most species of *Nectria*, can also exist as a saprophyte, and as such may live in the soil

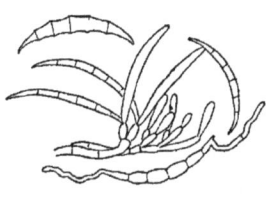

Fig 86 —Immature, ripe, and germinating gonidia

Unfortunately I have not been successful in reproducing the perithecium form of the fungus   On a slide numerous spheroid bodies which were the first stages of perithecia or pycnidia formed in the mycelium, but they always failed to mature   On this account I am unfortunately still unable to refer the fungus to a species

As regards measures that may be instituted with the view of preventing the spread of the disease, attention should in the first place be directed to the diminution of surplus moisture   If such are present, we should also remove all objects such as latticed frames, branches, &c , that have been laid down to shelter the plants   As it is certain that the fungus remains in the ground from one year to another, one must take care, in laying down new seed-beds, to avoid situations where the disease was prevalent in the previous year   If this cannot be done, one should interstratify the upper nine inches of soil with brushwood, dry turf, or some such material, and roast it, or at least raise its temperature to such a pitch that any spores present in it may be killed   Herr Mantel related to me how he had heated the soil of certain beds by burning dry wood in parallel trenches a foot deep and about a foot apart. The fire was kept up for two days, so that the soil was practically roasted to the depth of more than a foot Seed was afterwards sown on these beds as on the others On the beds so treated the plants remained sound for two years, but in the third year the old symptoms reappeared. It is most likely that the fungus again invaded the ground by means of gonidia carried from adjoining beds It would appear desirable, should circumstances make it advisable, that the above plan should be experimentally tested. One would thus discover whether infested seed-beds may continue to be utilized without incurring much expenditure, or whether it is better to change the ground

VALSA (MONOSTICHA) OXYSTOMA[1]

In Alpine-districts a disease is very prevalent on *Alnus viridis*, which, superficially examined, reminds one strongly of the ravages of the larvæ of *Cryptorhynchus lapathi* Numerous stems and branches contract the disease and die. It is chiefly in August that the leafy branches become infected The withering of the cortex attracts attention to the presence of the fungus, and directly afterwards small black tubercles appear on the dead tissues The stage of the development of these pustules depends upon the length of time that has elapsed since the branch died Thus, although the presence of the fungus may be detected on branches that are still living, it is met with in its highest development only on such as are perfectly dead. The progress of the disease down the tree is indicated by a sharp line between the diseased wood, which is brown, and that which is still sound As the disease advances, other lateral branches become affected An exceedingly vigorous and very tough mycelium is easily discoverable in the moribund wood, and especially in the vessels. The lenticular tubercles consist of black pseudo-parenchyma situated beneath the periderm. Owing to their rupturing the periderm at the highest point

---

[1] v Tubeuf, *Forstlich-naturwis Zeitschrift*, October 1892

of their concave surface, a small roundish aperture is formed.
Numerous perithecia, with very small tubes and hyaline spores,
form in the dead cortex underneath the lower surface of the

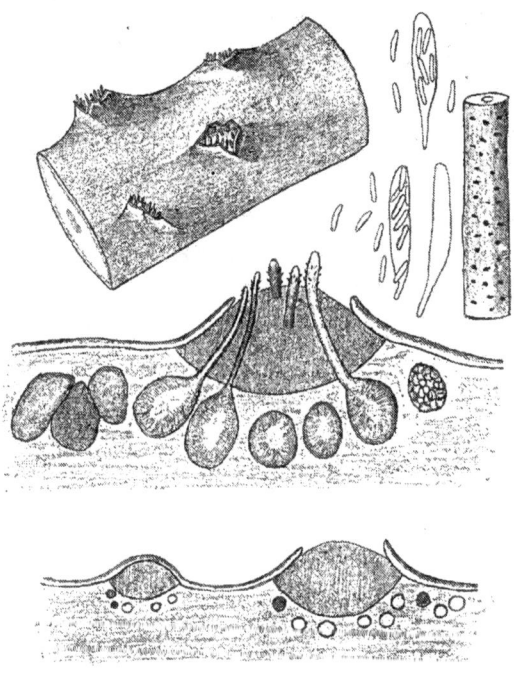

FIG. 87.—The upper left-hand figure represents a portion of a branch of *Alnus viridis*.
The periderm has been ruptured at four places by the stroma of *Valsa oxystoma*,
on which the necks of the perithecia are visible. To the right are seen the asci
and spores. The upper right-hand figure represents a piece of a smaller branch
whose periderm has also been ruptured by the stromata, but on which the perithecia have not yet developed. The central figure shows the microscopic section
of one of the stromata of the upper left-hand figure, and the lowest figure a similar
section taken from the branch shown in the upper right-hand corner.

lenticular tubercles. The perithecia push a long stout flask-
shaped neck through the lenticular stroma. On account of the
black necks finally protruding to some extent from the stroma,
each tubercle shows a considerable number of them.

BASIDIOMYCETES

The *Basidiomycetes* constitute the third group of fungi. In their case all spores originate by abscission.

UREDINEÆ.* RUST-FUNGI

The rust-fungi are true parasites, and develop their mycelium, which is usually intercellular, in the tissues of the leaves and cortex (and also, though less frequently, in the wood, *e.g. Coleosporium Senecionis*) of phanerogams, and abstract their nutriment by means of haustoria from the interior of the cells. Their course of development is characterised by most species producing sporocarps, which are usually cup-like in shape. The bottom of these so-called æcidia is lined by a hymenium consisting of numerous, usually club-shaped, basidia, each of which at its apex abjoints a series of spores which are usually reddish yellow in colour. These are united to each other by so-called intermediate cells, which are dissolved before the formation of the spores is completed. The basidia that are situated at the periphery of the hymenium, instead of forming spores, grow together to form an envelope called the peridium, which opens at the apex or by a longitudinal fissure. The peridium may, however, be entirely absent.

Before the formation of æcidia, spermogonia with spermatia usually originate, the latter probably playing the part of male sexual cells.† It is probable that the æcidium is the result of a preceding sexual act, and is therefore a true sporocarp, like the perithecium and apothecium of *Ascomycetes*. However, there are also rust-fungi in which the æcidium is entirely absent (*Chrysomyxa Abietis*).

*[The British species have been worked up into a monograph by Plowright (*Brit. Uredineæ and Ustilagineæ*, Kegan Paul, 1889), who has also devoted attention to the experimental investigation of some of the heterœcious forms.—ED.]

†[Researches into the morphology and physiology of these and other organs of the Uredineæ by no means support this conclusion. Brefeld's statements, as well as those of De Bary, much as they differ in detail, point to the opposite view—that there is no probability of sexuality in this group. The curious and interesting homologies are well put forth by Von Tavel.—ED.]

Besides the æcidium, a kind of gonidium is almost always formed, which, being designed to carry the fungus over from one year to another, has great capacity for retaining its power of germinating This is known as a resting-spore or teleutospore, and, instead of directly forming a mycelial filament, it first produces a promycelium, on which a number of small cells, called sporidia, develop, and it is these which produce the disease by infecting new host-plants The teleutospores are unable to produce infection, because they are usually in such intimate contact with the substance of the host-plant that their distribution by the air is almost entirely precluded The mycelium that is developed from the sporidia again produces spermogonia, and —after fertilization—sporocarps (æcidia). Thus an alternation of generations between the two forms of æcidia and teleutospores is presented, which, however, in the case of many rust-fungi, is further complicated by the fact that a form bearing teleutospores is not directly produced by the germinating æcidiospores, but that numerous generations of gonidia of another kind—namely, uredospores—often originate These at once germinate, without forming a promycelium, and reproduce the form bearing uredospores During summer they serve for the rapid distribution of the fungus, till the teleutospores are produced by the mycelium, as usually happens in autumn The cycle of development of many rust-fungi is interesting, from the fact that not only the uredo form but also the æcidium form may possess a facultative character , that is to say, these forms may develop only under certain favourable circumstances, and in the absence of such conditions they may be entirely omitted without the existence of the parasite being thereby imperilled

The generation which forms the æcidia, and that which produces the teleutospores, are either to be found on the same plant (autœcious parasites), or, with the alternation of generation, there also occurs a change of the species of host-plant (heterœcious parasites). In the case of the heterœcious rust-fungi the discovery of the related forms which belong to one and the same species of fungus naturally presents great difficulties This is sufficient to explain why we are not at present acquainted with the æcidia of many teleuto forms, and, on the other hand, do not yet know to which teleuto forms many æcidium forms belong

On this account it will be necessary, as in the case of the *Ascomycetes*, to append a list of imperfectly known rust-fungi, to which, depending on the development form, the provisional names of *Æcidium*, *Cæoma*, and *Uredo* are given.

The rust-fungi are divided into several families, of which we are here interested only in the *Pucciniæ* and *Melampsoreæ*. The former are characterised by the teleutospores being situated singly, or several together on a stalk ; whereas, in the case of the latter, the teleutospores are united to each other in large numbers to form a firm palisade-like layer.

PUCCINIÆ

The genus *Puccinia*, which is rich in species, is characterised by the teleutospores containing two cells and remaining attached to the basidia, which at the same time serve as the stalk. They appear as small brown or black brown heaps of a round or oblong shape.

Puccinia graminis * is the commonest kind of rust amongst cereals, occurring everywhere, not only on our various kinds of grain but also on many grasses. The teleutospores, which are disposed in narrow ridges, hibernate on the common grasses, though, if they have been produced on the lower parts of the stems of cereals, they may also be left on the stubble fields. In spring, when the sporidia that originate on the promycelia gain a footing on the young leaves of the barberry, *Berberis vulgaris*, they produce the barberry fungus, *Æcidium Berberidis*. The æcidium form—whose spores germinate on cereals and other species of grasses, and produce the wheat-rust, *Uredo linearis*— is distinguished from the black ridges of teleutospores of *Puccinia graminis*, which occur later, by the reddish brown colour.

This destructive cereal rust may be most effectively combated by rooting out the barberry. This measure must not, however, be confined within narrow limits, because the spores of the barberry-fungus can be widely distributed by wind.

*[This, the common rust of wheat and other grasses, is of classical interest, since it was this species in which De Bary first established the remarkable phenomenon of heterœcism.—ED.]

Puccinia striæformis (*straminis*) produces a cereal rust on rye, wheat, and barley It closely resembles the foregoing disease, from which it differs, however, by the ridges being smaller and less elongated, and by the very short-stalked club-shaped teleutospores remaining hidden by the epidermis The æcidium form is *Æcidium asperifolii*, which develops on the leaves of *Anchusa officinalis, Borago, Echium*, &c.

Puccinia coronata produces a rust on cereals, especially oats Its teleutospores are provided at the shoulder with a girdle of punctiform thickenings of the spore membrane. The æcidium form *Æcidium Rhamni* is well known by the peculiar rich golden yellow swellings which it produces on the leaves, flowers, and stalks of *Rhamnus cathartica* and *R frangula* in which it develops

Of the large number of species of *Puccinia*, the only other one that need here be noticed is *Puccinia Asparagi*, which completes its course of development on the asparagus alone The asparagus rust, which may seriously devastate asparagus-beds, is best combated by burning the halms in autumn, and by the timely removal of the shoots that are first diseased

PHRAGMIDIUM ·

The species of this genus are distinguished from the species of *Puccinia* by the teleutospores being stalked and consisting of a number of cells The groups of teleutospores which develop on the under side of the leaves are preceded by uredospores, whose orange red powder often covers the under side of the leaves in large quantity The course of development of the various species has not yet been sufficiently studied *

· *Phragmidium incrassatum*, the rust of the bramble, induces the formation of red blotches on the leaves of *Rubus fruticosus* and *R cæsius*, and the organs consequently die prematurely

Phragmidium Rubi Idæi produces similar pathological symptoms on the leaves of *Rubus Idæus*

Phragmidium subcorticum produces the rust of the rose.   ·

*[All occur in this country —ED]

GYMNOSPORANGIUM [1]

The species of this genus with which we are acquainted are perennial in the cortical tissues of various species of *Juniperus*. They induce local increase in growth, which takes the form of peculiar swellings on the branches and parts of the stem that are attacked.* Each autumn the teleutospores are developed under the outer cortical layers, and in spring and early summer they break through the cortex in large numbers and appear as fructifications which are conical or sausage-shaped, yellow or brown, and mucilaginous or cartilaginous in texture. These fructifications consist of the very long filamentous basidia whose outer wall has been converted into mucilage, and of the two-celled resting-spores which they bear at their apex. The formation of the promycelium and sporidia takes place in the mucilaginous mass, which in the end is completely dissolved by rain-water. The sporidia gain a footing on the leaves of various pomaceous trees, where they produce the æcidium form of the genus *Ræstelia*.

It appears to me desirable that the forms which are already known and described should be subjected to further examination, because the few test trials that I have undertaken have at once led to results which are at variance with what has been accepted. I append here a short description of the three recognised species, without, however, being able to vouch for its accuracy on the strength of my own investigations.†

GYMNOSPORANGIUM CONICUM (JUNIPERUM)

Teleutospore layers on *Juniperus communis*. They are hemispherical or conical, golden yellow, later swelling up to very large, variously shaped (spherical, pear-shaped, ovate, &c.) bodies. Spores spindle-shaped, some brown with a thick endosporium, 75 microm. long and 27 microm. broad ; others yellow, with a

---

[1] Oersted, *Bot. Zeit.*, 1865, p. 291 and elsewhere.

* [These are often called Cedar-apples in America. See Farlow, *Mem. Boston Soc. of Nat. Hist.*, 1880.—ED.]

† [A good deal of work has been done on the various and very confusing species of late years, most of which occur in this country. See Plowright, *l.c*, and Von Tubeuf (*Cent. f. Bakt.*, 1891, and *Zeitschr. f. Pflanzenkrankh.*, B. II. p. 110). Also Farlow, *l.c.*, &c.—ED.]

thinner endosporium, about 66 microm. long and 17 microm broad The æcidium form has been observed as *Ræstelia cornuta* on *Sorbus Aucuparia*, *S. torminalis*, *Aronia*, and other pomaceous plants. The æcidia are situated on orange yellow or red swollen blotches, which are united in various numbers into round or oblong groups. The peridium, which has the shape of a very long-necked bottle, is yellowish, or yellowish brown, twisted like a horn, up to 8 mm long, open at the shoulder, serrulated, and either not or only ultimately slightly and irregularly lacerated

GYMNOSPORANGIUM CLAVARIÆFORME

Teleutospore-layers on *Juniperus communis*. They are cylindrical, tongue-shaped or band-like, often bifurcated, twisted, and bent, somewhat cartilaginous in texture, yellow, and up to 12 mm long Spores spindle-shaped, contracted at the middle, bright golden brown, 70—120 microm long, and 14—20 microm. thick. The æcidium form, *Ræstelia lacerata*, is met with on species of *Cratægus*, and occurs abundantly in smaller or larger groups on orange yellow swollen blotches —though frequently covering large areas, especially on fruit— and is usually accompanied by contortions and other deformations Peridia, flask-shaped when young, later cylindrical cup-shaped, dirty white, rupturing longitudinally to various depths into numerous erect or somewhat outwardly inclined lobes

GYMNOSPORANGIUM SABINÆ (SYN G FUSCUM)

Teleutospore-layers on *Juniperus Sabina*, *J. virginiana*, *J phœnicea*, *J Oxycedrus*, and *Pinus halepensis* When fresh they are abruptly conical or cylindrical, often slightly compressed laterally and expanding somewhat towards the top, sometimes pectinate, red brown, 8—10 mm long Spores broadly elliptical, either not contracted at the middle or contraction scarcely observable, chestnut brown, 38—50 microm. long, and 23—26 microm thick The æcidium form, called *Ræstelia cancellata*, is found on *Pyrus communis*, *P Michauxii*, and *P tomentosa* In shape the æcidia are like very short-necked bottles, about 2—2½ mm high, and several are situated together on orange

yellow, roundish or irregular, cushion-like swollen blotches
Pseudo-peridium yellowish white, closed at the shoulder,
ruptured on the side by numerous longitudinal fissures, which
extend to the surface of the leaf These longitudinal fissures
are bridged over by short transverse rodlets, whence the whole
peridium appears grated In this connection I may remark that
I have repeatedly observed the pear-rust in great abundance
in places where no examples of the above-mentioned host-
plants of the teleuto form were to be found within a wide
radius

GYMNOSPORANGIUM TREMELLOIDES

To the three above-mentioned species a fourth falls to be
added, whose æcidium form is very abundantly met with in
the Bavarian Alps on *Sorbus Aria* and *S Chamæmespilus*, and
which as *Æcidium penicillatum* has already been described as an
independent form (Fig 88)

In equal abundance one meets in the same region with a
teleuto form on *Juniperus communis* which does not agree with
any of the above-named species, but whose connection with the
æcidium form on *Sorbus Aria* has been proved by infection-
experiments in the garden of the Munich institute of forest
botany

The teleutospore-layers appear in May on *Juniperus communis*, as hemispherical orange yellow to yellowish brown masses,
which, as in the case of *Nostoc communis*, are mucilage-like
in texture and capable of swelling (Fig 89, *a a*) They
easily drop off when the branches are shaken, and then pale
yellow smooth scars remain, which are often 1 cm. in diameter
(Fig. 89, *b b*). The spores are all about the same size, being
approximately 40—45 microm long and 20—25 microm broad.
The two short abruptly conical cells, whose height is about
equal to their greatest diameter, are provided with smoky-
grey walls Some of them coalesce all along their base, others
are to a certain extent separated owing to contraction—in fact,
it not unfrequently happens that the two parts of a teleutospore
become completely disunited. Most of the cells possess three
germ-pores, which, when situated near the transverse septum,
frequently alternate with those of the second cell (Fig 90).

The æcidia appear on *Sorbus Aria, S. Chamæmespilus, Pyrus Malus,* and *Sorbus torminalis* (?).

The cushion-like stroma, on which the æcidia are often arranged in circles, is very thick, and luxuriantly developed. The pseudo-peridia are somewhat cup-shaped, and are split up as far as the base into a large number of filaments 1 mm. in length, which bend out somewhat. The aperture of the

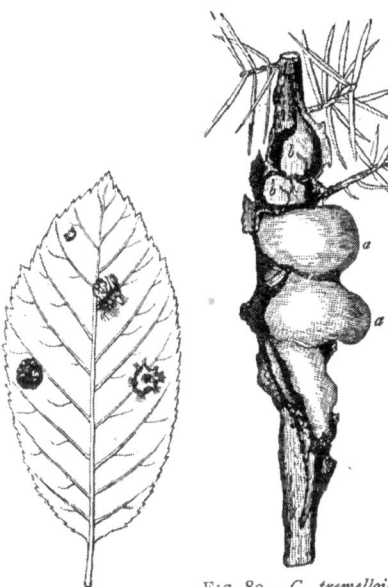

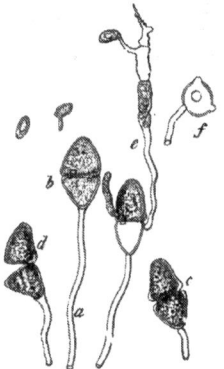

FIG. 90.—Teleutospores of *G. tremelloides. a,* basidium ; *b,* spore that has not yet germinated ; *c,* a similar spore, showing contraction along the centre ; *d,* ditto with the cells separated ; *e,* a germinated teleutospore with promycelium and sporidium ; *f,* basal view of a teleutospore showing three germ-pores, the one from which the germ-tube is issuing being closed by a lamella.

FIG. 88.—Æcidia of *G. tremelloides* on a leaf of *Sorbus Aria.*

FIG. 89.—*G. tremelloides* on *J. communis. a a,* teleutospore-layers ; *b b,* scars which are left after the mucilaginous mass has dropped off.

æcidium is distinct, and is black in colour owing to the dark spores. Material sent by Herr Nawaschin, of Moscow, shows that this species also occurs in Russia, where the teleuto form develops not only in the cortex but also on the leaves of *Juniperus communis,* forming an oblong cushion-like stroma which extends over about half of the leaf. In that country the æcidia occur on the leaves of the apple-tree.

MELAMPSORA (CALYPTOSPORA) GOEPPERTIANA [1]

The fungus which attacks the cowberry, and its æcidium form, *Æcidium columnare*, which produces the columnar rust of the silver fir, are indigenous wherever silver firs abound. The first-mentioned form, indeed, is also met with in districts from which the silver fir is absent, and this furnishes a proof that the æcidium form possesses only a facultative character.

Specimens of *Vaccinium Vitis Idæa* that are attacked by the parasite are at once distinguishable from healthy plants by their manner and habit of growth. Whereas the latter rise but a short distance above the ground, individuals that are infested by the fungus grow quite erect, display an unusually vigorous height-growth, and develop two shoots even in the same year. The diseased plants, singly or in groups, tower above the healthy plants, whose height they exceed in some cases by a foot. At the same time they exhibit a striking appearance, the greater part of the stem being swollen to the thickness of a quill, while only the upper part of each shoot retains its normal dimensions (Fig. 91). At first the thickened spongy part of the stem is of a white or beautifully rosy red colour, which soon, however, changes into brown, and later be-

FIG. 91.—A plant of *V. Vitis Idæa* which has been infected by *M. Goeppertiana. a*, the infected stem containing the mycelium. The new shoots *b*, in the year succeeding that in which the plant was infected, undergo abnormal thickening under the influence of the mycelium; the apex alone retaining normal dimensions. *c*, the youngest shoot; *d*, a dead portion.

[1] Hartig, *Lehrbuch der Baumkrankheiten*, 1st edition, pp. 56 *et seq.*, Table II.

M

comes almost black. The lower leaves of each shoot are dwarfed, while the upper ones develop normally. If one infects a healthy cowberry plant with the æcidiospores of the columnar rust of the silver fir—which will be described presently—the stem remains unaltered during the first year, although the mycelium spreads in the tissues of the cortex. Next year, however, the young shoots are affected in the manner just described. The mycelium grows into the young shoots, where, by the exudation of a ferment, it stimulates growth in all the cortical cells. This effect, however, can only be produced so long as the cells of the new shoots are still young. But on account of the slow upward growth of the mycelium in the shoot, it only reaches the apex at a time when the cells of the cortex are completely matured, and when, consequently, it is no longer able to stimulate to increased growth.

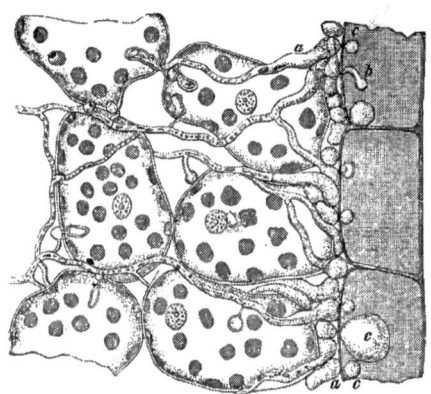

FIG. 92.—Cortical parenchyma and epidermal cells from the stem of *V. Vitis Idæa*. The mycelium grows in the intercellular spaces, and pushes short branches, which swell at the apex, against the outer wall of the cells. A delicate prolongation at the apex of these branches penetrates the cell-wall, after which a sac-like haustorium develops in the interior of the cell. Underneath the epidermal cells the hyphæ enlarge in a clavate manner, *a a*. Haustoria, *b*, and teleutospore-mother-cells, *c c*, develop in the epidermal cells. Magnified 420 times.

The mycelium, however, pushes up as far as the topmost bud, which may be stimulated to shoot out even in the same year as that in which it is formed. The mycelium, which is perennial, is intercellular, and abstracts nutriment from the parenchymatous cells by means of haustoria (Fig. 92). It ultimately reaches the epidermis, underneath which it swells up in a clavate manner (Fig. 92, *a a*).

Haustoria (*b*) are also pushed into the epidermal cells, which may at once be distinguished, by their shape, from the young spore-mother-cells (*c c*), which are also developed there.

From four to eight, usually six, such mother-cells are produced in each epidermal cell. These increase in size till they occupy the whole space, and then divide each into four teleutospores, which are arranged side by side in a palisade fashion (Fig. 93, *a*). During wet weather in May of the following year, each teleuto-spore germinates *in situ* to produce a promycelium (*b*), on which the sporidia develop on short sterigmata (*c*). Should these reach the silver fir they penetrate the young leaves by means of a germ-tube, and four weeks later the mycelium produces two rows of æcidia on the under side of each leaf, which are characterised by an extremely long peridium (Fig. 94). The peridia burst open in various ways at the apex, and allow the æcidiospores to escape (Fig. 95). These are characterised by the unusual length of the intermediate cells, which separate the individual spores from each other. The æcidiospores germinate when they reach the epidermis of *Vaccinium Vitis Idæa*, and produce either a tube which remains of uniform thickness, though it sometimes branches, or a germ-tube which enlarges in a sac-like fashion towards the extremity. Infection is accomplished by means of a fine hypha which springs from the germ-tube.

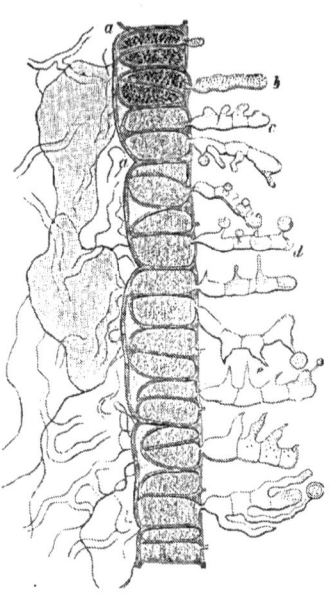

FIG. 93.—Epidermis and cortex of *V. Vitis Idæa* containing ripe teleuto-spores of *M. Goeppertiana*, some of which are germinating. The mother-cells, each of which forms four teleuto-spores, are usually found six together in an epidermal cell, *a*. A germinating teleutospore produces a promy-celium, *b*, on which, after the formation of three transverse septa, four sporidia, *c*, usually develop on short sterigmata. Magnified 420 times.

The infected leaves remain green for a considerable period, and only fall off in the course of the summer. Even in

M 2

August I have found green leaves beset with the withered æcidia.

Serious damage is done only when the young silver firs are situated amongst badly infested cowberry-bushes, and when the greater part of the leaves contract the disease. The æcidium form possesses a facultative character—that is to say, it may be absent without endangering the existence of the parasite whose

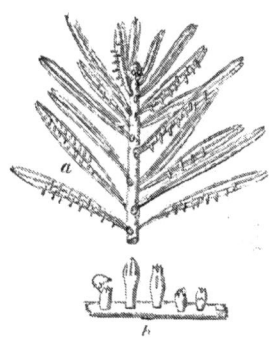

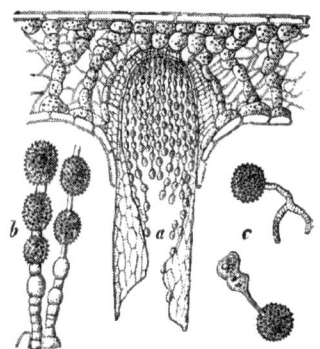

FIG. 94.—*a*, the branch of a silver fir on the under side of whose leaves two rows of the æcidia of *M. Goeppertiana* (*Æcidium columnare*) have developed ; *b*, the æcidia magnified.

FIG. 95.—An æcidium of *M. Goeppertiana*, *a*, in the tissues of a leaf of the silver fir ; *b*, the strings of æcidiospores with intermediate cells ; *c*, germinating æcidiospores.

sporidia are capable of germinating on, and of directly infecting cowberry-plants.

Where damage is to be apprehended from the columnar rust of the silver fir during the regeneration of a wood, one may reduce the chances of an outbreak by rooting out diseased cowberry-plants. On account of their striking appearance, these are not difficult to find.

MELAMPSORA TREMULÆ *

Under the name *Melampsora populina*, the Poplar-rust, are denoted the fungus-forms belonging to this genus which are met with on various species of poplars, and which await more thorough and exact investigation.

Forms are met with on *Populus tremula* whose cushion-like

* [Occurs in England, and requires investigation.—ED.]

stromata are distinguished by their smaller size from those which occur on *P. balsamifera* (*M. Balsamifera Thüm.*), and it would also appear that the form *M. populina Jacq.* which is often met with in luxuriant development on *P. nigra* is distinct from the first two. Owing to the development and increase of the uredospores in the course of the summer, the foliage may appear quite golden yellow in August, and poplars sometimes suffer so severely from this rust that even in September the trees may be entirely leafless.

The teleutospore-layers are primarily concealed by the epidermis of the leaf, but ultimately appear above the surface as smooth brownish-yellow cushions, which afterwards become dark brown (Fig. 96); while the yellow uredo-layers, after rupturing the epidermis, may be recognised as loose clusters of spores.

It would appear desirable that these various forms of poplar-rust should be made the subject of more exact investigation, seeing that their æcidium forms have not yet been determined with certainty.

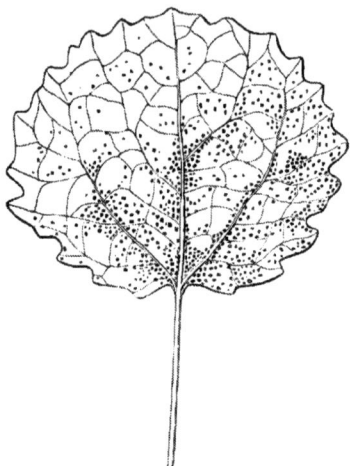

FIG. 96.—Aspen-leaf showing the teleuto-spore-layers of *M. Tremulæ*.

I have, so far, investigated only the *Melampsora* that affects *Populus tremula*. Even as early as 1874[1] I drew attention to the fact that, with scarcely an exception, aspens present in young Scotch pine woods are infested by *Cæoma pinitorquum*, and that some connection might possibly exist between *Cæoma* and some fungus that occurs on the aspen.

I indicated that such a connection was doubtful in the case of *Melampsora Tremulæ*, because this fungus occurs in districts where *Cæoma pinitorquum* is unknown. In the interval, however, Rostrup proved experimentally the connection

[1] *Wichtige Krankheiten der Waldbäume*, p. 91.

between these two fungi, and this I was able afterwards to confirm   At the same time I proved that *M. Tremulæ* produces *Cæoma Laricis* on the larch

Then Rostrup also obtained *Cæoma Mercurialis* by infection with *M Tremulæ*   Rathay believes that he has also obtained *Æcidium Clematitis* on *Clematis vitalba* by infection with spores of *M populina*

As regards *Cæoma pinitorquum* and *C Laricis*, I obtained the æcidia of both by infection with sporidia from the same aspen-leaf, and, further, I have infected *Pinus* with teleutospores of *Melampsora* which I had raised by sowing *Cæoma Laricis* on the aspen

Thus, although it appears to me that the identity of these two species of *Cæoma* has been conclusively proved, still it would be desirable to have this confirmed   Even more pressing, however, is the solution of the problem whether *Cæoma Mercurialis* also originates in the same species of *Melampsora*, or whether various species occur on the aspen to which these æcidium forms belong. Further, it is necessary to discover whether the species present on *P nigra*, *P alba*, and *P balsamifera* are identical with those on the aspen ; and, finally, it remains to be determined whether the æcidium forms possess a facultative character, as appears to me most probable   I have described below the two diseases produced on conifers by *M. Tremulæ*

First Form on **Pinus sylvestris** *with* **Cæoma pinitorquum.** *The Pine Shoot Twist Disease.* **Melampsora Tremulæ pinitorquum**

This disease is distributed throughout the whole of Germany, being most prevalent in the north, where it has proved exceedingly destructive, especially from 1870 to 1873   It may attack young pine seedlings even at the stage when they are just appearing above ground   In such a case longish pale yellow sporogenous layers rupture the epidermis and appear upon the surface of the stems or leaves   The disease is most frequently observed in pine woods from one to ten years old, infection being brought about by the teleutospores of *M. Tremulæ* which develop on aspen-leaves that are lying about on the ground   The disease may be recognized by the fact that in the beginning of June, sometimes even in the end of May, at the season when the apex of the green leaf-fascicles on the young shoots is projecting somewhat from the leaf-sheath, pale yellow patches ⅜ to 1⅛ inch long and ⅛ to ⅔ inch broad appear upon the green cortical tissues of the shoots (Fig. 97), and on these, with the help of a pocket lens, numerous small rather deeper yellow tubercles, the spermogonia, may be made out. These are formed partly in the epidermal cells, and partly between them and the cuticle, the latter being raised up to cover the spermogonium (Fig. 98). The *Cæoma*-layer originates in the second or third row of cortical cells, and is formed by the intercellular mycelium growing outwards from the interior of the stem to produce a sporophore in that region. The æcidiospores are afterwards distributed by abscission from the apex of basidia in the usual way. While the formation of this internal sporogenous

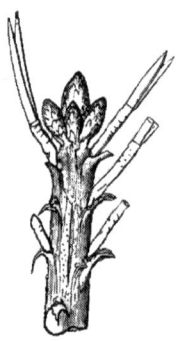

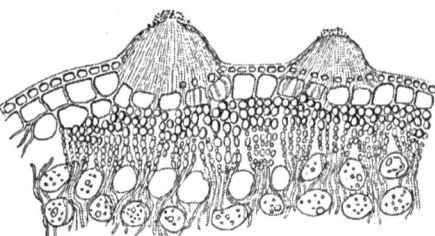

Fig. 97.—Apex of a young pine-shoot showing the sporogenous layers of *C. pinitorquum* through the ruptured cortex. Natural size.

Fig. 98.—Transverse section of a sporogenous layer of *C. pinitorquum* before the cortex has ruptured. Two tubercular spermogonia are visible in the epidermis.

layer is proceeding, the surface of the part of the cortex affected is constantly assuming a deeper golden yellow colour, while, at the same time, it forms a cushion-like elevation which results in the development of a longitudinal fissure (Fig. 97) in the external layers of the cortex through which the spores are shed. The tissues of the cortex beneath the sporophore afterwards die as far in as the wood, and a callus is formed, under favourable circumstances, in about a year.

During the development of the spores, and for some time afterwards, the young shoot continues to elongate normally, except at the seat of the disease. The result is that the diseased shoot bends over a little at the place occupied by the spore-layers. In many cases, however, the ultimate contortions, which have earned for the parasite the designation Pine Twister, *C. pinitorquum*, are due to the weight of the young shoot, whose apex, in the case of lateral branches that are considerably damaged on one side, is bound to be depressed. Later on the apex again grows up, and thus S-shaped contortions arise. If the weather is normal, a few such sporophores are formed

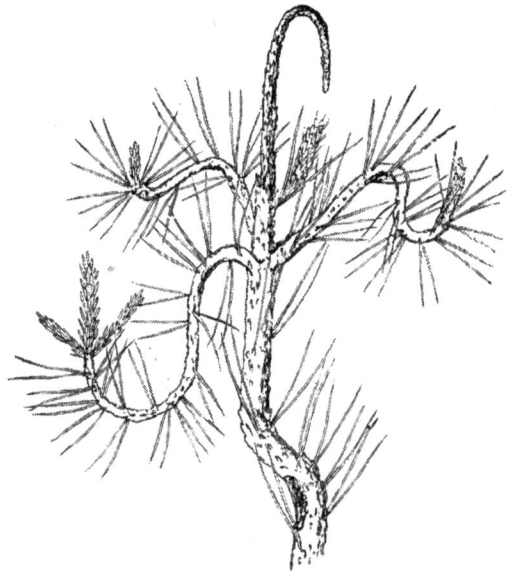

FIG. 99.—Apex of a pine which has been attacked by *C. pinitorquum*. The leading shoot has been killed almost to the base. The branches of the whorl, as well as the main shoot-axis, show diseased spots and contortions which have existed for a considerable time.

annually on the young shoots, while in very dry weather the sporogenous layers wither up as soon as formed, and no external damage is visible. Should May and the beginning of June be very wet, the sporophores develop so abundantly and luxuriantly that the shoots, with the exception of the base, die off and dry up completely (Fig. 99). A badly diseased young Scotch pine wood appears in the end of June as if a late frost had killed and contorted all the young shoots. Next year the dormant eyes of the leaf-fascicles that survive at the base of the shoot develop into shoots, and these afterwards become diseased like the rest. The fact that a pine that is once attacked by the fungus suffers from the disease year after year during successive decades justifies the assumption that the mycelium of the fungus is perennial in the shoots. From the part of a pine wood that is first attacked—the focus of the disease—the disease continues to spread each year in a centrifugal manner. The point is to be emphasized that very young woods—those from one to three years old—suffer most from the disease. Pines that become diseased at a later period are sometimes so badly crippled as to hold out but faint hope of a healthy wood, but as a rule a dry spring occurs sooner or later which retards the development of the fungus, and so, a few years' mitigation of the disease being granted, the plants gradually recover, although they again suffer in unfavourable seasons. About the thirteenth year the disease spontaneously disappears. Clearing out the aspens from the young pine woods is the surest method of combating the disease

Second Form on **Larix europæa** *with* **Cæoma Laricis.**[1] **Melampsora Tremulæ Laricis**

The larch-leaf-rust is distributed throughout the whole of Germany, and is frequently so common that a large part of the foliage is destroyed by the fungus.

It is often overlooked on account of the damage bearing a certain resemblance to that due to *Chermes Laricis*. In the month of May numerous spermogonia first of all appear on the leaves, amongst which the *Cæoma*-layers break through the epidermis of the leaf in the form of long or short yellow cushions.

FIG. 100.—Larch-leaves attacked by *Cæoma Laricis.*

After the spores have been shed the leaves wither and fall off. Felling the aspens in the neighbourhood of larch woods protects the latter against the disease.

[1] *Wichtige Krankheiten der Waldbäume*, 1874, p. 93, and *Allgemeine Forst- und Jagd-Zeitung*, 1885, p. 326.

MELAMPSORA SALICINA.[1] THE WILLOW-RUST

Several species of *Melampsora* occur on the various willows, and these, until a short time ago, were grouped under the common collective name of *M. salicina*. By means of the form of the teleutospores and uredospores, Thümen was the first to distinguish a number of species, which ought to be thoroughly investigated for the sake of verification. Rostrup [2] has, in the interval, succeeded in obtaining the æcidia of two species, which will now be more particularly described.

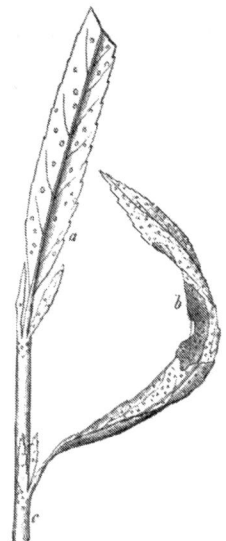

FIG. 101.—*M. Hartigii* on *Salix pruinosa. a*, a living leaf with sporophores ; *b*, a leaf which has been killed at places ; *c*, sporophores on the stem close to the base of the leaf.

MELAMPSORA HARTIGII

The uredospores appear sometimes as early as the end of May or the beginning of June, in small reddish yellow clusters on the lower surface, more rarely on the upper surface, of the leaves of *Salix pruinosa*, *S. daphnoides*, *S. viminalis*, and other willows. The disease spreads rapidly, partly owing to the internal growth of the mycelium, which penetrates the cortex of the shoots by way of the leaf-petioles, and partly by means of the uredospores which are carried by the wind. These germinate very quickly, and produce numerous new uredo-clusters, generally on the eighth day after they have been sown on a sound leaf. Leaves that are attacked soon become marked with black blotches, and drop off. Before the leaves fall off or die numerous teleutospore-layers, about the size of a pin-head, develop beneath the epidermis of the leaf (Fig. 101). These occur more especially in late summer

---

[1] Von Thümen, *Mittheilungen aus dem forstlichen Versuchswesen Oesterreichs*, ii. p. 41 *et seq.* Hartig, *Wichtige Krankheiten der Waldbäume*, pp. 119 *et seq.*

[2] Rostrup, *Fortsatte Undersøgelser over Snyltesvampes Angreb par Skovtraeerne Kjøbenhaven*, 1883.

and in autumn   These small cushion-like bodies, which are at
first pale brown and later very dark brown in colour, pass the
winter in the tissues of the decaying leaves that are lying on the
ground, and produce promycelia and sporidia in spring   These
sporidia are carried by the wind to the leaves of the young willow-
shoots, and induce the disease afresh   They produce *Cæoma
Ribesii* on the leaves of *Ribes alpinum, R. Grossularia, R rubrum,*
and *R nigrum*   This æcidium form appears, however, to possess merely a facultative character, for we annually meet with
numerous instances of the disease, especially in autumn, even in
places where no examples of *Ribes* are to be met with for long
distances

Hitherto I have met with serious infestations of the fungus
only on *Salix pruinosa* (syn *caspica, acutifolia*), numerous osier-
beds being entirely destroyed by repeated premature defoliation
The best preventive measures consist in raking together and
burying or burning the fallen fungus-infested leaves from
autumn till spring, and in careful attention to the osier-beds
during summer   As soon as the rust appears sporadically it is
advisable to cut off and bury the infested shoots. In place of
the glabrous-leaved *Salix pruinosa*, which suffers most from the
fungus, the cultivation of the hybrid *S pruinosa* × *daphnoides*
is to be recommended, the latter being pubescent, and thus better
protected against infection.

MELAMPSORA CAPREARUM

This willow-rust is very common on *Salix Caprea, S cinerea,
S aurita, S. longifolia, S. repens,* and *S reticulata*   It produces
the æcidia of *Cæoma Evonymi* on *Evonymus*

Then we also meet with *Melampsora epitea* on *S alba,
S. incana, S. purpurea, S. nigricans,* and *S. retusa ;* and *M
mixta* on *S. triandra, S hastata,* and *S silesiaca.*

M. betulina occurs on various species of *Betula.*

M. Carpini	„	„	*Carpinus Betulus.*
M. Sorbi	,	„	*Sorbus Aucuparia* and *S torminalis.*
M. Ariæ	„	„	*Sorbus Aria.*
M. Padi	„	„	*Prunus Padus*
M Vaccinii	„	„	*Species of Vaccinium* *

* [Several of these are recorded for this country, and are much in need of
thorough investigation.—ED.]

COLEOSPORIUM SENECIONIS

The genus *Coleosporium* ,is distinguished from the preceding one by the teleutospores being formed out of several super-imposed cells, each of which produces a unicellular promycelium with a single sporidium.

According to the investigations of Wolf and Klebahn, three species of this genus produce æcidia on the leaves of the pine. These include not only *C Senecionis*, which occurs on various species of *Senecio* (according to Wolf), but also *C. Euphrasiæ* and *C Tussilaginis* (according to Klebahn). The æcidium forms are known under the names of *Peridermium Pini acicola* or *Peridermium oblongisporium*, the pine-leaf-rust.[1]

In the months of April and May the æcidia may be observed on the one- and two-year-old leaves chiefly of younger pines,

FIG 102 —The æcidia and spermogonia of *Peridermium Pini acicola* on the leaves of a pine

occasionally also of old trees. The spermogonia are found scattered amongst the reddish yellow vesicles (Fig 102), which are only a few millimetres in size   The former become brown with age, and thus look from the outside like small black blotches   The mycelium develops in the interior of the leaf, where it passes the winter, and in the following year it may again produce æcidia without killing the leaf   Seeing that the leaves which are infested by the æcidia do not die prematurely, or at least not to any great extent, the injury done by this form of the fungus is insignificant   Discoloured spots are merely formed upon the leaves

Several species of *Cronartium* produce æcidia and spermogonia in the cortical tissues of pines   These have hitherto been grouped under the name *Peridermium Pini corticola* *   The disease, which occurs both in young and old woods, is very prejudicial to the health of the trees   How infection takes place —whether it must always be preceded by an abrasion of the cortical tissue, such as is induced by insects, woodpeckers, hail-

---

[1] R Hartig, *Wichtige Krankheiten der Waldbaume*, 1874

* [This disease occurs every year on pines in this country —ED]

stones, &c.—remains for the present undetermined. Parts of the stem older than 20—25 years appear to be incapable of receiving infection. The mycelium of the fungus spreads by intercellular growth amongst the cells of the cortex and of the bast, from which it proceeds, by way of the medullary rays, into the wood to the depth of about four inches.

Wherever the mycelium obtains access, the starch-grains and other cell-contents disappear, their place being taken by drops of oil of turpentine, which form on the inside of the walls, or saturate the wall-substance itself. The cells are, of course, killed, death however being unaccompanied by browning of the tissues. The whole stem, to a depth of some three or four inches, is completely saturated with resin, a section of wood, as much as one to two inches in thickness, being more or less translucent. As the mycelium penetrates the resin-ducts as well, killing the surrounding tissues, there is no doubt that a portion of the turpentine finds its way down from parts of the stem situated at a higher elevation. The assumption that direct conversion to turpentine of the cell-contents and of the wall-substance of the parenchymatous cells also takes place is, however, justified by the complete resinous saturation, and by a frequent voluminous outpouring of turpentine from the cortex, which detaches itself from the tree after death.

Each year the mycelium spreads from the diseased part into adjoining tissues, the rate of progress being usually somewhat more rapid longitudinally than horizontally. In proportion as the mycelium spreads, so is the passage of the plastic materials confined to the sound side of the tree, in consequence of which the cambium in that region is stimulated to such a degree of activity as to produce exceptionally broad annual rings. Fig. 103 exhibits the cross section of a stem which, when fifteen years old, was

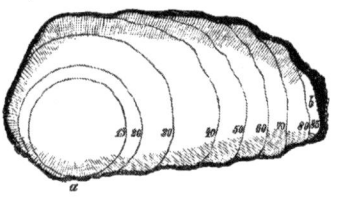

FIG. 103.—Transverse section from the upper part of the stem of a pine which, seventy years previously, had been infected at *a* by *P. Pini corticola.* The crown of the tree died in the year immediately preceding that in which the section was removed, and at that time the only portion of alburnum that was not saturated with resin or attacked by the fungus was the portion marked *b.* The portion of the wood saturated with resin is shaded in the figure. One tenth natural size.

infected at *a*, but which, with the part of the crown situated above the point of infection, only succumbed in its eighty-fifth year. The top of a diseased tree is specially liable to die during a dry warm summer, when the wood, having for the most part undergone resinous degeneration, is unable to allow sufficient water to pass to compensate for the rapid evaporation from the crown.

For the most part æcidia are formed only in that region of the cortex which has become diseased during the preceding year. They break

FIG. 104.—Portion of the stem of a young pine showing the vesicular æcidia of *P. Pini corticola* breaking through the cortex. At three places which are darker shaded spermogonia are situated beneath the periderm. Natural size.

FIG. 105.—A pine-branch which has been infested by *P. Pini corticola* for several years. The branches on the left side, which were the first to be attacked, are already dead. From these the mycelium has spread backwards on to the main branch and the other lateral branches. One fifth natural size.

through the outer dead cortical layers in the months of May and June as hemispherical, oblong, sausage-shaped, yellowish white vesicles filled with reddish yellow powdery spores (Fig. 104). Amongst these one recognizes with difficulty the flat spermogonia which are about the size of a pea. These consist of innumerable fine sterigmata which are situated between the deepest periderm-layer and the living cortex, being arranged at right angles to the former. The small spermatia are abjointed from the apex of these sterigmata.

Branches and twigs of the crowns of the older classes of trees often die in a few years, after which the parasite frequently spreads downwards from the base of the branch to the main axis of the stem (Fig 105) Even should the latter die the tree will still remain alive, provided there are branches and twigs well provided with leavès beneath the canker-spot These branches constitute a kind of new leader, and the dead crown forms the " resin-top " or " resin-leader " (" bird-resin "), which was regarded by Ratzeburg as the result of injury caused by the Pine Beauty Moth, and designated as " spear-top "

The disease has also been described by this observer as " moth-wither," or, in other words, as the result of the attack of *Phycis abietella* (*Tinea sylvestrella*, Ratz).

Three species of pine-blister-rust are to be distinguished in the cortex of trees, viz. :—

(1) *Peridermium Strobi*, which occurs only in the cortex of *Pinus Strobus* The æcidium form is *Cronartium rubicula*.

(2) *Peridermium Cornui*, which occurs in the cortex of *Pinus sylvestris*, has for its æcidium form *Cronartium asclepiadeum* on *Asclepius Vincetoxicum*.

(3) *Peridermium Pini* This is probably the most destructive species, and it is to be regretted that so far the plants have not been determined on which the teleutospores are produced Until we discover the teleuto form preventive measures must be confined to felling pines that are attacked

CHRYSOMYXA

The genus *Chrysomyxa* is closely related to the preceding one, in that here also each teleutospore consists of a row of cells, the terminal one of which produces a multicellular promycelium with four sterigmata and sporidia. The sporophore consists of a dense orange yellow cushion-like body of varying shape. The uredo and æcidium layers are similar to those of the genus *Coleosporium*.

CHRYSOMYXA ABIETIS,[1] THE SPRUCE-LEAF-RUST

This is a disease of the spruce which is met with throughout the whole of Germany, with the exception of the higher Alpine regions It occurs on old as well as on young spruces,

[1] Reess, *Bot Zeit*, 1865, Nos 51 and 52, and Willkomm, *Die mikroskopischen Feinde des Waldes*, 1868, pp 134—166

and is frequently so prevalent on the youngest shoots as to kill a large proportion of the leaves, which subsequently drop off.

The fungus is autœcious, the uredo and æcidium layers being entirely absent. Its teleutospore-layers alone are developed on the spruce-leaves. In the month of May the sporidia germinate on the delicate leaves of the young shoots, inside which they produce the mycelium, which contains numerous drops of yellow oil. By the end of June the part of the leaf that is infested may be recognized by its pale yellow colour. The diseased portion may occupy the base, middle, or apex of the leaf. As autumn approaches it constantly becomes deeper lemon yellow in colour, while the rest of the leaf remains green. In autumn formation of the teleutospore-layers begins on both the

under sides of the leaf. These take the form of oblong, somewhat prominent cushions, which are at once to be recognized by their more golden yellow colour. In this condition the fungus hibernates on the tree, and in the following spring the teleutospore-layer still further develops (Fig. 106), until finally the epidermis ruptures longitudinally and exposes a golden yellow stroma. The promycelia with their sporidia next develop from the cells of the teleutospores, as is shown in the case of *C. Rhododendri* in Fig. 107, and as this occurs in the month of May, at a time when the young shoots of the spruce are forming, the sporidia have the opportunity of germinating directly on the young leaves.

FIG. 106.—A spruce-leaf attacked by *C. Abietis*, the golden yellow spore-layers of which have not yet ruptured the epidermis.

It is probable that spruces which are very backward in growth at the time when the spores ripen escape infection, and this explains why many individuals of a wood remain entirely free from the fungus while others are very badly attacked. Such cases have frequently inspired non-professional minds with the belief that the fungoid disease is dependent upon a predisposition to disease on the part of particular spruces. After the sporidia drop off the teleutospore-layers wither, while the leaves themselves soon afterwards die and fall from the tree. As a rule the tree suffers but little from the loss of leaves, because a sufficient supply of foliage is always left on the older parts of the branches as well as on the youngest shoots As the meteorological conditions are not always equally favourable for the germination of the sporidia, and as the teleutospores may germinate at a time when most of the spruces are either too far, or not far enough, advanced in development to be infected by the sporidia, it very seldom happens that the disease maintains its intensity throughout a long series of years. With the exception of a spruce wood in the Saxon Erzgebirge, I have never come across very serious damage due to *Chrysomyxa Abietis* Certain years occur, and not uncommonly, when the disease is very scarce, and when the spruces are in a position to clothe themselves with a full stock of leaves On this account I am not able to agree with Willkomm, Frank, &c, in their recommendations regarding measures for combating the fungus, because felling the diseased trees, and such like measures, would have worse consequences than the disease itself

It may be not uninteresting to note that in the severe winter 1879-80 it was noticed that in many districts the diseased leaves dried up so that the development of the fungus was prevented. And, further, it not unfrequently happens that *Hysterium macrosporum* is encountered along with *Chrysomyxa*, the result being that the development of the leaves is interfered with, and they acquire black blotches

CHRYSOMYXA RHODODENDRI [1]

The Rust of the Rhododendron is of special interest in that it is heterœcious, developing its teleutospore- and uredo-layers in clusters in the form of small roundish and oblong cushions on the leaves of rhododendrons, while the æcidia (*Æcidium abietinum*, the Spruce-Blister-Rust) develop on the leaves of the young shoots of the spruce.

The occurrence of the disease on spruces is consequently dependent on the presence of rhododendrons,[2] although, of course, the spread of the sporidia, by means of wind and rain, from high elevations into the valleys or otherwise is not impossible De Bary, to whom we are indebted for our know-

[1] De Bary, *Bot. Zeit*, 1879.
[2] In the Alps *R hirsutum* and *R ferrugineum* are the common species

N

ledge of the biology of this parasite, has, however, proved that
the æcidium form may be dispensed with. Where spruces are
absent the sporidia germinate directly on the leaves of the
rhododendron to produce the uredo layers, and these serve
to maintain and spread the fungus during summer, until, in
autumn, teleutospore-layers are again formed on the leaves of
the youngest rhododendron shoots. These hibernate, and in the
following spring the germination of the teleutospores results in
the rupturing of the leaf-epidermis (Fig. 107).

At first the development of the parasite in the spruce-leaf
resembles that of *Chrysomyxa Abietis*, but even in July and

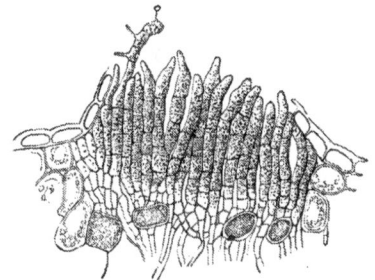

FIG. 107.—Teleutospore-layer of *C. Rhodo-*
dendri on *R. hirsutum.* The development
of the promycelia has caused the epidermis
of the leaf to rupture.

FIG. 108.— Spermo-
gonia and æcidia
of *C. Rhododendri*
on a spruce-leaf.

August numerous small spots, the spermogonia, are to be
observed on the yellow parts of the leaves. Shortly afterwards
one sees the yellow vesicles of the æcidia breaking through the
epidermis, and these bear a close resemblance to those produced
by the pine-blister-rust on the leaves of pines (Fig. 108). In
August and September, when the peridia burst at the apex, the
æcidiospores are liberated in such numbers that if a diseased
spruce is shaken the air is filled with a dense cloud of spores.
In the course of the same year the diseased leaves die and drop
off. This distinguishes the parasite at once from *Chrysomyxa*
Abietis, which, in an immature state, hibernates on the tree. On
lateral branches it is usually only the leaves that are situated on the
upper side that are diseased. The leaves on the under side, being
preserved against infection by those above, escape the disease.

CHRYSOMYXA LEDI [1]

This parasite induces the same pathological symptoms in the spruce as the preceding one, but it differs in producing its teleutospores and uredospores on the leaves of *Ledum palustre* * Letters received from Russia mention that the fungus occurs in extraordinary abundance in that country, and I have also recently had it forwarded from the district of Königsberg. It has also frequently been observed in other parts of Germany, with the exception of the south, but of course only where *Ledum* occurs in the immediate neighbourhood

In the case of the parasites about to be described, the æcidium forms alone are as yet known, so that the investigation of the course of development of what are probably all heterœcious forms of fungi is work for the future.

ISOLATED ÆCIDIUM FORMS

From amongst the æcidium forms of whose teleutospore-forms we are so far ignorant, attention will here be directed only to those species which occur on forest trees

ÆCIDIUM (PERIDERMIUM) ELATINUM [2] †

This fungus is parasitic on the silver fir, where it produces the so-called witches' brooms and canker-knobs which may be seen anywhere in Germany where woods of silver firs occur.[3] As I have always noticed small wounds on one- or two-year-old witches' brooms close to their base—near the point, namely, where they have developed from a bud—it may in the meantime be assumed that infection occurs at such wounds. The mycelium of the fungus, which stimulates growth in a very marked manner, is perennial in the cortical and bast tissues of the stem, and even penetrates the cambium and the wood Should infection occur

---

[1] De Bary, *Bot Zeit.*, 1879   [2] *Ibid.*, 1867.

[3 Very common also in many parts of Britain, *e g* the south-west of Scotland —*Trans*]

*[An Ericaceous plant found on moors, &c , in N E Europe.—ED.]

† [The cankers occur in various Silver Firs grown in English gardens, though they often seem devoid of the Witches' Brooms and æcidia I have seen both, however, on *Abies Pinsapo* and other species —ED]

at a part of a stem or branch where there are no buds capable of developing, the stimulated growth of the cambium induces the formation of a knob-like swelling at that place, which is due both to the increased formation of wood and to the more vigorous development of the cortex (Fig. 109). With the spread of the mycelium the swellings or canker-spots increase in size, and if present on the stem of a vigorous tree they may attain to large dimensions. At such places the tissues of the cortex and bast soon become fissured (Fig. 110), and dry up here and there as far in as the wood, so that in course of time a

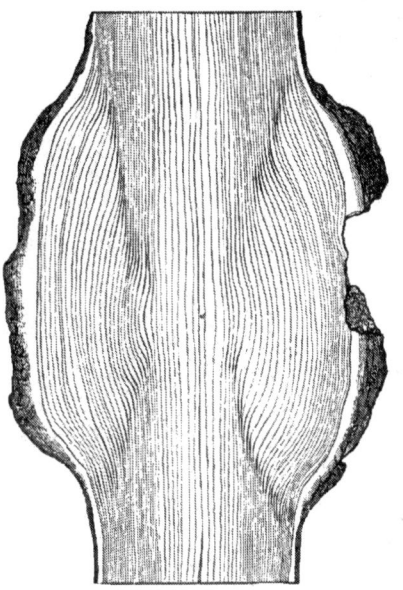

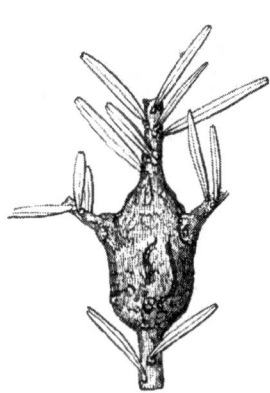

FIG. 109.—Swelling on the silver fir, but without the formation of a witches' broom. Natural size.

FIG. 110.—Longitudinal section of a silver fir showing a swelling, one third natural size, which had originated by infection thirty-one years previously, when the stem was four years old. On the right side the cortex, which has been dead for three years, has withered and dropped off. At the infected part the growth of the cortex and wood has been stimulated.

door is opened for the entrance of wood-parasites. One of the commonest of these is *Polyporus Hartigii*, which produces a kind of white rot. A species of *Agaricus* also—namely, *A. adiposus*—frequently appears as a wood-destroying parasite. In consequence of the decomposition of the wood, storms and snow often break the trees. One not unfrequently finds swellings which have originated without any connection with witches' brooms (Fig. 109), and on such swellings no formation of spores ever occurs.

More frequently infection occurs on or in the immediate neighbourhood of a bud. When the bud proceeds to grow it forms a young witches' broom—that is to say, a shoot whose cortex is stimulated to growth by the advancing mycelium, and whose young leaves are so affected by the parasite that they remain small, are somewhat round in cross-section, and show

FIG. 111.—Branch of a silver fir, with a witches' broom two years old, *a*. The mycelium in advancing through the tissues of the branch has so stimulated a dormant eye that it has developed into a shoot a year later, *b*. The portion of the branch that has been invaded by the mycelium is much swollen.

scarcely any chlorophyll. They remain yellowish, and in the beginning of August two rows of æcidia appear on their under side, which open and shed their spores in the end of the month (Fig. 111). Soon afterwards the leaves die and fall off. The witches' broom is consequently deciduous. Each year the mycelium advances into the new shoots, to produce the phenomena already described. The twigs of branches which show this peculiar symbiosis* anastomose abundantly, and for the most part incline upwards, so that they appear amongst the ordinary branches of the silver fir like perfectly independent

* [Symbiosis signifies the fact that two organisms are living together—a dual existence.]

organisms, somewhat after the manner of the mistletoe. The mycelium also spreads slowly backwards in the cortical and bast tissues, so that a swelling or canker-spot, such as I have already described, is formed on the stem or branch to which the witches' broom is attached (Fig. 112). This swelling increases independently, even after the witches' broom, as such, is dead, an event which is sometimes delayed for twenty years or more. In young woods all trees that show cancerous swellings on their boles should be removed in the thinnings, even in cases where they belong to the larger class of trees.

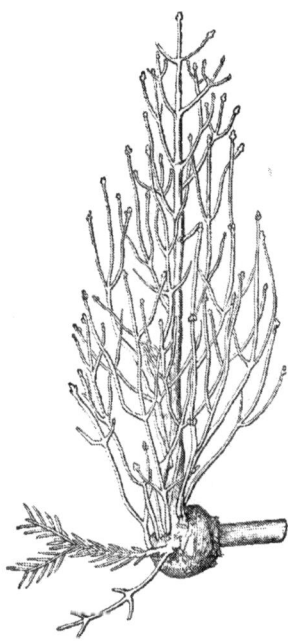

FIG. 112.—The appearance of a witches' broom, seven years old, in winter, when, being deciduous, of course it is leafless. Above the point from which the witches' broom springs the fir branch has almost ceased to exist.

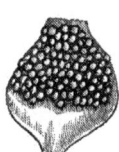

FIG. 113.—Æcidia of *A. strobilinum* on the upper side of a scale of a spruce-cone.

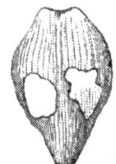

FIG. 114.—The outer side of the scale of a spruce-cone, showing two pale patches which had previously been occupied by the æcidia of *A. conorum Piceæ*.

ÆCIDIUM STROBILINUM [1]

This æcidium form develops its mycelium in the green living carpellary scales of the spruce. It destroys the organs of the flower, and produces dark hemispherical brown æcidia, which are densely crowded, for the most part on the inner side of the scales, though to some extent also on the outer side. These æcidia usually rupture transversely (Fig. 113). When such cones fall to the ground they are easily recognized by the fact

[1] Reess, *Die Rostpilzformen der deutschen Coniferen.*

that they open even in damp weather, whereas sound cones remain tightly closed. This cone-disease occurs throughout the whole of North Germany, reaching as far south as the spurs of the Alps.

ÆCIDIUM CONORUM PICEÆ

This cone-infesting fungus differs from the former by the fact that only two large æcidia are situated on the outer side of each scale of the spruce-cone. After the pale peridia have ruptured and the spores have been scattered, pale spots are left on the scales (Fig. 114).

ÆCIDIUM CORUSCANS [1]

When this rust-fungus, which is common on spruces in Sweden and Finland, attacks a young shoot, the whole of the

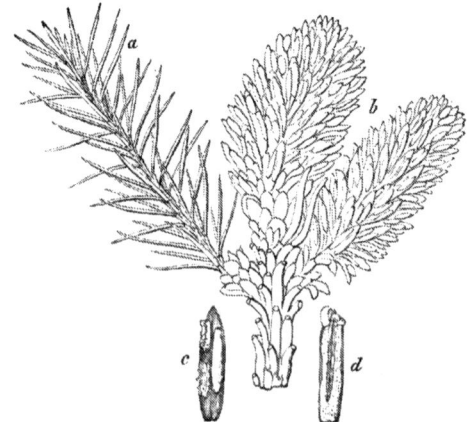

FIG. 115.—A spruce-branch, one shoot of which, *a*, has developed normally, while two shoots, *b*, have been attacked by *A. coruscans*. All the leaves of the diseased shoots are short and fleshy, and bear æcidia on all their four sides. The lower sides, *c*, and the upper sides, *d*, of a diseased leaf showing the æcidia, the peridia of which are still present at *c*, but have mostly disappeared at *d*.

leaves are affected. They become occupied by a peridium, which ruptures in places or along the whole length of the leaf, and displays the golden yellow æcidia underneath. Such leaves make the shoot look like a fleshy cone (Fig. 115). These "cones" are eaten in Sweden under the name "Mjölkomlor."

[1] Reess, *Die Rostpilzformen der deutschen Coniferen*, p. 100.

CÆOMA ABIETIS PECTINATÆ [1]

This disease closely resembles the vesicular or columnar rust, *Æcidium columnare* (*Melampsora Goeppertiana*), from which it is distinguished by the presence of numerous spermogonia, and by the absence of a peridium. It occurs on the lower side of the leaves of the silver fir, usually in the form of linear sporogenous layers, which are situated on both sides of the mid-rib (Fig. 116). It is very abundant in the Bavarian Alps and in the woods near Passau, and is probably to be met with wherever the silver fir is indigenous.

FIG. 116.—A fir-leaf showing *C. Abietis pectinatæ.*

The damage which it causes takes the form of the diseased leaves falling off in the first year, but the injury is comparatively unimportant.

HYMENOMYCETES (CAP-FUNGI *)

Most of the *Hymenomycetes* are saprophytes, and develop their mycelium in soil that is rich in humus, or in the interior of the dead parts of plants, and especially in dead wood; while the sporophore, which is often of large proportions, appears on the surface of the ground or on the outside of the plant. Only relatively few of the *Hymenomycetes* are undoubtedly parasitic in character, and, in the case of many, more exact investigation must determine whether they are to be classed as parasites or saprophytes. The peculiarity in the production of the spores consists in their being simultaneously formed in fours at the apex of basidia, and that these basidia constitute a more or less dense layer (hymenium), which may occupy a part or the whole surface of the hymenophore.

[1] Reess, *Die Rostpilzformen der deutschen Coniferen*, p. 115.

*[These include the " Mushrooms " and " Toadstools " in the wider sense: we are still in want of a good English general term for them, and the translation of the German *Hut-pilze* does not really meet this need.—ED.]

EXOBASIDIUM

The genus *Exobasidium* induces the formation of character-istic galls on the leaves, flowers, and stems of various ligneous plants. The basidia originate on the mycelium, which is chiefly intercellular, and force their way outwards between the cells of the epidermis, on the surface of which they form a hymenial layer. No special sporophore, in the narrower sense of the term, is produced.

EXOBASIDIUM VACCINII [1]

This parasite produces swellings on the leaves, flowers, and stems of *Vaccinium Vitis Idæa*, *V. Myrtillus*, and *V. uliginosum*. These are partly of a beautiful white colour and partly of a bright rosy hue, and are to be distinguished from the swellings due to *Melampsora Goeppertiana* by their being dusted over with the

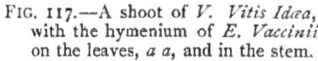

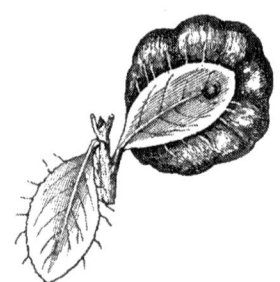

FIG. 117.—A shoot of *V. Vitis Idæa*, with the hymenium of *E. Vaccinii* on the leaves, *a a*, and in the stem.

FIG. 118.—"Alpine-rose apple" on *Rhododendron hirsutum*.

white spores, whereas, in the case of the latter, the lustrous epidermis hides the sporogenous layer ; and further by their occurring more frequently on the under surface of the leaves or on the racemose inflorescence than on the stem (Fig. 117). A microscopic examination at once reveals the fact that the long somewhat bent spores are situated on four delicate sterigmata at the apex of the clavate basidia.

This fungus, which was formerly described as a separate

---

[1] Woronin, *Verhandlungen der naturf. Gesellschaft zu Freiburg*, 1867, IV.

species under the name *Exobasidium Rhododendri*, produces the familiar "Alpine-rose apples" (Fig. 118) on the leaves of the Alpine rhododendrons. These bear a strong resemblance to many of the galls on oak-leaves which are caused by various species of *Cynips*, and are to be met with in all Alpine districts where rhododendrons occur.

TRAMETES RADICIPERDA[1]*

T. radiciperda is undoubtedly the most dangerous of all the parasites met with in coniferous woods, not only because it produces the worst kind of red-rot, but also on account of its being the most common cause of gaps in both young and old plantations. I have had the opportunity of observing it on various species of pines, especially *P. sylvestris* and *P. Strobus*, and also on other conifers, notably *Picea excelsa*, *Abies pectinata*, and *Juniperus communis*. It is true that I have also occasionally met with its sporophores on the roots of old stools of *Betula*, and on beeches that have been damaged by mice, still I doubt if it occurs on dicotyledons as a parasite.

Not unfrequently the disease appears in plantations which are not more than five to ten years old, though it also occurs in woods of a hundred years' standing. Here and there individual trees showing luxuriant growth suddenly become pale, and die. We shall afterwards see that identical pathological symptoms are displayed by trees infected by *Agaricus melleus*. In the neighbourhood of a tree that has been killed—no matter whether it is left standing or has been felled—other trees soon die, and so in the course of years the death-circle constantly extends outwards. Large gaps and openings are thus formed in woods which were previously quite close. At first one generally

---

[1] R. Hartig, *Zersetzungserscheinungen des Holzes*, pp. 14 *et seq.*, Tables I.—IV. Under the name *Polyporus annosus*, Fr., a number of different species of fungi have been described, *Trametes radiciperda* amongst the others. This mode of description has, however, been accepted as sufficiently accurate even in the second edition of Fries's *Systema*, which appeared some years after I had described *T. radiciperda*. The name *T. radiciperda* is thus entitled to priority, and is also to be preferred, as it prevents any confusion.

* [Brefeld, *Unters. aus dem Gesammtgeb. der Mykol.* VIII., re-names this *Heterobasidion annosum*, and describes its second kind of spores—conidia.— ED.]

observes only one or a very limited number of diseased spots in a wood, but when these have been allowed to extend for some years one notices new seats of disease establishing themselves all over the wood.

When the dead trees are examined about the roots, one finds the sporophores, with their snow-white hymenial surface, appear-

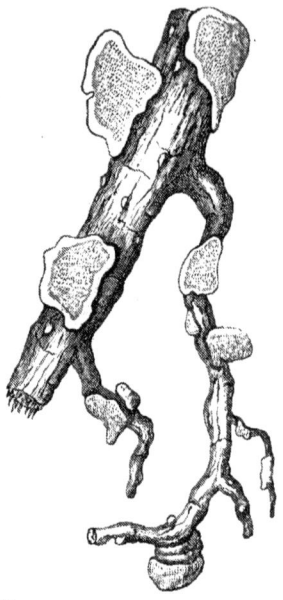

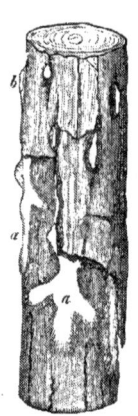

FIG. 120.—The mycelium of *T. radiciperda* on the root of a spruce. The outer bark-scales have been removed from the lower portion so as to show the felted mycelium, *a a*, while in the upper portion only cushion-like mycelial masses, *b*, project from between the scales. Twice natural size.

FIG. 119.—The sporophores of *T. radiciperda* on the roots of a spruce. Natural size.

ing between the bark-scales as very small yellowish-white cushion-like structures (Fig. 119). These coalesce with similar adjoining cushions, and in exceptional cases attain to a diameter of twelve to sixteen inches. In the case of pines the sporophores are usually to be found on the stool close under the surface of the ground, though sometimes also on the deeper roots, while in the case of the spruce they are almost always to be found only on the roots. Between the bark-scales one finds the ramifying felted mycelium, which is distinguished from that of *Agaricus melleus* by its extremely delicate texture (Fig. 120). It scarcely

attains to the thickness of the finest tissue paper, and only where
it penetrates between the bark scales does it swell up to form
yellowish-white bodies varying in size from a pin-head to a pea.
Decomposition (red-rot) spreads from the roots up into the
interior of the stem to a considerable distance. It is only in
the case of the Scotch pine that the rot does not ascend into
the stem from the stool.

Shortly described, the biology of the parasite is as follows.
The spores, which are formed in the hymenial layer of the
subterranean sporophore, do not as a rule spread from the place
where they originate, unless they are brushed off by a passing
object. As sporophores are especially liable to be formed on
diseased roots at the point where they abut on mouse-holes,
it appears to be a likely supposition that the mice, or other
burrowing animals, carry away the spores on their fur, possibly
for long distances, and afterwards rub them off on healthy roots.
The spores soon germinate in warm humid air, and the mycelium, entering between the bark-scales, will probably reach
the living cortex at some point or other. From this time its
course of development is in two directions. It forces its way
into the wood, in which it very rapidly travels up the stem. The
contents of the parenchymatous cells are killed and turned
brown by the action of the ferment that is exuded by the
mycelium, while a violet colour in the wood is the visible
symptom of this stage of the decomposition. With the
disappearance of the protoplasmic contents of the cells the violet
colour is replaced by pale brownish yellow, except for a few
dark blotches which persist. The latter afterwards become surrounded by a white zone, and simultaneously the wood gradually
becomes lighter and more spongy. Ultimately numerous holes
are formed, the tissues become dismembered, sodden, and pale
brownish yellow, but never dark brown.

The hyphæ of the fungus travel upwards in the lumina of
the elements of the wood, and easily pierce the walls of the cells.
As they send off lateral branches they also invade the cells of
the medullary rays, as well as adjoining tracheides. As already
mentioned, the first perceptible change in the wood occurs in the
contents of the living cells, which become brown and partly
disappear. This is succeeded by the conversion of the lignified

cell-wall into cellulose, a change which begins on the side next the lumen, and advances outwards The cellulose is soon completely dissolved, and at last the delicate skeleton of the middle lamellæ also disappears At certain points this process proceeds with great rapidity. Here and there, for instance, one finds that the tracheides, in immediate proximity to the medullary rays, are filled with a brown fluid, which has probably originated in the latter, and which discolours and nourishes the mycelium to such an extent that a brown " mycelial nest " is formed So energetic is the action of the ferment in the neighbourhood of these bodies that the encrusting substances entirely disappear from the adjoining tracheides, which, to the distance of several millimeters, are completely transformed into cellulose, and thus become colourless—in other words, white Almost immediately after being converted into cellulose the middle lamella disappears entirely, and the individual elements of the wood thus become isolated, so that, when disturbed by a needle, they fall apart like the strands of asbestos Gradually they are dissolved, and holes, which are constantly increasing in size, are formed in the crumbly wood

While the mycelium thus decomposes the wood, sometimes to a height exceeding eight yards, the parasite advances much more slowly in the cortex, where its presence is betrayed by three distinct phenomena From the point of infection the mycelium spreads both towards the root-apices and towards the stem. It kills the cortex, and consequently the root, and when, after some years, it has reached the stem, it spreads from the stool on to roots that have hitherto remained sound. As soon as these are also attacked by the disease, the tree dies.

A second function of the mycelium that grows in the cortex consists in the formation of sporophores, which appear here and there between the bark-scales of the roots or stool These lead to the production of fresh seats of disease in the plantation, as has been already described

A third function is concerned with the spread of the disease subterraneously owing to infection by the mycelium Where a diseased root comes into contact with the sound root of an adjoining tree (Fig 121), or where the two are positively grown (grafted) together—as may very frequently be observed in a dense wood—the mycelium, which appears as a small cushion between the scales, grows into the cortex of the neighbouring tree. It is easy to induce infection artificially by taking a piece of cortex containing a portion of living mycelium still capable of growth, and binding it firmly to the cortex of the root of another tree.

Owing to the mycelium spreading subterraneously from tree to tree, these well-known gaps, which increase in size each year by the death of the marginal trees, appear in woods. At one time no reason whatever could be assigned for the peculiar behaviour of these gaps. On account of the decomposition of the wood proceeding rapidly and advancing far up the stem, and

FIG. 121.—The thinner root has been killed by *T. radiciperda*, and the stronger one has been infected at the point of contact. The disease has spread as far as the dark shading. One eighth natural size.

as it is succeeded by the death of the tree, the disease is to be classed with the most dangerous forms of "red-rot." It is very abundant in the pine forests of North Germany,[*] and quite as much so in the spruce woods, especially where these are situated in hilly districts. There is this difference to be noted, however, that when pines are killed by the parasite it is usually only their roots that are affected and rotten, the stem, with the exception of the stool, showing no signs of decomposition. The wood of the stool is generally strongly impregnated with resin, and I believe I am right in concluding that it is the abundant resinous contents of the pine, which are especially prominent in the lower part of the stem, that form a barrier to the upward growth of the mycelium of the fungus. In the case of the spruce, on the other hand, and of the Weymouth pine, which is poor in resin, decomposition of the wood spreads high into the stem.

It appears to be necessary to keep a watchful eye upon coniferous woods at all stages of their growth, so that diseased or dead trees may be instantly removed. In the case of the older woods, one may isolate the diseased spots by surrounding them with narrow trenches, and by severing all roots that may be encountered. In order to attain this end we must, of course,

* [It is also by no means uncommon in this country.—ED.]

form the trenches at such a distance from the diseased gaps as to warrant the assumption that all trees already infected are included in the isolated area As a rule it suffices to include the trees nearest to the margin of the gap If the workman notices that a dead root crosses the trench, then it will be necessary at that point to divert the course of the trench farther into the wood, otherwise the labour will be in vain Although this operation is a certain preventive when it is properly performed, its careful supervision is so difficult when conducted on a large scale that I am doubtful if a general adoption of the practice is to be recommended in commercial sylviculture The objection that the sporophores develop in the trenches does not appear tenable, because it is a simple matter to examine the trenches once a year and to remove such sporophores * When the fungus appears at many points in a wood, even the most careful isolating is of no avail The gaps should either be filled up with dicotyledonous trees, or if, for any reason, this is deemed impracticable and conifers must be employed, then the young trees must be carefully watched so that infected plants may be rooted out and the disease be promptly checked

TRAMETES PINI[1]

This parasite is exceedingly abundant in the pine woods of North Germany.† In South Germany, where it is less common, it is met with chiefly in spruce woods It also occurs in the spruce woods of the Harz, the Thuringian Forest, and Schleswig, as well as in the larch and silver fir woods of the Riesengebirge

It produces a so-called bark-shake, ring-shake, or heart-shake, which nearly always commences at a branch, and therefore usually in the crown of a tree

The brown woody sporophores, which attain an age of fifty years, vary in shape between an incrustation and a bracket. In the case of pines and larches they occur only on the part of a stem where a branch has fallen off (Fig 122), while in spruces

---

[1] R Hartig, *Wichtige Krankheiten der Waldbaume*, p 43 *Zersetzungserscheinungen des Holzes*, p 32, Tables V. and VII

*[If Brefeld's account of the conidial fructification is correct, this may be a more difficult matter than appears —ED]

†[Also occurs in this country —ED.]

and silver firs they may spring directly from the bark as
well.

The spores which are annually produced in these sporophores
are scattered by the wind, and should they gain a footing on a
fresh branch-wound which is not protected by a covering of
resin they push their germ-tube into the stem, and the mycelium

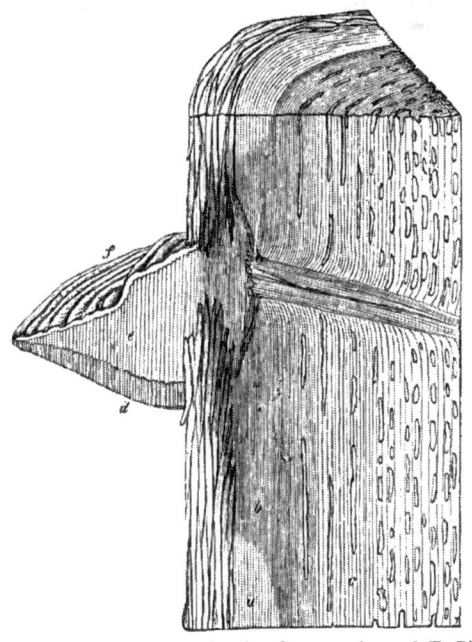

FIG. 122.—Part of the stem of a pine bearing the sporophore of *T. Pini*. *a*, healthy
alburnum ; *b*, wood saturated with resin in the neighbourhood of the sporophore ; *c*, decomposed wood ; *d*, the canals in which the spores are produced ;
e, older canals which have become filled up by fungus-tissue ; *f*, the upper
surface marked by zones. One half natural size.

spreads partly upwards and partly downwards. The younger
class of trees enjoy immunity from infection, because in their
case wounds are very quickly protected by an exudation of
turpentine. From the time when the heart-wood becomes
comparatively dry, turpentine ceases to exude from the central
part of a branch-wound, and this consequently becomes liable to
attack from the spores of the fungus. This accounts for the

disease not usually appearing upon trees younger than fifty
years.

The mycelium shows a preference for growing longitudinally in
the stem, while its distribution horizontally is most pronounced
in some particular annual ring. On this
account decay often takes the form of ring-
shake—that is to say, it is most pronounced
in peripheral zones which encircle a part or
the whole of the stem. At first the wood
becomes somewhat deeper red brown in
colour, and then white blotches or holes
appear here and there. In the case of
the pine especially, these are largely confined to the spring wood of some particular annual ring, in which they enlarge
parallel to the longitudinal axis of the
stem, the result being that the resinous
zone of autumn wood may persist alone
for a long time, until it also is destroyed
by decomposition.

A resinous zone is formed along the
boundary between the alburnum and the
decomposed wood, and this interferes with
the outward progress of the mycelium of
the fungus. In those specimens which I
have examined, this zone is absent only in
the comparatively non-resinous silver fir
and in spruce-branches, and thus, in their
case, the fungus is able to reach and penetrate the cortex with ease. The action of
the ferment of the parasite produces white
spots, similar to those that have been described in the case of *T. radiciperda*. The
lignin is extracted from the cell-walls, and
pure cellulose is left. The middle lamella

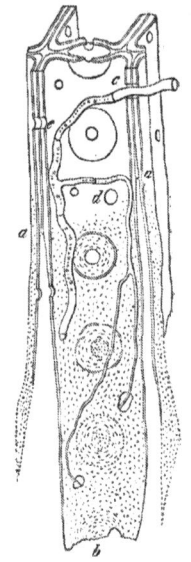

FIG. 123.—A tracheid
of *P. sylvestris* which
has been decomposed
by *T. Pini*. The prim-
ary cell-wall has been
completely dissolved as
far as *a a*. In the lower
portion of the figure the
secondary and tertiary
walls consist of cellu-
lose alone, in which
granules of lime are
distinctly recognizable,
b; filaments penetrate
the walls and leave
holes behind, *d, e.*

is completely dissolved as soon as the lignin disappears, and
thus the tracheids become isolated before being finally dissolved
(Fig. 123, *a a* to *b*). The lamella which is nearest to and bounds
the lumen persists the longest, and before it is dissolved the

O

ash-constituents of the wall impart to it a finely granulated appearance

The fungus is only in a position to produce sporophores when it has developed luxuriantly in the interior of the tree In that case the mycelium pushes its way outwards at a place where the base of a dead branch opens a passage through the alburnum At such a place the sporophores are produced, and should these be forcibly removed a number of new ones are, as a rule, formed in a short time

It is thus seen that nothing is gained by removing the sporophores, but trees infested by the fungus should always be removed in the thinnings and other fellings We thus remove the danger of infection, and utilize the trees before they are rendered entirely valueless by the advancing decomposition It frequently happens that, although fungi are visible on the upper region of the tree, the disease has not extended down to the lower and valuable part of the stem, so that, after cutting off the upper portion, some good useful timber is available. If one waits till the final felling before removing the fungus-infested trees, all that one gets is very worthless rotten wood Of course a stop must also be put to pilferers breaking or sawing off green branches, as this practice increases the probabilities of infection. Old branches that have died naturally cannot be attacked by the fungus

This disease is most prevalent in the neighbourhood of towns and villages, where the pilfering of branches is common, and in woods that are much exposed to the wind, and where, consequently, branches are frequently broken off.

POLYPORUS HARTIGII (ALL)

When I first described this parasite of the silver fir and spruce, I made the remark, "Whether this is a new species distinct from *Polyporus fulvus* can only be decided by a careful study of the allied species of this genus In the meantime it may pass under the name of *P fulvus*."[1] Since then it has been recognized as an undoubtedly new species, and has been introduced into the literature of the subject by Herr Allaschen under the name *P. Hartigii.*

[1] R. Hartig, *Die Zersetzungserscheinungen des Holzes*, p 40

This fungus produces a kind of white-rot in silver firs and spruces, and is very frequently encountered in association with *Æcidium elatinum* Apparently infection is most liable to occur naturally on those parts of the cancerous swellings where the cortex has ruptured and exposed the wood The mycelium, which is at first very vigorous, is yellowish in colour, and produces numerous short lateral branches, which are twisted in a worm-like manner, and are apt to fill up the cavities of the bordered pits of the tracheids. This vigorous mycelium gives off a few exceedingly delicate lateral hyphæ, which bore through the walls, in which they form very minute holes Only in the later stages of decomposition is the disappearance of the middle lamella effected, after which the inner walls are also dissolved, having first been greatly attenuated and then temporarily isolated At this stage the mycelium is of extraordinary fineness The wood of the silver fir appears yellowish, clear oblong patches being observable if carefully looked for on a smooth surface The vigorous yellow hyphæ induce the formation of narrow dark lines at the boundary of the sound wood

As the silver fir cannot form a strongly resinous zone, it is unable to prevent the progress of the mycelium into the youngest layers of wood The mycelium consequently grows outwards with ease into the cortex, and, having advanced far enough, it produces the sporophores on the surface These are at first hemispherical, but in the course of years they become more and more bracket-like in shape. Externally they are yellowish brown on the hymenial surface, but elsewhere they are ashy grey, almost smooth, display no zones, and are beset with exceedingly minute punctures or pits. The interior, which is tawny and lustrous, shows distinct zones, except in the region of the pore-canals, which increase in length each year at their lower extremity

As it is found that silver firs with cancerous swellings sooner or later break at the diseased spot owing to snow or storms, it has become the custom in many districts—for instance, in the Black Forest in Wurtemberg—to fell all cankered trees during the thinnings, even when such trees belong to the larger class. In this way the spread of *Polyporus Hartigii* can best be prevented

POLYPORUS BOREALIS[1] *

This fungus produces an exceedingly characteristic form of white-rot in the spruce. In the Salzburg and Bavarian Alps, and in the spruce woods near Munich, it is the commonest form of decomposition in the spruce, and I have also noticed it in the Harz. Infection takes place, and the sporophores are produced, above ground. On account of their white colour the sporophores are conspicuous even at a distance. They are annual, more or less bracket-shaped, and frequently superimposed the one above the other and grown together. They are very watery, somewhat sodden on the upper surface, and destitute of zones.

The colour of the wood is but little altered by the decomposition. It becomes brownish yellow, and horizontally disposed holes filled with mycelium appear in vertical rows in the spring wood. These holes, which stand 1 to 1½ mm. apart, impart to the wood an appearance which reminds one of the finest graphic granite. The wood constantly becomes lighter and more friable, but the peculiar appearance is retained till the end of the final stage of decomposition.

Should the wood be exposed, without drying, when decomposition is beginning, the mycelium will grow outwards to form a white skin, the mycelial strands of which are chiefly disposed in a horizontal direction.

Growth and decomposition are in several ways characteristic. The hyphæ, which in the first stage of decomposition are yellow and stout (Fig. 124, a, b), are replaced by more delicate filamentous mycelia as decomposition proceeds, until at last the hyphæ which are formed can only be seen by the aid of a very powerful microscope. The mycelium has a marked tendency to grow to some extent in a horizontal direction, at right angles to the long axis of the elements (Fig. 124, t), the chief result being the formation of the above-mentioned horizontal holes in the wood. Why these are formed only at definite distances from each other I have not been able to determine. Dissolution of the

---

[1] R. Hartig, *Zersetzungserscheinungen*, pp. 54 *et seq.*
* [This is quoted as a British species.—ED.]

cell-wall begins at the lumen and proceeds outwards, being preceded by the conversion of certain layers of lignin into cellulose.

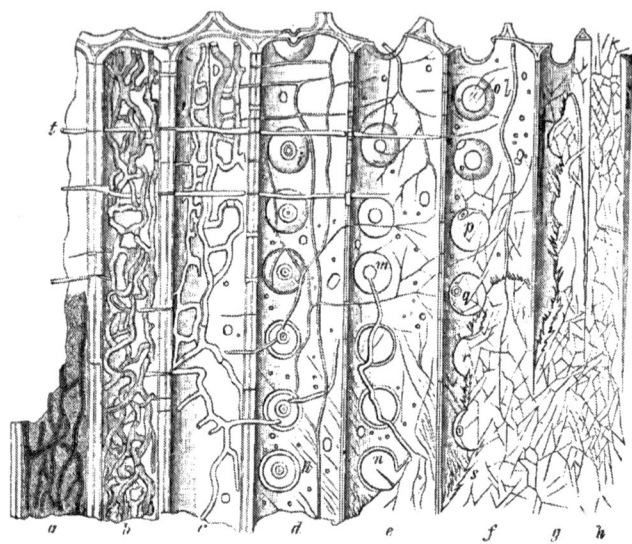

FIG. 124.—Decomposition of spruce timber by *P. borealis*. *a*, a vigorous mycelium in a tracheid containing a brownish yellow solution which has originated in the medullary rays. In *b* and *c* the mycelia are still brown in colour and very vigorous. At *d* and *e* the walls are much attenuated and perforated, and the mycelia, not being so well nourished, are very delicate. At *f* the pits are almost entirely destroyed. At *g* and *h* only traces of the walls remain. The destruction of the bordered pits is to be followed from *i* to *r*. At *i* the bordered pit is still intact, at *k* one wall of the lenticular chamber has been largely destroyed, its inner boundary being marked by a circle. At *l* one side of the bordered pit has entirely disappeared. A series of pits is shown from *m* to *n*, in each of which only a single delicate wall has been preserved—namely, that which is provided with the closing membrane. In preparing the section a crack has formed in this wall. From *o* to *r* pits are shown where both of the walls have been partially or completely dissolved, and only at *p* and *q* does one perceive the thickened portion of the closing membrane. At *s* one can plainly see the spiral structure of both cell-walls, which when united form the common wall between two tracheids. At *t* mycelia are to be seen traversing the tracheids horizontally.

The thin middle lamella persists longest, being converted into cellulose and dissolved only after the internal portion of the wall has entirely disappeared.

POLYPORUS VAPORARIUS [1] *

The decomposition produced by this and the following parasite, *P. Schweinitzii*, bears a very strong resemblance to that caused by the dry-rot fungus *Merulius lacrymans*.

P. vaporarius is exceedingly common on spruces and pines, both roots and wounds above ground being attacked. It very frequently effects an entrance through a wound due to the barking of red deer. The wood becomes reddish brown, dry, and fissured, and as time goes on the resemblance to half-charred timber becomes more and more apparent. When rubbed between the fingers it crumbles into yellow dust. The mycelium is specially liable to develop in cracks, or between the dead wood and the bark, in the form of snow-white much-branched woolly felted strands, similar to many of the mycelial growths of *Merulius lacrymans*. Although I have made no direct observations on the point, still I think it probable that the mycelial strands which grow on dead roots and stools may convey the disease subterraneously to adjoining trees. The sporophores, which are pure white, form incrustations, but never brackets. These originate on decayed wood or dead bark, or on luxuriant mycelial growths or strands. This fungus very frequently appears on the timber of buildings where, on account of its luxuriant mycelial growths, which have sometimes a fasciated, sometimes a strand-like appearance, it is usually confounded with *Merulius lacrymans*, whose mycelial growths, however, always assume an ashy grey colour shortly after being formed. As regards its importance as an agent in inducing decay in buildings, I may refer to the remarks which I shall have to offer when discussing *M. lacrymans*.

POLYPORUS SCHWEINITZII †

In describing this parasite in *Zersetzungserscheinungen des Holzes* [2] I have called it *Polyporus mollis*. This mistake was

[1] R. Hartig, *Zersetzungserscheinungen*, pp. 45 *et seq.*, and Table VIII.

[2] P. 49.

* [Very common on dead wood, and I have found it on the decayed wood of a green-house.—ED.]

† [Quoted as British.—ED.]

due to my having access only to old dry sporophores, which rendered the correct identification difficult. In the interval Professor Magnus has correctly identified the fungus as *P. Schweinitzii*. It appears on the Scotch pine, the Weymouth pine, and the larch.

The decomposition which it produces very closely resembles that due to the preceding species, but in the present case the white branching mycelial strands are absent, the mycelium at most growing out of the fissures as a fine chalky incrustation. The smell of the wood, which is very characteristic and intense, reminds one of the smell of turpentine, without however being perfectly identical.

The sporophores, which appear on the dead wood or project from the bark-fissures of living trees, take the form of reddish brown cushions, which afterwards assume a somewhat bracket-like shape. The porous layer, which is yellowish green when young, assumes a deep red colour if ever so slightly abraded.

As decomposition advances the tracheids exhibit spiral cracks and fissures (Fig. 125). Apparently these cracks are due to the shrinkage of the wall-substance, which always remains fairly dry. It is owing to these cracks that the wood is so easily pulverised.

P. vaporarius also induces cracks and fissures in the cell-walls, but, instead of extending completely round the cell-lumen, these are small, and are arranged in large numbers in vertical rows.

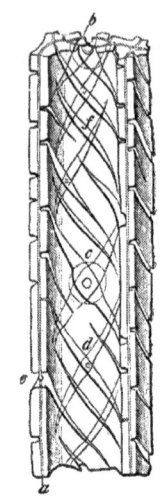

FIG. 125.—Tracheid of *Pinus* destroyed by *P. Schweinitzii*. The cellulose has been largely extracted, the walls consisting chiefly of lignin. Cracks occur in the secondary wall when dry, while the primary wall, *a b*, remains intact. The spiral structure of the secondary wall is the cause of the fissures in the walls of adjoining cells crossing at the bordered pits, *c*, and at the punctures, *d*, *e*. Where pits and punctures are absent the fissures are simple, *f*.

POLYPORUS SULPHUREUS[1]*

This is one of the most widely distributed parasites of the oak, *Robinia*, alder, tree-willows, poplars, walnut, and pear   It also occurs as a parasite on the common larch   Infection takes place through a branch-wound, and the mycelium spreads rapidly in the wood, causing it to become red brown and dry   The wood reveals numerous cracks, into which the mycelium grows, to form large sheets of felted hyphæ.   In the case of dicotyledonous trees the vessels become filled, in the early stages of decomposition, with a dense fungoid growth, so that, on a transverse section, they appear as white spots, and, on a longitudinal section, as white lines.   The walls of the elements of the wood become brown and very rich in carbon, and shrink greatly, but on being treated with dilute caustic potash they swell up and become almost completely dissolved   The spiral cracks, which always ascend from right to left in the interior of the fibres, never extend into the middle lamella

Whenever old snags, or any kind of wound, admit of the mycelium reaching the surface, a group of sporophores is annually formed   These are succulent, of a pale sulphur-yellow colour beneath, and pale reddish yellow on their upper surface, and by their size and strikingly luminous colour they readily attract attention   The pileus is internally of a white colour and cheesy consistency   The pores reveal a hymenial layer with clavate basidia   The mycelium of this fungus very frequently develops numerous round gonidia in the wood itself, and during my early investigations on this parasite I regarded these as belonging to a different species of fungus   It very frequently happens that before diseased trees are overthrown by storms, their tissues, on one side or other, die as far out as the bark, and the latter, withering, drops off and allows the red-brown decayed wood to fall out from the inside of the tree   Thus it is not impossible that the gonidia may be carried into the air along with the dust of the decayed wood, and so assist in the distribution of the parasite

---

[1] R Hartig, *Zersetzungserscheinungen*, pp 110 *et seq*   De Seynes, *Recherches pour servir à l'histoire naturelle des végétaux inférieurs*, 1888

* [Very common in this country. I have frequently collected it in Windsor Park and elsewhere —ED.]

POLYPORUS IGNIARIUS [1] *

This is the parasite most frequently met with on the majority of dicotyledonous trees. My investigations on its destructive effects on wood have been conducted for the most part on the oak.

Infection may occur on branches or on bark-wounds, and the mycelium spreads rapidly in the wood. At first the wood assumes a deep brown colour, and this is succeeded by yellowish white decomposition, which is the commonest kind of white-rot in the oak. The yellowish white wood constantly becomes lighter and softer, and resembles in its properties the cellulose that is used in paper-making. The hyphæ, which are at first very strong and afterwards extremely delicate, completely fill up the elements, and induce a form of decomposition which is characterised by the inner layers of the walls being converted into cellulose and dissolved, before the middle lamella, which persists for a long time as a delicate skeleton, undergoes similar changes. It will thus be seen that the process of decomposition bears a close resemblance to that described under *P. borealis.* The sporophores, which usually spring directly from bark that is infested by the mycelium, are at first hemispherical, but afterwards become more or less hoof-shaped. Although they are familiar enough, it may be mentioned that they differ from those of *P. Hartigii,* which they resemble in external appearance, by exhibiting concentric zones, and frequently cracks as well, on their upper surface, while internally the layers of pores are also interrupted by the zones.

POLYPORUS DRYADEUS [2] †

This fungus of the oak produces a form of decomposition in which oblong yellowish or white blotches occur, surrounded by firm wood which displays the original colour of the duramen.

---

[1] R. Hartig, *Zersetzungserscheinungen,* pp. 114 *et seq.,* and Tables XV. and XVI.

[2] *Ibid.,* pp. 124 *et seq.,* and Table XVII.

*[One of the commonest fungi in Windsor Park and neighbourhood, especially on old Beeches.—ED.]

†[Common in Britain.—ED.]

The white blotches consist of elements which have been con-
veited into cellulose, and which have become isolated by the
solution of the middle lamella   The yellowish parts, on the
other hand, reveal a form of decomposition of the cells which
is exceedingly like that due to *P. igniarius*, and which is cha-
racteiised by the middle lamella persisting the longest   The
white patches are the first to be dissolved, and thus holes, surrounded by very hard sides, are formed   When freely exposed
to the air the wood assumes a cinnamon brown colour, and is
replaced by a mass of firm biòwn hyphæ.

The large hoof-shaped annual sporophores are of a cinnamon
brown colour, and appear on the bark or on the spots previously
occupied by branches   They possess so little durability that
one but seldom meets with a perfect specimen

Should *P. dryadeus* and *P. igniarius* simultaneously attack an
oak, and should their hyphæ come into contact, a peculiar kind
of decomposition occurs along the line where the hyphæ of the
two species meet • The wood becomes yellowish white, the
decomposition being similar in appearance to that which is
induced by *P igniarius* alone   All the longer medullary rays,
however, are represented by snow-white bands, which, on being
investigated, are often found to consist of nothing but unaltered
starch-grains, while the cell-walls have been almost entirely
dissolved, or have been converted into cellulose

HYDNUM DIVERSIDENS [1] *

A parasite is frequently met with on oaks and beeches whose
yellowish white sporophore takes the form of an incrustation or
bracket, and which is distinguished by the hymenium being
disposed on downward-directed spines of unequal length   The
hymenium, which is at first simple, periodically increases in
thickness by the hyphæ growing through the last layer to form
a new hymenium   In the lower portion of the spines especially
this process is repeated five to eight times, the result being that
the spines increase greatly in thickness, and the hymenium
displays five to eight layers.

In this case also the decomposition, which spreads from

[1] R. Hartig, *Zersetzungserscheinungen*, pp. 97 *et seq*, and Table XII
*[This is also British —Ed]

infected wounds on the stem, takes the form of a white-rot. The colour is yellowish ashy grey, alternating with stripes of a pale brown colour, which generally persist longest in the medullary rays. In the later stages of decomposition snow-white masses of felted mycelium occur where a zone of spring wood is much decayed.

The peculiarity of the action of the ferment consists in the inner layers of the cell-walls swelling up into a gelatinous mass, without being converted into cellulose, before they are completely dissolved ; the middle lamellæ being the last to disappear.

THELEPHORA PERDIX[1] *

A form of disease which is very common in the oak throughout the whole of Germany is known as "partridge wood," on account of the peculiar discoloration which it induces in the wood, and which reminds one of the white-speckled feathers met with on certain parts of the body of the partridge. At first the diseased wood assumes a deep red brown colour, and then white blotches on a dark ground make their appearance which stand in a certain relationship to the large medullary rays. These blotches afterwards become transformed into sharply defined cavities with a white lining. As the cavities, which are separated from each other by firm brown wood partitions, increase in size, the wood looks as though it had been attacked by ants, and, as a matter of fact, the symptoms are often mistaken for the work of these creatures. It is to be noted that each cavity usually remains distinct until the stage of complete decomposition is reached. In the wood of the oak the mycelium first induces the contents of the parenchymatous organs to become brown. Gradually proceeding inwards, the starch-grains fail to give a blue reaction with iodine, colourless granules persisting for some time in the central cells of the medullary rays, until they also are at last destroyed (Fig. 126).

Where the white blotches make their appearance, as also in the partitions of the white cavities, all the organs are converted into cellulose, and the middle lamellæ being dissolved the

[1] R. Hartig, *Zersetzungserscheinungen*, pp. 103 *et seq.*

* [I do not know this as British, but a specimen of diseased wood sent from India was marked in exactly the way Hartig describes.—ED.]

individual elements of the wood become isolated (Fig. 126, *e—h*). It is remarkable that the process of decomposition in the neighbourhood of the cavities undergoes a change when these have become enlarged. The latter no longer appear white but greyish yellow, and reveal abundant felted mycelia, which pierce the walls at numerous places. Instead of a conversion into

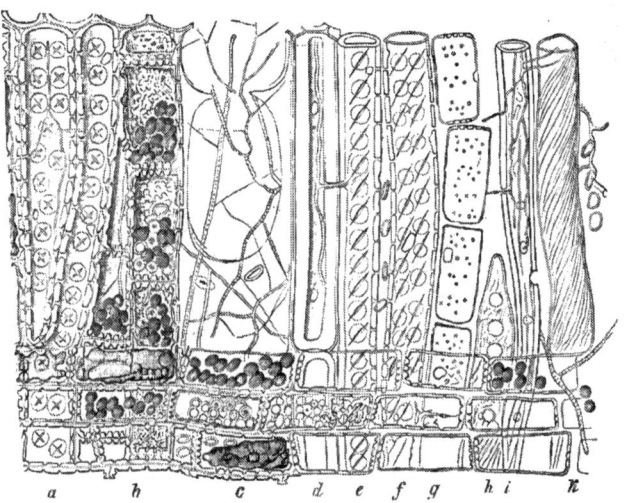

FIG. 126.—Decomposition of oak induced by *T. Perdix*. *a*, tracheids containing some filamentous mycelia, and showing a few perforations on their walls ; *b*, wood-parenchyma containing starch which is partly undergoing solution, the outer granules being the first to disappear ; *c*, vessels containing hyphæ of the fungus ; *d*, sclerenchymatous fibres containing fungus-filaments, and showing perforations in the walls ; *e* and *f*, tracheids which are completely isolated by the solution of the primary wall. The thickened rings of the bordered pits are also seen to be isolated between the tracheids. As the elements are isolated, the cracks no longer cross at the bordered pits. *g*, cells of wood-parenchyma which are completely isolated and almost completely dissolved ; *h*, a tracheid just before final solution ; *i*, sclerenchymatous fibre much decomposed ; *k*, a tracheid whose wall has been dismembered by cracks before being dissolved.

cellulose resulting, the wood-substance is dissolved, partly by the enlargement of the perforations and partly by the centrifugal attenuation of the cell-walls.

The sporophores of the parasite occur as incrustations in fissures or other cavities in the diseased wood, or on the outside of dead branches. The incrustations, which vary in thickness from $\frac{1}{25}$ to $\frac{2}{5}$ inch, are brownish yellow in colour, and consist of a layer of hyphæ disposed at right angles to the surface. The hyphæ end in somewhat club-shaped basidia, which are covered by peculiar hair-like outgrowths. Only a certain number of the basidia produce spores (four in each case), those which remain sterile producing a new hymenium in a succeeding period of growth, and in doing so they anastomose here and there by lateral budding. On a transverse section a sporophore, depending on its age, shows more or less distinct strata, of which only the youngest possesses a pale colour, the others being of a deep brown hue. When dead the whole of the sporophore appears dark brown.

STEREUM HIRSUTUM [1] *

A very striking and characteristic form of decomposition in the oak is produced by *S. hirsutum*. In practice such wood is called "yellow piped" or "white piped." Usually a brown colour first makes its appearance in certain concentric zones, which to begin with are confined to one side but afterwards encircle the whole of the stem, and later on a longitudinal section will show detached snow-white or yellow stripes which appear as white spots on a cross section ("fly wood"). When the oxygen of the air has free access, as in the alburnum, branch-snags, &c., the whole of the wood is frequently converted into a uniform yellow mass. It scarcely seems to admit of doubt that this fungus also plays an important part as a saprophyte, and finds its way on to branches that are dying naturally. In the white stripes the mycelium converts the wood into cellulose, and when the middle lamella disappears the elements become isolated. In the yellow parts of the wood, on the other hand, the solvent action proceeds from the lumen outwards, as in the case of *P. igniarius*, and this is not preceded by a conversion into cellulose. The sporophores, which usually develop on the bark, appear first as a crust, but afterwards their upper edge—which is brown, faintly zoned, and covered with stiff hairs —projects in a distinctly horizontal direction.

[1] R. Hartig, *Zersetzungserscheinungen*, pp. 129 *et seq.*, Table XVIII.
*[Very common in England.—ED.]

POLYPORUS FOMENTARIUS *

The familiar tinder-fungus, which occurs on beeches and oaks, produces a form of white-rot, and its mycelium has a tendency to form luxuriant patch-like or skin-like growths in fissures of the decayed wood. So far it has not been made the subject of thorough investigation

POLYPORUS BETULINUS [1] †

Occasionally *P. betulinus* is to be found abundantly developed on the birch. Its hirsute sporophore, which is white beneath and brownish grey above, is at first globular, but afterwards takes the form of an inverted bracket with a convex upper surface The decomposition induced by the parasite is a form of red-rot

POLYPORUS LÆVIGATUS [2]

This parasite produces a form of white-rot in the birch Its sporophore appears on the surface of the bark as a dark brown porous incrustation

Numerous other species of *Polyporus* doubtless occur as parasites on the wood of trees, but these, so far, have not been subjected to investigation

The following fungi are also worthy of mention *Dædalea quercina* ‡ is met with everywhere on old oak-stumps, where it forms large bracket-like sporophores which bear the hymenium partly in pores and partly on lamellæ During decomposition the oak-wood assumes a grey brown colour Having found the fungus vigorously developed on branch-wounds of the older classes of oaks, I suspect that it is also a parasite

Fistulina hepatica the Beef-steak Fungus, produces a deep red brown decomposition in the wood of the oak

All the above-mentioned wood-parasites, which obtain an entrance through wounds above ground, can only be combated in one or other of the following ways First, great care must be

---

[1] D H Mayr, *Bot Centralblatt*, 1885   [2] *Ibid.*

* [Common in Britain.—ED]

† [I have frequently collected this in this (Cooper's Hill) part of England —ED]

‡ [Both this and the next occur in Surrey and elsewhere in Britain.—ED]

taken to do nothing that will cause the formation of wounds in trees, of which more will be said in the section on wounds ; and, secondly, where wounds are intentionally produced on trees, as in pruning, the necessary prophylactic measures must be at once put in force, and in particular an antiseptic dressing in the form of a covering of tar should be provided

At the same time woods should be kept tidy and free from decaying wood, which may bear the sporophores of parasites, but this must not be taken to mean that all old oaks that are already decayed are to be felled without regard to other considerations   For the sake of effect the forester should allow old trees and picturesque bits of timber to stand where deemed desirable in the neighbourhood of frequented paths, even although the benefits of so doing may not be at once manifest in the shape of hard cash

AGARICUS MELLEUS [1]* THE HONEY AGARIC

This fungus belongs to the most widely distributed and destructive of parasites   It lives parasitically on all European conifers, besides destroying those that have been introduced from Japan, America, &c, and I have even recognized it in the fossil wood of *Cupressinoxylon*   Amongst dicotyledonous trees it appears to occur as a parasite on *Prunus avium* and *P. domestica*, while as a saprophyte it is to be met with everywhere, not only on the dead roots and stools of all dicotyledonous and coniferous trees, but also on the structural timber of bridges, conduits, mines, &c   It has frequently been asserted that it also occurs as a parasite of the vine, but I have had no opportunity to convince myself of the correctness of this view   Those rhizomorphs whose occurrence I have hitherto observed on the vine belonged to *Dematophora necatrix.*

The disease often manifests itself on plants only three to five years old, though it also destroys spruces, pines, &c., a century old.   One recognizes it by removing the bark at the collar

---

[1] R Hartig, *Wichtige Krankheiten der Waldbäume*, 1874, pp 12 *et seq* , Tables I. and II.   R. Hartig, *Zersetzungserscheinungen*, pp 59 *et seq* , Table XI , Figs 1—5.

*[This is one of the commonest of British fungi, and its rhizomorphs and sporophores are well known --ED]

and on the roots, when a firm snow-white mycelium (Fig. 127, *c c*) is observed, which, in the case of the older class of trees, sometimes ascends under the bark while the tree is still alive to the height of ten feet or more. Brownish black lustrous strands, $\frac{1}{25}$ to $\frac{1}{12}$ inch in thickness, which occasionally anastomose, are observed in greater or less abundance adhering to the roots. These are met with in conjunction with the sheets of white mycelium under the cortex, though sometimes they merely embrace the roots externally.

A great deal of turpentine and resin frequently adheres to the outside of the stronger roots, and this, mixing with the particles of soil, forms a firm mass round the collar (Fig. 128). The diseased trees speedily succumb, and are seldom to be recognized more than a year before their death by their pale colour or stunted shoots. If we carefully dig up a plant that appears to be perfectly healthy, in the immediate neighbourhood of one that is manifestly diseased or dead, we will as a rule discover on the roots one or more places of infection where a black rhizomorph strand has bored into the cortex (Fig. 127, *a*). When the cortex is carefully removed the strand will be observed expanding from the place of entrance into a snow-white body (Fig. 127, *b*), which spreads in the cortical tissues and causes browning and death, as far as it reaches (Fig. 127, *c c*). The mycelium that grows in the living cortex

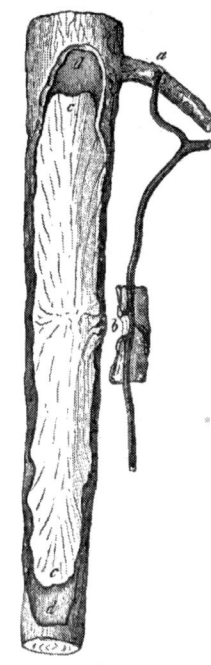

FIG. 127.—The living root of a spruce, showing two spots, *a*, *b*, where the rhizomorph has entered and infected the cortex. The cortex has been removed from the larger root, *d* to *d*, in order to show the mycelium, *c c*, which has gained an entrance at *b*.

is characterised by its fasciated and skin-like appearance. It very easily resumes the round strand-like form, which may either grow to the outside of the roots or proceed to develop between the wood and cortex. When, owing to the death of the tree, the shrinkage of the cortex affords space for the development of these strands, they anastomose abundantly, like so many twigs, and envelop the wood of the stem in a reticulate fashion. The rhizomorphs that spring from the roots progress underneath the surface of the ground, at a depth seldom exceeding four inches, and bore into any sound roots of conifers that they may encounter, and thus the disease is spread from tree to tree (Fig. 127). In autumn, from the end of August till

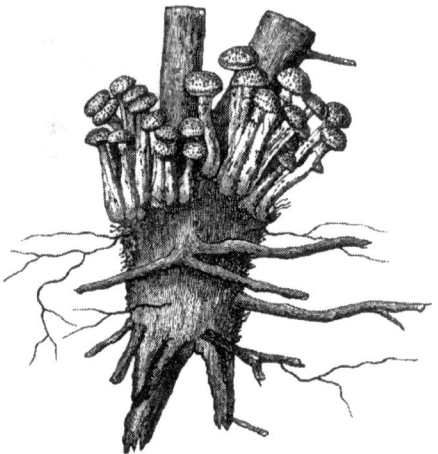

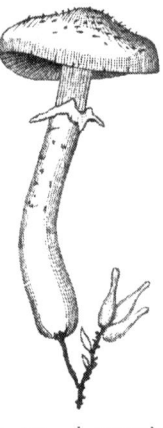

FIG. 128.—A young pine which has been killed by *A. melleus.* Numerous sporophores are seen which have broken through the cortex at the surface of the ground. Branching rhizomorph-strands are present on the roots.

FIG. 129.—A sporophore of *A. melleus* which has developed on a rhizomorph, a lateral branch of which has produced only abortive sporophores.

October, the large familiar sporophores (Fig. 129) may be observed developing on the rhizomorphs which grow independently in the ground, or projecting from the cortex, especially the collar (Fig. 128), of trees that have been killed by the parasite. For further details I may refer to what I have published in the works already alluded to. The white spores of this Hymenomycete, which are spread either by the wind or by being brushed off by passing objects, develop first of all a filamentous mycelium, and from this the mycelium form designated *Rhizomorpha* is produced, as is easily proved by

P

sowing the spores in a decoction of plums. The pathological
symptoms can only be explained in the light of the peculiar
organization of the mycelial growth that lives in the cortical
tissues.   The apex of the rhizomorphs (Fig. 130) consists of
delicate pseudo-parenchyma, which, elongating by the division
and growth of the cells, produces delicate hyphæ on the inside
at a certain distance from the point, whereby a felted tissue,
called the medulla, is produced in the interior. The outer parts
of the pseudo-parenchyma (Fig. 130, c), on the other hand,
coalesce to form the so-called rind (Fig. 131, d), which when
young gives off numerous delicate hyphæ, and these, taking
advantage of the medullary rays, penetrate the wood, and
especially the resin-ducts, should such be present. In the wood
the growth is upwards. This filamentous mycelium, which
progresses much more rapidly in the interior of the wood
than the rhizomorphs which grow in the cortex, completely
destroys the parenchyma that exists in the neighbourhood of
the resin-ducts, and to all appearance this is accompanied
by a partial conversion of the cell-contents and the cell-walls
into turpentine (Fig. 131). The turpentine sinks down under
its own weight, and in the collar, where the cortex is
withered, having been killed by the rhizomorphs, it streams
outwards, pouring partly in between the wood and the cortex,
and partly into the surrounding soil at places where the cortex
has ruptured owing to drying. On this account the disease was
formerly called " Resin-flux " or " Resin-glut." In the upper
parts of the stem, where the cambium and cortex are still sound,
the turpentine also flows laterally, by means of the ducts of the
medullary rays, from the injured canals towards the cambium and
cortex.   In the latter this accumulation induces the formation of
large resin-blisters. When, during the summer, the cambium is
forming a new ring, the plethora of resin has the effect of causing
the production of numerous resin-canals, which are unusually
large and abnormally constructed, and these impart to the wood-
ring formed during the year of sickness a very striking and
characteristic appearance.

   The mycelium gradually spreads from the cells of the
medullary rays and from the resin-ducts into the vascular
elements of the wood, where it produces a form of decay which

may be termed a variety of white-rot. During the progress of the decomposition from the surface of the stem inwards a certain stage is reached, which is highly favourable to the

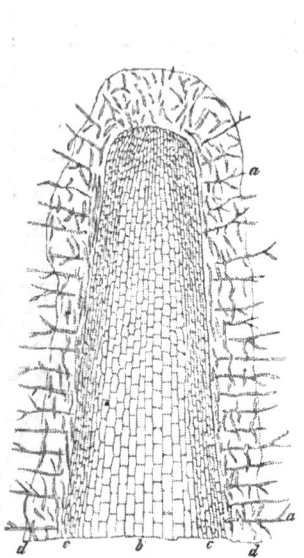

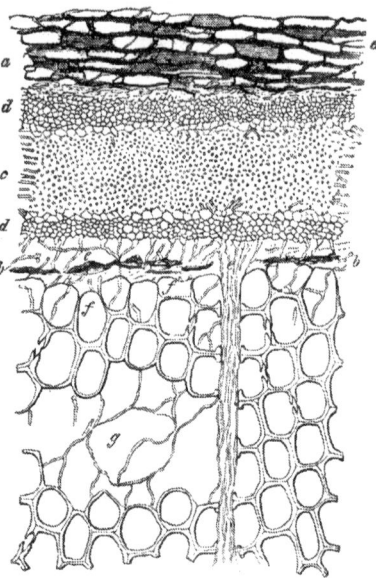

FIG. 130.—Longitudinal section through the apex of a rhizomorph from the outer hyphæ of which numerous hair-like filaments, *a a*, spring. In the interior the central cells enlarge greatly, *b*, at a short distance from the apex, while the cells of the hyphæ situated towards the periphery, *c*, remain smaller, to form the pseudo-parenchyma of the "rind"; *d d* indicates the boundary of the mucilaginous layer which envelops the strand.

FIG. 131.—Transverse section through the cortex and wood of a pine-root which has been killed by a rhizomorph. *a*, the dead tissues of the bast; *b*, the dead cambium; *c*, the medulla of the rhizomorph; the pseudo-parenchyma of the rind he rhizomorph; *e e*, filamentous hæ which have grown from the rhizomorph into the wood; *f*, dead immature wood-cells; *g*, a resin-duct which has been completely destroyed, the parenchymatous cells which surround it being also dissolved.

development of the mycelium. While previously it was simply filiform and furnished with numerous lateral hyphæ, it now develops large bladder-like swellings, and at the same time the hyphæ change into a kind of large-meshed parenchyma, which, like the tyloses in the vessels of many dicotyledonous trees, completely fills up the lumina of the tracheides. On account of the mycelium assuming a brown colour when in this condition, it makes the portion of diseased wood which it infests appear to the naked eye like a black line. As this kind of mycelium soon dies off and is dissolved, being replaced by a delicate filamentous mycelium, it seldom happens that the zone which it occupies exceeds the breadth of 3—4 tracheids. The walls of the elements of the wood afterwards display a cellulose reaction, and speedily dissolve from the lumen outwards.

On account of the trees drying up, after the rhizomorphs have spread from the point of infection on the roots into the stem, and again from the stem into the hitherto sound roots, decomposition of the stem usually ceases before the mycelium has advanced from the alburnum into the duramen. It is only in the stool and roots that decay rapidly spreads throughout the whole of the wood.

The practical preventive measures to be enforced in the case of this parasite are the same as those which I have already recommended for *Trametes radiciperda* (see pp. 190-91).

THE DESTRUCTION OF STRUCTURAL TIMBER BY FUNGI

Although, strictly speaking, the diseases of felled timber should not be discussed in a text-book of the diseases of trees, still an abbreviated summary of the results of my investigations on this subject may not be altogether out of place.[1]

As regards the management of squared and round timber before it is utilised—that is to say, in the forest and during transport—one should in the first place take all reasonable precautions to see that, after felling, only sound wood is retained as structural timber. Of course it is always possible that now and again a log or beam will be retained that turns out to be diseased during subsequent manipulation. This may be due to the fact that a parasite which has entered through a branch-wound has not spread up or down to one of the sectional surfaces, so that it is impossible to recognize the destructive effects of the fungus when the timber is despatched. It is often

[1] *Der ächte Hausschwamm (Merulius lacrymans)* (Berlin, Springer, 1885), and *Die Rothstreifigkeit des Bau- und Blochholzes und die Trockenfäule. Allg. Forst- und Jagd-Zeit.*, November 1887.

the case, however, that the diseased portion of a tree which is easily recognized—as, for instance, owing to brownness, &c —is cut off till the saw-cut appears to the naked eye to be perfectly sound   The apparently sound portion of the tree is afterwards disposed of, say as a log   Now, it may easily happen that the parasite has already penetrated into the portion of the tree that was regarded as free from attack, and consequently an infected piece of timber is sold as sound   Should such wood retain a portion of its moisture for a considerable period, the parasite will continue to grow until it destroys not only the wood that contained the filamentous mycelium at the time the tree was felled, but frequently also very considerable portions of the timber that was primarily sound

Polyporus vaporarius, which occurs on spruces and pines even when alive, and which I have described at page 198, is the commonest and most destructive of these fungi   Frequently when investigating the destructive effects of "dry-rot" I have found the cause to be not *Merulius lacrymans* but *P. vaporarius*, whose mycelium forms snow-white sheets on beams and deals, and produces stiff strands several yards in length   Should timber which is infested by this parasite be applied to structural purposes, and should it not dry quickly enough, the fungus develops more or less luxuriantly, and in a short time completely destroys all the wood-work   This fungus is apt to be specially prevalent in cellars, and in the wooden floors of the ground flat of houses that are unprovided with cellars

Perfectly sound timber may, however, also be infected during the time it is lying in the forest   The danger is greatest in the case of peeled timber that is in immediate contact with the ground   Various wood-fungi, and amongst them *Merulius lacrymans*, may induce disease in felled timber when it is stored for a considerable time on the ground in the forest   At the time of issuing my publication on *Merulius lacrymans*, I stated that it was doubtful whether this fungus occurs in the forest at the present day   Since that time I have received genuine specimens of *M lacrymans*, from Herr W Krieger, Königstein, Saxony   Peeled timber that is exposed to air-currents by being piled upon supports is much better protected, because the surface layers soon dry, and render the entrance of the fungus impossible　　In the case of peeled stems that are freely exposed, drought in a few weeks induces the formation of cracks in the alburnum　　These occur about an inch apart, and penetrate to a depth of an inch or more　　The rain-water enters these cracks, carrying with it any spores that it may contain　After pro- longed rain the wood swells owing to the absorption of water, and the cracks close　　During wet years, or long storage of the timber, decomposition may begin even in the forest, the spores that have entered by the cracks germinating and causing the wood to become brown along both sides of the fissure

As a rule, however, spores that enter cracks in the alburnum do not germinate in the forest, because when the rain ceases the superficial layers of the wood quickly dry again, so that even if the cracks should have closed they subsequently reopen　Should such wood be removed from the forest to the building or saw-mill in a dry condition, it remains sound, even although the spores in the cracks retain their power of germinating for a long time If, on the other hand, the wood is floated, so that it has the opportunity to become again fully saturated with water, a very undesirable pathological symptom makes its appearance, which is known to saw-millers, timber-merchants, &c, as "the red stripe," and represents the first stage of what is popularly called „dry-rot."

It is a familiar fact that there is no essential difference as regards durability, or resistance to the attack of *M lacrymans* and other wood-fungi, between coniferous timber that is felled in summer and that which is felled in winter.　The attempt that has been made to show that the destructive effects of *M. lacrymans* are modified by the varying chemical composition (as regards potash, phosphoric acid, &c) of wood felled in summer and in winter must be described as total failures　On the other hand, it is an undoubted fact that wood which is felled in summer suffers far more from dry-rot than that which is felled in winter　This apparent contradiction is easily explained Winter-felling takes place in the lowlands and in the less elevated mountains　In these districts the timber is chiefly removed from the forest by land, after it has lain for a longer or shorter period with or without its bark.　Such timber is either free from spores, or, should it contain spores that have entered by cracks formed in the alburnum during drying, it afterwards remains dry, and therefore sound, because the spores are unable to germinate in the dry wood. On all the higher mountains, on the other hand, felling takes place in summer. The wood is at once peeled and piled on supports, and in winter it is conveyed on the snow to the streams, to be sent off in rafts in spring. The timber is dried in the first summer—that is to say, directly after being felled and peeled—when cracks form through which the spores of fungi enter. During floating the logs become saturated with water, and the cracks close. When the wet logs arrive at the saw-mills they are piled up in thousands, to be sawn up in the course of the summer. The logs that are sawn up in May are, as a rule, perfectly sound, but from June onwards the number of "red-striped" specimens constantly increases, until in autumn it frequently happens that more than 50 per cent. of the logs are so decayed as to furnish but few serviceable boards. This is easily explained, if one considers that the saturated logs are prevented from drying owing to the way they are piled up on one another, and that the high summer temperature is suitable for the germination of the spores present in the cracks, and favours the destructive development of the fungi.

The owners of saw-mills in the Bavarian Forest calculate that they lose 33 per cent. of their total timber by logs becoming red-striped. For some years I conducted extensive investigations not only at Zwiesel in the Bavarian Forest, but also at Marquardstein and Freising, partly to determine the cause of timber becoming red-striped, and partly with the object of discovering a means of preventing the mischief. This is not the place to go into the details of these arduous investigations. I have shortly described the causes of the phenomenon above. As regards the prevention of the disease, it was found to be possible to obtain perfectly sound logs by protecting them against rain by a covering of boards or spruce-bark. Unfortunately this only induces another evil—namely, the excessive cracking of the timber, which means a very serious shortage in good boards. The rejected red-striped boards are used in houses for underflooring and for false floors. As it very often happens that the wood has not been sufficiently dried to kill the enclosed fungus-mycelium, the latter continues to grow in the presence of moisture, and the wood is still further destroyed.

Squared timber that has been floated suffers quite as much from red-stripe as that which comes straight from the saw-mill As nowadays it hardly ever happens that perfectly dry timber is employed for structural purposes, there is great danger of the so-called "dry-rot" appearing in a destructive form.

The greatest danger attaches to the ends of joists that are built into a wall If the latter contains water, it is transmitted to the wood, so that joists which may have been fairly dry are again rendered so wet as to enable any fungus-mycelium contained in the cracks of the wood to develop and destroy timber that was perfectly sound when placed in the building Should the ends of the joists have originally shown any appearance of red-stripe, the danger of total decay is of course increased One ought therefore to endeavour, as far as possible, to avoid using red-striped joists, or at least their use should be confined to the highest story of a building, where the walls being thinner dry faster Under any circumstances, however, one should never neglect to apply several coats of creosote (common coal-tar oil) or some special carbolic preparation to the ends of the joists for a distance of three feet, before they are built into the wall Tar cannot be recommended, because it does not penetrate far into the wood, and it forms a covering which prevents the joists from drying

The other parts of the joists are not so much exposed to danger Even when they are red-striped they usually dry so soon in properly constructed buildings as not to suffer further damage from any fungus that they may contain, though of course their strength is reduced in proportion to the extent of the disease

The name "dry-rot" is unhappily chosen, in so far that it is characterized as occurring only in wet or damp wood, in which the fungi can find sufficient moisture for growth. *Merulius lacrymans*, on the other hand, may destroy perfectly dry wood by imbibing and conducting the water requisite for growth from other parts of the building, and either parting with it to the woodwork or letting it escape in the form of drops or "tears" The disease has, in fact, acquired the name "dry-rot" because it is usually only noticed in a building when it, and consequently the woodwork also, has become practically dry.

Frequently, however, dry-rot appears in new buildings to such an extent that not only the joists but also the boards of the false and true floors decay. When this is the case the cause is usually to be found in gross negligence on the part of the contractor. Most frequently the mistake is committed of placing wet deadening material ("pugging") on the false floor and covering it over too soon, either with the boards of the sub-floor or of the true floor. I have thoroughly discussed the subject of deadening material in my work on *M. lacrymans*. It must be as dry as possible, and free from humus or anything that will condense moisture. Clean gravel or coarse dry sand suits best. Anything of the nature of coal-dust should on no account be used.

It is a great mistake to cover the floor too soon with oil paint or with parquet, because this prevents the evaporation of any moisture that may have been originally present in the boards, or that may have been imparted to them by the packing material. The water that is contained in the packing material and in the woodwork cannot afterwards escape upwards. All that is possible is an extremely slow evaporation downwards— that is to say, through the ceiling of the room beneath. Between the false ceiling and the matchboard ceiling the air becomes saturated with moisture, and this space offers conditions which are extremely favourable for the growth of fungi. The flooring boards, being saturated with moisture derived from the packing material, decompose under the action of the spores which are brought from the forest in the cracks of the wood. In two years' time, when the building has become perfectly dry, the moisture n the boards also disappears. The withdrawal of water induces very great shrinkage in the already decomposed wood of the lower side of the boards, while the upper side, being exposed to the air or protected by paint or varnish, is not similarly affected. The result is that the upper side of each board becomes convex in the middle, and the nails are easily wrenched out of the partially rotten joists. Open joints are thus formed, which may be large enough to admit of the entrance of one's finger.

The repairs thus rendered necessary are very expensive, and

give rise to vexatious litigation between the architect, builder, carpenter, and timber-merchant. Nor are the distinctions between this form of dry-rot and that induced by *Merulius lacrymans* sufficiently appreciated as a rule, although the ravages of the latter may be easily recognized since the publication of my work on the subject.

As a rule the term "dry-rot" is applied to those forms of decomposition in structural timber where the fungus that does the damage is invisible to the naked eye. This want of conspicuousness is accounted for by the fact that such fungi, instead of covering the wood or of filling up cracks in the timber or spaces between the woodwork and the walls with mycelial growths, distribute their fine hyphæ in the substance of the wood itself. But in a series of fungi which destroy structural timber a luxuriant mycelial growth is produced outside of the wood, and it is to these that the term "House Fungus" is generally applied. These fungi vary exceedingly as regards appearance and life-history. Of them the most important and destructive is *Merulius lacrymans*. Then we have also *Polyporus vaporarius*, which has already been described, and a number of other fungi which I am at present busily engaged in investigating.

Space may also be found here for a few remarks on the soundness and quality of timber furnished by conifers that have been entirely defoliated by caterpillars, and especially by *Liparis monacha* and *Gastropacha pini*. When spruces or pines have been completely defoliated during spring or summer, the leafless branches as well as the top of the tree die in the course of the following autumn, winter, or spring, while the more valuable parts of the stem remain perfectly sound till the middle of the succeeding summer. As a rule it is not till the beginning of July that the inner cortex, especially on the south-west side of the tree, begins to show brown patches and die. During the devastations committed by the nun moth in recent years, the older classes of spruces were almost all dead by autumn—that is to say, the cortex was brown. Underneath the dead cortex the wood of the alburnum became discoloured, and rapidly decomposed under the influence of numerous fungi. The timber of all those trees which were felled and immediately barked before the beginning of July of the year in which the havoc was committed was found to be of exceptionally high quality, and showed no blemishes. This was the case even after the barked trees had been piled for a whole year before being removed from the forest. Owing to the stores of carbo-hydrates having been nearly all used up by the cambium in the formation of the wood-ring during the summer of the first year, such timber offered less suitable conditions for the growth of fungi than the wood of trees that had not been defoliated. It was only after the cortex had died, or had been perforated by wood and bark beetles, that fungi could gain an entrance, when the high temperature and abundance of moisture offered favourable conditions for their growth. The low repute in which timber furnished by trees destroyed by insects is held is entirely due to the fact that such trees are often left standing in the forest till the cortex is dead. Trees that have been stripped of their leaves should therefore be felled and barked not later than the beginning of July of the year succeeding the defoliation.

I now return to the consideration of the true dry-rot fungus, *Merulius lacrymans*.

Although this plant has been encountered at least once on the old stool of a conifer in the open forest, it is usually associated with man. It is probable, however, that it has hitherto escaped notice in plantations, and that it is more generally distributed than is usually supposed. Although it lives chiefly on coniferous timber, it also grows on oak, and the oaken boards of parquet floors are liable to be infected.

The filamentous mycelium which is invisible to the naked eye grows inside the wood, from which it abstracts the proteids necessary for its growth. At the same time it dissolves the coniferin and cellulose of the cell-walls, and leaves behind a brown residue consisting of lignin, tannin, and oxalate of lime. So long as sufficient moisture is present these substances enable the wood to retain its original volume, but whenever water is withdrawn the wood becomes traversed by numerous fissures running at right angles to each other, and frequently breaks up into regular cubes.

As the wood decomposes it becomes brown in colour, a result which is probably due to the higher oxidation of the tannin. Although soft when damp, the wood bears some resemblance to charcoal when dry, and may be rubbed down between the fingers into an impalpable yellow powder An important property which it possesses is its great sponge-like power of absorbing water. This is chiefly due to the fact that, owing to the cell-walls having been perforated by the filamentous mycelia, the air is enabled to escape in front of the water which enters by capillarity Thus it happens that when a house is attacked by *M. lacrymans* the woodwork is able to absorb water with great ease, and to transport it to considerable distances. Thus the capillarity of the diseased wood makes it possible for liquid water to be conveyed from the ground floor of a house to the upper stories, which it may render damp by evaporation So far wood that is decomposed by *M lacrymans* resembles that which is attacked by what is popularly called dry-rot

M lacrymans is, however, capable of growing out of the wood in which it feeds, if only the surrounding air remains sufficiently humid to prevent the advancing mycelial filaments drying up Where, therefore, the air is stagnant and humid, the mycelium grows out of the wood, at first taking the form of a snow-white loose woolly growth, which spreads over the wood and covers its surface These white fungus-growths also spread on to other objects from which they can obtain no nutriment, provided they are situated in the neighbourhood of the wood-work Thus they creep up the walls, and spread over the damp ground, flag-stones, &c Later on stouter branching strands of the same colour occur amongst the masses of floccose fungoid hyphæ These may attain to the thickness of the finger, and are of immense importance in the life-history of *M. lacrymans.*

Before proceeding to describe these stout strands, I may mention that the woolly mass of mycelia attains more consistency as it gets older, and forms a lustrous silky ash-coloured sheet which may be detached from the substratum The ashy grey colour of this mycelium enables us to distinguish it from that of *P vaporarius*, already described, which always remains white

The mycelial strands of *M. lacrymans* consist of (1) firm fibres, which make them to a certain extent untearable, (2) filaments rich in protoplasm, which in humid air may send out buds in all directions, and (3) organs resembling vessels with large lumina, which contain a plentiful supply of proteid substances. Not only water but also large quantities of nutritive substances are apparently conveyed in these vessel-like organs from the nutrient substratum—that is to say, the woodwork—to the more remote portions of the growing mycelium. Now, as these strands attain to a length of many yards, and by taking advantage of depressions in walls mount from the cellar to the ground floor, and from there to the upper stories, it is easily seen that the fungus may occur in parts of a building in which there is absolutely no woodwork, without having encountered any nourishment—that is to say, wood—on its way. Of course those strands do not advance as such. It is the delicate filamentous mycelium which, supplied with water and nourishment from the strands behind, and taking advantage of every crack and cranny, grows through walls, soil, &c. The chink in a wall which was entered at first by a delicate floccose mycelium later on contains a thick strand, which, however, has gradually developed from the former. Should the mycelium during its progress again gain access to woodwork, it destroys the latter, the delicate filaments entering and abstracting the nourishment, and thus gaining strength for more vigorous development. It is characteristic of *M. lacrymans* that it is able to destroy even dry woodwork. This is rendered possible by the strands conducting enough water from other damp parts of the building to soak the dry wood, and thus make it suitable for attack. In muggy rooms, when wood is not available to absorb the water, the fungus parts with it in the form of drops or "tears," which has gained for it the name of the "weeping" house-fungus (*lacrymans*).

If sufficient space be available, and as a rule in the presence of more or less light, though this is not absolutely necessary, the familiar sporophores are formed. Though they vary in form, these are usually of a flat saucer-like shape. The fungus-mass, which is at first white and loose, assumes a reddish colour in places, and displays vermiform folds, which soon become so covered with rusty spores that the whole surface is coloured deep-brown. The brown spores, which are so small that about sixty-five thousand millions can be contained in a cubic inch of space, display a germ-aperture in the thick wall at one end, which is closed however by a clear lustrous plug.

The spores of *M lacrymans* can germinate only when this plug has been dissolved or has disappeared in some way, and this seems to occur only under the action of some alkali. I succeeded with germination experiments only when I had added some ammonia or salts of potash or soda to the infusion in which the spores were placed. These salts are not to be regarded as nutritive in their effects, but merely as rendering possible the removal of the spore-pellicle that covers the germ-aperture. Every seed and every spore contains a certain quantity of nourishment which has been derived from the parent plant, and which is instantly available for use   Only when this has been used up during germination is further development dependent upon a supply of nourishment from the environment I will not contest the possibility that now and then a spore of *M. lacrymans* may germinate directly on wood, which of course contains minute traces of alkalis, still I have only succeeded in inducing spores to germinate on wood by adding a little alkali   This explains why injuries from *M lacrymans* are specially apt to occur in places where urine, humus, wood ashes, coal-dust, and such like are present

Wood is the natural food of *M lacrymans*, and in this respect there is no difference between summer-felled and winter-felled timber   The causes of the frequent complaints regarding summer-felled wood have already been discussed

Soil that is very rich in humus also offers nourishment to *M. lacrymans*, though only in small quantity   It is probable, although not certain, that when the mycelium is growing in contact with walls it dissolves and consumes minute quantities of lime, but in any case these are so small that no direct damage can be ascribed to this cause

When alive or still fresh, *M lacrymans* has a very pleasant odour and delicate flavour, though this is succeeded by a somewhat astringent taste   When sporophores, especially large ones, decompose, they disseminate a highly repugnant and very characteristic smell   There is no doubt that the gases generated by the decaying fungus are highly injurious to the health of human beings inhabiting rooms exposed to them   In addition to this, large quantities of water are evaporated from the fungus, and thus rooms are kept damp.

Even under the most favourable circumstances, *M. lacrymans* can only appear after infection by spores or pieces of mycelia, and on this account it is important to determine how the spores or mycelia are distributed and carried about.

I have already mentioned above that, under certain circumstances, the spores may be brought with the timber from the forest. Such cases, however, must be extremely rare, at least under the conditions of forest conservancy that obtain in Germany, where large quantities of timber are seldom stored in the forest to admit of the development of *M. lacrymans*, which has hitherto been observed but once in such a situation. That timber may be infected and attacked by *M. lacrymans* during long storage in the forest naturally follows from what has been said. But as a rule infection occurs only in the towns, either in the wood-yards of carpenters, cabinet-makers, &c., or in houses. It happens often enough in wood-yards that the timber of old houses, which is still useful for certain purposes, is stored beside sound wood, so that the rain washes any loose spores and bits of mycelium on to the sound wood. Workmen, especially carpenters—who, let us say, have been executing repairs in a structure affected by *M. lacrymans*— easily introduce the spores into new buildings, by proceeding from the one to the other without changing or cleaning their clothes, boots, or tools.

For *M. lacrymans* to appear it is not merely necessary that spores or mycelia should be present, but the conditions necessary for their development must also be favourable. The spores germinate only in the presence of alkalis. This explains the disastrous consequences of employing humus-substances or wood or coal ashes as packing materials, or allowing the workmen to pollute the building with urine. The further growth and vigorous development of the fungus are, however, most encouraged by the use of damp materials, *e.g.* damp wood, damp packing, damp stones, &c., because moisture is necessary for the growth of *M. lacrymans* as well as every other plant.

This is no more the place to go into further details regarding preventive measures to be taken in building a house than it is to describe the measures to be instituted when *M. lacrymans*

appears in a structure.   In the book which I have quoted I have ·
thoroughly discussed all these matters.

Amongst   the   saprophytic   wood-fungi,   *Peziza æruginosa*
excites a general interest   Although belonging to the *Dis-*
comycetes, it may be mentioned in this place, as it is to it
that the so-called "green-rot" of wood is due   When much-
decayed wood, of the oak and beech especially, less frequently
of the spruce and birch, lies constantly soaked on the ground
of the forest for a long time, it frequently assumes an intense
verdigris-green colour.   This is due to the wood being occupied
by the mycelium of the above-named fungus, which, along with
the saucer-shaped sporophore, is vividly green in colour.   The
green pigment, which may be extracted, is also present in the
walls of the elements of the wood

On account of its indestructibility the green colouring matter
finds employment in the arts, and · recently experiments have
been instituted to produce green-rot in wood on a large scale by
artificial propagation.

The   so-called   "blueness"   of   coniferous   wood   is   due   to   a
Pyrenomycete, *Ceratostoma piliferum* (*Sphæria dryina*), whose
brown mycelium enters the stem by the medullary rays, and very
rapidly reaches the pith   It is specially common in pine woods
on unhealthy trees, such as those which have suffered from
caterpillars, or it may appear in a heap of damp fagots
Probably on account of deficiency of moisture it rather avoids
the duramen, whereas the alburnum is often quickly occupied by
the mycelium, and destroyed.

SECTION II

WOUNDS

NUMEROUS wounds are produced annually in plants which are the result of normal biological processes. Thus leaves are shed in autumn, certain twigs are naturally cast off (*e.g.* in poplars and oaks), and the outer layers of the cortex die. The plant makes preparation some time in advance for all such wounds as occur naturally, so that at the moment when the wound is formed the process of healing may be regarded as completed. This preparation consists in a periderm being formed in the tissues along the plane which the surface of the wound ultimately occupies. In its origin and structure this periderm entirely agrees with the periderm of uninjured shoots, or with the peridermal covering that gradually forms on wounds which have resulted from an accident. In many cases a protective covering of gum is first spread over the wound, and later on the formation of a periderm is gradually accomplished. Only such wounds as are due to external mechanical causes, which have exposed the internal living tissues to the prejudicial influences of the environment, come into the category of pathological phenomena.

HEALING AND PRODUCTION OF NEW TISSUES IN GENERAL

In order to understand the processes of healing and the production of new tissues, we must first cast a glance at the different kinds of tissues and their capacity to produce new growths.

On the young parts of plants the protective covering is represented solely by the epidermis, which usually consists of a single cell-layer. But before this has entirely lost its power

Q

of expanding, and has been ruptured by the growth in thickness of the stem, a new protective covering is formed beneath it, which protects the inner living cortical tissues against drought. This periderm—on whose structure and characteristics it would be out of place here to enlarge—is formed from a layer of phellogen (cork-cambium), which results from the tangential division either of the epidermal cells while still alive, or of a layer of cortical cells which is situated at a greater or less distance beneath the epidermis. The radially arranged cells, which are being constantly formed by division, die and become converted into cork, and thus a protecting envelope, more or less thick, is formed on the outside of the living tissues. By division of the phellogen-layer the envelope is constantly being renewed on its inner surface, whereas the oldest cork-cells on the outside are being lost by the exfoliation or detachment of compact layers of cork-cells. In the case of most trees *bark* is formed sooner or later, owing to the older layers of the cortex and bast losing their power of expansion.* When this occurs new cork-layers form in the interior of the cortex, and these separate the inner layers from the outer layers of cortex, immediately before the latter die, dry up, and rupture.

It is evident that an injury to the dead periderm or bark is unaccompanied by any prejudicial results. The only way in which it can affect the growth of the tree is that by diminishing the pressure it stimulates the cambium to increased activity. Where the dead bark has been mostly removed in a broad zone from pines, for the purpose of laying on a ring of tar with the object of intercepting caterpillars, the trees during succeeding years grow distinctly faster at the barked region than either above or below. In the event of the layer of living phellogen being injured, a new zone of phellogen and cork, which is continuous with the cork layer along the edge of the wound, is formed from the uninjured cells which are situated deeper in the cortex or phelloderm.

The cortical parenchyma (Fig. 132, *b c*) which lies beneath the

* ["Bark" is, therefore, all the dead tissue situated outside the phellogen; it may be represented by the corky layer of the periderm only, or may include this and dead tissues of the cortex, which the periderm has cut out as well. —Ed.]

periderm possesses sufficient power of cell-division to enable it to keep pace with the increasing thickness of the stem. In the case of a wound, however, its reproductive capacity is confined to the development of a periderm close beneath the surface of the exposed tissues. This layer of cork, which is also formed along the boundary between the sound and dead tissues when plant-parasites induce diseases of the cortex, is called "Wound

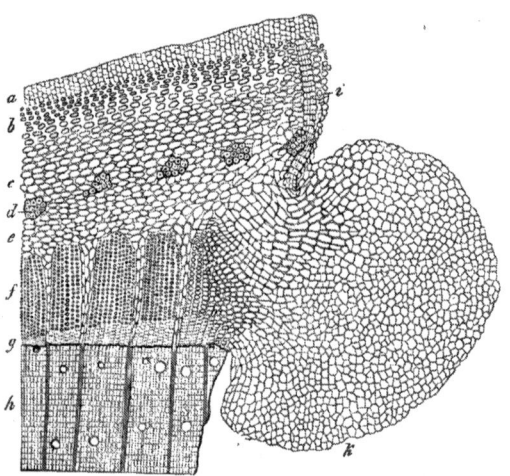

FIG. 132.—The formation of callus on the edge of a wound on an oak-branch. *a*, periderm ; *b*, collenchyma ; *c*, outer cortex ; *d*, primary bundles of hard bast ; *e*, cortical parenchyma ; *f*, soft bast ; *g*, cambium ; *h*, wood ; *i*, "wound-cork" formed by the outer cortex ; *k*, callus.

Cork" (Fig. 132, *i*). Its formation does not depend on the season of the year, for even in winter, should the weather be favourable, it is formed soon after the occurrence of a wound.

Only that portion of the cortical parenchyma which is situated nearest to the cambium, or the soft bast, or in other cases merely the deepest-lying and youngest organs of the soft bast, take part in the reproductive processes that are about to be discussed.

As wood consists for the most part of empty elements—viz. fibres, tracheids, and vessels—it possesses only a very limited reproductive capacity. The cells of the wood that retain vitality consist of the parenchyma of the medullary rays and the wood-parenchyma, but these are so surrounded by the elements above mentioned that they are scarcely able to exercise even the limited reproductive capacity which they do possess. This capacity is exhibited in but two forms—first, in the production of tyloses or "filling cells" in the vessels of the wood whenever these are injured, and, secondly, in the development of so-called "intermediary" tissue ("cementing tissue") during the process of engrafting.[1] When the cut surfaces of the scion and stock are bound together in a sufficiently fresh condition, any empty space which may exist between the two portions of wood becomes filled with parenchymatous tissue, which originates in the above-mentioned parenchymatous cells of the wood itself.

FIG. 133.—Surface of a beech-stem from which the cortex has been removed, and on which an investing layer has been partially formed. Natural size.

Wood that is exposed by a wound has the power of producing cortex and wood only if the cortex is removed during the season when the cambium is active, and the cambium layer or the young wood is protected against drought. In such a case the regeneration of the covering layers is effected. The region of the cambium, with its delicate cells and abundant protoplasm, consists, during the period from May to August, of initial cells, mother-cells that have been formed from these by division, and young embryonic cellular tissue (young bast and young wood) which is still capable of growth. When exposed to the air this region dries up very easily, and only during rainy weather, or when the air is saturated with moisture, does this tissue survive, and, by the transverse division of the elongated elements of the cambium, become converted into a healing tissue consisting of parenchymatous iso-diametric cells.

Owing to energetic cell-division this gives rise in a few days to an investing layer (Fig. 133), which, under the influence of light, assumes a green colour. Frequently the cambium that covers the surface of a wound withers, with the exception of the

[1] Göppert, *Ueber innere Vorgänge bei dem Veredeln*, Cassel, 1874.

cambium of the medullary rays, so that the clothing of the surface of the wound is almost exclusively undertaken by the latter, giving the impression that the medullary rays have grown out of the wood. The healing tissue, which is originally homogeneous, soon shows a certain amount of differentiation. The elements which abut upon the old wood change into wood-cells, while towards the outside a new bast region forms amongst the layers of cells that are assuming the form of parenchymatous cortical

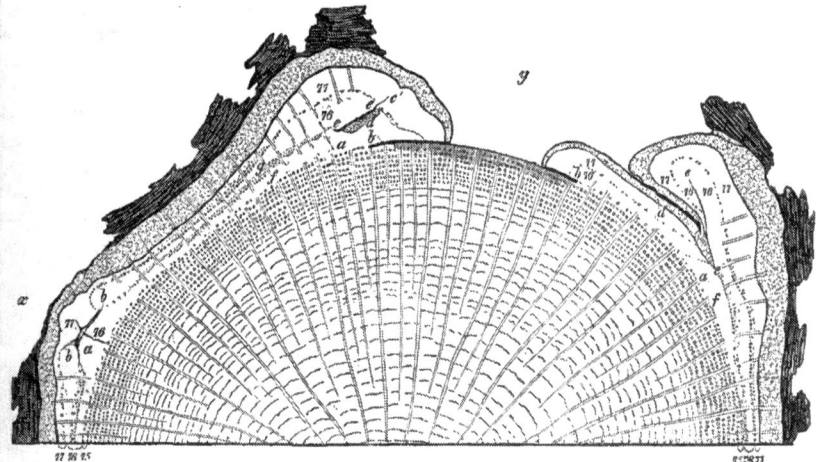

FIG. 134.—Cross-section of the stem of an oak which, two years before being felled, had ruptured at several places in the cortex in consequence of much-augmented growth. *x* and *y*, two places where the cortex had ruptured; *a* to *b*, new investing layers formed by occlusion with their cortex, *d*; *c*, callus; *e* to *e*, lower surface of the loosened cortex, the cambium of which has also produced new growth.

tissue. A portion of tissue between the wood and bast preserves the character of meristematic cambium, while a new epidermis forms on the surface of the cortex.

In the accompanying woodcut (Fig. 134), which represents the cross-section of an oak whose bark became separated from the stem two years before felling, the portion of the surface of the wound situated between *b* and *b* has dried up. Beneath the shelter of the loosened cortex, *e e*, on both sides of the wound new healing tissues (*a b*) have been formed on the wood, and these have already attained an age of two years (1876–77).

Should the loosened cortex be supplied with nourishment by remaining in organic union with the tree, new tissue may of course also be formed on its under surface, to which some cambium will also have adhered. In such a case the process of cell-division proceeds normally in the cambium, after it has been converted as explained above into short-celled cambium. It is in this way that the new tissues have been formed during the two years which have succeeded the loosening of the flaps of bark, *e e* (Fig. 134).

The wood which is formed on the surface of the exposed wood of the stem and on the inner surface of the detached bast is distinguished from ordinary wood by its abnormal structure, and especially by the shortness of its cells and the absence or scarcity of vessels. H. de Vries,[1] who was the first to direct attention to this abnormality, designated such wood with the name "Wound-Wood."

The formation of new cortex in the manner above described has been made use of on a large scale in the cultivation of cinchona bark under MacIvor's system. Strips of cortex several yards long are separated from the wood along the cambium zone, alternate strips of the same breadth being left *in situ*. The whole is then covered with moss. The system can only be practised during the rainy season. The fresh growth contains twice as much quinine as the original bark.*

When the cambium on the portion of a stem that has been deprived of its cortex dries up before it can produce an investing layer, or should cambium be entirely absent from the surface of a wound, as, for instance, in the case of branch-wounds, &c., the only regenerative process that is possible is the formation of callus from the edge of the wound.

Under the so-called Javanese method the cortex is removed, with the exception of a thin layer which contains the cambium and youngest bast. In a short time a layer of periderm forms beneath the surface, and prevents the loss of moisture. By this method, which may be practised at all seasons, the tree does not require to be bound round with moss.

[1] Hugo de Vries, *Ueber Wundholz*, Flora, 1876.

* [This system of "mossing" has been much in vogue among the planters in Ceylon.—ED.]

The process by which callus is formed begins in the soft bast, and in the embryonic tissue along the edge of the wound— namely, the cambium (Fig. 132, *g*). It is a purely mechanical process, and results from the bark-pressure on these tissues being reduced. The annual growth in thickness of the stem produces distension of the cortex and bast, which, however, is balanced for the most part by the living cells of these tissues dividing and growing, and so keeping pace with the increase in the periphery of the stem, while the dead external portions become fissured longitudinally. Nevertheless there is always a certain amount of tension in the cortical mantle, whereby a considerable pressure is exerted on the cambium. Should this pressure on the cambium be locally reduced by a wound reaching to the wood, the processes of cell-division and growth are accelerated not only along the edges of the wound but also at greater distances. In Fig. 132 this is visible as far as *g*. Wherever the pressure has been reduced (in Fig. 134 this may be perceived at a distance of some inches from the points *a a*), the normal cambium changes into " wound-cambium " with short cells, which produces a luxuriant growth of " wound-wood," destitute of vessels and without distinct medullary rays. The process of cell-division proceeds most energetically in the direction of the surface of the wound, where of course there is absolutely no counter-pressure, and one may perceive the cushion-like callus appearing between the wood and the cortex Either in the year in which it originated, or not till later, the wound-wood assumes a normal character, whereas the cortex of the callus remains thinner and more expansive for a series of years, and exerts less pressure than old cortex or bark. The increased rate of growth is consequently not confined to the first year, but is often maintained till the various callus-cushions which advance from the edges of the wound come into contact and coalesce.

This coalescence is retarded, if not rendered absolutely impossible, in the case of trees which at an early stage clothe the callus with dead bark.

Should the cortex of callus-growths that have come into contact be thin, living, and free from dead bark, it is squeezed out during further growth, so that cambium abuts upon cambium, and complete coalescence results.* Thick bark may retard this coalescence for many decades, as, for instance, in the case of the pine (Fig. 138).

When one considers that the pressure exerted by the bark in consequence of the peripheral enlargement of the stem acts for the most part horizontally, like the pressure of a barrel-hoop upon the staves, it is evident that the formation of callus must proceed much more vigorously in the case of a longitudinal incision in the cortex than when the incision is a transverse one. This sufficiently explains why callus is most vigorously produced along the lateral margins of branch-wounds.

Should an injury produce little or no reduction in the bark-pressure, as in the case of bruises caused, for instance, by one tree knocking against another during felling, the formation of callus is either absolutely prevented or proceeds with great slowness. The dead cortex, which, without becoming detached from the uninjured portion, retains its position on the bruised and lifeless spot, does not admit of a reduction of pressure along the edge of the wound, and consequently no formation of callus takes place.

Finally, it may be mentioned that the shape of the wound may be recognized on the surface of the tree for many decades, the boundary between the old and new cortex being usually visible for a long time.

It need hardly be mentioned that coalescence of the wood exposed by a wound, with the wood of the callus that is subsequently formed over it, is impossible, and especially so as the external wood-layers of the wound have previously died, dried up, and become decomposed to a greater or less depth.

This leads us to the consideration of the changes that occur in wood which is exposed by a wound. In the case of those conifers which are furnished with resin-ducts, the surface of the wound is more or less perfectly protected, owing to the outer layers of wood becoming impregnated with resin.

The resin-ducts, into which resin mixed with turpentine is shed from the surrounding parenchymatous cells which

---

* [I have proposed to call all such cases of covering over of wounded surfaces by the agency of a callus, "occlusion": the wound is said to be "occluded."—ED.]

produce it (resiniferous cells), are disposed in the wood both vertically and horizontally—that is, radially. I was the first to show that the latter, which are known as medullary-ray canals, communicate freely at certain points with the vertical canals. This is owing to the fact that at those places where the two sets of canals come into contact the parenchymatous epithelial cells, instead of remaining coherent to each other, become widely separated (Fig. 135, *e*).

By means of these intercellular spaces the resin of the vertical canals can with ease gain access to the radial canals, and should the latter be opened by a wound on the outside of the tree the resin is enabled to flow freely out to the surface. This explains the abundant outpouring which takes place when conifers are partially barked in order to procure the resin.

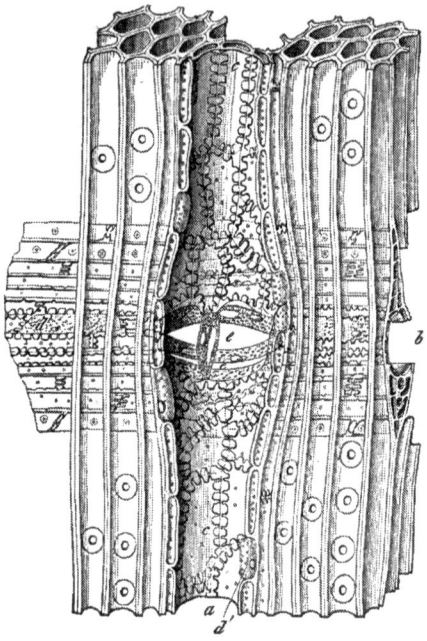

Fig. 135.—Manner of communication between a vertical resin-duct, *a*, and a duct in a medullary ray, *b*, in the Norway spruce. The epithelial cells of both canals are for the most part empty and furnished with very thick walls; the walls between adjoining epithelial cells being abundantly pitted, *c c*. Only a small proportion of these cells retain thin walls, protoplasm, and a nucleus, and serve for the preparation of turpentine, *d d*. At the point where the back of the vertical canal facing the reader, *a*, comes into contact with the horizontal canal behind, *b*, the epithelial cells of both canals are provided with very delicate walls, and are separated by large intercellular spaces, *e e*, the latter providing the means for the passage of the turpentine from the one canal to the other.

Under the oxidising influence of the air the resin that oozes from the wounded surface soon forms a hard incrustation; and of course the partial volatilization of the turpentine also contri-

butes to the induration of the exposed mixture of resin and
turpentine.

If a conifer be felled or a branch removed, either during
summer or winter, one very soon perceives an exudation of resin
from the alburnum ("sap-wood") of the cut surface. But in
the case of the pine, spruce, and larch no resin exudes from the
older parts of the wood, although these parts are frequently
more resinous than the alburnum. I believe that this state of
things may be easily explained by the fact that not only are
the cell-walls of the alburnum completely saturated with water,
but the lumina of the tracheids are more than half full of water.
In spite of its volatility the turpentine contained in the resin-
ducts is unable to distribute itself throughout the wet wood,
and in the case of a wound is forced out of the canals. When
the wood, with advancing age, loses its power of conducting
water, and so becomes drier—no matter whether this is accompanied by the formation of duramen ("heart-wood") or not—
there is nothing to prevent the turpentine spreading throughout
the wood. Not only does it spread into the cell-walls and
impregnate them with resin, but it is also deposited in the form
of drops on the walls in the lumina of the tracheids, and in
fact the lumina are not unfrequently completely filled with turpentine or resin. In this way old pine-wood is frequently so
saturated with resin that sections as thick as one's finger become
partially transparent. Should a section be made of old wood
that can no longer conduct water, there will be no exudation
of turpentine, for the reason that it has become a part of the
walls of the tracheids, or has been deposited in their lumina.

This also explains why the alburnum becomes completely
impregnated with resin when, in consequence of a wound, its
outer layers are exposed and dry up. The water that is lost
by evaporation is at once replaced by turpentine, which is
conveyed in abundance from other parts by means of the resin-
canals. The resinous impregnation of these outer layers forms
a protection against further injury from the environment.

The resinous saturation of the old stools of conifers, and the
distribution of the turpentine in trees whose wood is being
decomposed by parasitic fungi, are very peculiar. The
turpentine moves from the decomposed parts to the boundary

between the sound and diseased wood. One is inclined to assume that when the cell-walls are destroyed by the mycelium of the fungus the turpentine in the interstices of the micellæ is again liberated and becomes volatile, and so penetrates such cell-walls as are either wholly or for the most part free from decomposition. As a matter of fact, those parts of the wood which are the last to be attacked by the parasite become completely saturated with resin, whereas mere traces of resin are to be found in the decomposed portions. Thus, when the alburnum has been destroyed, the duramen of old pine-stools is very resinous. So far there is no proof to support the view that the cell-walls are converted into resin during the decomposition of the wood.

When wounds due to pruning, barking, &c., expose the wood of a dicotyledonous tree, the tree protects itself against the unfavourable influences of the environment in two ways. In the first place, the vessels become completely plugged up by tyloses,* which both prevents the entrance of rain-water and the evaporation of any water that may be present in these organs. In the second place, gums are formed in abundance in the neighbourhood of the wounded surface, and these fill up and close the lumina of the organs, especially the vessels, thereby protecting them to a certain extent against the prejudicial influences of the environment. It is probably to the direct action of the oxygen of the air that the brownness of the wood under the surface of the wound is due, tannin and its allies especially assuming a brown colour in the higher stages of oxidation.

The foregoing protective agencies are, however, insufficient to afford absolute security to the exposed wood against decomposition and decay. On this account wound-diseases are much more liable to occur in dicotyledonous trees than in the resinous conifers.

In the previous section attention has already been directed to wound-diseases due to parasites, and I shall again refer to this subject when dealing with the pruning of trees. But besides

---

*[Tyloses are ingrowths of the cells surrounding a vessel, which push their way through the bordered pits into the cavity, and may there divide and grow further.—Ed.]

the forms of decay in wounds which are induced by parasites, there are other forms of decomposition in wood in which parasitic fungi take no part. It is rather to the saprophytic fungi, in conjunction with atmospheric influences, that a variety of forms of decay in wood are to be ascribed. In the meantime I propose to apply the collective term "Wound-rot" to those various forms of decay which have not yet been explained.[1]

The many forms of decomposition which are embraced under this term have not yet been subjected to scientific investigation. Should a large portion of the stem become functionless and die, saprophytic fungi belonging to the *Hymenomycetes* or *Ascomycetes* induce decomposition, especially when their growth is stimulated by the unrestricted entrance of rain-water. This state of things exists in the case of snags destitute of buds, the stools of felled trees, trees that have lost large patches of bark by game, sun-scorching, &c., and which soon die to a considerable depth owing to the effects of drought. When water and air find easy access to a wound, as in the case of root-wounds, and branch-wounds that have not been tarred, decomposition spreads fairly rapidly in the direction followed by the water in the elements, although this wound-rot certainly does not progress nearly so rapidly as that which is due to parasitic fungi. The so-called false duramen of the beech always proceeds from a wound, and not only are all the vessels filled with tyloses, but the tannin is also so changed as to produce brownness in the heart-wood. Saprophytic fungi slowly advance from the wounds, and produce decomposition in the false duramen. The sooner a wound is closed, either artificially or naturally, the better for the tree. When air and water are excluded, wound-rot advances so slowly as only to reach a depth of half an inch in a century, as is shown by the occluded branch-wound of an oak in my collection.

The treatment of wounds follows from what has been said. Two objects have to be kept in view—first, the process of healing, and, secondly, protection against wound-diseases, both infectious and non-infectious.

The most perfect form of healing—namely, the re-clothing of the wound with a new cortex—can only be looked for when the

[1] *Zersetzungserscheinungen*, &c., p. 63.

injury is due to the separation of the cortex during the season of cambium-activity, and provided the cambium can be preserved against drought by the immediate application of a bandage, which, however, must not come into contact with the cambium. The only practicable means consists in binding moist oil-cloth, straw ropes, moss, or such like round the stem.

Should there be no prospect of a new cortex forming, everything should be done to favour the production of a callus. All dead and crushed portions of cortex which may press injuriously on the edge of the wound should be removed with a sharp knife, only those portions of cortex which remain uninjured on the surface of the wound, and which are nourished through a connection with the edge, should be carefully retained. From these a callus is formed quite as quickly as from the edge of the wound proper.

In order further to guard against wound-diseases, all loose portions of cortex along the edge of the wound should be removed, as moisture lingers for a long time between them and the wood, and is absorbed by the latter. The moisture itself hastens decay in the wound, and moreover it induces conditions that are favourable for the germination of the spores of infectious fungi, which thus gain an entrance into the interior of the tree.

In the case of those conifers which are supplied with resin-ducts, wounds need be protected only when a thick branch which possesses duramen is cut or broken off, or when the cortex has become detached by pruning or the barking of game during summer. The spruce is most exposed to wounds of this character.

The wounds of dicotyledonous trees require protection at all seasons. In order to form a waterproof covering over the wound, grafting-wax is used by gardeners and coal-tar by foresters. I have never observed any injurious effect of the tar on the tissues, as has been repeatedly asserted by practical men; in fact, I can affirm that it is only the ruptured organs and their walls that are penetrated and impregnated by the tar. Cells in the immediate neighbourhood of vessels, and libriform fibres that were filled with tar, remained healthy and perfectly sound after a number of years.

"Preventitious" buds are also to be reckoned amongst the regenerative phenomena that follow on injuries to trees, and which compensate for portions that have been lost. Only a limited number of the axillary buds of a shoot develop in the following year to form new shoots. The majority of these buds, and especially such as are situated in the axils of the bud-scales and of the undersized leaves towards the base of the shoot, remain imperfectly developed, and do not, as a rule, shoot out in the following year. It is these which constitute the dormant eyes, or "Preventitious Buds" of Theodore Hartig, so called because they are present on any given portion of stem from the first year of its existence. Only under certain circumstances do these burst forth into new shoots, *e.g.* epicormic * branches and the like. Preventitious buds is a term employed in contradistinction to adventitious buds, the latter indicating *new* buds that are formed under certain conditions.†

These axillary buds may remain alive for a hundred years and more, especially in the case of trees with a smooth rind, such as the beech, &c.

It is only as regards apical growth that the preventitious buds (Fig. 136, *a*) are inactive, for they display a peculiar form of growth in length, which Theodore Hartig has called "Intermediary Growth." Each year the delicate vascular bundles, which extend from the medulla to the buds (Fig. 136, *b*), increase in length to the same extent as the portion of the stem on which the buds are situated increases in thickness. Such growth is perfectly analogous to the growth of the sucker-roots of *Viscum album*, or to the growth in length of medullary rays. The bud-axis that is embraced by the stem possesses its own cambium, ‡ at the point where it crosses the cambium of the stem.

The cambium of the axis of the bud, which divides at the same rate as the common cambium of the stem, annually produces two portions of tissue—namely, a larger one on the inside

---

* [Shoots which develop in this way on the trunk are known as Epicormic shoots. Such shoots are very common on old Elms, &c.—ED.]

† ["Adventitious," because they arise in places where they would not normally be expected.—ED.]

‡ [Embryonic tissue, which adds new tissues to those already existing in the suppressed bud.—ED.]

whose length corresponds to the breadth of the wood-ring, and a smaller one on the outside equal in length to the thickness of the new bast. A cambium region persists between these two portions till the dormant eye dies, when the bud-axis, which is disposed at right angles to the main stem, ceases to grow and is overgrown and enveloped by the advancing wood-rings.

Numerous bud-axes traverse the wood of dicotyledonous trees, exactly as is the case with medullary rays. Should these be stimulated to form shoots (Fig. 136, *c*), the latter produce their own growth of wood, and both they and their medulla form an acute angle with the main axis of the stem.

In the case of some trees, more particularly the beech, a certain proportion of the dormant eyes develop in a peculiar manner after the cessation of intermediary growth. Concentric growth in thickness of that portion of the wood of the bud-axis which is situated in the cortex and bast gives rise to the familiar wood-balls, or " spheroblasts " (Fig. 137), which project from the surface of the stem and frequently exceed the size of

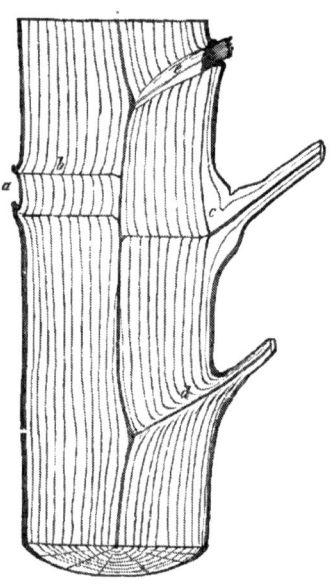

FIG. 136.—Longitudinal section of a beech-stem, twelve years old. At *a* two dormant axillary buds are shown whose vascular bundles, *b*, stand at right angles to the main axis. A third dormant eye, *c*, had burst forth to form a shoot two years previously. A dwarf shoot, *d*, has been formed by the unfolding of a bud when the main shoot was a year old ; *e*, a shoot that has been dead for four years. Natural size.

rifle bullets. As they have no connection with the wood of the stem, they may be detached by a slight pressure.*

In the case of our conifers, almost all axillary buds are in the

* [These " Spheroblasts " are very common on the old Beeches in Windsor Park, Burnham Beeches, and elsewhere.—ED.]

habit of developing into dwarf shoots,* and consequently dormant
eyes are very scarce on these trees. In the case of old pines
only one or two buds remain dormant in each whorl, and in rare
cases a dormant bud may be perceived to burst forth at the base
of a shoot where the dwarf shoots (foliar spurs) are absent.
Should a pine be so injured, by the repeated attacks of caterpillars, that not only all the foliar spurs with their dormant
buds but also the youngest shoots with their whorls of buds
wither, the only buds that the tree retains are the dormant
whorl-buds of the older shoots. These elongate to form the
so-called " Rosette Shoots," which however
are unable to preserve the life of the tree.
The rosette shoots either bear simple lance-
olate leaves alone, or along with these a few
foliar spurs.

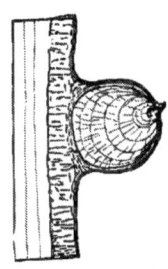

FIG. 137.—Globular
shoot ("sphero-
blast") of a beech
which has been
formed from a
dormant eye after
the latter had be-
come disconnect-
ed from its vas-
cular bundles.

In the case of the larch only about 10 per
cent. of the leaves of the one-year-old shoots
have buds in their axils, all of which develop
to normal or dwarf shoots (leaf-fascicles). A
lost leader can be replaced only by the
vigorous development of one of these dwarf
shoots.

The spruce and silver fir are also but
sparingly supplied with axillary buds, some
of which, however, remain dormant until
special circumstances stimulate them to shoot
out. These dormant buds are frequently to
be found in a whorl at the base of the annual shoot.

The conditions under which dormant eyes may be stimulated
to form vigorous shoots vary, but all agree in this, that the buds
receive an accession of nutriment. As examples of stimulating
conditions I may mention pruning, coppicing, light-thinning,
defoliation by insects, late frost, &c.

Adventitious buds are, generally speaking, comparatively
scarce. Their first inception is not in the axil of a leaf but at other
points of the stem, roots, or leaves, where they originate in after
years, and are therefore supplementary to the axillary buds.

* [e.g. The pairs of leaves on a Scotch or Austrian Pine arise each on such
a dwarf shoot or "foliar spur."—ED.]

It but rarely happens that adventitious buds originate above-ground on uninjured portions of a plant, whereas endogenously developed buds occur regularly on the roots of many species of trees (root-suckers). On the other hand, their occurrence on the callus or investing layer of a wound is a frequent phenomenon (Fig. 151). There they originate close beneath the surface in the meristematic parenchymatous tissue, where they form their ring of vascular bundles, which internally are in intimate union with the wood of the callus.

Adventitious roots, which may occur endogenously both on the uninjured cortex and on wound-tissues, have a precisely similar origin.

THE VARIOUS KINDS OF WOUNDS [1]

Of the endless variety of wounds, we need select for discussion only a few of the more generally interesting.

BARKING BY GAME

Barking (peeling) by red deer is usually confined to conifers, though dicotyledonous trees, for example the beech, are also similarly attacked less frequently. Fallow deer, on the other hand, abrade most if not all of our forest trees, though certain trees, *e.g.* the ash, are specially liable to attack. Roe deer, hares, and rabbits also bark trees under certain circumstances. Roe deer cause a special form of injury by rubbing off the bark of young trees with their newly formed horns.

During winter, game bark trees for want of food, the starchy cortex of smooth-stemmed trees being nibbled to satisfy hunger. In summer, when trees are easily peeled, the more characteristic feature of the injury consists in the separation of large flaps of cortex, and this is frequently done to a considerable height. Views differ as to the motive of peeling during summer. It appears to me most probable that the game regard the rich store of sugar in the cortex as a toothsome morsel. Some believe that the animals find an important aid to digestion in the tannin of the cortex. Game are also said to peel trees for the sake of the lime contained in the bark. Excellent results attended the feeding

---

[1] R. Hartig, *Zersetzungerscheinungen*, pp. 67 *et seq.*

of red deer in the forest district of Ramsau with a substance
containing bone meal, as well as with a special powder (Hofeld's)
consisting chiefly of phosphate of lime and oak-galls   It was
reported that the trees were not afterwards barked   Others
again believe that summer peeling is merely the continuance
of a mode of obtaining food which necessity taught the animals
during winter, and that game thus get into the habit of barking
during summer even when other food is present in abundance

On account of their periderm remaining smooth for a long time
up to the height of four, or five feet, bark being formed only
comparatively late in life, the spruce and silver fir are longest
exposed to the danger of barking.   In the case of these trees,
therefore, it often happens that barking is repeated after an interval
of several years (Fig 139), and stems are not unfrequently to
be met with which show evidences of having been barked at
various ages as often as five times

As the Scotch pine and larch, especially the former, produce
rough bark early in life, they are exposed to the danger of
barking only for a short period   It is only that portion of the
stem of the Scotch pine which is from three to five years old
that is barked   The portions that are younger are protected by
the leaves, and those that are older by the thick bark

The damage which results from barking varies with the species of tree, time of year, and dimensions of the wound.   The
resinous pine suffers but little, unless the stem is completely
barked round   The exposed wood dries and becomes so
abundantly impregnated with turpentine and resin that further
decomposition is prevented, and evaporation of water from the
internal layers is retarded.   The wounds, however, close with
great difficulty, because the coalescence of the callus-cushions
is interfered with by the early formation of rough bark
(Fig. 138)

The spruce, on the other hand, suffers much more from
barking, partly because it is not usually attacked till a later
period of growth, when much larger wounds are formed, and
partly—and more particularly—because the wounded surface is
not impregnated with resin to the same extent as in the case of
the pine   Less damage is done by barking during winter than
during summer, not only because in the former case the wounds

are usually smaller, but also because the wounds have the opportunity to become impregnated with resin before the season when a higher temperature favours the formation of wound-rot, or the germination of the spores of parasitic fungi.

Should parasites gain an entrance, decomposition spreads rapidly in all directions, and results in the destruction of the tree. In other cases the wound-rot merely induces the inner layers of wood to become brown, without, however, attacking the wood that is formed in succeeding years. Should the wound remain long open, wound-rot may assume very serious propor-

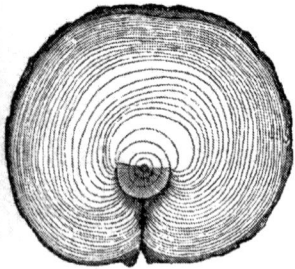

FIG. 138.—Transverse section of a pine-stem showing a wound caused by the peeling of red deer over which a callus has formed, but which, after twenty-four years, is not yet quite closed. One third natural size.

FIG. 139.—Transverse section of a spruce-stem showing three wounds due to the barking of game. One half natural size.

tions. As a rule it ascends in the stem only to the height of a few yards, so that, when this is the form of "Red-rot," the timber is sound after the removal of a few short lengths. As the spot where the bark has been removed offers the least resistance, it is evident that should the tree be loaded with snow it will break most easily at that point.

BARKING BY MICE

The wood-mouse (*Mus sylvaticus*) and the field-mouse (*Arvicola arvalis*[1]) especially injure young dicotyledonous trees by gnaw-

[1] *A. arvalis* is not a native of Britain, but other species of the same genus do considerable damage to trees in this country.—*Trans.*

ing the cortex during winter. Young beech woods especially frequently suffer very severely. If one allows the injured plants to remain standing, most of them will develop in spring apparently in a perfectly normal manner, because the sap is conducted up through the wood as before. In the course of the summer the exposed wood generally dries up, the outer layers being the first to be affected, and wound-rot also makes its appearance. Should the cortex have been removed right round the stem above the collar, the plant loses the power of conducting water at the injured part, and withers. If one delays cutting over the plant till this has occurred, it seldom happens that any stool-shoots are produced. If, on the other hand, one examines the young plantation before the leaves appear, and cuts over all injured plants close to the ground, vigorous shoots will be produced, at the expense of the store of reserve materials present in the roots, and in a short time the young wood will be almost as promising as before. The more vigorous plants may remain alive for several years, and adventitious roots may even be formed above the wound, as is represented in Fig. 140.

BARKING DUE TO THE DRAGGING AND CARTING OF TIMBER, THE GRAZING OF CATTLE, &c.

Abrasions of the bark which are caused during the process of removing timber from the wood, especially on declivities, are amongst the commonest form of wounds to which shallow roots and the lower parts of stems are subjected. During the dragging of timber, and especially when water is in active movement in the tissues, large portions of cortex are detached from the base of growing trees. Where cattle are grazed or folded, and where roads occur in a wood, the shallow roots are subjected to all sorts of injuries, and from these, in the case of the spruce, the wound-rot ascends in the stem, attaining to a height proportionate to the amount of moisture that enters the wound from the soil. On this account wounds that are covered by moss or humus are much more dangerous than those which are perfectly exposed.

The majority of the brown patches of red-rot that are observable on the cut surface of the stool of the spruce, and which disappear when one or two short lengths of the tree are removed, may be traced to such wounds on the root or collar (Fig. 141). Should the mycelium of *Agaricus melleus* gain an entrance into such root-wounds, decomposition proceeds much more rapidly, and the lower part of the stem may become perfectly rotten.

When wood-ants (*Formica herculeana*, or *F. ligniperda*) take possession of these wounds, they frequently form

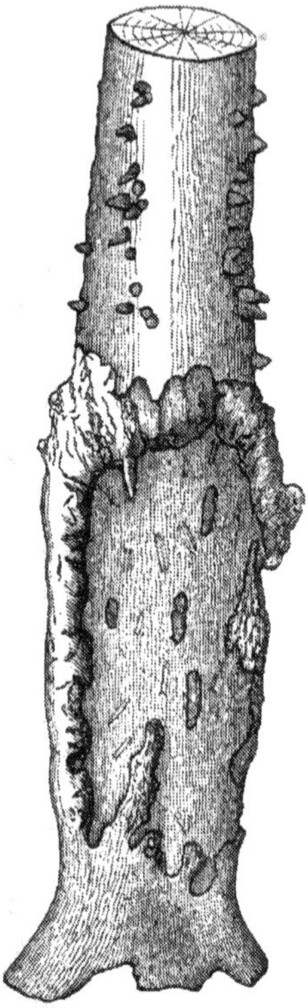

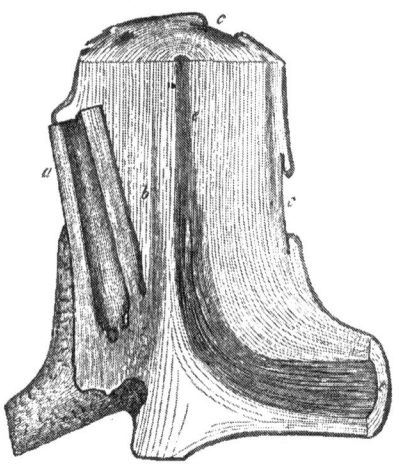

FIG. 140.—A beech which has been severely barked by mice above the collar. On the left side a stripe of cortex has been left. Numerous adventitious roots are seen breaking through the uninjured cortex above the wound. Natural size.

FIG. 141.—The stool of a spruce that had formed two stems. One of the stems, *a*, had been removed in the thinnings, and from it decomposition subsequently spread downwards into the sound stem, *b*. At *c c* wounds have been formed in the cortex during the dragging of timber, and at *e* wound-rot has spread upwards from a damaged root into the stem. One tenth natural size.

galleries which extend far up into the sound part of the stem, and rapid decomposition succeeds their excavations.

Intentionally or unintentionally, man is accountable for the most varied forms of bark-wounds. Take, for example, the carving of figures or letters. Should these be formed in the cortex the wound will be of the same shape as the figure, and the latter may be recognized for many decades, even after callus has been formed, owing to the difference in the appearance of the old and new cortex. If, on the other hand, the cortex is first removed from a considerable surface of wood, and the figures are carved in the wood itself, they disappear when the wound closes. All that can afterwards be perceived is the boundary between the old cortex and the place from which the cortex had been removed.*

When it is intended to remove a ring of dead bark from the Scotch pine for the purpose of laying on a band of tar, the living bast, and even the wood, are frequently unintentionally cut into as well. Even after the tar has been laid on, turpentine and resin continue to exude from the wound and form a white covering on the black tar. This has given rise to the erroneous impression that the tar partially dissolves the cortical tissues and causes wounds in the bast.

Precisely similar wounds result from the removal of bark from old pines for the purpose of obtaining fuel for laundries, as occasionally happens in the neighbourhood of towns. When climbing irons are used for scaling trees wounds are also extensively formed, and especially so during the harvesting of cones, and the cutting down of spruce-branches for litter.

WOUNDS DUE TO CRUSHING

During the felling of timber in a close wood, it often happens that a falling tree, or one of its branches, strikes an adjoining tree, stripping off and crushing the cortex. During pruning the top rung of the ladder crushes the cortex of the branch against which it is laid. In dealing with insect ravages it was formerly a common practice to shake the trees by beating them violently with the back of an axe so as to frighten the caterpillars and make them drop off. In consequence of crushing due to these

* [Such cut letters, &c., are often found deep down in the wood many years ater, the successive annual rings formed by the occluding callus having covered them completely over. The burying of wire, nails, chains, &c., deep n the wood is due to similar occlusion by a callus which gradually forms wood over the edges of these objects.—ED.]

causes the cortex dies, and growth ceases at the injured spot. But more than that, the dead cortex remains for a long time in union with that which is living and uninjured, and no formation of callus can take place, because growth is stimulated along the edge of the wound only when the bark-pressure is reduced The formation of wound-rot is encouraged by water collecting behind the dead cortex, which becomes locally fissured owing to shrinkage consequent on drying, and finally rots away, but only after the lapse of many years

WOUNDS CAUSED DURING THE COLLECTION OF RESIN

Turpentine and resin are procured from conifers in various ways. In the case of the silver fir, it is only the turpentine that is gathered This collects in vesicles in the cortex, which sometimes attain to the size of a pigeon's egg (Strasburg Turpentine)

In the case of the larch, large holes are bored into the stem, and these being afterwards plugged up collect the "Venetian Turpentine" which flows down from the vertical resin-ducts of the wood In the case of the black Austrian pine, the cortex is removed from the stem in fairly broad stripes, the turpentine that exudes freely from the canals of the medullary rays being collected in a receptacle that is cut in the stem below the wound, while the resin is scraped from the wound after it has solidified On account of the exposed wood soon becoming impregnated with resin, and the canals of the medullary rays becoming choked up with the same substance, it is necessary from time to time to remove fresh portions of cortex at higher points on the stem.

In the case of the spruce, vertical strips of cortex, one to two inches in breadth and extending from the base of the stem to a height of about six feet, are detached from the tree When the tree is small the resin is taken from one side only, but as it gets thicker four sides may be utilized (Fig 142). When the flow of resin ceases, the callus that has been formed along both sides of the wound since the last time of stripping is removed, and thus a new set of resin-ducts is opened, from which resin continues to flow

In the course of years the exposed wood dries up, and decay begins to make its appearance, being greatly favoured by the larvæ of *Sirex*, which bore from the surface of the wound deep into the wood, and thus enable rain-water to reach the interior of the tree. Decomposition frequently spreads from the wound high up the tree, and does so much damage that in woods where resin is collected the yield of timber may be reduced from seventy

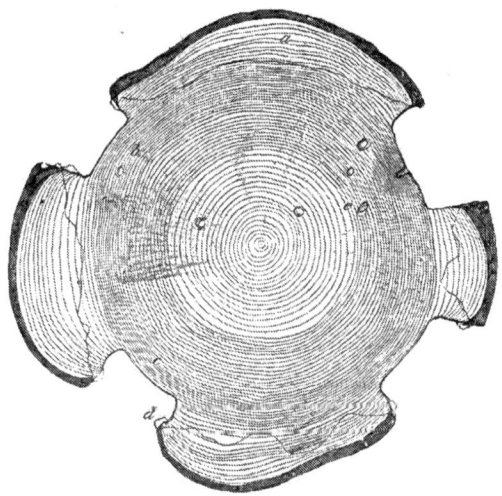

FIG. 142.—Transverse section of the stem of a spruce which has been tapped for resin on four sides for ten to fifteen years. The only wood that is capable of conducting water is those portions of alburnum, *a*, which are marked off by lines between the four gutters. The wood, *b*, beneath the two upper gutters is much decomposed, whereas the wood, *c*, beneath the other gutters has remained sound. Numerous galleries, *e*, formed by *Sirex* are seen proceeding from the upper gutters. One fifth natural size.

to twenty or thirty per cent. of the gross output. It has not been proved that trees that are tapped suffer in growth, nor is it to be expected that such will be the case, seeing that trees cannot utilize turpentine for growth. Tapping, however greatly reduces the value of timber, because the quality to a large extent depends on the amount of resin which it contains.

RING-WOUNDS

These are often caused by game and mice, though they may also be due to human agency, as, for instance, in a mixed wood, where it is desirable to protect a valuable species against its more vigorous neighbours. Their effects upon the tree are not always alike. It is known that, if even a narrow band of cortex be removed completely round the stem, the cambium below the girdled portion ceases to be nourished, and there, as a consequence, growth in thickness comes to a stand-still. As the tree even where ringed retains its power of conducting the ascending sap, it remains alive as a rule for some years. What the conditions are that limit the duration of life of the portion above the ring-wound has not yet been fully made out.[1] In June 1871 I selected fifteen equal-sized Scotch pines 120 years old which were standing close together, and from these I completely removed the cortex to the height of some six feet. While certain of the trees died in 1872, several were still perfectly healthy in 1877. As this shows that it is not the desiccation of the exposed portion of the stem from the surface inwards that is the sole cause of death, investigation should be directed to the question whether the cessation of growth beneath the ring-wound may not prejudicially affect the absorption of water by the roots.

Those cases where ringed trees remain alive for a long period may possibly be explained by root-engrafting, the roots of the girdled stem being thus nourished by neighbouring trees.

PRUNING [2]

Although the pruning of trees is a subject that has often been treated in forestry literature, still the views regarding its admissibility are so diverse that a somewhat full discussion of the operation may not be out of place here.

The natural pruning of trees is accomplished by shade, which causes the branches to become functionless, and ultimately to

[1] This is not the place to discuss bicollateral fibro-vascular bundles, where the plastic materials may descend in the bast organs near the pith.

[2] R. Hartig, *Zersetzungserscheinungen*, pp. 68 *et seq.*

die. The dying twigs and branches are more or less quickly decomposed by saprophytic fungi.

The rate of decomposition and the period when the branches will drop off are most of all regulated by the condition of the wood. Branches of dicotyledons which consist only of alburnum drop off much sooner than branches which contain duramen. On account of the shaded branches of young Scotch pines consisting of soft broad-ringed wood, these trees clean themselves much sooner than the spruce and silver fir, the wood of whose branches is tough, firm, and durable. The thicker, more resinous, and narrower-ringed branches on the upper part of the stem of the Scotch pine, on the other hand, retain their position for a long time, and are more or less embraced or overgrown at their bases by the growth of the stem. This embracing of dead branches is the general rule in the case of the silver fir and spruce, and as they have no organic connection with the adjoining wood-layers they drop out of boards as loose knots when the wood shrinks in drying.

The embracing of dead branches would be a much commoner occurrence, were it not for the fact that the base does not die, and in the case of the thicker branches it often remains alive for a distance of about two inches (Fig. 143). The base of the branch, being nourished from the stem, remains alive, and is capable of growing in thickness. When, after some years, the increase in thickness of the bole of the tree has become equal to the length of the living basal part of the branch, the dead part of the branch will have become so much decayed as to drop off under the action of wind, snow, &c. (Fig. 144). After the wound has healed over only a small dark brown blotch remains in the interior of the tree to indicate the limits of the enclosed stump.

It is in the manner just described that the tree protects itself against the dead stumps of branches being overgrown. It is only the larger branches that frequently do not drop off until a portion of the dead base has been embraced by the stem. In the case of conifers this portion is saturated with resin, and in the case of dicotyledons it is more or less decomposed. Afterwards, when the branch has become completely rotten and has dropped off, a hole remains behind which is only partially filled by the occluding callus, and which of course greatly reduces the value of the tree for technical purposes (Fig. 145).

Thus it is always a good plan, in the case of every variety of tree, to remove as early as possible all the larger dead branches that have succumbed to the natural shading processes. I do not

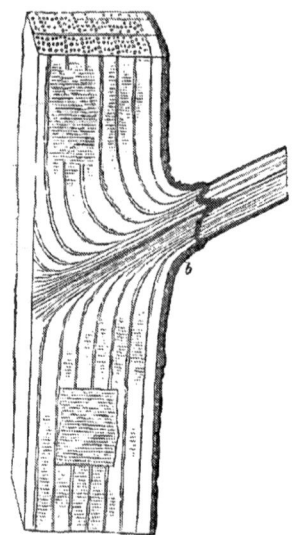 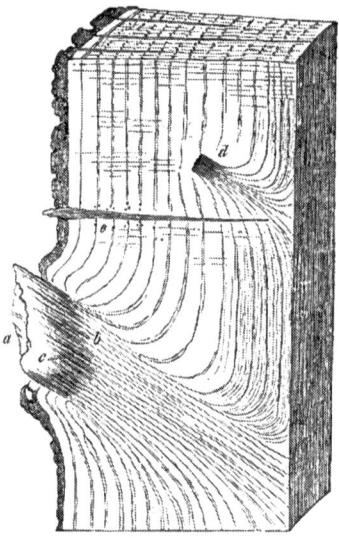

FIG. 143.—An oak-branch which has succumbed to the natural process of shading, its base, *b*, however, still receiving nourishment from the main stem.

FIG. 144.—The snag of an oak-branch which has dropped off after being killed by the natural process of shading. The basal portion, *b*, of the branch which remained alive, and originally projected from the stem, has been grown over. After a callus has formed, the dark brown zone, *c*, between the living, *b*, and the much-decomposed wood, *a*, remains unchanged in the interior of the tree, as is shown in the case of a small branch at *d*. The axis of the stem of a latent bud is shown at *e*.

propose to enter into the technique of the operation, merely remarking that it is evident that the expense should be incurred only in the case of such trees as promise to yield high-class timber. With this limitation there is no doubt that as forestry advances the pruning of dead branches will become general.

The contention that such pruning is too costly is justified only
when it can be proved that the difference in value between a log
free from knots and one where they are abundant is not equal to
the cost of pruning *plus* interest on the outlay.

When we come to consider the removal of green branches—
that is to say, branches or twigs that are living and provided with
leaves—we find that, except in a few exceptional cases which
will be presently discussed, a loss of growth attends the operation. This is the case no matter whether the separation
from the stem be effected
by the hand of man or
by such natural agents
as storms, accumulations
of snow, &c. If one re-
duces the number of the
organs of assimilation
(the foliage leaves), the
products of assimilation
generally suffer to a like
extent. As I have proved
conclusively,[1] it is only
in the case of trees that
are growing in a per-
fectly open situation,
whose stems are branch-
ed to the ground, and
which have a very large
mass of foliage, that
limited pruning may be performed without diminishing the
amount of growth. In the case of such trees there is a greater
extent of foliage than is necessary to effect the metabolic
processes in the plant-food that is taken in by the roots. Of
course the amount of growth depends essentially upon the
quantity of such food. Under such circumstances a reduction
in the extent of the foliage merely results in more active
assimilation in the leaves that remain.

In the great majority of cases the practical operation of
pruning is followed by more or less considerable reduction in

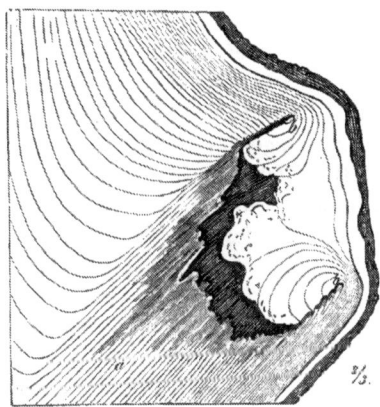

FIG. 145.—The dead and rotten stump of an oak-
branch over which an occluding callus has
formed. Two thirds natural size.

[1] *Das Holz der Rothbuche.* Berlin, Springer, 1888.

growth. This becomes evident in the lower region of the stem, where in fact, if pruning is carried far enough, growth may cease altogether, as I have also proved to be the case with trees that are very much overcrowded.

One must always bear in mind that as pruning generally interferes with growth there must be important reasons for performing the operation if the loss of growth is to be compensated for. Amongst these may be mentioned, on the one hand, the improvement of the form of the stem and the production of a clean bole, and, on the other, the admission of light to underwood.

If, for the purpose of obtaining smooth stems, pruning is carried further than the mere removal of a few branches, one must remember that in such a case there is not only reduction of growth, but that there are also indirect dangers consequent on such pruning. The first of these dangers is connected with the retardation of the healing of the wounds. It is evident that the formation of callus over a branch-wound depends to a large extent on the supply of plastic substances with which the cambium along the edge of the wound or the callus-cushion is provided. Very severe pruning will seriously interfere with the formation of callus, and consequently with the occlusion of wounds. This leads us to consider whether the pruning of the stem to the desired height should not be accomplished in two operations, separated by an interval of several years. If one first of all removes the branches from the lower half of the portion of the stem that it is desired to clear, the diminution of the products of assimilation does not interfere to such an extent with the formation of callus, and the wounds may be covered over in a few years. The more vigorous development of the crown compensates to a certain extent for the branches removed by pruning, so that when the operation is repeated the new wounds close sooner than would have been the case had the whole operation been performed at one time.

By dividing the operation in this way there is also much less chance of an excessively large number of epicormic shoots being produced. Such shoots originate partly in the adventitious buds of the callus along the edge of the wound, and partly in dormant eyes. In the latter case, it is chiefly the buds that are situated on the basal portion of the severed branch that is embraced by the stem which produce the shoots.

When a spruce is pruned, numerous shoots spring apparently from the cortex of the main stem. These are chiefly due to the vigorous development of small weak dwarf shoots, which originated at the base of the branches in their first year, and which have become occluded during the increasing thickness of the stem. I have not been able to prove that true adventitious buds are formed in the case of this tree.

If in pruning green branches one leaves the stump of a branch (snag) without any foliage, the same state of things occurs as when branches are suppressed naturally. The snag dies, except for an inch or two at the base, and the formation of callus is either rendered impossible or is so much interfered with and delayed that the dead stump has time to become completely rotten. If the bark is removed from the snag, the conditions are rendered more favourable for the formation of callus, and a covering will more easily grow over the snag from the base than is possible when the dead and dry cortex remains *in situ* on the stump. In Fig. 146 I have represented the progress of the formation of callus on a thick snag, where for clearness the bark has been mostly removed. The bark of the dead snag presses firmly on the wood, and the formation of the new growth (*a*, *b*), which already covers more than half the stump, has been rendered possible only by its pushing in like a wedge and separating the dead cortex from the dead wood, so that the thin and primarily non-vascular edge of the living tissues has been enabled to grow into the space that has thus been formed. The familiar curled growths on the stumps of branches are formed when the new tissues advance unequally, as is most frequently the case when they are growing over an irregularly fractured surface (Fig. 146, *x x*, in the upper part).

As a dead snag interferes with occlusion, the general rule in pruning is to cut as close as possible and to make the cut parallel to the stem. If this is attended to, a callus is formed in the way already described, its formation proceeding most rapidly from the lateral edges of the wound. For obvious reasons the bark is there most easily raised, much more easily, in fact, than along the upper and lower edges. The upper edge, however, is greatly favoured as compared with the lower edge, because the plastic substances during their passage down the stem are conveyed directly to the former, whereas the latter lies out of the stream as it were, and is but sparingly supplied with nutriment (Fig. 147).

There is, however, a much more important reason for the

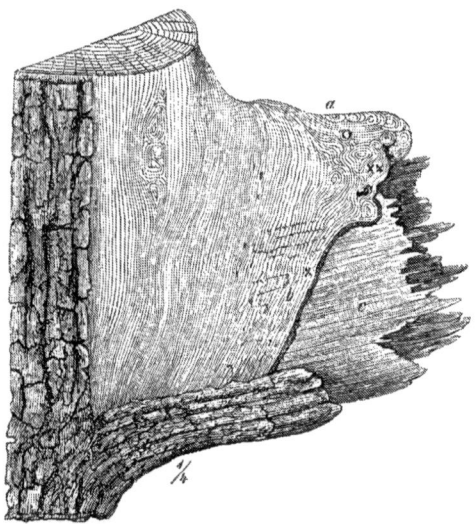

FIG. 146.—A fractured oak-branch. The wound is being gradually occluded by a callus which is slowly advancing beneath and pushing off the thick cortex. At *a* the new growth shows curls, while at *b* it pushes its thin non-vascular edge forward regularly over the dead wood. The dead wood is represented at *c*. One fourth natural size.

slow formation of callus on the lower part of a wound. In that region the cortex is, as a rule, loosened from the wood during the operation of pruning. At the time when the cambium is active, it is quite impossible to prevent the cortex being loosened, the friction of the saw being sufficient to account for it. But the main cause is to be traced to the fact that, in order to prevent the cortex being torn off, a cut is first of all made underneath, and during the sinking of the branch the lower edge of the wound is subjected to severe pressure.

The cortex of the lower edge of the wound forms a pivot round which the sinking branch turns, and, although the effects may not be immediately visible, still the crushing and tearing at that point kills the cambium for an inch or two back from the edge of the wound. Of course, in such a case, the new growth—namely, the callus—is not formed at the edge of the wound, but at a considerable distance from it, where it is covered by the cortex (Fig. 148). The result is that the cortex, which was originally in intimate contact with the wood, becomes detached,

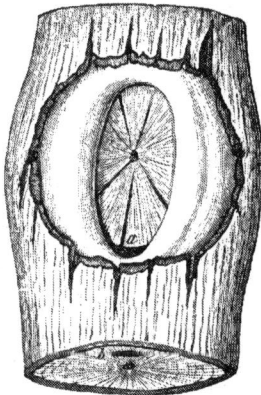

FIG. 147.—A branch-wound on an oak which has been half occluded by a callus.

FIG. 148.—The lower edge of a branch-wound one year after being formed. The cortex, *a*, that has been crushed during the sinking of the branch, dies as far as *b*, at which point the formation of callus, *c*, begins, and the cortex is gradually separated from the wood. Natural size.

so that a cavity is formed beneath the wound between the wood and the dead tissues. This cavity acts like a gutter to catch the rain-water that flows over the surface of the wound, as well as all the organisms that it may contain. This forms a specially suitable place for the germination of the spores of parasitic fungi, and it is from here that water containing the soluble products of decomposition finds its way by means of the medullary rays into the interior of the wood. This cavity is a gutter in every sense of the term, and at the same time the point of attack for fungi. Even although the surface of the wound may have been coated with tar immediately after pruning, this spot remains unprotected, and indeed it is only formed after the cortex has been separated from the wood by the advancing callus. It is in fact the Achilles heel of the branch-wound. In pruning, the main object must be to prevent its formation, but this is possible only if pruning be confined to autumn and winter, when growth is at a stand-still, and when the cortex is least liable to be detached from the wood. If one also takes the precaution to support the branch during sawing, and at the moment of separation to push it clear of the wound, danger is reduced to the minimum.

The rate at which a wound is occluded depends entirely upon the vigour of the tree and the size of the wound. A callus forms on young trees, with their relatively broad annual rings, faster than upon old trees, and the faster too the higher on the stem the wound is situated, because with few exceptions the breadth of the rings increases as we ascend. It is equally apparent that occlusion will be accomplished sooner where the situation is good than where bad. In the case of dicoty-ledonous trees, especially the oak, to which my investigations have hitherto been confined, branches of a greater diameter than 4—5 inches should not be removed.

The effects of pruning as regards the health of the tree depend chiefly upon the period of the year in which the opera-tion is performed. So far as my observations go, it is always highly dangerous to prune the spruce during summer, as rapidly advancing wound-rot is an almost invariable con-sequence. It may be mentioned, however, that in all the cases which I examined, the cortex had been injured during the process of pruning. This may be avoided by pruning during autumn or winter, and as the cut surface becomes immedi-ately covered with a resinous exudation the wound is almost certainly safe from rot. It is only in the case of the older branches, where the heart-wood emits no turpentine, that parasitic infection is liable to occur. It thus appears to me that conifers may be pruned in autumn and winter, if the wounds caused by the removal of the larger branches be coated with tar, but since in the case of these trees the branches are generally small this will seldom be necessary.

When the wounded surface of a dicotyledonous tree has not been tarred, one first observes a brown colour penetrating to a

S

depth of an inch or two, and this is succeeded in a few years by wound-rot, which, however, ceases to make progress when the wound closes (Fig. 149). If pruning has been done in summer, it will be found that beneath the wound brownness appears in the youngest annual ring, and often spreads down the stem for four or five yards. If one omits to apply a coat of tar, the danger of infection by parasitic fungi is naturally increased. These, however, penetrate even into tarred wounds should they

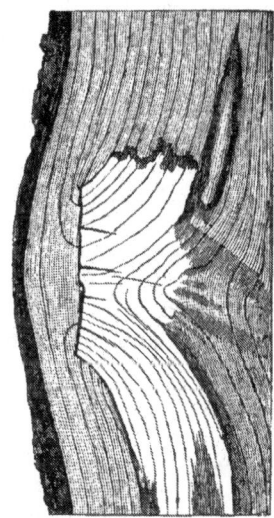

FIG. 149.—Oak pruned in July. Rot has spread from and beneath the untarred surface of the wound far into the stem. One third natural size.

FIG. 150.—The occluded branch-wound of an oak which has been infected by *Hydnum diversidens*. One half natural size.

be formed in spring or summer, because at that time the germ-tubes are able to enter beneath the lower edge of the wound (Fig. 150).

Tarring produces satisfactory results only when pruning has been done in late autumn or in winter, because it is only then that the tar is absorbed by the surface of the wound. It would appear that the absorption of the tar is due partly to the diminished amount of water in the wood during autumn, and partly to the consequent negative pressure of the air in the tree.

When pruning is undertaken in spring or summer, the tar altogether fails to enter the wood, and the thin superficial layer does not prevent the cut surface from drying later, and forming fissures into which water and fungi may gain an entrance. And then, again, the separation of the crushed cortex from the lower edge of the wound frustrates the object of tarring.

From what has been said, it follows that dicotyledonous trees may be best pruned in the months of October, November, and December—perhaps also in January and February—and that a good coat of coal-tar should at once be applied to the wounds.

Hitherto pruning has usually been undertaken in summer, and this explains why the operation has caused such enormous damage to trees, especially the oak. It is, however, desirable from every point of view that the subject be further investigated with scientific accuracy. Several species of trees should be taken in hand, because the trials which I conducted were confined to the oak, and even in their case sufficient time has not yet elapsed to make it possible to furnish conclusive answers to all the questions that have just been raised.[1]

SHORTENING OF BRANCHES

The shortening of the branches of plants from three to ten or twelve feet in height differs from pruning proper only as regards the size of the branches. Most of what has been said in connection with pruning may be applied here. It therefore follows that all shortening of branches is an evil which can only be excused when important objects are to be gained. The dressing of the younger classes of plants is most admissible at the time of transplanting, when the number of the roots has been considerably reduced. In the early part of the season when foliage is scarce, and when transpiration of water proceeds but slowly, the quantity of roots may suffice; whereas in summer the diminished mass of roots may be unable to provide sufficient

[1] It is very desirable that observations be continued on some 240 pruning experiments that I carried out in 1875 in the woods attached to the Forest School of Eberswalde.

nourishment for the undiminished crown, which consequently withers. The danger is avoided, and the plant gets over the loss in a short time, if equilibrium between the roots and the foliage is restored at the very first by shortening the longer branches.

A second reason for shortening the branches is the improvement of the shape of the plants, whether in the nursery or in the wood. I do not intend in this place to enter upon the technique of the subject, but will merely say that so far as the growth of the plant is concerned the usual time—namely, summer —is the least suitable. If we dress a plant in spring or autumn we remove, in the main, only the branches, the reserve materials being left in the storehouses of the stem. But if summer be selected for the operation, the reserve materials of the stem, being partially utilized in the production of shoots and leaves, are lost. If one waits till autumn, the leaves of the branches to be removed will have assimilated materials for the following year, and these will have been partly deposited in the main stem. It appears desirable to institute investigations in this direction, and the question whether wounds are least attacked by parasitic fungi, such as *Nectria*, during summer or, during autumn and spring should also receive careful attention. This question has special force with respect to *Acer*, *Tilia*, and *Aesculus*, seeing that these genera suffer most from *Nectria cinnabarina*, and in their case even small wounds should be protected by grafting-wax.

The practice of leaving snags destitute of buds on the main stem is justly condemned, for the reason that if growth is rapid they are partly embraced or completely enveloped when dead and withered. On the other hand, it is a mistake to suppose that decay spreads in the wood from such snags in after years, for I have never been able to observe such a state of things even in oaks that had been pollarded or coppiced in youth.

As the wounds are small and are usually soon occluded by a callus, the application of tar is scarcely necessary, except in the case of the above-named trees, which are specially liable to suffer from *Nectria cinnabarina*. The technical properties of timber are not interfered with by the small brown wounds in the body of the stem, for it must be borne in mind that numerous wounds of a similar character are also formed when branches drop from trees naturally.

As has been already stated, it sometimes happens that parasitic fungi, especially species of *Nectria*, enter through branch-wounds and produce cancerous diseases, which afterwards spread in the stem.

REMOVING DOUBLE LEADERS FROM THE SPRUCE

When the spruce is grown in open lines in the nursery, it tends to develop a double leader when about three or four years old, so that instead of a single stem we find two. If one of the two stems is not removed till the first thinning, the base dies and decays exactly like the snag of a branch (Fig. 141), and becomes enveloped more or less by the other stem. The wound-rot spreads easily from the stump to the other stem, in which it may ascend to the height of four feet.

In order to avoid this injury, one of the shoots should be removed in early life, as is easily done by means of a knife with a long handle and a bent blade. In rare cases the technical properties of the timber are reduced by a double leader again forming in later life. Such an occurrence, however, happens but seldom, and probably only when the tree occupies a very open situation.

Less damage is done by removing, during the first thinning, a stem that has grown into another at the collar, as sometimes happens in a very dense wood. Such cases of natural grafting occur most frequently in woods that have been formed by planting the young trees in bunches. Seeing that the stems are separated by their cortex up to the twentieth or thirtieth year, when the first thinning takes place, the coalescence is usually only apparent, and the removal of one stem scarcely injures the survivor.

COPPICING

When trees are cut over close to the ground, various phenomena of regeneration which vary with species and age make their appearance. Amongst conifers the Scotch pine produces stool-shoots from dormant eyes only when very young.

In the case of that tree the axillary buds of the primary leaves preserve their vitality until the formation of bark begins, usually about the fifth year, when they perish, and with them the power of producing stool-shoots is lost.

Those American pines which have three leaves in the sheath, for instance *P. rigida*, retain the power of producing stool-shoots till a late age. This is owing to dwarf shoots being developed partly in the whorls, and partly on the main axis midway between the whorls. These dwarf shoots grow each year to an extent corresponding to the growth in thickness of the stem, and produce but few leaf-fascicles. It is these that give rise to an abundant growth of stool-shoots. On account of the absence of dormant eyes that are capable of producing shoots, the regenerative power of the stools of conifers is a very limited one, if we except those cases that have been quoted. The formation of adventitious buds in the callus of wounds is also very exceptional, and it is only in the case of the silver fir that I have occasionally observed new buds and shoots produced from the callus of the stool. On the other hand, it frequently happens that the stools of conifers—more especially those of the silver fir, spruce, and larch, very rarely those of the Scotch pine—live for several decades, and form callus more or less energetically along the edge of the cut surface, so that in certain cases the whole of the transverse section may be occluded. It is probable that the formation of callus on the stool is generally due to the natural grafting of the roots of the tree that has been felled (the nourished stem) with those of an adjoining tree (the nourishing stem). There is, however, no getting over the case quoted by Th. Hartig, where a larch-stool showed a growth of callus notwithstanding the fact that the tree had stood in a large gap in a wood, so that the possibility of nutriment being transferred from a neighbouring tree was absolutely precluded. This case can only be explained by supposing that in the course of years the reserve materials stored up in the roots and stool were dissolved and applied to the nourishment of the cambium.

If the cortex and cambium have not been destroyed for some distance back, by the drying up and decay of the wood, the stools of dicotyledons develop a callus and numerous buds during the year succeeding that in which the tree was felled.

These adventitious buds frequently produce vigorous stool-shoots (Fig. 151), which, however, fail to become self-rooted, and suffer from the advancing decomposition of the parent stool. The stool-shoots that are formed from dormant eyes are much more serviceable, and also more abundant. As it is very desirable that these should become self-rooted, so that the new plants may be unaffected by the health of the parent stool, it is an advantage to have them as low down on the stool as possible. For this reason coppice poles are cut as low as possible, and in order to destroy all shoots that have formed too high up on the stools, and thus encourage the formation of deeper shoots, it is a common practice in oak coppice to char the stools by burning any ground vegetation.

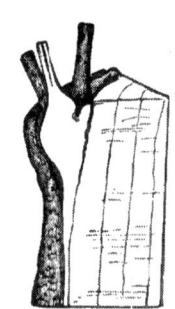

As the dormant eyes preserve their vitality for only a limited period, no shoots need be expected from old stools. The stools of the older class of birches produce abundant shoots, which however usually succumb after a year or two. The reason for this is that the extremely hard bark does not yield to the growth in thickness of the shoots whose base it envelops. The result is that when, on account of the base of the shoots being nipped by the bark, the supply of water fails to keep pace with the accelerated transpiration, the shoots formed early in the year succumb about midsummer.

FIG. 151.—Shoots that have formed from adventitious buds on the one-year-old callus of a beech-stool. Natural size.

When young dicotyledonous trees that have become stunted in growth are cut over close to the ground, the young shoots often grow so satisfactorily and persistently that the plan is frequently practised with good results as a cultural measure. Although this matter has not yet been made the subject of scientific investigation, it seems probable that after the tree has been cut over the reserve materials present in the roots and stool are utilized in stimulating root-growth, so that when the roots have penetrated to a deeper, fresher, and richer layer of the soil the plant continues to grow satisfactorily. Stunted oaks that are situated on ground that is covered by weeds or heather are often induced to throw out strong shoots, and to show vigorous and persistent growth, by setting fire to the whole wood.

INJURIES TO THE ROOTS

These are partly due to animals, *e.g.* mice, but are mostly caused during cultural operations, and are always prejudicial to the plants. The greatest care must therefore be exercised to preserve the roots during lifting, transport, and planting.

Pruning the roots is always an evil, and is admissible only in two cases. The first occurs when roots are crushed, nipped, or broken off during the process of lifting. A clean cut immediately above the damaged part encourages the formation of a callus from which adventitious roots are produced, and also prevents or reduces the chances of decay in the roots. The second case where shortening the roots is admissible occurs where it would be too expensive to preserve the whole root-system during the operations of lifting and planting. It may be mentioned that many plants suffer less from their roots being shortened than from their being doubled back during planting. In order to induce the formation of a dense mass of roots by the production of numerous roots in the neighbourhood of the collar, repeated shortening of the roots may be necessary where the attainment of extra large plants is the object in view.

The practice, which is unfortunately still so common, of aimlessly cutting back the roots is in the highest degree reprehensible.

Other forms of root-injury are occasioned by removing litter from woods, tearing up roots, the attack of cockchafer grubs, mice, &c.

CUTTINGS

The growth and future success of parts entirely destitute of roots, *e.g.* slips, pole-cuttings, &c., depends essentially upon the greatest possible restriction of evaporation from the plants until they have produced an abundant supply of roots. For this reason one at first suppresses the development of leaves by almost entirely burying the cutting, so that only the highest bud is able to produce a shoot; or, in other cases, and more especially in Horticulture, the rootless cuttings are placed in a chamber where the air is saturated, with moisture.

Cuttings of the Caspian willow, that appear to have rooted perfectly, frequently die off on sandy soil in the height of summer, or in the autumn of the first year The reason for this is that in the early part of the season adventitious roots appear both upon the cortex and the callus of the cutting, and when the upper layers of the loose sandy soil dry up the greater portion of the roots on the cortex, most of which are disposed horizontally, die off. When this is the case, it often happens in the height of summer that the roots which have originated in the callus of the wound, and which always penetrate the soil obliquely, are unable to supply sufficient water to satisfy the wants of the leafy shoots, which consequently wither On this account the soil of osier-beds should be worked to as great a depth as practicable, so as to encourage the roots to go deep

GRAFTING

A technical discussion of the various operations connected with the transference of a living shoot or bud from one plant to another would be entirely out of place here It is sufficient that we should shortly consider the internal changes[1] that are associated with the process If we except grafting by approach, where two adjoining plants are so united to each other at one or more places that similar wounds in the cortex of both plants are brought into and retained in intimate contact till complete coalescence has taken place, we find that all grafting operations agree as regards the main principles. A portion of a plant provided with buds but destitute of roots, the so-called scion, or only a portion of cortex furnished with a bud (the shield and eye), is united to a rooted plant, called the wild plant or stock, in such a way that when coalescence takes place water and food-materials will be transferred from the stock to the scion, as well as plastic materials from the scion to the stock

The operation succeeds, as a rule, only when, on the one

[1] Goppert, *Innere Zustande der Baume nach aussern Verletzungen* Breslau, 1873

hand, the cambium of the stock is active, so that immediate coalescence may take place between the callus-tissues produced by its cambium and by the cambium region of the scion, and when, on the other hand, the scion or bud is at the same time inactive. The coalescence, in fact, demands a certain time. Should the scion become active before coalescence has been effected, or should its buds even be swollen at the time of the operation, it withers in consequence of transpiration from the young leaves before it can obtain a sufficient supply of water from the stock. On this account the scions are prepared as early as February, and are preserved in such a manner that by repressing the tendency to growth as far as possible they will still be inactive at the time when the stock has burst into leaf. As is well known, budding is usually undertaken in summer, after the new axillary buds have been formed, the buds being united to the stock at a time when cell-division is still active in its cambium.

The scion and stock are united in such a way that their cambium layers are brought into as intimate contact as possible, care being also taken that no considerable interspaces are left between the cut surfaces of the wood. According to Göppert's investigations, coalescence is due to two distinct processes, for not only does union occur between the cambial layers, or the callus-tissues that are produced from them, but also between the cut surfaces of the wood. The cells of the parenchyma, both of the medullary rays and of the wood, are stimulated to divide, and so form a connecting or intermediary tissue, which completely fills up the space between the two cut surfaces.

If the operation has succeeded and the scion has grown, the latter is in future supplied with the raw food-materials that are absorbed from the soil by the roots of the stock. On the other hand, the plastic materials that are elaborated in the scion nourish the cambium both of the scion and the stock. Of course the new elements that are produced by the cambium cells of the scion are the characteristic elements of the scion, and similarly with regard to the elements produced by the cambium of the stock. The plastic materials produced in the scion afford assimilable nourishment to both scion and stock, just as cow's milk may serve as nourishment not only to a calf but also to a child. But the latter does not on that account assume the pecu-

liarities of a cow, nor does the stock assume the peculiarities of
the scion, although it is nourished by the metabolic products of
the latter. If the cambium cells of the stock naturally divide
more actively than those of the scion, the former will increase in
thickness more rapidly than the latter, and *vice versâ*. The line
which marks externally the point of union between the fast-
growing and slow-growing portions of the stem has been called
by Göppert the "External line of demarcation," and is often
recognizable by distinctions in the cortex and bark. Internally
there is of course also
a corresponding line of
demarcation, along which
the wood of the stock
and scion unite, and
which may often be re-
cognized by a difference
in the colour of the wood
(Fig. 152).

Many cases are known
where it must be ad-
mitted that the scion
exerts an influence on
the stock. It has been
observed, for instance,
that when a scion with
variegated leaves has
been used, variegated
leaves have sometimes
been produced on the

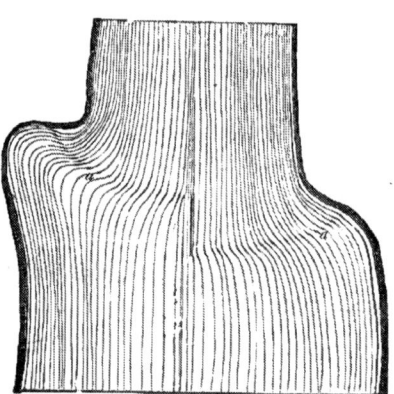

FIG. 152.—Transverse section through the region
where *Sorbus Aria* has been grafted on
S. Aucuparia. The boundary line, *a a*, between the slow-growing *S. Aria* and the fast-
growing *S. Aucuparia* is known as the internal line of demarcation. One fourth natural
size.

shoots that have afterwards formed on the green-leafed stock.
Such a case forces us to the conclusion that the plastic materials
produced in the variegated leaves of the scion possess peculiar
properties which act upon the cambium cells of the stock in
such a way as to induce variegation in the leaves of the new
shoots. It is not my intention now to discuss the still more
potent influences which the scion has been known to exert in
certain cases on the stock, merely remarking that hybrid forms
have been obtained by grafting different varieties of potatoes on
each other.

DEFOLIATION OF TREES BY INSECTS[1]

The effects on dicotyledonous trees of defoliation by insects depend on the season when it occurs. When the young shoots as well as the leaves are destroyed in spring, fresh shoots are soon produced by the dormant eyes of the older branches, or by the buds that may have escaped at the base of the young shoots. Should defoliation occur in June or July, the trees reclothe themselves during August with leaves which spring from the buds of the defoliated shoot itself. When defoliation takes place still later, fresh leaves are either not produced at all or only very sparingly. In the following year it usually happens that the effects of the defoliation are entirely obliterated. The wood-ring formed during the year of defoliation is narrow, and the growth of the succeeding year is usually also below the normal. The effects on the larch are similar to those met with in dicotyledons. In mixed woods of beeches and conifers, the former often suffer very severely from bark-scorching after the conifers have been stripped of their leaves.

As compared with dicotyledons, evergreen conifers usually suffer very severely from defoliation, but in their case also much depends on the season of the year when the damage is done. Should this occur in spring, before the new shoots have been formed, or in autumn, after the wood-ring has been nearly or entirely completed, the life of the tree is not endangered. The new shoots, being prevented from deriving any nourishment from the leaves of the older branches, do not indeed develop so vigorously as those of trees that have not been defoliated, still a sufficient quantity of foliage is produced to enable such a tree to regain its normal condition in a few years. Fatal results, on the other hand, attend total defoliation at, or shortly after, the time when the new shoots are formed—that is to say, in May and June. On account of their tender condition, the young shoots are either totally destroyed or a portion persists long enough for the buds to develop. In any case there is a reserve supply of dormant buds, which the defoliation may stimulate to further

---

[1] R. Hartig, *Das Erkranken und Absterben der Fichte nach der Entnadelung durch die Nonne. Forst. naturwiss. Zeitschrift.* Nos. 1, 2, 3, 7, 10. 1892.

development, and some of which may even produce short shoots
The trees are, however, unable to reclothe themselves with a
permanent supply of leaves, for the following reasons During
the year in which defoliation takes place, all, or nearly all, the
reserve supplies of plant-food that are stored up in the tree are
made use of by the cambium in the formation of a wood-ring
No growth takes place in the following year The reserve
supplies in the young shoots also are quickly consumed by the
cambium, so that the buds are prevented from forming shoots
In the course of the autumn and winter, especially during
long-continued winter drought, all, or nearly all, the twigs and
branches of the crown die for want of water The bole of
the tree maintains its vitality till the middle of summer—that is
to say, for a full year after defoliation During that period,
however, no growth takes place Then the inner cortex begins
to become brown, and the bole dies This is largely due to
the high temperature of the tree, which is induced by the lack of
shade in a wood that has been entirely defoliated by the ravages
of insects Especially is this the case with spruces, whose bark
is but ill-adapted for mitigating the action of direct insolation.

Should the defoliation not have been complete, the wood
may slowly recover This is most likely to occur when a
mild wet winter follows the season in which the ravages were
committed New shoots are formed on those branches which
have retained a large proportion of their leaves, and which have
therefore been in a position to produce reserve materials
even while the insects were at work, and to store them up
for use during the succeeding season The thin-barked spruce,
however, is apt to succumb to bark-scorching, consequent on
direct insolation. Trees which are to a certain extent protected
against the action of the sun by the foliage of their neighbours
may gradually recover, even after having lost a great deal
of their foliage, but not after complete defoliation

DISEASES DUE TO CONDITIONS OF SOIL

SINCE science has recognized that the occurrence of all infectious diseases is perfectly independent of the chemical composition of the soil, that section of plant-pathology which deals with diseases induced by peculiarities of soil has been greatly restricted in extent.

SOIL IN RELATION TO WATER AND PLANT-FOOD.

The supply of water and food-materials in the soil has a great influence on the rate of growth of a plant, although it is only in rare instances that it produces disease, in the restricted sense of the term explained at page 5.

One such form of disease is the condition where the tree is said to become " **stagheaded** " or " **top-dry**," * and which is usually to be traced to considerable diminution of the supplies of water or food-materials in the soil, and this prevents sufficient nourishment being continued to plants that have grown up under more favourable conditions.

In beech woods this disease is specially liable to occur, in consequence of the removal of litter, and often appears as early as the pole-wood stage. The reduction in soil-fertility first makes itself noticeable in a general diminution of the rate of growth, though frequently also in the withering of the upper portion of the crowns, while the lower portion remains green.

In alder woods top-drought follows excessive draining. When oaks that have grown up in a dense wood of beeches,

---

* [*i.e.*, the topmost branches become completely leafless, and die off, and remain as dry sticks, like antlers projecting above the foliage.—ED.]

and that have but poorly developed crowns in consequence, are isolated by the removal of the beeches, they clothe their stems abundantly with epicormic branches For some years these as well as the crowns thrive perfectly satisfactorily In the process of time, however—and especially on the lighter classes of soil which are subject to rapid drought or are liable to produce weeds —a portion of the topmost branches of the crowns die, and the oaks become stag-headed If the ground is protected in time, by under-planting, the top branches either do not die or the disease soon fails to make any progress, and the stag-headed condition may entirely disappear owing to the dry branches dropping off

It is difficult to demonstrate the causes of these phenomena experimentally, but the following explanation may be accepted as sufficiently accounting for the disease Directly the oaks are isolated the amount of soluble food-materials in the soil is augmented, owing to the accelerated decomposition of the humus that covers the ground, and, at the same time, the leaves of the crown, being more exposed to direct sunlight, are enabled to assimilate more rapidly These two causes combine to produce considerable increase of the plastic substances, and consequently an increase in growth, and the dormant axillary buds are also enabled to develop into shoots

The first impulse to activity is probably communicated to the dormant eyes by the increase in the products of metabolism, while their further development into shoots is rendered possible by the intensified action of the light When the crowns and branches have grown vigorously for a few years, the stock of humus becomes exhausted, while the soil dries up in summer to considerable depths, owing to the upper layers being deprived of their protective covering The result is that the processes by which plant-food is rendered available are interfered with, and the stock of soluble food-materials in the soil is reduced Such a state of things is commonly expressed by saying that the ground has " become wild "

The years when plant-food is abundant are followed by a period of famine Owing to the reduced supply of water and nutriment, the upper part of the crowns is starved, the lower branches appropriating the whole of the water and plant-food

Provided the crowns have not been too severely crippled, they may recover under the influence of an increased supply of food-materials, consequent on the improvement of the soil by under-planting Trees that were possessed of well-developed crowns before the wood was light-thinned produce but few, if any, epicormic branches, nor do they become stag-headed. The reason for this is that, owing to vigorous development, the crowns are able to make use of the excess of nutriment that is produced during the years immediately following the light-thinning No epicormic shoots are produced, so that there are none to interfere with the nourishment of the crowns during the years of famine No doubt the general health of the crowns suffers, but at all events their upper branches do not die.

It follows from what has been said that if top-drought is to be avoided there must be no temporary reduction of soil-fertility. The discovery of the means by which the soil may be protected and its fertility conserved falls within the province of sylviculture

In the case of agricultural plants we are familiar with a number of pathological phenomena which are primarily due to the effects of drought on the soil. Here I will only mention the "going off" of cereals—namely, the withering of the straw before the grain has formed—and the premature ripening of grain, where the plants wither after the seeds have formed, but before all the nutritive materials have been stored up in the grain

Under exceptional circumstances it may also happen that the growth of plants is interfered with by excess of nutriment I would, however, again utter a word of warning against hastily ascribing sickly appearances to the soil, in the absence of scientific evidence. A sudden increase in the supply of plant-food, and the consequent important augmentation of the plastic substances, may, under certain circumstances, cause the outer tissues to rupture, and this occurs when their extension has been unable to keep pace with the growth of the internal tissues It occasionally happens, when some cultural operation has suddenly induced considerable increase of growth in trees, that the bark, especially on the main stem, is ruptured on all sides owing to the powerful internal pressure that is set up When hornbeams [1] that were mixed with beeches in a wood were suddenly isolated in the seed-felling, their annual sectional growth at breast-height

[1] *Untersuchungen aus dem Forstbot. Inst* , Vol III. pp 141—144.

increased in a few years from 0·186 sq. in. to 2·124 sq. in.,
and even more. This caused such high tension in the outer
periderm that longitudinal rupturing was finally induced at
numerous points. Owing
to subsequent shrinkage the
fissures extended to the wood
(Fig. 153, *a*), and it sometimes happened that the
whole of the cortical tissues
became detached from the

FIG. 153.—Diagrammatic representation of
two ways in which the cortex may rupture
when the rate of growth is suddenly
increased.

wood along the cambium region for some distance on each side
of the fissure (Fig. 153, *b*). The consequence was that the whole
of the cortex warped like a board that has been dried on one
side. Most of the numerous wounds healed very quickly in

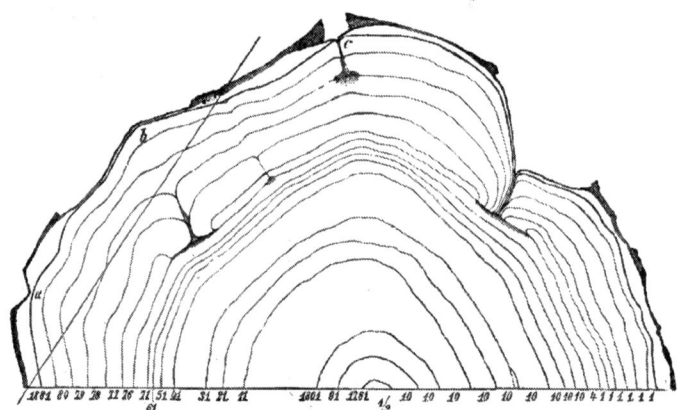

FIG. 154.—Transverse section of the stem of a hornbeam whose cortex had been
ruptured in 1876 owing to sudden acceleration in the rate of growth. *a*, a fissure
in the cortex which does not extend to the wood; *b*, an occluded fissure; *c*, a
fissure which has not yet been completely occluded. The figures correspond to
the annual rings, these being very narrow in the years 1861—1871. One half
natural size.

about a year, though some not till later (Fig. 154), but for a
long time the cortex of such hornbeams exhibited an unusual
appearance (Fig. 155).

I have frequently observed the cortex of oaks[1] to be similarly

---

[1] *Op. cit.*, vol. i. pp. 145—150.

T

ruptured, when trees that have grown for a long time in a wood, overcrowded owing to neglect in thinning, have been suddenly isolated, or when trees that have been reared in restricted light have been suddenly exposed by the removal of the standards.

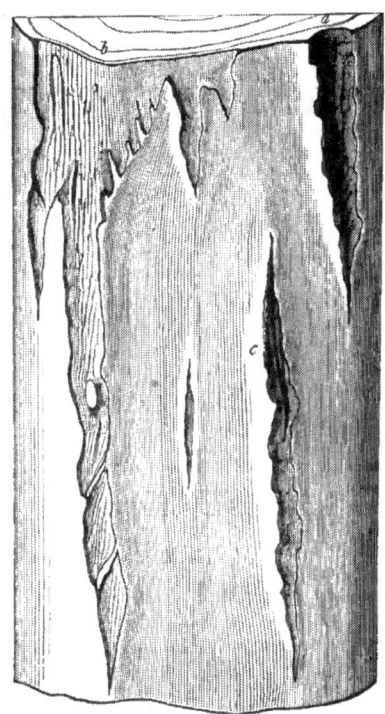

FIG. 155.—Hornbeam whose cortex has been ruptured. *a*, a crack which does not extend to the wood; *b*, a fissure reaching to the wood, but which has been occluded by the formation of callus (see Fig. 154, *b*); *c*, a crack which extends to the wood only in the upper portion. One half natural size.

The augmented supply of food-materials in the soil, and the intensified action of the light, resulted in such an acceleration of growth that fissures of various sizes were formed all over the stem. Fig. 156 represents the transverse section of such an oak a hundred years old, and exhibits the interesting manner in which new tissues are produced as a result of the formation of the fissures. These wounds are injurious, not only because the resulting cicatrization and formation of callus interferes with the splitting of the wood, but also because they offer a means of ingress to parasitic wood-destroying fungi. They may almost always be avoided by strongly thinning the plantation some years before it is intended to "lighten" it.

It being taken for granted that roots rot and the whole plant dies when excess of stagnant water in the soil prevents the entrance of air to the roots, and, further, that the same cause induces the formation of injurious humic acids, increases the danger of frost in the case of many plants, and conduces to seedlings being thrown out by frost, &c., the subject need not be further discussed.

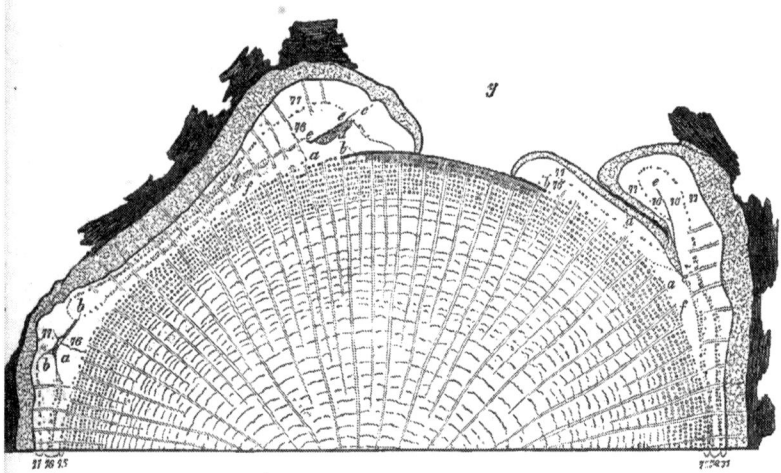

FIG. 156.—Transverse section of an oak which in consequence of much accelerated growth has ruptured in two places, *x* and *y*, two years before being felled. At the three places marked *a b* the cambium has occluded the surface of the wood with new tissues, which are possessed of an independent cortex, *d d*. The loose flaps of cortex have at *e e* formed new wood on their inner surface. This has formed a kind of callus-cushion at *c*, which constitutes the edge of the wound. The wood-ring formed underneath the cortex in 1876, the year in which the cortex was ruptured, is a sort of double ring, and consists of two parts, *f* and *g*, both of which contain a porous zone and a zone where vessels are comparatively scarce. The porous zone of the inner of these two parts, namely *f*, was formed in the spring before rupturing had taken place.

CIRCULATION OF AIR IN SOIL [1]

The metabolic processes in the roots demand an abundant supply of oxygen. The roots die owing to asphyxia if they are excluded from a constant supply of this element. Oxygen is necessary not only for growth but also for the formation and solution of reserve materials, processes which are specially active in roots. The air in the soil is impoverished to an extent corresponding to the amount of oxygen thus abstracted. Under normal conditions the loss is abundantly compensated for, partly by the variations of temperature in the

[1] R. Hartig, *Zersetzungserscheinungen*, pp. 75 *et seq.*

superficial layers of the soil, partly by the processes of diffusion, and partly by the entrance of water containing dissolved oxygen. The greater the daily and annual variations of temperature in the upper layers of the soil, and the greater the depth at which they operate, so much the more thorough is the interchange of gases, or, as it is sometimes called, the "respiration" of the soil. As is well known, the temperature of the soil depends, in a great measure, on its specific heat. The lower the specific heat, so much the more quickly is the soil heated or cooled. Water and humus possess a high specific heat, and the more of these substances a soil contains the greater will be the quantity of heat required in order to raise its temperature. A forest soil that is unprotected by umbrage, that is easily dried owing to exposure, and that has lost the greater part of its humus, is much more easily warmed than a soil that is protected by a dense wood, is constantly moist, and contains abundance of humus.

It is further evident that a forest soil which is exposed to direct insolation is much more easily warmed, though it also cools much more easily owing to radiation of heat, than one where the crowns of the trees and a covering of leaves and humus afford a double protection.

So far as the diffusion of air in the soil is concerned, we know that it only occurs to a considerable extent in porous soil which is not over-wet. In the case of dense, firm wet soil the mixing of gases proceeds with extreme slowness. It may happen, under certain circumstances, that the interchange of gases in the soil is so limited as to induce asphyxia and decay in the roots of plants. I have applied the term "Root-Rot" to cases where the roots die by asphyxia, in contradistinction to infectious root-diseases.

ROOT-ROT [1]

This disease is specially destructive in the young Scotch pine woods of the north of Germany. It seldom appears before the twentieth year, usually not till the thirtieth, and is characterized by the trees appearing unhealthy for a short time and then falling over while still perfectly green, after snow or a strong gale has supplied an external impulse. The tap-root will be

[1] *Op. cit.*, pp. 74 *et seq.*

found to be wet and rotten almost back to the stool, while on the other hand all or most of the shallow lateral roots remain perfectly sound   Only in rare cases is the withering of the tree due to saturation of the stool with resin, consequent on the decay of the tap-root   Root-rot is to be distinguished from the ravages of *Trametes radiciperda*—both being frequently met together in pine woods—by the tap-root rotting and the lateral roots remaining sound, whereas in the case of the parasite the tree is killed, though not thrown, owing to the lateral roots being attacked

The disease is also to be met with in spruce woods growing on decidedly shallow soils that contain stagnant water. Under such circumstances, however, it is less destructive, because the shallower root-system of the spruce makes the tree more independent of the decay of the few roots that penetrate deep into the soil

In the case of pine woods, root-rot appears only on soils where, at a short distance from the surface (usually about $1\frac{1}{2}$ ft), a stratum is encountered which offers no obstacle to the entrance of the tap-root when the trees are young, but which is of such a texture as to prevent the free circulation of air after the wood has become close. This stratum, which usually consists of argillaceous loam or of very fine-grained quartz (alluvial loam), is so difficult to work with the spade as to necessitate the use of the pick. As such conditions of soil are also unsuitable for agricultural purposes, we very frequently find such strata where farming has been replaced by forestry. For this reason the subsequent disease of the pines has been erroneously ascribed to the previous tillage operations. At first young pine woods thrive admirably on such soils   The tap-roots penetrate to the deeper layers of the soil, to which at first the circulation of air also extends. It is only when the branches begin to interlace and to form a dense umbrageous canopy which protects the soil summer and winter, and when a thick layer of leaves and humus forms on the ground, that the circulation of air in the soil is interfered with   Insolation becomes impossible, and both heating and cooling are rendered alike difficult. As the soil remains constantly moist, while the air is largely excluded from soil that is argillaceous and very impervious, or consists of dense sand, the processes of diffusion proceed but slowly. Although it may not be for some decades, this interference with the air-circulation may ultimately induce asphyxiation of the deeper roots, by preventing their obtaining a sufficient supply of oxygen.

Root-rot never occurs in dicotyledonous trees, and only with extreme rarity in pines that are mixed with dicotyledons. Possibly this may be explained by the fact that during half of the year the soil is subjected to the minimum of umbrageous shelter, and consequently there is more air-circulation than in a wood composed entirely of conifers.

This brings us to the immediate consideration of the best means of prevention. These must always be directed towards securing better aëration of the soil. The circumstances of any particular case must determine which of the following courses is to be taken: cultivating mixed woods of dicotyledons and conifers, or, should this be impracticable, the pine may be replaced by the shallow-rooted spruce; the removal of excessively large accumulations of leaves in hollows; or the abstraction from the soil of stagnant water by drainage.

The death of the deeper roots on trees that have been too deeply planted may to a certain extent be described as a variety of root-rot. The heavier the soil, so much the more dangerous is it to plant deeply. It is best that such a tree should succumb at once, but in most cases it lingers through several decades without being able to produce new roots to replace those that have rotted off. Only a few trees, such as willows, poplars, and especially shrubs, develop a plentiful supply of adventitious roots immediately beneath the surface of the ground, by means of which a new root system is formed, as in the case of cuttings which are absolutely destitute of roots.

Similar conditions are induced when the roots of older trees are covered with a thick layer of earth, as often occurs during the operations attending road-making, mining, &c. In such cases less damage is done if the air can get at the roots from the side, as usually happens when trees grow on sloping ground, but if the entrance of air to the roots is rendered a matter of great difficulty the trees either die off entirely, or at all events their growth is seriously impaired. I found close beneath the surface of the earth-heap that adventitious roots were being abundantly produced from the uninjured cortex of smooth-barked tiees, such as the beech and hornbeam, even when the stems were eight inches in diameter

Where it has been deemed desirable to preserve valuable trees, excellent results are said to have been got by ringing the stems a short distance beneath the surface of the ground, or at least by removing the bark in patches as far in as the wood. From the callus that formed at these places numerous roots were produced, which by ramifying close beneath the new surface of the heaped-up soil preserved the life of the tree

· It is scarcely necessary to mention that failure in the natural regeneration of beech woods is often to be traced to the insufficient aeration of soil that is covered with a thick layer of humus. Small seeds especially, that are buried too deeply, frequently fail to produce plants on account of the supply of air being insufficient to replace the carbonic acid gas that is produced during germination   The familiar fact that unsatisfactory results are almost always got when the germination of alder- and birch-seeds is tested in a room, although these seeds germinate splendidly when they are sown outside, is probably due to the circumstance that it is only outside that the air in the neighbourhood of the seeds is constantly being changed, owing to the daily variations in the temperature of the soil.   In the room the temperature is uniform and the air is comparatively still, so that the carbonic acid gas which is given off during germination cannot be removed quickly enough from the neighbourhood of the seed.   Death occurs in heaps of germinating seeds for similar reasons.

Analogous to the root-rot that has already been described is also the decay of the roots of plants that are cultivated in glazed pots, which render the free circulation of air impossible.

POISONOUS SUBSTANCES

In the narrower sense of the term poisons are taken to mean only such substances as are directly injurious to plant-cells and effect their destruction.   Such substances may be naturally present in the soil, but are more often imported into it.   As a rule, the meaning is extended to include innocuous soluble substances —which may even be valuable constituents of plant-food—when the solutions in which they are present in the soil are in a too concentrated form. The endosmotic process by which the roots take in water can go on only if the cell-sap of the roots is so much more concentrated than the solutions in the soil that it can absorb water rom the environment. On this account any strong solution of food-materials in the soil will prove injurious, and may even attract water from the roots. The result is that the plants wither. Such a state of things may be frequently observed when very soluble mineral manures are applied in excessively large quantities. Other soluble salts which are innocuous in themselves may also cause plants to wither.

When spring tides have inundated woods situated behind dunes, the water, being unable to return, has slowly percolated into the soil, and the chloride of sodium which sea-water contains has frequently proved extremely injurious.[1] The pine, alder, oak, and beech succumbed altogether and were found to suffer most, while the birch was least affected. In July 1874, along with Herr Schütze, the chemist at Eberswalde, I instituted investigations on the action of common salt, using solutions of the strength of the water of the Baltic (2·7 per cent.) and of the North Sea (3·47 per cent.) The Scotch pine, spruce, false acacia, and beech were selected for experiment, beds of seedlings and transplanted trees being sprayed with the salt water, each square yard receiving 2·57 gallons at a time. One- and three-year-old spruces succumbed both to the weak and the strong solutions, while six-year-old plants were only killed by the stronger solution, though they became partially brown under the action of the other. When spruces some six feet high each received fully three gallons of the stronger solution, some were killed, while others showed only a temporary brownness and ultimately recovered. False acacias one year old were also killed by the weaker solution, while, strange to say, in the case of thirty-year-old beeches it was only the points of the leaves that died, some time after the solution had been applied.

[1] Schütze, "Untersuchung von Boden und Holz aus Beständen, welche durch Sturmfluthen der Ostsee beschädigt sind," *Zeitschrift für Forst- und Jagdwesen*, 1876, p. 380.

In this experiment the Scotch pine proved least sensitive, a result which was possibly due to its deeper roots.

The injurious effects of urine on plants are generally well known, and may be sufficiently explained from its saline contents

Many acids and leys act as true poisons, and are sometimes conveyed to the soil in large quantities in the impure water that flows from factories. As experience proves, they are highly injurious, but this is not the place to discuss the many poisons that may occur in such contaminated water.

A certain amount of interest also attaches to the injurious influences exerted on vegetation by continuous exhalations of carbonic acid gas from the soil At the baths of Cudowa in Silesia many springs of water containing carbonic acid are distributed throughout the park At such places one finds only grass, shrubs being unable to grow This is probably due to the soil being so permeated by free carbonic acid that the respiratory processes of the roots are rendered impossible Grass, however, is enabled to grow because the circulation of air close beneath the surface of the ground is sufficient to maintain the roots alive.

It has been proved that the roots of trees are injured by coal gas when it escapes from pipes into the soil in large quantity. The unhealthy condition or death of trees that line the streets of towns is, however, not altogether to be attributed to this form of injury The cause is rather to be found in the close paving of the streets and footpaths, which precludes the entrance of water and even air, so that the tree-roots suffer both from want of moisture and of air

It may be shortly mentioned here that coal gas also interferes considerably with the cultivation of flowers in rooms This is the case even when but little gas is burned, for small quantities are always escaping from the pipes Camellias, azaleas, and ivy are very sensitive to gas, the least sensitive plants being palms and *Dracæna* *

* [In many cases, at least, these injuries are due to the sulphurous anhydride of which traces are frequently present —ED]

SECTION IV

INJURIES DUE TO ATMOSPHERIC INFLUENCES AND FIRE

THE ACTION OF FROST

THE action of frost on plants, whether fatal or otherwise, can be understood only when one has gained a clear idea of the sources of heat of which plants can avail themselves.

The metabolic processes which make the more highly developed animals independent to a greater or less degree of the influences of external heat constitute a factor in the vegetable kingdom which may be neglected, in comparison with the effects exerted on plants by the heat of the surrounding media. In the case of the older classes of trees, especially those which are covered by thick bark, the temperature of the lower and inner portions of the tree is chiefly determined by that of the soil. The temperature of the surrounding air has, however, most influence on branches and twigs.

At the time of active growth, and in fact whenever transpiration of water is proceeding energetically, the temperature of the interior of a plant is brought into conformity with that which prevails in the soil by means of the water that is absorbed by the roots. This has been placed beyond the shadow of a doubt by the following experiment. Two trees alike in all respects and equally exposed to the sun were selected, of which one was deprived of its branches. It was then found that the temperature of the tree that had been left intact was 18° F. lower than that of the tree which had been pruned. When the former was also pruned, and the ascent of water consequently stopped, the temperature at once rose 18° F. When the soil is frozen so that no water can enter by the roots, the tree receives heat from the soil only by the process of direct conduction This, however, is always of sufficient importance to explain why the temperature of the interior of a tree, even during prolonged cold, rises as we descend, and also why a deep soil, in which the roots descend to long distances, has a more favourable thermic effect on trees than a shallow soil. This also explains why a natural or artificial covering on the soil is so useful in enabling fruit and ornamental trees to resist the winter's cold The reason also why certain trees that are easily frosted when young are apparently less sensitive to cold in later life—or become "hardened," as it is called—is to be traced to the greater amount of heat which the roots receive when they have penetrated to greater depths

The extraordinary rapidity with which shrubs and trees become green in spring after a heavy shower of warm rain is also due to the rise in temperature of the soil Finally, the early appearance of leaves on the smaller classes of trees in a wood, as compared with the larger trees, is due to the fact that the soil-strata in which the roots of the former are chiefly distributed experience a rise in temperature at a time when the cold of winter still prevails in the deeper strata, and it is from the latter that the stronger and more vigorously developed roots derive their heat

It is the temperature of the surrounding air that chiefly determines the temperature of twigs and branches, as well as of all the more delicate parts of plants generally Heat penetrates with extreme slowness into the interior of those portions of a stem which are covered with a very thick periderm or a layer of bark It is only when insolation is uninterrupted that the side of a tree which is exposed to the sun's rays may become heated to such a pitch as to induce such pathological phenomena as "Bark-scorching" and "Sun-cracks" As opposed to the heat which plants receive, we have the loss of heat which they experience Owing to the evaporation of water, heat is directly abstracted from the tissues where this process is active The process of assimilation is also connected with loss of heat

The rate of cooling is, however, most influenced by radia-

tion of heat. This proceeds most energetically in the more
divided up parts of plants, where the surface is large in
proportion to the mass of the organ. The depression of temperature consequent on radiation of heat not only explains the
phenomena of hoar-frost, dew, &c., but is also in most cases
accountable for late frosts which not unfrequently occur during
still clear weather, even when the temperature of the air is
above the freezing-point. From what has been said it is
sufficiently evident that the readings got from thermometers
inserted in holes of different trees are the result of the joint
action of various heat-producing and cold-inducing factors. The
determination of the internal temperature of trees at the Forestal
Meteorological Research Stations has absolutely no scientific
value, and represents a waste of time on the part of the observer
that is quite unjustifiable.

When the temperature of any portion of a plant sinks below
the minimum necessary for the production and continuance of
the chemical processes of metabolism—that is to say, for the
calling into action of the vital forces—a period of rest ensues,
which continues until the necessary thermal conditions are again
restored in the tissues. Should the temperature sink considerably
below 32° F., the plant is frosted; in other words, a portion of the
water of imbibition in the cell-walls and a portion of the water
of the cell-sap separates in the form of ice crystals, while a
more concentrated solution with a lower freezing-point remains
behind in the liquid form.

In the wood of a tree, where for the most part intercellular
spaces are absent, the water of the cell-walls can only separate
out to form ice crystals in the lumina of the cells, while the
walls themselves become drier but do not freeze. As the lumina
of the wood-cells contain abundance of air besides water, there
is ample space to admit of the expansion which the water
undergoes in changing into ice. The lower the temperature
sinks, so much the more water leaves the walls, and so much
the drier do they become. This explains why trees shrink in
exactly the same way during intense cold as felled timber does
on drying. The volume of the cell-walls is reduced proportion-
ally to the water that is withdrawn, and the stem ruptures
longitudinally and displays frost-cracks or frost-fissures. These

are most abundant on the north-east side of trees, because intense cold usually occurs with a north-east wind. As a rule, frost-cracks are formed only when a great reduction of temperature occurs suddenly, and when the interior of the tree is therefore relatively warm, so that excessive shrinkage is confined to the outer layers of the wood.

It is a familiar fact that, when such frost-cracks have closed up with the restoration of a higher temperature, they become occluded by the callus that forms along their edges. The reduced pressure of the bark causes the formation of new tissues along both sides of the crack, and these project from the surface as a "frost-rib." On account of the thin callus-layers being easily ruptured, it requires but a few degrees of frost in succeeding years to re-open the crack. Repeated opening and closing of the wound sometimes induces the formation of strikingly prominent frost-ribs.

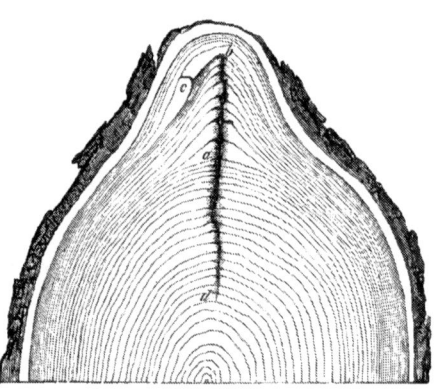

FIG. 157.—An oak-stem showing a frost-crack which has been produced in the winter before the wood-ring, *a*, was formed. Originally the crack extended from *a* to *d*. For nine years in succession the crack has been annually reopened, so that the frost-rib, *a* to *b*, has been formed, and this has ruptured laterally at *c*. During the last five years the crack has remained closed. One half natural size.

Should several mild winters occur in succession, a frost-crack may close up entirely, as is seen in Fig. 157.

In the interior of old oaks I have sometimes noticed numerous radial and peripheral cracks which did not extend to the outside of the stem, nor had they reached the surface even at the time when they were formed. At present it is uncertain whether these cracks are also to be attributed to the action of frost, and no satisfactory explanation has been given as to the circumstances under which they originated.

When the tissues of the leaves and cortex, and in fact when any parenchymatous tissues are frosted, pure water is withdrawn into the adjoining intercellular spaces, but the cells themselves do not generally freeze. The result is that the cells lose their turgidity, and at the same time begin to droop. This explains the familiar phenomenon of lilies, hyacinths, &c., which have been caught by late frost, being prostrated on the ground, until the ice melts and the cells reabsorb the water into their interior and again become turgid, when the plants resume an erect position.

Cells which contain a concentrated solution, part with water only under the influence of very intense cold, and I have often found that the cortex and bast of trees showed no signs of ice when the wood was hard frozen.

As a rule, when living plant-tissues that contain much water are frosted—and this applies especially to young leaves and shoots that are affected by late frost—large masses of ice are formed in certain regions, and notably underneath the epidermis of leaves and shoots, and in the medulla. The tissues, however, remain entirely free of ice, merely shrinking in proportion to the quantity of water that is lost. These masses of ice consist of parallel prismatic crystals, which are arranged at right angles to the tissues from which the water has been abstracted. The cortical parenchyma of the shoot usually contains numerous intercellular spaces, especially along the line that marks the limits of the collenchymatous tissues of the outer cortex. Owing to the formation of a sheet of ice in this region, a separation of the cortical tissues may take place, which however may occasion but little damage to the plant. I have noticed after a late frost that the epidermis on the under side of the leaves of the sycamore was pushed out into numerous vesicular swellings, but it was only after the lapse of several weeks that this forcible separation exercised any prejudicial influence on the health of the leaves.

On account of its numerous large intercellular spaces, it is evident that the spongy parenchyma of the under part of the leaf offers specially favourable conditions for the formation of ice. In the case of the false acacia and other trees that are still green when the first frost occurs in autumn, a sheet of ice forms in the layer of cells that has previously been formed across the petiole of the leaf Simultaneously with the formation of the ice the connection of the leaf with the tree is severed, the result being that on the following morning there is a general fall of leaves

When a thaw occurs in the frosted parts of a plant, the tissues usually regain the condition which characterized them before the frost appeared As the water is set free by the melting of the ice it is slowly absorbed by the cell-walls and the cell-contents. In many cases, however, it is found that the parts have been killed Instead of the chemical processes that are revived under the action of a recurrence of heat inducing normal metabolism, they initiate chemical decomposition The views are divided as to the time when frost proves fatal While Goppert concludes that death occurs during the continuance of the frost, Sachs is of the opinion that the tissues die only after they have thawed, and that a fatal issue depends very much on the manner and rate of thawing The two views may to a certain extent be reconciled, for it is possible that during winter death occurs during the continuance of the frost, whereas in the case of a late spring frost it appears at the moment of thawing

The death of a plant under the action of frost during winter bears a close resemblance to the effects of drought on the tissues No matter whether the deficiency of water in the tissues is due to the action of frost, or to evaporation being in excess of the absorption of water by the roots, the cells must die if the deficiency exceeds a certain limit. A change is induced in the molecular constitution of the protoplasm, the main feature of which is that the protoplasm is rendered incapable of retaining any considerable quantity of water This change is probably connected with the dissociation of molecular groups in the protoplasm in consequence of the abstraction of water. In a living condition the micellæ * of the protoplasm are surrounded by water, the water and the micellæ being held together by that kind of molecular attraction whose action in an organic substance is spoken of as the force of imbibition It

*[The hypothetical structural units of an organized body have been termed, among other names, micellæ each micella is supposed to have its own molecular structure also, much as a crystal has —ED]

may be assumed, although it cannot be demonstrated, that the arrangement or grouping of the ultimate particles of the protoplasm suffers a change during excessive abstraction of water, and that, when the supply of water is again restored, they are unable to regain their original position. Should the critical limit of drought not be overstepped, the cell passes from the condition of plasmolysis * into that of turgescence ; but, on the other hand, a cell withers and is unable to regain its normal vital condition if the limit of drought has been exceeded. The same holds true when the loss of water is induced by frost. A cell is able to bear a certain amount of cold with impunity, the molecular derangement that causes the death of the plant—that is to say, the changes in the normal properties of the protoplasm —occurring only when the loss of water due to the action of frost or drought has exceeded a definite limit.

In order to illustrate the molecular derangement of the protoplasm, reference may be made to the familiar changes that occur in starch-paste under the action of frost. When that substance freezes it parts with more or less of its water, and the comparatively dry residue suffers a molecular change which prevents its reabsorbing as much water as it originally possessed. When the thaw occurs, the clear water remains outside the disorganized paste, which consequently loses its glutinous character.

In the condition of vegetative inactivity our perennial plants are capable of withstanding our coldest winters without perishing from frost. In other words, our winters are never so cold that our forest trees succumb to a molecular disorganization of the protoplasm of the cells. On the other hand, trees that have been introduced from warmer countries—and these include most of our fruit trees—perish from frost during unusually severe winters. The winter 1879-80 furnished a lamentable instance of this fact. Exotic plants exhibit every degree of hardiness, down to the point which is reached even in our mildest winters, and which precludes the possibility of their passing the winter out of doors. Apart from specific peculiarities, we also find

*[Plasmolysis is a condition of collapse of the living contents of the cell, so that water escapes : the cell cannot grow until it is again distended with water (turgescent).—ED.]

individual differences, and it is this fact that makes it possible for us to acclimatize plants As the capacity to resist frost varies amongst individuals of the same species, just like any other physiological or morphological peculiarity, it becomes possible to acclimatize a tender plant by propagating hardy varieties It is also probable that hardier varieties are produced in the struggle for existence that takes place along the line which limits the natural geographical distribution of a plant, where the increasing severity of the climate bars the way to a further advance From this it follows that in attempting to introduce a certain species it must be advantageous to procure the seeds from such frontier regions

Indigenous shrubs and forest trees suffer from winter frost only under very exceptional circumstances The roots of young trees, more especially oaks up to four years old, may be killed if severe and long-continued frost finds the lighter classes of soil unprotected by snow or any other covering The periderm on roots is thinner than that on stems, and consequently the former are less protected and moreover growth is active for a longer period in roots, where it frequently continues till the middle of winter, so that when frost occurs the tissues are not in the inert condition which assists them to resist cold Such plants burst their buds in spring, but wither up whenever transpiration from the delicate young shoots has exhausted the stock of water

Shoots that have not completed their growth, especially the Lammas shoots of the oak, suffer from winter frost This is a matter, however, that belongs to the second division of our subject, which treats of the phenomena induced by frost in plants that are affected while in a state of vegetative activity.

Even our indigenous trees, more especially evergreen di-cotyledons and conifers, may succumb during winter owing to their supplies of water being abstracted not by cold but by transpiration [1] The absorption of water by the roots ceases when the ground is frozen to a depth that is reached by the roots of young plants No harm is done if the trees are protected above-ground against evaporation, by snow or any other covering They die, however, if they are exposed for

[1] R Hartig, *Untersuchungen*, I p 133

U

months to the action of air and sun, as was the case, for instance, in the winter of 1879–80. In this case drought alone was accountable for death. Even in the course of the winter 1879–80 the leaves of middle-aged spruces and silver firs became brown and died where the foliage was exposed to the direct rays of the sun, and where constant air-currents encouraged transpiration, as, for instance, on the southern edges of woods, on railway embankments, or on spruce hedges, &c. It was said that in Alpine regions which were much exposed to the south wind even old woods of silver firs succumbed entirely to the influence of the frost. In my opinion these phenomena can only be explained by the circumstance that repeated thawing and accelerated transpiration are induced in the leaves by the direct action of the sun during the bright wintry weather that usually prevails in these parts, or by the warm south winds, as the case may be, and that the leaves wither because they are unable to obtain any water from the stems which have been frozen under the influence of long-continued and severe cold. Many of the phenomena accompanying the defoliation of pines, as well as the death of the branches of old pines, may also be explained in this way. The injurious effects of repeated thawing and freezing, long-continued frost, or strong drying winds are to be explained by the scarcity of water that results from the interrupted or at least reduced passsage of water.

The limits of forest growth in northern latitudes and in mountainous regions are determined not so much by the low temperature as by the action of drought on those parts of the tree that project from the snow during the long period of vegetative inactivity. On this account, too, we find that the limits of tree-growth are reached at a considerably lower elevation on south and west slopes, where the action of the sun, augmented as it is by reflection from the snow, is stronger than on north and east slopes.

We are still awaiting a satisfactory explanation of the familiar fact that trees, especially exotic conifers, are more easily killed by frost in a wet situation than in a dry one, and that in general the more succulent parts of plants are more liable to succumb to frost than those portions which are comparatively dry. When trees have suffered from frost during winter the injurious effects manifest themselves in a variety of ways which have not hitherto been sufficiently investigated. After very severe and long-continued winter cold, the cortex, bast, and cambium, and the wood-parenchyma as well, die and become brown. The trees either fail to produce leaves in the following season, or if they do bear leaves, flowers, and even fruit they wither up entirely in the course of the summer or autumn. As the wood does not lose its power of conducting water all at once, trees that are injured by frost may be able to produce leaves. The power, however, disappears as decomposition spreads from the parenchymatous cells to the conducting organs, or as the wood dries up from without inwards. Sometimes the cortex and bast are only killed in patches, and when this is the case a callus may gradually form over the damaged parts.

It sometimes happens, especially in the case of exotic conifers, occasionally also in dicotyledons, that the cortex, bast, cambium, and frequently also the youngest annual wood-rings exhibit immunity from frost ; the wood-parenchyma, especially that in the neighbourhood of the medulla, being alone destroyed. In such a case conifers usually die suddenly from drought in the beginning of May ; whereas dicotyledons, whose cambium becomes active during the bursting of the buds, frequently remain alive. This result is due to the fact that the cambium, having remained unaffected, forms a new wood-ring before the old frosted wood has lost its power of conducting sap ; or else the youngest annual rings escape the frost and suffice for the transference of the sap. Although the shoots and leaves are but poorly nourished for some years after the occurrence of the frost, such trees ultimately recover. Under such circumstances it often proves an excellent plan to prune severely, so as to bring evaporation into proportion with the diminished quantity of water that finds a passage through the wood. In very dry years, however, many trees ultimately succumb to the after-effects of the frost.

When frost affects plants during the season of growth—and this is the case with late and early frosts—a fatal issue no longer depends on the hardiness of the plant, but upon the manner of thawing. When in a state of vegetative inactivity, our indigenous trees can withstand the most severe cold of winter with

U 2

impunity, whereas if the leaves have appeared they suffer from a few degrees of frost. In this case the view is undoubtedly correct that death from frost only occurs with the thaw. When plant-tissue is frozen during active growth, it exhibits the conditions that have already been described. Should the plant thaw very gradually, the water is absorbed by the walls and contents of the cells at the same rate as it is formed from the ice-crystals by the gradual accession of heat, so that when the cells have attained the temperature at which chemical processes are possible the normal conditions of imbibition have also been again restored, and the metabolic processes which were temporarily suspended are resumed under the influence of the higher temperature. The case is different, however, when the frosted parts of plants are rapidly thawed, as occurs, for instance, when they are brought into a warm room, or are touched by the warm hand, or are suddenly warmed by the sun. The rapid accession of heat induces the ice in the intercellular spaces to thaw rapidly, and the ice-water, being but slowly absorbed by the cell-walls and protoplasm, flows into the intercellular spaces, and drives out the air, with the result that leaves which are suddenly thawed become translucent. The normal conditions of imbibition have not been restored when the chemical processes start afresh under the influence of the rise in temperature. Instead of these processes assuming the normal features of metabolism, they lead to chemical decomposition in the comparatively dry and withered tissues ; in other words, they induce death from frost. It is therefore emphatically to be recommended that plants affected by late frost should be protected against a too rapid thaw.

It often happens, even in the case of our indigenous trees, e.g. the oak, that after a cold wet summer the vigorous Lammas shoots have not ceased growing when the first early frost appears. Exotic trees, whose vital processes demand more heat for their normal maintenance than our climate has to offer, find themselves every year in an unprepared condition on the advent of winter. The youngest organs of the annual shoots have not completed their development (and especially is this the case when growth in height continues till the latter part of summer, as happens with *Ailanthus*, &c.), the youngest elements of the wood-ring are still in an embryonic condition and with their walls unlignified, and the plastic substances have not yet been converted into reserve materials. Such trees display the same sensitiveness to winter frost that our indigenous trees do to late spring frost. After a rapid thaw the interrupted chemical processes induce decomposition.

Numerous pathological phenomena in plants have been erroneously attributed to frost, and in particular so-called tree-canker has frequently been ascribed to this cause.* Most of the forms of canker are infectious diseases, and it is only in a few extremely frosty localities that I have had the opportunity of noticing cancerous spots which were undoubtedly due to frost. These were met with on a great variety of dicoty-ledonous trees, and in order to distinguish this form of disease from the work of can-ker-inducing fungi I have designated it "Frost-canker." [1]

Frost-canker always occurs at the base of a lateral branch that has been killed by severe late frost. The first symptoms are found in the callus which surrounds the base of the dead branch. Should the locality (frost-hollow) be visited by late frosts during a series of years, the callus, which has not had time to protect itself by a dense firm periderm, is killed in the month of May by frosts which occur after

FIG. 158.—The branch of a beech showing frost-canker in the vicinity of the base of a shoot that has been killed by frost. The wood is brown internally. Natural size.

the tissues have resumed the state of vegetative activity. The tissues often die to the distance of half an inch or more from the base of the branch (Fig. 158). Subsequently a new callus forms under the dead and rapidly decomposing cortex. Should the plant be unaffected by late frosts for several successive years, these canker-spots may heal up completely. But, on the other hand, should such frosts recur, the canker-spot increases in size with each unfavourable year. The fact that frost-canker makes

[1] R. Hartig, *Untersuchungen*, I. p. 135, Table VII.
    *[See Sorauer, *Pflanzenkrankheiten*, B.I. 1886, for the arguments in favour of this view.—ED.]

progress only in a frosty year distinguishes it from fungoid canker, which spreads every year. It is further to be noted that the late frost also kills the wood at the exposed region as far in as the medulla. The products that result from the decomposition of the contents of the dead cells distribute themselves more or less both up and down the stem, whereas in the case of fungoid canker the exposed wood usually becomes brown only on the surface.

In the case of many trees, especially exotic dicotyledons, the small fissures in the cortex which are induced by cold prove the primary cause of canker.

BARK-SCORCHING, SUN-CRACKS, AND DEFICIENCY OF LIGHT

In science and in practice two entirely different phenomena are referred to under the first of these terms. The more frequent phenomenon, which I shall specially designate bark-scorching, is caused during the months of July or August by the action of unusually strong sunshine on the bark of smooth-stemmed trees which have been suddenly exposed after growing up in a close wood.

The trees that suffer most from bark-scorching are the beech, hornbeam, spruce, Weymouth pine, and silver fir.* The commonest causes of exposure are the formation of roads, railways, or rides, or the retention of certain trees for the production of seeds, or as standards.

The injury to the bark by drying up and exfoliation occurs almost always on the south-west side, the reason being that this is the side on which the sun's rays impinge at the time of the maximum daily temperature.

The extensive clear-felling of spruce woods that had been entirely or largely defoliated in Upper Bavaria by the nun moth afforded an opportunity for some careful observations on the temperature of isolated trees. On August 18, the warmest day of 1892, when the thermometer registered 96·8° F. in the

---

* [These injuries occur not unfrequently even in our climate. It should be noted that the word "bark" is here used in a somewhat loose sense : true bark is dead, and it is the living tissues below which suffer.—ED.]

shade, and 104 9° F on a felled area that was not exposed to the wind, it was found that on the south-west side of eighty-year-old spruces fully exposed to the sun the temperature was 131° F between the wood and the bark   Four weeks later the whole of the south-west side of most of the trees had died. The high temperature may possibly be explained by the fact that the trees had small crowns, and that consequently but little water found its way up the younger wood-rings   By comparing the temperature of the cambium of beeches, spruces, and pines of the same age and thickness, the influence of the cortex and bark in modifying the temperature of trees fully exposed to the sun was determined   On September 30, at 10 A.M, when the temperature of the air was 69 8° F, the temperature on the south-east side of the thin-barked beech was 98 6° F, of the thin-barked spruce 82 4° F, and of the thick-barked pine 68° F   This would appear to indicate that in trees with thin periderm or bark the branches on isolated individuals come well down the stem, so as to afford protection against the sun, a state of things that one does not find to the same extent in trees with thick bark.

On standards in a young wood bark-scorching first appears, and is most severe, near the surface of the ground.   There are two reasons for this   First, the rays reflected from the ground increase the temperature, and, secondly, the air-currents that assist so materially in cooling those parts of a tree which are exposed to the sun are interfered with by the young trees

Even the parenchymatous tissues of the injured parts of the stem succumb to drought, and the alternate desiccation and saturation with external moisture induces rapid decomposition, which of course speedily affects the internal portions of the stem   Should parasitic tree-fungi effect an entrance, the tree may be rapidly killed, but otherwise the decomposition retains the simple character of wound-rot

I investigated and described a disease which I found in a wood of Weymouth pines about forty years old [1]   This disease both agrees with and differs from bark-scorching, and may be designated "bark-drought"   The extraordinary drought of 1876 had reduced the supplies of water in the trees of a wood growing

[1] *Untersuchungen*, III pp 145—149

on dry ground intermixed with a silicious moor-pan, to such an extent that the cortical and other living tissues beneath the bark exposed to the drying winds became completely withered. This occurred on the south and west sides of the trees, and especially at a height of from three to six feet, although portions both above and below these heights were also affected. The Weymouth pine is found naturally in marshy situations, and, adapting itself to the natural habitat of the tree, its cortex is but poorly protected by periderm and bark. It is thus easy to understand that on a dry soil and in a hot dry year the wood is unable to furnish the cambium and cortical tissues with sufficient moisture. It follows therefore that this species of tree should not be cultivated on excessively dry ground, especially where water cannot be expected to ascend from the subsoil.

Of quite another character is the pathological phenomenon appropriately called "sun-crack," which is sometimes met with in late winter or spring in the beech, hornbeam, *Acer*, and oak.[1] In spring, fissures varying in length form in the cortex, which separates from the wood for an inch or more on both sides of the wound. In the case of the beech, with its thin cortex, the rind* not only becomes detached but also dies. Owing to the vigorous formation of callus, such a sun-crack frequently heals up after a few years, whereas in the case of bark-scorching it is very seldom that healing occurs. Fig. 159 represents, in one half the natural size, the cross section of the upper part of an oak taken from the south side of the stem. The tree, which was about 170 years old, and was taken from a light pole-wood of beeches on a fairly steep north slope, showed that numerous sun-cracks had been formed all over the stem, at various periods of its existence.

The cold ground, which in spring was hardly affected by the sun even at midday, must have kept down the temperature of the wood of the oak to a low point, even when the stem was intensely heated by the sun's rays. It is probable that the cortex had become so warm at certain places under the

---

[1] *Untersuchungen*, I. p. 141.

*[The word "rind" is here used in a general sense to denote all the tissues outside the cambium.—ED.]

influence of the sun's rays that it expanded violently, and so became detached from the wood. The question, however, has not yet been settled by experiment, and unfortunately it is scarcely possible in this way to determine the factors that combine to produce sun-cracks.

As a further result of dryness of the air and of excessively strong sun, the premature withering and fall of leaves may here be mentioned. In 1876 I had the opportunity of observing this in an intensified form in all the beech woods on south and west

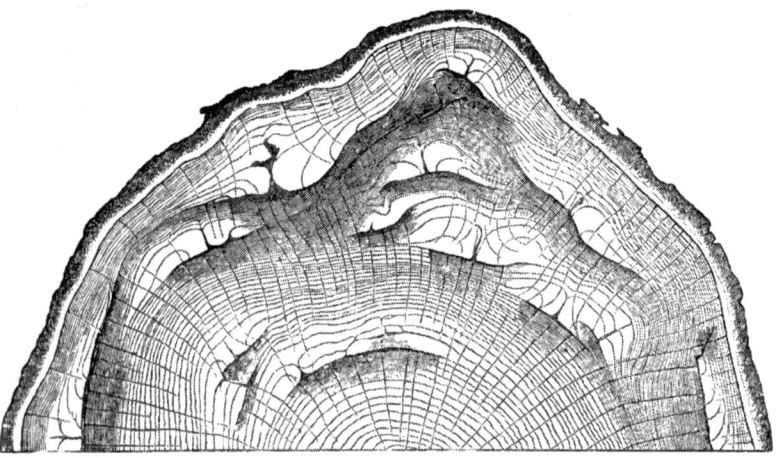

FIG. 159.—Transverse section of an oak-stem showing numerous sun-cracks. One half natural size.

slopes in the northern Harz. The beech pole-woods were almost entirely defoliated in the end of August—that is to say, nearly two months before the normal time of the fall of the leaf. As this state of things was manifest even on fairly fresh ground, it must be attributed to an abnormal rate of transpiration from the leaves during the hot dry summer, to compensate for which water could not be conveyed quickly enough from the ground.

When plants have been kept in a humid atmosphere, as, for instance, in a forcing-house, a conservatory, or under the shade of a close wood, the shoots, but especially the leaves that are produced under such circumstances, are peculiar in possessing an epidermis which is comparatively non-tuberous.* On this account it is ill-adapted to prevent the excessive transpiration which is encouraged by air-currents and a dry atmosphere, and such plants wither or lose a portion of their leaves prematurely.

A sudden accession of light in too large quantity has also a prejudicial influence on the health of plants, and especially on the leaves of trees, whether dicotyledons or conifers. Under normal conditions the chlorophyll-corpuscles protect themselves against the action of too bright light, which would destroy their green colouring matter, by so arranging themselves in the cells of the leaf that their narrow edge only is exposed to the intense illumination. The leaves of plants that have been reared in shade become yellow or brown when suddenly exposed to the action of direct sunlight. In such a case, however, it is always difficult to determine how much of the damage is to be ascribed to the accelerated transpiration induced by the intense sunlight, and to the consequent withering of the cells.

On the other hand, it is a familiar fact that pathological phenomena may also be induced by deficiency of light. A plant that has grown up in unrestricted light possesses a certain stock of the products of metabolism which have not, so far, been utilized in the construction of cells. These may take the form of reserve materials which have been stored up in the plant, or of active plastic substances which are distributed throughout the leaves and organs of the stem. By means of these substances a plant is able to grow for a certain time even without light, until, in fact, the substances have been utilized and the supply has been exhausted. Shoots and leaves that have been produced in the dark are, however, abnormally constructed. They are spindly, and " drawn," and display the phenomenon of so-called etiolation. As chlorophyll can normally be produced only under the action of light, and as the supply of nutritive substances is insufficient, the shoots and leaves are yellowish and not properly developed. Seeing that light cannot exert its retarding influence, the shoots become abnormally elongated. Such drawn shoots,

* [There are other anatomical differences also in the cellular tissues of such shade leaves, as Stahl has shown, which are calculated to make them less resistent.—ED.

being unprovided with a properly developed epidermis, wither or easily succumb to other influences when the plants are again fully exposed to the light, and are incapable of developing into normal shoots

The laying of cereals is the result of the shading of the lower internodes in consequence of thick seeding or heavy manuring The restriction of light that results from drilling seed thickly stimulates spruces, pines, and other plants to make increased height-growth, but this is secured at the expense of the lateral shoots and the health of the plants

MECHANICAL INJURIES

Reference may here be made in a few words to such mechanical injuries as are due to atmospheric precipitations and violent gales, and especially as these often lead to other diseases

Flowers and leaves are damaged by heavy hail, which may also severely injure the cortex of trees, especially when the rind is smooth At the places where the hailstones strike, the rind is crushed, or, it may be, knocked off altogether Although as a rule a callus very soon forms over such wounds, still it not unfrequently happens that the injured portion of the stem dies In young spruce woods in the neighbourhood of Munich I found that the leading shoots which were affected by hailstones died— a result doubtless due to the excessive evaporation from the wood, which in many cases was stripped of its cortex on one side of the shoot to the distance of about an inch

It very frequently happens that the wounds caused by hailstones form an entrance for parasitic fungi The spores of *Nectria ditissima* are specially apt to germinate on such places, and to produce canker in the beech (Fig 39, page 93) Larches, too, are often similarly infected by *Peziza Willkommii*

There is not much to be said about the damage that is induced by snow-crushing For obvious reasons, this occurs almost exclusively in woods of evergreen conifers, where it takes the form either of the breaking off of the tops and branches, or of the fracturing of young poles It may be worth noting, however, that wounds are very often formed at the base of branches which are bent down by a load of snow Should the ground be covered with snow, and should the apex of such a branch become frozen into the upper layers, it may readily happen that during the gradual melting and shrinking of the snow the branch is forcibly detached from the stem altogether. Such wounds frequently form the means of entrance for the above-named parasitic fungi.

Gales may fracture stems or tear trees up by the roots, but such injuries fall rather within the limits of a treatise on sylviculture or forest management than of pathology.

INJURIES DUE TO FIRE, COAL SMOKE, AND LIGHTNING

Attention may here be directed to the fact that the destructive effects of the passage of fire over the ground of a wood depend not only upon the intensity and duration of the conflagration, but also upon the species and age of the trees, or, in other words, upon the amount of protection afforded by the cortex and bark. As is known, the lower portions of the bark of old pines may be perfectly black and charred without the cambium being killed. This is due to the low conductivity of the bark for heat.* If ro brownness is to be observed in the younger layers of the bast, it is evident that the fire can have done no damage. On the other hand, trees with thin bark are very sensitive to fire, and by making a few incisions in the cortex one may determine whether it has been killed or not. Although trees whose lower cortex is damaged may produce fresh leaves, one must not be deceived by such a state of things. Trees that are no thicker than one's arm become green in spring when the lower cortex is charred or withered right round. A similar state of things occurs with beech-saplings that have been barked by mice, but in both cases the trees ultimately wither up entirely. During the growing season the starch that is stored up in the stem at a lower level than the dead cortex is utilized by the cambium—which is no longer nourished from above—in the formation of the wood-ring, so that when the trees die in the course of the summer the stools, being destitute of reserve supplies, are unable to produce

---

* [In cases where the cambium is scorched for some distance, but not entirely, round the stem, the remnant of living cambium may slowly creep round and form callus over the injured side : years afterwards, on felling such parts of the stem present " ring-shakes."—Ed.]

fresh shoots. Shoots are produced much better from the stools
of trees that have been entirely consumed, or that have been cut
over close to the ground directly after the injury occurred   In
such a case the whole of the plastic materials stored up in the
subterranean parts•of the tree are at the disposal of the new
shoots   If the injured stem is sufficiently young to hold out the
prospect of stool-reproduction at all, it can only do harm to
delay cutting it over

SULPHUROUS ACID IN COAL SMOKE AND THE SMOKE FROM IRON-WORKS[1]

In the neighbourhood of extensive blast furnaces or similar
centres of industry, where large quantities of coal are consumed,
it has always been noticed that vegetation suffers from the
smoke   To such an extent is this the case that in industrial
towns like Essen scarcely any vegetation exists   In the direction
of the prevailing winds very serious damage is not unfrequently caused even for a distance of two miles from the furnaces   The views at one time held that the damage was due to
metallic poisons (arsenic, zinc, lead) present in such smoke, or
to the soot deposited on the leaves, have proved to be incorrect
The investigations of Stockhardt[2] and Schroder[3] have shown
that the damage is due entirely to the sulphurous acid present
in the smoke   It has been determined by experiment that the
sulphurous acid being absorbed by the surface of the leaves
induces local death and brownness in the tissues   The tissues
prove most resistant in the neighbourhood of the larger ribs
Although the leaves of conifers absorb less sulphurous acid than
those of dicotyledonous trees, still, on account of their being
longer exposed to the prejudicial influences, they generally
suffer more than the foliage of deciduous trees * If one examines

[1] Hasenclever, *Ueber die Beschadigung der Vegetation durch saure Gase*
Berlin, 1879.

[2] Stockhardt, *Tharander forstl. Jahrbuch*, 1871, p 218

[3] Schroder, *Landwirthschaftl Versuchsstationen*, 1872 and 1873

* [I have investigated many such cases, and find the Larch suffers greatly
The cases are complex, and it is by no means clear that the action of the
acid-gases is merely local on the leaves , there is evidence to show that the
damage is largely due to the gases passing through the stomata and into the
lacunæ of the living leaves —ED]

spruces that are still living, though fully exposed in the neighbourhood of blast furnaces, it will be found that it is only on the youngest shoots that the leaves are still green. The farther one moves from the seat of the mischief, so do the annual crops of leaves that still maintain their position on the spruce-shoots increase. It is thus evident that the duration of the leaves depends in large measure on the intensity of the action of the smoke. Amongst dicotyledonous trees the beech is the most sensitive, after which come the oak and the sycamore, while the elm, ash, and mountain ash, and, amongst conifers, the black pine are some of the most resistant. In towns where it is only in winter that large quantities of coal are used as fuel, the conifers alone suffer. In summer the air is almost free from sulphurous acid, and it is only on the approach of cold weather that the deleterious influences begin to make themselves manifest. At this time the deciduous trees have shed their leaves, so that it is only the conifers that are affected. The sulphurous and sulphuric acids that collect in large quantities in snow that has covered foliage for some time prove injurious to the trees.

The ease with which sulphurous acid is oxidized to hydrated sulphuric acid not only explains how this plant-poison is constantly being removed from the atmosphere, but also indicates how we may remove sulphurous acid from the smoke of blast furnaces and factories generally. To some extent this has already been put into practice. By leading the sulphur gases through moistened hydrated lime 90 per cent. is rendered innocuous. Another plan is to conduct the gas through a long pipe in which a stream of water flows in the opposite direction. By this process a conversion into hydrated sulphuric acid is effected.

According to recent observations the chlorine and soda fumes that are produced in certain factories also prove injurious to vegetation.

THE EFFECTS OF LIGHTNING

Up to the present the way in which lightning affects the health of trees remains unexplained.

When lightning strikes a wood, its effects may be confined to a single tree, or they may be noticeable on a whole group of trees As regards the former case, we find that all trees are subject to be struck by lightning, but that some are more liable to suffer than others Oaks and the Lombardy poplar would appear to be struck most frequently, though the Scotch pine is also very often affected ; whereas the beech enjoys comparative immunity from such injury Even in trees of the same species the form of damage varies exceedingly As a rule the injury is confined to the separation from the wood of a strip of cortex about an inch in breadth This lightning score, which begins in the crown, is frequently interrupted over considerable portions of the stem It may leave one side of the tree and appear on another, again to return to the original side at a different level In stems with straight fibres it runs straight, but in trees showing spiral growth it follows a similar course At the bottom of the tree it disappears between two roots close to the surface of the ground ; or it runs for some distance along the under side of a strong lateral root, and then suddenly disappears By this treatment the health of the tree is in no wise affected The narrow strip of wood is either wholly uninjured or else reveals a small crack down the centre. Externally it shows but little brownness, and in a few years it becomes entirely covered over by a callus.

In other cases trees (pines) that are struck by lightning reveal externally the same form of injury, but in a few days the entire cortex—with the exception of that on the collar, the roots, and the upper part of the crown—dies and becomes brown Such trees generally wither up after an interval varying from a few months to a year or so, although they may remain alive for four or five years, to die at the end of that period In some cases the electric current barks the tree and leaves the stem almost naked, or it splits the stem longitudinally into several parts, dismembering it almost entirely, and scattering large splinters to a distance of one hundred yards In certain cases all that is left in the ground is a short stump

It is only when the tree is perfectly dry, or possesses dry branches or at least dry rotten wood, that the lightning sets it on fire Combustion does not follow in a fresh living tree

So far no explanation is forthcoming to account for the death of the trees over considerable areas that have been affected by lightning, a state of things that I have several times observed both in young and old pine woods.[1] In such cases it was remarkable that death, instead of affecting the whole area simultaneously, spread centrifugally and radially from a given point, and frequently continued to carry off the trees for five years or more. An investigation of the trees showed that only one or a few examples revealed traces of lightning, but that between the crown and the collar of such trees, and many others in their vicinity, the cortex was dead. In an old pine wood the dead bark hung loose from the boles, while the crowns retained perfectly green foliage. In a younger wood about thirty years of age I found three stems showing traces of lightning along the margin of the devastated area which had been steadily extending for five years previously. The first of these had died within the past year, the second still possessed a green crown although its cortex and bast had died between the heights of one and a half and eight feet, while the third, in spite of the lightning having detached a broad strip of cortex, was perfectly healthy in all parts. I confess that in face of these observations I am unable to offer an explanation of the action of the lightning. The fact that trees struck by lightning sometimes remain alive for five years is to be explained in the same way as the frequent survival for several decades of pines that have been girdled. The water and plant-food move upwards in the wood, and the crown, utilizing the products of metabolism, remains healthy, and forms new organs. Death occurs only when the exposed wood of the bole has gradually dried up to such an extent that water is unable to pass upwards in sufficient quantity. That a tree scored by lightning may remain perfectly healthy, while a neighbouring tree not so marked may die, may possibly be explained by supposing that in the former case the electric current was confined within narrow limits, whereas in the latter it was distributed over the whole surface, or throughout the entire cortex, of the stem.

[1] R. Hartig, *Zeitschrift für Forst- und Jagdwesen*, 1876, pp. 330 *et seq.*

THE DISEASES DESCRIBED IN THIS VOLUME CLASSIFIED ACCORDING TO THE PLANT, AND PART OF THE PLANT, ATTACKED

The number placed after the name of a disease refers to the page in the text-book where a description will be found.

Abies

1. The seedlings droop and die : *Phytophthora omnivora*, 58.

2. Young plants in the nursery become yellow or die, the stems contracting suddenly close to the surface of the ground . *Pestalozzia Hartigii*, 136.

3. Young plants are enveloped by a brown fungus : *Thelephora laciniata*, 35.

4. The leaves bear numerous columnar æcidia on their under surface : *Melampsora Goeppertiana*, 161.

5. The leaves display long sporogenous layers on their under surface. These rupture and emit yellow spores : *Cæoma Abietis pectinatæ*, 184.

6. The leaves, which are deformed, are pale yellow, and bear æcidia. The branches form witches' brooms : *Æcidium elatinum*, 179.

7. The leaves are yellowish brown, while, on the under side, the mid-rib bears a black longitudinal ridge . *Hysterium nervisequium*, 108.

8. The leaves are yellow, and remain attached to the branch by being enveloped in white mycelial filaments : *Trichosphæria parasitica*, 72.

9. The branch or stem shows a spheroidal swelling : *Æcidium elatinum*, 179.

10. The branches bear mistletoe, or the stem shows perforations : *Viscum*, 25.

11. The cortex dies right round the branch or stem, and bears black tubercles : *Phoma abietina*, 138.

12. The stem bears irregular or bracket-shaped sporophores which show very fine pores : *Polyporus Hartigii*, 194.

13. The stem bears sporophores with large pores : *Trametes Pini*, 191.

14. The stem bears tawny yellow cap-shaped sporophores, which spring from rhizomorphs : *Agaricus melleus*, 207.

15. The roots bear white sporophores : *Trametes radiciperda*, 186.

16. The roots are attacked by rhizomorphs : *Agaricus melleus*, 207.

Acer

1. The seedlings show black blotches on the leaves or stem, and may decay : *Cercospora acerina*, 135 ; *Phytophthora omnivora*, 58.

2. The leaves show white blotches : *Erysiphe bicornis*, 70 ; *E. Tulasnei*, 70.

3. The leaves show black blotches : *Rhytisma acerinum*, 105.

4. In autumn the leaves show persistent green blotches, which ultimately bear black spots : *R. punctatum*, 106.

5. The branches wither, while a transverse section of the wood shows dark green blotches : *Nectria cinnabarina*, 96.

6. The branch or stem dies, while the cortex bears cinnabar-coloured fungus bodies : *N. cinnabarina*, 96.

7. The stems of young plants contract suddenly above the roots : *Pestalozzia Hartigii?* 136.

8. The branches show canker-spots : Frost-canker, 293.

9. The branches bear mistletoe : *Viscum*, 25.

Acer platanoides

The branches die in spring, and show oblong fungus-bodies : *Septoglœum Hartigianum*, 141.

Æsculus

The branches die, and bear cinnabar-coloured fungus-bodies on the cortex : *Nectria cinnabarina*, 96.

Alnus

1. The leaves show yellow vesicular swellings : *Exoascus flavus*, 133.

2. The leaves show greyish white downy corrugations : *E. epiphyllus*, 133.

3. The cones show pocket-like outgrowths : *E. alnitorquus*, 133.

4. The branches show canker-spots : *Nectria ditissima*, 91.

5. The wood shows red-rot : *Polyporus sulphureus*, 200.

6. The roots show fleshy outgrowths : *Schinzia Alni*, 39.

Alnus glutinosa

The leaves show vesicular corrugations   *E alnitorquus*, 133

Alnus incana

The branches bear witches' brooms   *E. borealis*, 133

Alnus viridis

The branches wither, and black tubercles appear on the dead cortex . *Valsa oxystoma*, 151.

Berberis

The leaves show golden yellow blotches · *Puccinia graminis*, 155.

Betula

1 The leaves show small yellow fungus-bodies   *Melampsora betulina*, 171.

2. The leaves show vesicular swellings . *Exoascus carnea, E. Betulæ*, 135.

3. The branches bear witches' brooms · *Exoascus turgidus*, 133.

4 The stem bears large bracket-shaped sporophores   *Polyporus betulinus*, 206.

5 The stem bears brown crust-like sporophores . *Polyporus lævigatus*, 206.

Brassica

The roots bear fleshy outgrowths   *Plasmodiophora Brassicæ*, 39

Carpinus

1. The leaves bear small golden yellow fungus-bodies : *Melampsora Carpini*, 171

2 The branches bear witches' brooms   *Exoascus Carpini*, 135.

3 Branches or stem show canker-spots   *Nectria ditissima*, 91 , Frost-canker, 293

Castanea

The branches show prominent swellings, and bear a "mistletoe" · *Loranthus*, 30.

Corylus

1. The leaves show small brown blotches . *Sphærella*, 88.

2 The leaves show white dusty blotches   *Erysiphe guttata*, 70.

3. The branches show canker-spots   *Nectria ditissima*, 91.

Cratægus

1 The leaves bear golden yellow swellings, which produce æcidia *Gymnosporangium clavariæforme*, 158.

2 The leaves show white dusty blotches . *Erysiphe guttata*, 70

3 The branches bear witches' brooms · *Exoascus bullatus*, 133

X 2

Cynanchum

The leaves show small yellow fungus-bodies : *Cronartium asclepia-deum*, 175.

Fagus

1. The seedlings show dark patches on the leaves and stem, and decay or wither : *Phytophthora omnivora*, 58.

2. The stem of young plants contracts suddenly close to the surface of the ground, and the tree withers : *Pestalozzia Hartigii*, 136.

3. Young plants in the nursery are enveloped by a brown fungus : *Thelephora laciniata*, 35.

4. The leaves show white blotches : *Erysiphe guttata*, 70.

5. The leaves show brown blotches : *Sphærella Fagi*, 88.

6. The cortex shows canker-spots : *Nectria ditissima*, 91 ; Frost-canker, 293.

7. The cortex is covered with a white woolly substance : *Chermes fagi*, 96.

8. The cortex shows pustular swellings : *ibid.*

9. The cortex of branches is ruptured longitudinally : *Lachnus exsiccator*, 96.

10. The cortex of the stem withers on the south side : Bark-scorching or Sun-crack, 294.

11. The stem bears large bracket-like sporophores : *Polyporus fomentarius*, 206.

12. The wood shows a verdigris-green colour : *Peziza æruginosa*, 224.

Fraxinus

The cortex shows canker-spots : *Nectria ditissima*, 91.

Gentiana

Gentiana asclepiadea shows yellow fungus-bodies : *Cronartium asclepiadeum*, 175.

Gleditschia

The branches bear mistletoe : *Viscum*, 25.

Gramineæ

1. Culm and leaves show fungus-bodies, which are first yellow and later brown : *Puccinia graminis*, 155.

2. The spikelets are covered with a sweetish secretion or produce black fungus-bodies : *Claviceps purpurea*, 98.

3. The spikelets produce dark brown powder : *Ustilago Carbo*, 68.

Hyacinthus

The bulb becomes soft and slimy, and emits a repulsive smell : *Bacterium*, 37.

Juglans

1. The branches bear mistletoe . *Viscum,* 25.

2 The stem bears sulphur-yellow sporophores. The wood shows red-rot *Polyporus sulphureus,* 200

Juniperus communis

1 Leaves and branches enveloped in dark brown mycelia : *Herpotrichia nigra,* 76

2. Branches show swellings which, in spring, produce abundant yellow or brownish spores *Gymnosporangium conicum,* 157 ; *G. clavariæforme,* 158 ; *G tremelloides,* 159.

3 Roots bear white sporophores . *Trametes radiciperda,* 186.

Juniperus Oxycedrus

Branches bear a " mistletoe " : *Arceuthobium Oxycedri,* 30.

Juniperus Sabinæ

Branches show swellings which, in spring, produce abundant yellow spores : *Gymnosporangium Sabinæ,* 158.

Laburnum

The cortex and branches die . *Cucurbitaria Laburni,* 87.

Larix

1. The seedlings droop and wither : *Phytophthora omnivora,* 58.

2. The young trees die, and reveal mycelia on their roots : *Rhizina undulata,* 123.

3 The leaves show yellow fungus-bodies : *Melampsora Tremulæ,* 164.

4. The leaves become brown, and show black fungus bodies : *Hysterium laricinum,* 117.

5. The cortex shows canker-spots *Peziza Willkommii,* 117.

6. The cortex, on its inner side, shows white mycelial sheets . *Agaricus melleus,* 207.

7 The cortex bears brown crust-like sporophores . *Trametes Pini,* 191.

8. The cortex bears large sulphur-yellow sporophores . *Polyporus suphureus,* 200.

9 The cortex bears cap-like tawny yellow sporophores : *Agaricus melleus,* 207.

10 The roots are dead, and show rhizomorphs · *ibid.*

11 The wood shows red-rot *Polyporus Schweinitzii,* 198.

12. The wood is decayed, and marked by white blotches *Trametes Pini,* 191.

13 The wood shows red-rot and luxuriant white fungus-growths . *Polyphorus sulphureus,* 200.

Ledum

The leaves are marked by brown blotches, and show small yellow fungus-bodies: *Chrysomyxa Ledi*, 179.

Medicago, see Trifolium

Picea

1. The seedlings droop soon after appearing: *Phytophthora omnivora*, 58; *Nectria cucurbitula*, 89.

2. Plants in the nursery become yellow and die, the stem being contracted close above the surface of the ground: *Pestalozzia Hartigii*, 136.

3. Young plants, or the branches of older trees, are enveloped in dark brown mycelia: *Herpotrichia nigra*, 76.

4. Young plants are enveloped in the sporophore of a fungus: *Thelephora laciniata*, 35.

5. Young and old trees die, their roots showing mycelia: *Rhizina undulata*, 123.

6. The leaves and branches wither in winter and spring: Frost, 291.

7. The leaves bear golden yellow vesicles: *Chrysomyxa Rhododendri*, 177; *C. Ledi*, 179.

8. The leaves become yellow, and show golden yellow longitudinal ridges on their under surface: *Chrysomyxa Abietis*, 175

9. All the leaves of a young shoot are abnormally short, and rupture on their four sides: *Æcidium coruscans*, 183.

10. The leaves become red, and later yellowish brown. They either show longitudinal black ridges, or fall prematurely: *Hysterium macrosporum*, 109.

11. The branches die in May or June: *Septoria parasitica*, 143.

12. The scales of the cones show numerous round brown swellings on their upper surface: *Æcidium strobilinum*, 182.

13. The scales of the cone show two large æcidia on their lower surface: *Æcidium conorum Piceæ*, 183.

14. The cortex shows dead patches beset with groups of red fungus-bodies: *Nectria Cucurbitula*, 89.

15. The cortex in the lower part of the stem shows resinous exudation: *Trametes radiciperda*, 186.

16. The cortex shows white mycelial sheets on its inner surface: *Agaricus melleus*, 207.

17. The cortex shows evidences of injury by sun: Bark-scorching, 294.

18. The root is dead, and bears small yellowish white fungus-bodies, or large white sporophores: *Trametes radiciperda*, 186.

19 The root shows red-rot and white mycelia *Polyporus vaporarius,* 198

20 The root is dead, and shows black mycelial strands which form white enlargements between the cortex and wood . *Agaricus melleus,* 207

21. Branch-wounds bear brown sporophores . *Trametes Pini,* 191 , *Polyporus Hartigii,* 194.

22 Wounds bear large white sporophores : *Polyporus borealis,* 196.

23. The wood shows white-rot *Polyporus Hartigii,* 195.

24 The wood shows white-rot. The pure white patches have usually a black spot in the centre · *Trametes radiciperda,* 186

25. The wood shows white-rot, and contains numerous cavities . *Trametes Pini,* 191.

26 The wood shows white-rot, and crumbles down into very small cubes *Polyporus borealis,* 196

27. The wood shows red-rot : *Polyporus vaporarius,* 198.

28. The wood shows dark brown blotches or cavities Wound-rot, 236, 243

29 The wood shows green-rot : *Peziza æruginosa,* 224

Pinus Cembra

The roots show numerous Mycorhizæ, 71.

Pinus montana

The branches with their leaves are enveloped and killed by dark brown mycelia : *Herpotrichia nigra,* 77. See also the diseases, 1, 6, 8, 10, 13, 16, 17, under *Pinus sylvestris*

Pinus Strobus

1. The leaves die, and display black fungus-bodies : *Hysterium brachysporum,* 117.

2 The cortex shows resinous exudation and golden yellow vesicles : *Peridermium Strobi,* 175. See also diseases 1, 4, 10, 13, 14. 16, 17, under *Pinus sylvestris*

Pinus sylvestris

1 The seedlings droop and die . *Phytophthora omnivora,* 58 ; *Nectria Cucurbitula,* 89.

2. Seedlings and older plants show brown blotches, which afterwards bear small black tubercles *Hysterium Pinastri,* 110.

3. Seedlings and older plants are entirely yellow and finally brown or the discoloration spreads gradually back from the apex of the shoots " Blight," 111

4. Young plants in their lower parts are enveloped in the brown sporophores of a fungus : *Thelephora laciniata*, 35.

5. The leaves become suddenly brown in summer : " Frost-blight," 111.

6. The leaves show golden yellow vesicles : *Coleosporium Senecionis, C. Euphrasiæ, C. Tussilaginis,* 172.

7. The young shoots in the end of May show golden yellow spots on the cortex. These afterwards rupture, and the shoots either die or become contorted : *Melampsora Tremulæ,* 164.

8. The cortex shows golden yellow vesicles filled with spores : *Peridermium Pini,* 172 ; *Cronartium asclepiadeum,* 175.

9. The cortex gradually dies, and shows resinous exudation : *ibid.*

10. The cortex dies, and shows large white sheets of mycelium on its inner surface : *Agaricus melleus,* 207.

11. Branch-wounds bear brown bracket-like sporophores : *Trametes Pini,* 191.

12. Wounds bear large reddish brown cushion-like sporophores : *Polyporus Schweinitzii,* 198.

13. The cortex close to the ground bears cap-like yellow sporophores : *Agaricus melleus,* 207.

14. The cortex close to the ground bears white cushion-like sporophores : *Trametes radiciperda,* 186.

15. The cortex or wood close to the ground bears white porous crust-like sporophores : *Polyporus vaporarius,* 198.

16. The roots are dead, and bear yellowish white cushion-like sporophores : *Trametes radiciperda,* 186.

17. The roots are dead, and show resinous exudation. Between the wood and cortex white mycelial sheets and black mycelial strands are found : *Agaricus melleus,* 207.

18. The roots are dead, and show white floccose mycelial strands : *Polyporus vaporarius,* 198.

19. The roots show mycelial growths : *Elaphomyces,* 71.

20. The leading shoot or the branches die above a black mark from which resin flows : *Cronartium asclepiadeum,* 175 ; *Peridermium Pini,* 172.

21. The wood shows white-rot, with numerous small round or oval holes : *Trametes Pini,* 191.

22. The wood shows red-rot, without much smell. Floccose mycelial growths and strands are found : *Polyporus vaporarius,* 198.

23. The wood shows red-rot, and emits a very strong smell of turpentine. Thin white mycelial incrustations are found in the cracks : *Polyporus Schweinitzii,* 198.

24. The wood shows holes, the branches bear mistletoe   *Viscum,* 25.
25 The wood (alburnum) shows a dark blue colour. *Ceratostoma pilifeum,* 224.
26. Old and young trees die, the roots showing mycelia   *Rhizina undulata,* 123.

Platanus

The leaves and young shoots die, or the former become brown along the ribs : *Glœosporium nervisequium,* 140.

Populus

1. The leaves show small yellow blotches, which afterwards become dark brown   *Melampsora,* 164.
2. The leaves show yellow vesicular swellings : *Exoascus aureus,* 135.
3. The branches bear mistletoe . *Viscum,* 25.
4. The flowers exhibit golden yellow much-enlarged ovaries : *Exoascus aureus,* 135

Populus pyramidalis

The branch and twigs die : *Didymosphœria populina,* 104.

Prunus Cerasus

1. The leaves are crumpled, and frequently also blood-red in colour : *Exoascus Wiesneri,* 132.
2. The leaves become prematurely yellow and die, and remain attached to the tree during winter : *Gnomonia erythrostoma,* 88
3 The branches form witches' brooms . *Exoascus Wiesneri,* 132.
4 The cortex bears brown sporophores *Polyporus igniarius,* 201.

Prunus domestica

1 The flowers show yellowish red fleshy blotches : *Polystigma rubrum,* 97.
2 The fruit forms "pockets " . *Exoascus Pruni,* 131.
3 The branches form witches' brooms · *Exoascus deformans,* 132.
4. The branches show black tuberous swellings : *Plowrightia morbosa,* 102.

Prunus instititia

The branches form witches' brooms *Exoascus Instititia,* 133.

Prunus Padus

1. The fruit forms " pockets ". *Exoascus Pruni,* 131.
2 The cortex shows canker-spots · *Nectria ditissima,* 91.

Prunus spinosa

1. The leaves show yellowish red fleshy blotches : *Polystigma rubrum,* 97.
2 The fruit forms "pockets " . *Exoascus Pruni,* 131.

Pseudotsuga

1 The young shoots die, and become brown: *Botrytis Douglasii*, 130.

2. The branches bear a "mistletoe," and show witches' brooms: *Arceuthobium Douglasii*, 30.

Pyrus communis

1. The leaves show yellow swellings, which produce æcidia: *Gymnosporangium Sabinæ*, 158.

2. The leaves show vesicular swellings: *Exoascus bullatus*, 129.

3. The stem bears brown cushion-like or bracket-shaped sporophores: *Polyporus ignarius*, 201.

4. The branches bear mistletoe: *Viscum*, 25.

Pyrus Malus

1. The leaves bear yellow swellings, which produce æcidia: *Gymnosporangium tremelloides*, 159.

2. The branches show canker-spots: *Nectria ditissima*, 91; Frost-canker, 293.

3. The stem bears brown cushion-like or bracket-shaped sporophores: *Polyporus ignarius*, 201.

4. The branches bear mistletoe: *Viscum*, 25.

Quercus

1. One- and two-year-old plants wither, and show mycelial strands and black tubercles on their roots: *Rosellinia quercina*, 78.

2. The leaves show vesicular swellings: *Exoascus cærulescens*, 135.

3. The leaves show round brown blotches: *Sphærella*, 88.

4. The cortex shows canker-spots: *Nectria ditissima*, 91; Frost-canker, 293.

5. The cortex of young oaks dies over large areas of the stem, and, should the trees have survived, a callus forms along the margin of the wound: *Aglaospora Taleola*, 99.

6. The wood is dry, and shows red-rot: *Polyporus sulphureus*, 200; *Fistulina hepatica*, 206; *Dædalea quercina*, 206.

7. The wood shows white-rot: *Polyporus ignarius*, 201; *Hydnum diversidens*, 202.

8. The wood shows red-rot with white stripes: *Stereum hirsutum*, 205.

9. The wood shows red-rot with white blotches and cavities: *Thelephora Perdix*, 203.

10. The wood shows irregular oblong patches of red-, white-, and yellow-rot: *Polyporus dryadeus*, 201.

11. The branches bear a deciduous "mistletoe" and prominent swellings: *Loranthus europæus*, 30.

Rhamnus

The leaves and shoots show golden yellow swellings. *Puccinia coronata*, 156.

Rhododendron

1 The leaves bear large galls *Exobasidium Vaccinii*, 185.

2. The leaves show brown blotches : *Chrysomyxa Rhododendri*, 177.

Ribes

The leaves show yellow swellings : *Melampsora Hartigii*, 170

Robinia

The wood shows red-rot   Sulphur-yellow sporophores appear upon the cortex · *Polyporus sulphureus*, 200.

Salix

1. The leaves show small yellow fungus-bodies, which become brown in autumn   *Melampsora salicina*, 170.

2. The leaves show large black thickened blotches . *Rhytisma salicinum*, 107.

3. The leaves show white dusty blotches   *Erysiphe adunca*, 70

4 The wood shows red-rot, and sulphur-yellow sporophores appear upon the surface of the stem . *Polyporus sulphureus*, 200.

Senecio

Leaves and stem show reddish yellow fungus bodies   *Coleosporium Senecionis*, 172.

Solanum

1 Leaves and stem show black blotches : *Phytophthora infestans*, 64.

2 The tubers show disease : *P. infestans*, 64 , *Bacterium*, 38.

Sorbus Aria

The leaves show fungus-bodies, which produce æcidia · *Gymnosporangium tremelloides*, 159

Sorbus aucuparia

1. The leaves show large golden yellow blotches, which produce æcidia : *Gymnosporangium conicum*, 157

2. The leaves show small yellow fungus-bodies . *Melampsora Sorbi*, 171

3 The cortex shows dead patches, which bear small fungus-bodies . *Cucurbitaria Sorbi*, 88.

4. The branches bear mistletoe : *Viscum*, 25.

Sorbus terminalis

The leaves show yellow blotches, which bear æcidia   *Gymnosporangium conicum*, 157.

Tilia

1. The twigs and branches die, and produce cinnabar-coloured fungus-bodies : *Nectria cinnabarina*, 96.
2. The cortex shows canker-spots : *Nectria ditissima*, 91.

Trifolium and Lucerne

1. Roots attacked by violet *Rhizoctoniæ*, 82.
2. Close to the root-collar white mycelia and black resting-mycelia may be detected : *Peziza ciboriodes*, 130.

Tsuga

The leaves and shoots enveloped in white mycelia, the former dying: *Trichosphæria parasitica*, 72.

Ulmus

The leaves show vesicular blotches : *Exoascus Ulmi*, 135.

Vaccinium Myrtillus

1. The young shoots die and the berries shrivel up : *Sclerotinia baccarum*, 130.
2. The leaves show small brown blotches : *Melampsora Vaccinii*, 171.

Vaccinium Vitis-idæa

1. The stem becomes much elongated, and attains the thickness of a goose-quill : *Melampsora Goeppertiana*, 161.
2. Leaves, flowers, and stem are swollen, and dusted with white spores : *Exobasidium Vaccinii*, 185.
3. Leaves, fruit, and young shoots become brown : *Sclerotinia Vaccinii*, 130.

Vitis

1. Leaves, stem, and berries show mildew : *Oidium Tuckeri*, 70.
2. The leaves show yellow blotches above and white blotches below : *Peronospora viticola*, 65.
3. The berries wither : *Physalospora Bidwellii*, 103.
4. The berries are pale in colour, and their stalks decay : *Coniothyrium diplodiella*, 103.
5. The roots are killed by Rhizoctoniæ and Rhizomorphs : *Dematophora necatrix*, 82.
6. All parts of the plant show brown or black blotches : *Glæosporium ampelophagum*, 104.

Zea

Leaves, flowers, and stem show black vesicles filled with spores : *Ustilago Maydis*, 68.

INDEX

INDEX

THE END

RICHARD CLAY AND SONS, LIMITED, LONDON AND BUNGAY

CPSIA information can be obtained
at www.ICGtesting.com
Printed in the USA
BVHW07*1012170718
521845BV00006B/54/P